CHAMPIONS

OF

EUROPE

The History, Romance and Intrigue of
the European Cup

Brian Glanville

GUINNESS PUBLISHING

BIBLIOGRAPHY

John Motson & John Rowlinson, *The European Cup 1955–1980* (Queen Anne Press, 1980)

Roger Macdonald, *Manchester United in Europe* (Pelham Books, 1968)

Bill Shankly, *Shankly: An Autobiography* (Arthur Barker, 1976)

Alvaro Marchini, *Io, Presidente* (Edizioni Teveri, 1976)

Matt Busby's Scrapbook (Souvenir Press, 1980)

Peter Taylor & Mike Langley, *With Clough By Taylor* (Sidgwick and Jackson, 1980)

Derek Hodgson, *The Manchester United Story* (Arthur Barker, 1977)

Tony Francis, *Clough* (Stanley Paul, 1987)

Stephen F. Kelly, *You'll Never Walk Alone* (Macdonald, 1987)

Brian Glanville, ed., *World Football Handbooks*, 1968–76 (Mayflower, Queen Anne Press)

Editor: Charles Richards
Text design and layout: Amanda Sedge
Cover design: David Roberts
Picture editor: Alex Goldberg

Published in Great Britain by Guinness Publishing Ltd, 33 London Road, Enfield, Middlesex

Typeset in Times by Ace Filmsetting Ltd, Frome, Somerset

Printed and bound in Great Britain by The Bath Press, Bath

Front cover: Franco Baresi (Milan) holds up the European Cup

'Guinness' is a registered trademark of Guinness Publishing Ltd

British Library Cataloguing in Publication Data
Glanville, Brian *1931–*
    European soccer.
    1. Europe. Association football
    I. Title
    796.334094

ISBN 0-85112-948-X

CONTENTS

1

THE ROMANCE OF THE EUROPEAN CUP

The European Cup, known elsewhere as the Champions' Cup, is an inspired paradox; the greatest of all club competitions, just as the Football Association Cup, without which it would never have happened, is the most historic. The FA Cup was the catalyst for the whole future development of the game in Britain; and, by subsequent extension, the world. Derived from the Cock House Cup tournament at Harrow School, it exerted its charm and compulsive allure almost immediately. It generated tremendous interest not just throughout England but also in Glasgow, where the gallant amateur club Queens Park, having contributed to buying the original trophy, competed with distinction.

From the FA Cup, in time and in turn, flowed professionalism and the foundation of the Football League, when the pro clubs found they hadn't enough matches to stay solvent. But the European Cup was a French idea, as so many of football's best have been: FIFA, the international ruling body, and the World Cup, once known after its chief instigator as the Jules Rimet Trophy. Gabriel Hanot, by turns international footballer, administrator and journalist, was the begetter of the European Cup. His mind, well into old age, was always awash with new ideas. Indeed Sir Stanley Rous, finest of all football administrators, was once heard to grumble, when President of FIFA, that if he had a New Year's wish, it was that Gabriel Hanot would stop publishing half-baked ideas. Some of them might have been. The European Cup emphatically wasn't.

That the English should snub the competition in its infancy was almost par for the course. They had, after all, snubbed FIFA and the World Cup. In 1903, M. Robert Guerin, a Frenchman, was sent to London by the six European countries which wanted to found FIFA. His mission, embarked on with high optimism, was to enlist England, the mother of the game.

Frederick Wall, the formidable secretary of the Football Association, who would be in office for another 31 years, heard him out silently and dispassionately, head buried in his hands. England, said Guerin, should take the initiative. Wall, at the end, promised he would refer the matter to his board.

Several silent months went by; then Guerin was summoned back to London. This time he was received by the venerable President of the FA, red-bearded Lord Kinnaird, once a legendary FA Cup fighter, a proponent of the art of hacking. 'It was,' said Guerin hopelessly, 'like beating the air.' FIFA went ahead without England.

When the World Cup was initiated, its first finals taking place in Uruguay in 1930, England, like the other British nations, was not a member of FIFA, and therefore ineligible. A short period in FIFA had terminated with a dispute over broken-time payments for amateurs. In 1938, just before the finals were due to be played in France, England were invited at the last moment to make up the number. Spain was in the midst of a civil war, while Austria had ceased to exist after the Anschluss, its best players now gobbled up by 'Greater' Germany.

England had just completed a most impressive European tour, thrashing Germany 6–3 in Berlin, beating France 4–2 in Paris. But England refused. It would be another twelve years before they at last participated in a World Cup – and lost in Belo Horizonte to the United States.

Thus, the reaction of the Football League to the birth of the European Cup was hardly surprising. It was insular, it was negative, it was wholly in character and, alas, it found, of all clubs, Chelsea as the malleable champions, for the first and only time in their somewhat exotic history. Joe Mears, scion of the family which had built Stamford Bridge stadium and founded Chelsea in 1905 – 'Chelsea will astonish the world!' it had been said – was, by ill fortune, then the Chairman of the Football League. A difficult position, which he might have used for the good of Chelsea and the good of English football. But Mears was not a strong figure. The dominant League official at that time was the Secretary, just as it was at the Football Association. There, Stanley Rous. At the League, Alan Hardaker. Chalk and cheese. Internationalist and isolationist.

The Football League 'advised' Chelsea not to take part in this new-fangled tournament. Chelsea did not have to take this 'advice' but they meekly, cravenly and shamefully did. It would certainly have originated with Hardaker, who once, in an unguarded aside, confided to me with a grin that he didn't much enjoy dealing with football on the Continent: 'Too many wogs and dagoes!'

Hardaker, an embattled Northerner, happy to keep the League headquarters in Lancashire rather than London, even when it moved at long last from Preston, was the last person to welcome foreign encroachment and the potential overshadowing of his competition. In a sense he was only doing his job and duty, even if the historical process was manifestly against him. Immense interest had been stirred up in England by Wolverhampton Wanderers' floodlit home victories over Honved of Budapest and Moscow Dynamo.

Hardaker would, in due course, reach an absolute nadir of embattled insularity when he kept Manchester United out of the European Cup in 1958. But perhaps in some ways this tension between the Football League and the far more cosmopolitan Football Association, under Rous, was productive. Defied and defeated by Manchester United's determination to play in Europe in 1956, Hardaker, a man who found it difficult to forgive, would take his petty revenge. But it would be the merest, irrelevant parenthesis; by then, the battle had been lost and won.

Perhaps the true begetter of the European (Champions') Cup was the Mitropa Cup, a club competition played in Europe between the wars, without benefit of British entry. Austria, Hungary, Czechoslovakia and Yugoslavia initiated it, in 1927. Later, it would be joined by clubs from Italy and Switzerland. Near the outbreak of war, there had been hopes and plans to extend the competition across the continent, but these were frustrated, and when the tournament was revived in the 1950s, it was somewhat marginal. Meanwhile in 1949 the Latin Cup had begun, with Spanish, Portuguese, Italian and French clubs involved in what was something of a sideshow. Life in the Leagues had grown altogether too real.

Then came Gabriel Hanot, who had the perfect platforms of *L'Equipe*, the French daily sports paper, and the equally influential weekly sister, *France Football*. In April 1955, eighteen of Europe's most celebrated clubs met in Paris and agreed that the European Champions' Cup should go ahead; though for its first version, certain famous teams who did not hold their national league title were invited to compete. There was a momentary problem over the chain of command. Both FIFA and the European governing body UEFA dealt only with national associations, rather than clubs. In the event, FIFA allowed the tournament to go ahead, provided that those clubs taking part had the authorisation of their national body.

The competition, it was decided, would take the form of a knock-out Cup, with home and away legs being played until the Final itself. Here, an attempt was being made to ease the paradox, if not to square the circle. For to achieve the European Cup, a club had to win its country's League Championship, the very antithesis of a Cup competition. But it then found itself not in a European League but in a European Cup, a knock-out affair.

The organisers mitigated this with their two-legged ties. In the most famous Cup competition of all, the FA Cup, this had been tried only once, in the season immediately following the last war, 1945/6, when two-legged ties were introduced up to the semi-final stage, teams winning through on goal aggregate. But the experiment had not been popular. It was instantly abandoned, and has never been tried again.

What it did, above all, was to weight the scales in favour of Goliath against David, when the whole magic allure of the FA Cup had been its opportunity for giant killing. The way little Walsall, of the Third Division South, had beaten mighty Arsenal in the Third Round of the Cup in 1933, the way non-League teams of the 1940s like Colchester United and Peterborough United had knocked out powerful opposition; this was classically the way of the Cup.

Now, the new competition was in effect giving major clubs two bites at the cherry. What would Walsall have done if in 1933, having hustled Arsenal out of contention on their own little ground, they had then had to come to the imposing spaces of Highbury for a second leg? So, from the start, romance in the European Cup was at a premium. David might connect with his first sling shot, but he was still vulnerable to Goliath's great bludgeon.

If there was romance in the first five years of the tournament, it was the romance of aristocracy, even royalty: of Real (which after all means Royal) Madrid. If there was a King, it was surely Alfredo Di Stefano; not even a European but a king from across the water, an Argentine. If there had to be an Emperor, it was the club's President, Santiago Bernabeu, father and inspiration of the club. Without his extraordinary drive, initiative and endeavours – and, let us whisper, without the patronage of the Franco regime – there could hardly have been a Real Madrid as we know it today.

But then, without Di Stefano, it would have had still less chance. It could never have dominated the European Cup as it did, never have managed the almost incredible feat of winning it for the first five years in a row.

As time went by, and the pressures of the game became more unbearably hectic, the European Cup would suffer in consequence, afflicted by what one might call a kind of shorthand. In the earlier years, teams which finished level on aggregate after the home and away legs played off in a third match, to decide which team should go through. That was much too fair and rational to last. The next step, to save time at the expense of justice, was to enact that teams which finished level on goal aggregate after two ties should have their fate decided by which had scored the more away goals. In crude terms, away goals counted double.

It was, I suppose, a rough and ready way of reaching a result. Worse was to come. If teams, after the two legs, remained level on goals and on goals scored away from home, it came down to a question of penalty kicks. Five were taken by each side, and if by the end of the 'shoot out' they were still level, then penalties continued to be taken, until a 'result' was achieved.

A packed Hampden Park was enthralled by Real Madrid's 7–3 demolition of Eintracht Frankfurt in the 1960 Final. Real had fallen behind early on to this goal from Richard Kress (Popperfoto)

Like the flowers that bloom in the Spring, tra-la, such an indulgence had nothing to do with the case. Yet in due course, we were actually to see European Cup Finals no longer replayed, if drawn after extra time, but themselves decided on penalties. There 'had' to be a result, had to be a winner. Time, precious time, time which was money, would not permit the decent sporting solution of a replay. So in 1984, Liverpool beat Roma on penalties to take the Cup. So Steaua of Bucharest in 1986, PSV Eindhoven in 1988, and Red Star Belgrade in 1991 won the Cup in the same profoundly anomalous and unsatisfactory way.

Two teams which had reached the Final first by winning their own national Championship – or the previous year's European Cup – and had then played no fewer than eight highly competitive games, were now reduced to the arbitrary fiasco of kicking penalties. They might just as well have tossed up in the centre circle or played scissors-paper-stone. It was hard not to reflect that if UEFA could not take this illustrious competition seriously, why should anybody else?

Santiago Bernabeu had never, from the outset, hidden his dream that it might one day turn into a European League. He compared the tournament with the essence of a great wine, from which still greater wine could be produced. Many of us, at one time or another, have shared that dream; and in Bernabeu's case, by contrast with the 'dreamers' of today, money was surely a secondary consideration. Perhaps his finest, proudest moment, and that of his club, came at Hampden Park on a mild May evening in 1960. Real had just annihilated Eintracht Frankfurt 7–3 in a memorable European Cup Final, and the Glaswegian public, connoisseurs and nationalists to a fervent man, gave Real a magnificent standing ovation. Certainly it was a moment that I, who was lucky enough to be there, have never forgotten.

In later years Gabriel Hanot, always the idealist, a figure from another, more altruistic, less financially frenetic time, came to see himself as something of a Frankenstein. His progeny, the European Cup, was turning into something he had never intended. Winning mattered too much. Far too much money was at stake. Instead of regenerating football, the European Cup could undermine and pervert it. The notorious Years of the Golden Fix would prove him only too abundantly right; and they have been followed by an era in which money talks with a stentorian voice; the whole great problem exacerbated by the presence of television. Everybody's El Dorado; nobody's friend.

But the European Cup, for all its scandals and anomalies, has provided any number of cherished moments, and has provided a fitting theatre for the finest playing talents of its time, both European and South American. Real Madrid alone would furnish the incomparable Di Stefano, sublime tyrant of their team, Ferenc Puskas, Raymond Kopa and 'Paco' Gento. Manchester United, before the horrific, pitiful air crash at Munich in 1958, produced the mighty young prodigy Duncan Edwards, to be followed in the 1960s by the glorious arabesques of George Best, the swerves and shots of Bobby Charlton, the acrobatic brilliance of Denis Law.

Internazionale may have been a deeply suspect and manipulative club in the same decade, but they brought together, under the baleful aegis of Herrera, a galaxy of admirable players. There was tall Giacinto Facchetti, the attacking left-back, proud of the fact that he could not only set up goals with his attacking forays but score them too. Luis Suarez, though he had his violent moments, was a Spanish international inside-forward of great all-round gifts and a stupendous shot, Jair a black Brazilian right-winger of exciting pace and swerve, and Sandrino Mazzola the equal of his famous father in attack, whether he led it or played off the centre-forward.

Benfica, in their short but brilliant period under Bela Guttmann, gave the game the astonishing Eusebio, from Mozambique, the quintessence of all that was best in sub-Saharan African football with his compound of pace, graceful skills and a right foot as explosive as Puskas' left. Indeed, the moment after the 1962 European Cup Final when Puskas gave Eusebio his shirt, having himself scored three memorable goals, was an historic one.

Milan had their own prodigy in Gianni Rivera, already a coveted inside-forward at the age of 16, supreme in his control of the ball and in his ability to use it with shrewd subtlety; all this compounded by a shot remarkable for one so slight. Then, with the 1970s, came the scintillating years of Total Football, perhaps the best ever played in the history of the game, when the European Cup was monopolised first by Ajax of Amsterdam, galvanised by their centre-forward Johan Cruyff, then by Bayern Munich, inspired by their captain Franz Beckenbauer, the true inventor of that ultra-modern game.

A host of other stars played for both teams. For Ajax, the attacking full-back Ruud Krol, who by the time he came to play in the 1978 World Cup Final would be a dominating sweeper, Piet Keizer and Rob Rensenbrink, each a remarkable outside-left in his time. For Bayern there was the ever-intransigent Paul Breitner, always his own man, an attacking full-back who'd later play as a midfield general; there was little blond Uli Hoeness, darting about in attack, and 'Der Bomber', Gerd Muller, phenomenally prolific in an age when defences were meant to be suffocatingly on top. Massive of thigh, not very tall, Muller could conjure goals out of nothing, a prince of the penalty area with a genius for finding space which never previously appeared to exist. In the air, he was no John Charles, no Tommy Lawton, yet some of his headed goals were perfection, marvellous little masterpieces of anticipation and deflection, or the fruit of his ability to drift away from defenders who thought they were marking him impeccably. To score well over 60 goals for his country, including the winner in a World Cup Final, when goals were supposed to be at a premium was the mark of an extraordinary player.

Heidi Rosendahl, a popular and successful West German athlete of the time, jealous of the fact that Muller had been voted Sports Personality of the Year ahead of her, said acidly that all he ever did was hang around the penalty area and score goals. As Beethoven might have hung around at home and written symphonies.

The English era would come; and be terminated by the second, horrifying tragedy connected with the European Cup, the Heysel stadium disaster of 1985. Drunken, violent fans of Liverpool, of all clubs, ran riot, 39 spectators died when a wall collapsed, and England's clubs were banned from Europe *en masse*. I say Liverpool of all clubs because Liverpool it was who had established the English domination of the European Cup, Liverpool who had boldly changed their traditional British style to encompass Continental skills and methods, Liverpool who had striven diligently to make all their matches safe.

The era of English supremacy was not, let it be said, a brilliant one. I wrote at the time, and displeased Liverpool's Bob Paisley in the process, that it coincided with a decline in the standard of European football. I still believe that. Liverpool could boast such splendid players as Kevin Keegan, a self-made star if every there was one, the immaculate Kenny Dalglish and the robust yet so skilful Graeme Souness. Nottingham Forest could rely on the majestic goalkeeping of Peter Shilton.

But so many finals then were such drab, dull affairs. Oh, the longueurs and the mediocrity of such dire games as Liverpool against Bruges at Wembley, against Real Madrid in Paris; of Nottingham Forest against Malmo and Hamburg. These were Finals won without flair, without panache. Liverpool's first victory, in Rome against Borussia Monchen-gladbach, was another cup of tea: strong and refreshing. Tony Morley's marvellous run, in Rotterdam, which dazzled Bayern Munich's defence and made the winning goal for Aston Villa, was inspired. But after the grand epoch of Total Football, this was anticlimax.

Which does not alter the fact that with the departure of the English clubs, the European Cup was gravely devalued. On the Continent this was acknowledged. No one wanted the English hooligans back but almost every country wanted the English clubs, with their robust commitment, their physical challenge. They had, after all, proved Johan Cruyff wrong in his view that while English soccer was fine to watch, open and ingenuous as it was, those very qualities militated against success in Europe.

If English clubs were a loss to Europe, then European football was a tremendous loss to the English game, which largely reverted to the worst of its old habits. Liverpool, pioneers of the 'Europeanising' of English football, were shining exceptions to prove the rule. They kept on trying, usually with great success, to play measured, scientific, intelligent, passing football. There were bad moments: above all the FA Cup Final of 1988 when they lost to Wimbledon, most blatant and unregenerate practitioners of the crude, long-ball game.

As long ago as 1932, when the greatest of all Anglo-Continental coaches, little Jimmy Hogan, brought his Austrian *Wunderteam* to Stamford Bridge, its players were shocked, four days before a famous match against England, to watch Chelsea play Everton in the League. Two of the greatest centre-forwards in the history of British football were on show: stocky little Hughie Gallacher of Scotland for Chelsea, big Dixie Dean, that superb header of the ball, for Everton. All the players of either side did throughout the game, Hogan related, was to bang the ball down the middle, high to Dean or Gallacher.

Long-ball football, for all the spurious rationalisations of its advocates, not least within the FA coaching department, is in essence the easy way out, a world made safe for the untalented player, himself playing the percentages. Boot the ball into the penalty area often enough, and sooner or later, someone will blunder, and a goal will come. Tactics which could never work in Europe.

When the European Cup began, we were still three years away from the 4–2–4 plan with which Brazil, never able to master zonal defence and the pivoting back three, would win the 1958 World Cup. The four-in-line defence would sweep Europe with a speed which quite outstripped that of the Third-Back Game, introduced by Arsenal after the change in the offside law in 1925. The new 4–2–4 would be modulated, by the time the Brazilians won the 1962 World Cup in Chile, to 4–3–3, and then again to 4–4–2.

None of these systems appealed, in those days, to Italian football, locked as it was for so many years in the grip of *catenaccio*, with its deeply negative sweeper. Internazionale won the Championship with it in the early 1950s, and Helenio Herrera refined – or exacerbated – it when he took the club over in the following decade. A clutch of embattled, misguided theorists, convinced that Italian players were physically inferior, helped to prolong its life: or life in death. Not until the 1980s would Milan and Roma, under Nils Liedholm, embrace zonal defence, on the four-in-line pattern. Meanwhile the dynamic excitements of Total Football had come and, alas, gone.

But football, in the last analysis, will always come down to players rather than tactics, and Real Madrid had fine players galore; including the finest of his time.

2

REAL MADRID

In the beginning was Santiago Bernabeu. Without him, Real Madrid might well, however strange it seems, have remained no more than a minor, mediocre club. And without Alfredo Di Stefano, he could never have built it into the club it became.

Bernabeu may perhaps be described as a grandee. They are still fashionable in Spain, and Spanish football, even though their origins may sometimes be obscure; even though, like the ineffable Jesus Gil of the rival Atletico Madrid, they may have been convicted for erecting buildings which collapsed.

Since we shall later be talking at length of Italian football and its comparable structures, it is perhaps useful to make certain distinctions. In Italy, one has the *commendatore* syndrome. The *commendatore* is the Grand Panjandrum whose patronage and approval are sought, at whose feet acolytes sit, sometimes almost literally: see how the journalists swarm around Gianni Agnelli, chief of FIAT, patron of Juventus, whenever he attends a match, collecting and printing his most banal or mischievous utterances. But if the Agnelli family made Juventus a great club, Santiago Bernabeu made Real, much later, not only a great club but a great team, far surpassing anything 'Juve' have achieved in European competition.

Real Madrid are themselves an old club, founded as long ago as 1898. On 9 March 1902, a group of students from the University had it officially incorporated, though it was not until 1920 that King Alfonso XIII sanctioned the Real, or Royal, prefix. Football, by then, had made substantial progress, and was no longer overshadowed by the older passion of bullfighting. Significantly, perhaps, it was in the shadow of the Bull Ring that Real Madrid first played. It was a long way, and several different grounds, from the mighty Bernabeu Stadium at Chamartin.

There was, for many seasons, the Velodrome, in the quarter of Ciudad Lineal, then the original Chamartin Stadium, with room for fewer than 20 000 spectators. Santiago Bernabeu himself played centre-forward, and joined the club as such in 1912, continuing to play for them until as late as 1926. It was in September 1943 that he became the President. By that time, he was a prosperous lawyer.

'We were in a rut,' he has recorded. Gates averaged just 16 000. On his fishing and shooting expeditions, Bernabeu's mind was full of schemes and plans to break out of such mediocrity. Finally, he conceived the quantum leap of building a magnificent new stadium in the hope, so to speak, that trade would follow the flag. It was an extraordinary ambition, for where was the money to come from? Certainly not from Real's bank, which turned the project down flat.

Bernabeu had recourse to the club's fans: 'It was to them I turned, with my hands oustretched!' The club had an unsuccessful team, and only three thousand members, but the hands did not go unfilled. Thirty million pesetas' worth of bonds to build the stadium were sold, almost miraculously, within hours, and the membership itself rose to 35 000. An imposing New Chamartin stadium was built, with a capacity for 75 000 seated fans. It was ready in three years and, after more fund-raising, was increased to a massive capacity of 125 000. Multi-tiered, it was an extraordinary, imposing sight when filled with jubilant supporters.

Though a multiplicity of other sports, notably basketball, are played under the aegis of Real Madrid, football has always been the fulcrum of the club. The stadium, unlike so many in Europe, was designed essentially for football. There is no running track and so no massive distance between the spectators and the pitch, which contributes enormously to atmosphere during a game, but clearly has its negative capacity, too. The violence of the notorious Ultras Sur, the hooligan fans behind the South goal, became a particular problem in the 1980s, when the club was far too slow to take action against them and to install close circuit television to help the police control them.

There was, indeed, a murmur from time to time that elements in the police force might condone their behaviour. In the event, Real would pay dearly for their laxity. A horrific bombardment of the Bayern Munich players and the brave French referee Vautrot during the second leg semi-final of the European Cup in 1987 led to Real being forced to play the home leg of the following competition's first round behind closed doors, the second round home leg in Valencia. Such passions would have been hard to predict in bygone years when Real, the most amateur of clubs, would not even enter the Spanish League and pay their players until 1929.

Alfredo Di Stefano arrived in 1953, the second great turning point in the history of the club. Raimundo Saporta, Real's treasurer and Bernabeu's right hand man, had much to do with it. He had joined Real at the age of 26 only a few months earlier, having gained Bernabeu's approval through the way he organised a basketball tournament to celebrate their 50th anniversary. Administration was his *forte*; as he told Bernabeu when he was approached, he knew little or nothing about football.

Di Stefano, then in his mid-twenties, was already a famous centre-forward in South America though, paradoxically, he had played only a few times for Argentina. This was because, like so many Argentine stars of the period, he had decamped to Colombia when that country pulled out of FIFA, thus enabling its clubs to acquire foreign players for nothing. Neil Franklin, George Mountford and Charlie Mitten, from England, were among those who had gone there in 1950, though unlike Di Stefano, they did not stay very long.

Blond, deep-chested and powerful, Di Stefano was recruited for the Millonarios club of Bogotá by a still more famous Argentine centre-forward, Adolfo Pedernera, though Di Stefano would eclipse him in time.

He was already celebrated not only for his skill and opportunism but for his extraordinary stamina, which he had built up, it was said, running in the streets of Buenos Aires. Seldom in the history of football had there been so complete a player, such a compound of energy and versatility, such a tireless pair of legs. It might well be said that Di Stefano was playing Total Football long before it was invented in Europe.

When Colombia returned to FIFA, Di Stefano and the other self-exiled players were, so to speak, up for grabs. Real ordered Saporta to go to South America and sign him. But Barcelona, their deadliest rivals, in political as much as sporting terms, had the same idea.

Their emissaries went their different ways; the situation was complicated and would call, in due course, for a judgement of Solomon. Saporta went to Bogotá, Barcelona's officials to Buenos Aires, where Di Stefano had begun his career with the illustrious River Plate club. Technically, legally, he was still their player. Each emissary obtained a 'yes'; Saporta from Millonarios, Barcelona from River Plate. But which 'yes' was valid?

Both of them, it seemed. Each club flourished an option. The decision was left, at last, to the Spanish Football Association, who dodged the column. Their ludicrous decree was that the clubs should share Di Stefano. He would play for them in alternate seasons, first for Real, then in Catalonia.

This absurd situation lasted but six weeks. Di Stefano, whether by accident or design, did not set Chamartin afire when he began to play for Real. Barcelona had him watched and eventually decided to sell out their share. They would live bitterly to rue it for many years to come. One mere day after he had become definitively a Real Madrid player, Di Stefano celebrated by scoring four goals – against Barcelona themselves! Real won the game 5–0, and so it would go on.

Alfredo Di Stefano, inspiration and driving force of the Real Madrid team which won the first five European Cups; almost superhumanly active

(Allsport)

As a player, Di Stefano was a remarkable mixture of arrogance and selflessness. He may not have been the first of the deep-lying centre-forwards – Nandor Hidegkuti was already doing it for Hungary, and Roy Bentley had done it with Chelsea in the latter 1940s – but he was by far the most effective and influential. 'As a centre-forward,' he was quoted as saying, 'I am always on the move: up, back and across, trying not to be fixed in one position and so allowing the defender to see too much of me. Or I may be trying to avoid "bunching" with other forwards. Or I may be reading what is to come, and be moving quickly to help the next man on the ball . . . For forwards should accept it as part of their job that they should help the defence. When the opposing attack is in possession, you obviously are out of the game. What do you do? Just accept that position, while the defence tries to come through a difficult time? If the defence fails, the forward's job becomes that much harder – he has to score more goals! So the obvious thing is to get back quickly and help the defence. It eases your own job over the whole game.

'I think nothing of popping up at centre-half or full-back, to cover a colleague who has had to leave his position. We are all footballers, and as such should be able to perform competently in all eleven positions.'

Could there be a more succinct exposition of Total Football? And has there ever been a footballer so superbly equipped to play it? I have so many vivid memories of Di Stefano, not least in that European Cup Final of 1960 in Glasgow when he bestrode the pitch, even if Ferenc Puskas scored four goals to his three. I remember him winning the ball with a tackle in his own penalty area then, almost at once, haring upfield with the ball for a crack at goal. I remember him sending Vidal, the young midfielder, clean through with a beautifuly judged defence-cutting pass. I remember him lashing the ball into the roof of the net with his right foot.

Two years later in Amsterdam, when Real lost that marvellous Final to Benfica, I recall the still more astonishing through pass which enabled tubby little Puskas, the Galloping Major, to trot rather than gallop half the length of the field, before driving the ball home with his ferocious left foot. Pointing, shouting, gesturing, Di Stefano ran the show, a more or less benevolent despot. The story is told that when Puskas, that shrewd Budapest urchin, joined the club, himself already trailing clouds of glory, he found himself dead level on goals with Di Stefano in the very last game; that towards the end, he found himself with an easy chance to score, but rolled the ball to Di Stefano for him to score instead.

If that story be true, then Puskas knew just what he was doing. Di Stefano brooked no rivals on the podium; a Toscanini of his time. Didi, that marvellous strategist, coal-black spirit of the Brazilian midfield and hero of two World Cups, came to Madrid, spent a season of well-paid, humiliating inactivity, and returned to Brazil – to shine again. Agne Simonsson, the blond, impressive young Sweden centre-forward who had scored against Brazil and Didi in the 1958 World Cup Final, arrived, took Spanish lessons, spoke solemnly about the time it would need to adjust, about his willingness to wait in the wings; and went on waiting. There was to be no place for him. Home he went, as well.

To his strength, stamina and electric change of pace, Di Stefano allied superb ball control on which, too, he put a premium. He was an absolute perfectionist. Another image springs to mind: Di Stefano playing in a friendly game at Crystal Palace, sending Paco Gento haring up the left wing with an exquisite backheel, utterly sure, even without looking, that Gento would be there, would have anticipated it, and that the ball would go just where he had wanted.

'My greatest pleasure is in hitting goals!' he said, and he scored them in superabundance yet made so many for other players. He was strong in the air, and could head goals as well as kick them. But woe betide the man who crossed him. He did play some matches for Spain, but it was never the same as when he played for Argentina. That was where his patriotism, not to say his nationalism, truly lay. I remember him sitting behind me in the Press Gallery at Wembley, during that notorious World Cup quarter-final of 1966, when Herr Kreitlein, the West German referee, sent off Argentina's Antonio Rattin 'for the look on his face', Geoff Hurst scored the only goal of the game, and Alf Ramsey said afterwards that he hoped, in the semi-final, England would meet a team that would be interested in playing football 'and not act as animals'. Di Stefano that day went bellowing mad.

He loved to play, and he would play when he was ill. He made plenty of money, but the game was the thing: 'I can never understand non-triers.' He would always try, always play if it were possible. 'Many a time, even once or twice when I have been running temperatures, I have still persuaded the managers to let me play. Football is a great game, and when one is with a great club it should be a privilege to play and give of one's best, a privilege hard to sacrifice.' Alfredo, the Great Insufferable, was ready for that.

The Real Madrid team which won the Spanish Championship of 1954/5, thus qualifying for the first European Cup, was not quite as coruscating as others which would follow, though Di Stefano was unquestionably a host in itself. Playing its own version of the 'W' formation, alias the Third-Back

Game, which Di Stefano himself regarded merely as a trampoline for his own amazing versatility, it had perhaps only a handful of truly outstanding players.

Francisco 'Paco' Gento was certainly one of them. This dark, stocky little outside-left, the possessor of fabulous pace and a fine left foot, came from the village of Guaranizo, near Santander. At the age of ten, when he was playing football on the beach, he was already a left winger, and so he remained for the whole of an astonishingly long career, in which he far out-lasted possibly greater stars such as Puskas and Di Stefano, for both of whom he had always the warmest praise.

The length of his career proves that he had a great deal more than just devastating speed. Even when it had gone he was still a most effective player. He played in no fewer than eight European Cup Finals for Real, the first of them in 1956, and he was still a member of the team 14 years later, when it lost its grip of European Cup and Spanish Championship alike. His ball control was remarkable for one who, in his prime, moved at such veloc-ity, and it served him well when that velocity waned.

Moreover, his use of pace was highly original. It did not merely take him past players, allowing him to deliver a telling cross, or to cut in for a shot at goal. He would sometimes employ it in short, diagonal bursts which if any-thing took him away from the goal, towards the touchline, but in the process created time and space for him. In more than 80 European Cup ties for Real, he scored many goals, but none was more important than the winner, in the second half of extra time, against Milan in Brussels in 1958. He had also scored Real's second goal against Fiorentina in the Final of 1957, played in Madrid itself.

His first club was called Nueva Montana, New Mountain, and his first bonus was the grand sum of 25 pesetas. Then he joined another local junior team, Astillero, and he was as old as 19 when at last the local League club, Real Santander, signed him on a five-year contract, with a modest salary. In 1953 came the crucial move to Real Madrid. Two years later, he made his debut for Spain against England on his home ground in Madrid, and had an outstanding match in Paris against Belenenses of Lisbon in the Latin Cup Final, a competition which mattered then, but was very soon to matter much less. Already his combination with Di Stefano was almost telepathic. In due course, he would succeed Di Stefano as captain of the club.

Hector Rial, a tall Argentine inside-left, was Di Stefano's perfect foil in Real's first European Cup team, and in the next three. He was also a benign influence on Gento, who said that Rial taught him how to use his speed and helped him to learn the game. Unselfishly, he saw to it that Gento had plenty of the ball.

At right-half played the tall, powerful Miguel Munoz, who would later become manager not only of his old club, but of Spain. Of Munoz, Helenio Herrera, later to become the scourge of Real as manager of Barcelona and Inter, wrote appreciatively: 'The veritable motor of his team. (*Did Di Stefano know this?*) A magnificent attacker, he is always going forward and shoots at goal with much power.' But, added Herrera, Munoz could struggle against a quick, counter-attacking player. Of the big centre-half, Marquitos, whose remarkable, if fortuitous, goal would win Real the first European Cup Final, Herrera said, 'A very virile player, quick over direct distances, he possesses a well-developed sense of anticipation. Very difficult to beat in the air.' And, Herrera might have added had he been less diplomatic, pretty ruthless in his methods. In time, Marquitos would produce a son, known as Marcos, deeply influenced by his father, who would play vigorously on the right wing for Atletico Madrid, Barcelona and Spain. Herrera also had a few words for Hector Rial, conveniently 'naturalised' in 1955 so he could play for Spain: 'Has the technical assurance of the South Americans, but also a sense of realism.' Which Herrera, himself an Argentine, possessed to a fault.

In a small field, Real had to overcome just three opponents to reach the first European Cup Final, in Paris. Seven goals went past Servette of Switzerland in two games: two away, five at home. It was interesting to see that Servette were managed by none other than the Austrian Karl Rappan, praised or cursed as the true inventor of *catenaccio*, alias *verrou*, which Herrera would use with such controversial success in the 1960s.

In essence, Rappan's scheme, developed and perfected – if that be the word – in Switzerland, involved the withdrawal of one midfield player to operate behind the marking defenders, to act as *verrouilleur* or *battitore libero*, libero for short – what the English would eventually call a sweeper, short for a sweeper-up. The notion being that anything which got through the bolt-defence – another name for it – would be dealt with by the *libero*. Or sweeper. Unused to such a strategy, Real found it a little hard to fathom at first against Servette, till a goal by Munoz, justifying Herrera's appreciation of him, unblocked the away game. The home game was a great deal easier. Rial, whose skill and intelligence compensated for a certain lack of speed, scored the second goal in Geneva.

Rial would miss a penalty in the second round second-leg game in Belgrade against Partizan, but it didn't much matter. Partizan won 3–0 on a freezing day, Real's players were bombarded with snowballs, and the superbly gifted inside-forward Milos Milutinovitch scored twice, once from the penalty spot. But Partizan's 3–0 win was academic; they had already lost the first leg 4–0 in Madrid on Christmas Day. In those far-off times, Christmas matches were commonplace.

In the semi-finals, Real's opponents were another club destined to play a powerful role in the European Cup: Milan. They had an excellent team, one I had watched and admired in Italy the previous season. Two of their celebrated Swedes, Gunnar Nordahl and Nils Liedholm, veterans now but highly effective, were still with them. The third, Gunnar Gren, with whom they'd made up the so-called 'Grenoli' trio, had left.

But if Gren, the studious 'Professor', had gone, Juan Schiaffino had arrived. He came from Uruguay in 1954, after playing superbly in the World Cup for his country in Switzerland. Slender, pale, an unlikely-looking footballer, his superb skills, his inspired passing and his elegant left foot – which had scored a vital goal in the 1950 World Cup decider against Brazil in Rio – made him formidable. Liedholm, meanwhile, had dropped from inside-left to right-half, where he remained highly influential and inventive. Gunnar Nordahl might no longer be young, but his powerful, square physique, his ability in the air, and his ability to hold up the ball and move it sweetly on, made him still a force.

Milan had faltered badly in their first ever European Cup game, at San Siro. Drawn against Saarbrucken – allowed to enter because the Saar, then, was counted as a separate country – and with no Nordahl, they floundered horribly under teeming rain. Throwing away a 3–1 lead, Milan were eventually humiliated by a 4–3 defeat. But Nordahl returned to help them win the away leg 4–1, and an imposing 7–2 win at home against Rapid Vienna in the second leg of the quarter-final showed their strength.

It was insufficient to withstand Real in the semi-final. After giving away a very early goal to Hector Rial in Madrid, Milan did manage to square the scores at 2–2, but then gave two more goals away and lost 4–2. It was too great a deficit to put right at San Siro, though a couple of penalties gave them a consoling 2–1 victory. This meant that the first European Cup Final, properly destined for Paris where the competition had originated, would be between Real Madrid and the French champions Reims, inspired by Raymond Kopa.

Little Kopa, born at Noeux-les-Mines, the son of a Polish miner, was injured himself down the mines as a boy. He began his professional career as a right winger with Angers and from there he went to Reims, where his superb balance, beautiful ball control, acceleration and intelligent passing soon made him a star – first of the Under-23 team then, from 1952 onwards, of the full French national side. Centre-forward, however, was much his favourite position, and by the time the European Cup came round it was there that he was playing, in a team cleverly managed by Albert Batteux and full of smoothly gifted footballers.

Like Di Stefano, with whom he presented a great physical contrast, Kopa interpreted the role of centre-forward very much in his own way, liking to advance from deep positions, compensating his lack of size and power in the air with a general's role; a Napoleon, as it were, small but commanding. His ability to beat opponents meant that he would often draw other defenders to him, thus contriving attacking situations with a 'man over'. He split a defence beautifully with his well-judged passing, and he scored many a goal himself.

It was perhaps a little ironic, even a little sad, that after this exciting Cup Final he himself should move to Real Madrid. There, the idea of playing the crucial role he did with Reims was out of the question. Didi's experience had shown as much. Kopa settled for more money and a subsidiary place, out on the right wing. He did well enough there, winning the European Cup medals which eluded him at Reims, but one never saw the best of him in Madrid.

This Parisian Final, then, resolved itself both in prospect and in actuality into a duel between Kopa and Di Stefano, and a very close-fought one it was, too. When it was over, Kopa disappeared into what might be called his gilded tunnel, only to re-emerge, a centre-forward again, for the World Cup Finals of 1958, when, to vary the metaphor, he frolicked in Sweden as joyously as Ariel, released from his long imprisonment in a hollow tree. Pulling the strings – or rather, making the perfect through passes – for the dark, rapid, stocky Juste Fontaine, Kopa enabled France to take a distinguished third place in the tournament.

Di Stefano wasn't there. It was years since he had discarded, or been discarded by, Argentina, and Spain hadn't reached the Finals. When he did at last go to the World Cup Finals in 1962, he wouldn't even kick a ball. Helenio Herrera had been called in as the Spanish team manager, and egos collided. Officially at least, Di Stefano was injured. I remember visiting the Spanish team's hotel down at Viña del Mar, where pelicans sat on the rocks below, and Di Stefano's elderly father said he'd urged him to use a liniment he'd brought from Buenos Aires. He himself, originally from Capri, had been a player in his day. But though Puskas played for Spain, Di Stefano didn't.

Back, though, to 1956, and that Final in Paris. How close Reims, and Kopa, came! Indeed, they were two goals up in twelve minutes. First Kopa took a free kick; Lesmes, the Real defender, swung at it, it flew off his boot to Leblond and was headed in. The claims of the Real goalkeeper, Alonso, that it had not crossed the line, were overruled. Then Templin, the outside-left, taking two bites at the cherry, made the score 2–0.

It was clearly time Di Stefano took a hand, and he did. Typically, he was involved in the beginning of a movement in his own half. Just as typically, he 'got on the end of it' with a tremendous, scoring shot from just inside the penalty area. Then with thirty minutes gone, Real won a corner; a header by Hector Rial and it was 2–2. Di Stefano continued to drop deep for the ball, and send Real away. After half time he released Joseito, playing on the right wing that day. Joseito shot home but Arthur Ellis, hero of the 'Battle of Berne' in the 1954 World Cup when Brazil and Hungary kicked lumps out of each other, gave the goal offside.

So Reims were able to go ahead, again. Both sides seemed vulnerable to crosses from set pieces and now it was Hidalgo, possessor of a proud Spanish name, who headed in another of Kopa's measured free kicks. Things began to look black for Real, however much Di Stefano was running. Strangely and unexpectedly, it was the arch-defender, Marquitos, who came to their rescue. He it was, never known as a polished player, who took a leaf out of Di Stefano's book, advanced from inside his own half, ran on and on, and shot at last – against a Reims defender.

But luck was with him and with Real. The ball hit his shin and rebounded into the net. With eleven minutes left, Gento, who would call this the hardest of all Real's winning European Cup Finals, streaked away to make the winner for Rial. There was still time for Templin to hit the bar.

By the following season there were certain changes of personnel, but with Di Stefano dominating the team, these never seemed to make much difference, any more than did a change of manager. Di Stefano was what the Italians were wont to call 'a manager on the field'. He worked harmoniously under – or alongside – Real's manager when the European Cup began, José Villalonga, a former Army officer. Helenio Herrera had still to emerge in all his shameless flamboyance, spawning any number of mini-Herreras down the years, and across the Old World.

The new reality in season 1956/7, when Real entered the European Cup as holders and Athletic Bilbao did so as the unexpected Spanish champions, was of course Kopa, at outside-right. In Paris, Di Stefano had clearly emerged as the winner of the implicit contest between the two, in every way. Gabriel Hanot himself, progenitor of the tournament, wrote as much in *L'Équipe*: 'Di Stefano eclipsed Kopa.' Kopa himself, all too germanely, wondered aloud why Real needed him at all.

This time there was, somewhat oddly, a so-called preliminary round, from which Real and other clubs were exempt, followed by a First Round proper, in which Real came up against Rapid Vienna and found the going hard. Indeed, play-offs being the fashion in those early days, it needed a play-off before Real could squeeze through. Had the present dispositions been in force, Rapid would have eliminated Real by virtue of their two away goals. What they did achieve was to show that Real were by no means invincible.

Though the superb Austrian international team of 1951 was now largely a mere memory, there was life on Prater yet, as Real would find out. Gerhard Hanappi, the superbly versatile 'Engineer', could play at half-back, full-back or even centre-forward, as one wished; and Ernst Happel, the blond, powerful centre-back, later to lead Holland to the 1978 World Cup Final, remained formidable. In the return leg in Vienna, Happel, who could strike a dead ball with tremendous power and accuracy, actually scored all three of Rapid's goals in a 3–1 victory which wiped out Real's 4–2 lead from Madrid. Though there were play-offs then, they did not take place on neutral grounds. Real cajoled Rapid into probable defeat by offering them a minimal £25 000 – a great deal of money at that time – if they would agree to play at Chamartin. They swallowed the bait and lost 2–0.

Nice, in the quarter-finals, were less of a problem for Real. Then came two memorable games against the so-called Busby Babes, the splendid young Manchester United side which had already scored ten goals against Anderlecht and eliminated Athletic Bilbao. Matt Busby, United's manager and mentor, had seen that the club defied the Football League to take part in the tournament. In Madrid, Real simply had too much experience and fire power for the United side, winning 3–1. At Old Trafford, they drew 2–2 in a vigorously contested match and were through to the Final against Fiorentina of Italy – at the Chamartin.

This time, money was not involved. Madrid had already been chosen as the venue for the Final. To stick to such a choice when the ground transpired to be that of one of the finalists seemed to me, from the first, to be badly mistaken. The policy would bear bitter fruit in the mid-eighties. Reaching the 1984 Final, scheduled for Rome, Liverpool found themselves playing Roma. They prevailed on penalties, but many of their supporters were viciously beaten up after the game by hooligan fans of Roma, and the horrific events of Heysel were a partial consequence as the Liverpudlians exacted a kind of perverted revenge.

Fiorentina, the Florentine club, had won the Italian championship for the first time in their history. They had an excellent pair of full-backs, first choice for Italy, in the big, dark Ardico Magnini and the compact Sergio Cervato, a tremendous striker of free kicks. There were two gifted South Americans in the side. Julinho, the Brazilian right-winger, had been one of the outstanding players in the 1954 World Cup; he was strongly built, superbly fast with a devastating swerve outside the full-back, and had a ferocious right-footed shot. Michelangiolo Montuori was an Argentine, born in Rosario, who had found his way to Chile and was playing in Santiago for Universidad Catolica when a priest spotted him and recommended him to Fiorentina. For a small fee, the club picked up an inside-forward of great skill on the ball and much creative flair. At centre-forward was the compact, muscular young Virgili, who'd made his name with Udinese and the Italian Under-23 team which, in the first ever match of its kind, beat England 3–0 in Bologna.

Magnini knew all about how to play Gento. I remember visiting him once in his apartment near the football stadium in Florence, when he told me, between intervals of jollying his old father, how, against so fast a winger, he would never mark him close but stand off and let Gento come to him. On this occasion Gento, with a goal, had the last laugh. But Fiorentina gave them a very hard run for their money, and who knows what might have happened had the game been played on a neutral ground, instead of before 125 000 Real fans?

Fiorentina, as might perhaps have been expected in the circumstances, set up their stall in defence and when Real did finally break them down it was with a thoroughly unsatisfactory goal. Mateos, the inside-right, broke clear only for a linesman to wave his flag for offside. Mysteriously, Leo

Horn, the well-known Dutch referee, allowed him to go on. When he was brought down in the box, Horn blew for a penalty. Di Stefano scored and Kopa, playing cleverly throughout, eventually sent Gento through for a second. General Franco himself presented the European Cup to Miguel Munoz. Appropriate enough. Real were, after all, his favourite team, and all Spain knew it.

The 1957/8 season brought a change of manager, and a new centre-half. The able, self-effacing Villalonga left, giving way to the Argentine Luis Carniglia, himself once a centre-half, for many years in French football. He'd been in charge of the Nice team whom Real had beaten on the way to their second European title. Real's new centre-half might be described as another bargain, again brought back from South America by the faithful gun dog Ramon Saporta. José Santamaria, Uruguay's centre-half in the 1954 World Cup, cost £45 000. Tall, muscular, blond, and ruthless when under extreme pressure, Santamaria took over from Marquitos, who now became a right-back. The contrast between the two was substantial. Both were big men but Santamaria was far more mobile and technically accomplished. He could use the ball, too, when he had intercepted it or won it. Miguel Munoz, who like Santamaria would manage Spain, now retired, giving way at right-half to Juan Santisteban.

Manchester United's young team was now entering its prime and there might, who knows, have been a memorable Final that year between them and Real Madrid. But in February 1958, the horrific Munich air crash broke United's splendid side asunder, nearly killed Matt Busby, and decreed that it should be Milan, not United, who figured in the Final.

Real got there with the loss of one game: to the surprising Hungarians Vasas, debutants in the competition. Real beat them 4–0 at Chamartin but lost the second leg in Budapest 2–0. They'd been prolific at home throughout the competition. Six goals against Antwerp, another eight against Seville, who qualified for the European Cup by virtue of being runners-up to Real, the holders, in the Spanish championship. Di Stefano scored four in that game, in which a man was sent off from each side.

José Santamaria made a large contribution to Real's progress. Though his nickname among Real's fans was 'The Wall', he thought 'a centre-half should be anything but that. In my opinion, football begins out of defence.' 4–2–4, which Real, in the current, overwhelming, fashion, were playing by now, 'in essence is a game of counter-attack, the strength of it based on the speed with which the ball can be sent up to the advanced forwards, assuming the forwards themselves are of the right type.'

Intriguingly, the Final in Brussels would pit Santamaria against a former, much-admired colleague in the Uruguayan 1954 team, Juan Schiaffino, the Milan inside-left or putative centre-forward, which was the role he filled in the Final, playing between Nils Liedholm of Sweden and Ernesto Grillo of Argentina. A skilled trio indeed. 'After our 3–2 win,' said Santamaria, 'I barely dared look Juan in the eye!'

Perhaps that was because Real were quite lucky to win, needing extra time to do so. There were 70 000 in the Heysel Stadium, destined to play so sinister a part in the history of the European Cup. For the best part of an hour, the two teams seemed to circle one another, like a couple of wary dogs. After half-time, however, the game came gloriously to life.

Milan went into a 1–0 lead and it was Schiaffino who got the first goal. Liedholm, who would shortly go on to play superbly in the World Cup for

Sweden, set it up for him after 59 minutes. Di Stefano needed another quarter of an hour before he squared the scores, Grillo four minutes to make it 2–1 for Milan, Hector Rial one minute to equalise again for Real.

So the game went into extra time, with an enormously lucky escape for Real when Tito 'El Loco' Cucchiaroni, Milan's Argentine outside-left, hit the bar. But it was the other outside-left, Paco Gento, who was enabled to win the game with a goal after 111 minutes. When first he shot, the ball was blocked and came straight back to him. Shooting again, he drove the ball through a knot of defenders and past an unsighted goalkeeper, Soldan, to make it 3–2 to Real.

Now came Ferenc Puskas, one more indisputably great player, who would comfortably co-exist with Di Stefano. He came in the close season of 1958, having got out of Hungary two years earlier. By a massive irony, the Hungarian authorities were hoist with their own petard. They had cracked down on the established clubs of Budapest and made Honved, the Army team, the be-all and end-all of the country's football by inducting a number of stars and giving them phoney commissions. But when they allowed Honved out on tour shortly before the Revolution broke, Puskas, Sandor Kocsis and Zoltan Czibor, three of the club's and the country's finest attacking players, stayed out. All of them found their way to Spain.

In the case of Puskas it was after a couple of years of vagabondage, waiting partly in Milan for his period of 'quarantine' to end. Able now to sign for Real, he looked plump and slow at first but Di Stefano never said to him, as he allegedly did to Didi, then 30, that he was 'too old and slow' to displace him. They were complementary from the start.

Puskas in fact was 32 by now, and a player who had long since entered into the history of the game. Captain of the marvellous Hungarian team which had thrashed England 6–3 at Wembley in November 1953, shattering the unbeaten home record against foreign teams into minuscule fragments, he'd failed to follow up with a World Cup victory in 1954.

Hungary's failure in Switzerland, their defeat in the Final, remains a matter of massive contention. Puskas, as domineering a figure as Di Stefano in his day, had been cruelly kicked by Werner Liebrich, the blond West German centre-half, when Hungary thrashed the Germans 8–3 in their initial World Cup game. That put him out until the Final, which the Germans, thanks to the vagaries of the competition, reached. Puskas insisted that he play, though he still was not fully fit. Moreover, he allegedly insisted on the exclusion of the right-winger Budai, who had done extremely well till then.

Hungary stuttered and lost, though Puskas probably had a goal quite wrongly ruled out for offside by the British refereeing trio. Now here he, and his fabulous left foot, were in Madrid. He had always been not only a marvellous striker of the ball but a superb tactician, playing well upfield in front of a deep lying centre-forward in Nandor Hidegkuti, making goals as well as scoring them.

'I am grateful to my father for all the coaching that he did *not* give me,' he once wrote. 'In Hungary boys, in their own enthusiasm, learn to control a ball almost from the time they can walk.' If I have a favourite, emblematic, memory of Puskas, it involves, curiously enough, a distant and remote city, and it did not occur on the field of play.

It was in Santiago, the night that Chile had won the third place game in the 1962 World Cup, and the streets swarmed with joyful, celebrating Chileans. There, standing in a shop doorway, quite unrecognised, eating monkey nuts out of a paper bag and grinning all over his urchin's face, was Puskas. He had played for Spain in that tournament, but how could it compare with the authentic thing, the Final of '54, when Hungary went down to defeat and his 'goal' was given offside?

It was another Hungarian, Emile Osterreicher, who in fact brought Puskas to Real. He had been added to Real's staff, a downy bird who knew his European football backwards and would sing a diplomatic song: 'I always told Santiago Bernabeu that Real had three great players: Di Stefano, Puskas . . . and Bernabeu.'

'I was charged with being slow after my early matches in Spain,' wrote Puskas. 'Modestly, I beg to point out that this was, and is, an illusion. Spain favours fast, driving football, which is to the appetite of our supporters. I, too, think football should be a fast game – but the ball should run faster than the man! Individual speed is a serviceable advantage. But to run madly and without purpose is of no value. The ball must be moved about quickly, preferably on first contact; to run with it is too often only wasting valuable attacking time.'

Puskas could certainly run with it when the need arose. His offside 'goal' in the World Cup Final was an example. So was one of the three he so magnificently but unavailingly scored in the 1962 European Cup Final. But then his technique was such that he could do anything and everything; except, perhaps, head spectacular goals.

When Hungary beat England at Wembley, he scored a memorable goal, pulling the ball back with the sole of his boot while England's captain, in the equally memorable words of Geoffrey Green in *The Times*, rushed past him 'like a fire engine going to the wrong fire.' Puskas insisted, with some justice, that he was 'as fast as the next man when I think it necessary to produce a sprint.'

What was beyond dispute was that he and Di Stefano, two great *maestri*, complemented one another supremely well, and never more so than in the triumphantly successful European Cup Final of 1960, when Puskas scored four and Di Stefano three. Puskas was already well used to playing with a deep lying centre-forward, since Nandor Hidegkuti had filled that role for years, not least when scored three in Hungary's success at Wembley. But Puskas long outlasted him. By the 1958 World Cup in Sweden, Hidegkuti looked a tired and used-up man. Puskas went galloping on for several splendid years.

Ferenc Puskas joined Real Madrid after escaping from Hungary, whose brilliant team of the early 1950s he captained. His left foot was devasting (Allsport)

Sandor Kocsis, alias Golden Head, who had played beside Puskas in the Hungarian and Honved teams, would, like Czibor, join Barcelona, an imposing rival to Real in Spain. But when Barcelona did knock out Real and reach the 1961 Final under Helenio Herrera, they lost, as we shall see, to Benfica.

Thus the 1958/9 Real Madrid side had three indisputably great players in attack: Puskas, Di Stefano and Kopa. And by ironic chance, it was Reims, the club for which Kopa had done so much and would do still more when he returned there, who were Real's opponents again in the European Cup Final. That was a pretty dull match in which Kopa himself was injured and largely reduced to hobbling about on the right wing. It was his last major game for Real before returning to Reims and almost, you might say, a symbolic one.

Much closer and far more exciting were the derby matches against the city rivals, Atletico Madrid, in the semi-finals. Again Real were taken to three matches, and again, had away goals counted double at the time, they would have gone out. They won the first leg, at home 2–1, but lost the second leg 1–0. Atletico then may have seemed the poor relations, but they were hardly poor in talent.

Above all, they had a splendid inside-forward trio consisting of the elegant Portuguese Mendonca, the dynamic Vavá, Brazil's centre-forward in the 1958 World Cup and scorer of two goals in the Final, and Joaquim Peiró, the Spanish international. Peiró, who played with his socks rolled down his long, lean, powerful legs, had splendid control, a fine left foot, and will enter this story again as the scorer of a goal against Liverpool which remains one of the most contentious in the story of the European Cup.

Atletico Madrid sturdily refused the poisoned chalice offered them by Real: the opportunity to play both legs at the Chamartin Stadium and make a great deal more money than if they were to play the home leg on their own ground. In the initial match, at Chamartin, it was ultimately a tale of two penalties. Chuzo got the opening goal for Atletico, to shock Real. Hector Rial wiped that out, then Puskas' mighty left foot whacked in a penalty. Vavá had the chance to do the same thing for Atletico but Real's new Argentine keeper, Rogelio Dominguez, saved his kick.

One says new, but the term was relative. Dominguez, a seasoned Argentine international, had in fact come to Madrid as long before as 1957, but Juan Alonso was the incumbent, and remained so for a year and more. Dominguez, significantly, admitted that when he arrived in Madrid he wasn't, for all his major experience, in the habit of coming off his line to collect the ball. 'I was slow to make up my mind to leave my line, and instead of giving the ball a hearty punch, I would only finger it away.' When Alonso contracted lung trouble, Dominguez at last had his chance. He won two European Cup medals.

Atletico won the second leg of the semi-final through a goal by their Spanish international winger Enrique Collar. Puskas didn't play in that game but Kopa, who had missed the first leg through injury, did. The play-off would not, this time, conveniently take place at the Chamartin; Atletico knew a trick worth two of that. Zaragoza was the venue, but Real won just the same. Collar scored again, after Di Stefano had given Real the lead, but this time Puskas was again on parade and he it was who got the winner, five minutes before half-time, beating Pazo with a shot into the left-hand corner.

So to Stuttgart for the Final, and a rather banal one at that. Puskas did not

Real overcame Reims and Juste Fontaine (right), top scorer in the World Cup Finals the previous year, in the 1959 Final at Stuttgart's Neckarstadion (Popperfoto)

play, Rial was the inside-left, Mateos and Di Stefano scored the two goals and Mateos threw away the chance to score a second when he missed a penalty. Kopa was, in his own words, 'savagely and deliberately fouled' by none other than Jean Vincent, the left-winger who had thrived on Kopa's passes the previous year when France took third place in Sweden. Later, Vincent would make a name for himself as a manager in the Far East and Africa, and a rather more equivocal name during the 1982 World Cup in Spain.

There, after his Cameroon team had drawn a strange game with Italy in Vigo, he sent his wife back to France carrying, according to the testimony of a go-between, a bag full of money from different currencies. When Vincent tried to apologise to Kopa after that game, he got short shrift. A strange, unpleasant episode, and hardly characteristic of Vincent, the player.

In 1960 came crescendo, or what in retrospect we can see as such: Real's amazing fifth consecutive win, followed by the unsuspected end of their domination. Barcelona and Benfica, who would contest the 1961 Final, waited on the horizon. It would be another six years before Real regained the Cup, with a team fustian by comparison with the unquestionably great one which won Glasgow's applause on that extraordinary evening.

Managers continued to come and go. After Carniglia, there was Fleitas Solich, the Paraguayan; after Solich, who was deemed old-fashioned, came Miguel Munoz, who not long before had been Real's right-half and captain. Solich, in fact, was regarded by many in South America as the inventor of 4–2–4, which he had introduced as a club manager in Rio; hardly the hallmark of an obsolescent manager. Paco Gento wrote of him: 'In most respects, Solich was an experienced and shrewd trainer. But he never really accepted that in a team of the highest standards, the creative power is generated among the players themselves, who could achieve an intimacy of mind and movement to which no trainer ccu1d possibly condition them. To be frank, Solich failed with us on that one major count – he did not understand the team.'

A major count indeed. So Solich, poor fellow, was dismissed, between the quarter and the semi-finals, to be replaced by Munoz, who was an immediate success with the team he had, after all, so successfully captained. 'Training now,' said Gento blissfully, 'is perfect and beautifully balanced. He is alert to our physical condition, our behaviour, and the subtleties of the technical side. He never panics, nor shows that he is upset. . . . He understands us as a team, and has a sure grasp of our problems individually.' But if the honeymoon endured, success would not.

What needs to be emphasised is that Real, in the Final, did not crush just anybody. The Eintracht Frankfurt team they overwhelmed was in fact on a return visit to Glasgow having, in the semi-finals, themselves crushed the opposition in a 6–3 win over Rangers, whom they had already destroyed 6–1 in Frankfurt. Moreover, this was one of the most dazzling of all European Cup competitions, with Barcelona, under Helenio Herrera, grinding Wolves into their own Molineux mud, then falling twice to Real in the semi-finals, 3–1 at home and 3–1 away.

Herrera had built a remarkable, polyglot team. In it were such seemingly disparate elements as the famous Hungarian attackers Zoltan Czibor and Sandor Kocsis, the serpentine Brazilian inside-forward Evaristo, and the Paraguayan attacker Eulogio Martinez, the scourge of goalkeepers like Real's Dominguez. Half admiringly, Dominguez spoke of Martinez's habit of cunningly blocking a goalkeeper at the moment the ball entered the penalty area, enabling fellow forwards to score.

However unorthodox and contentious his methods, Helenio Herrera had unquestionably welded Barcelona into a magnificent team. Their 5–2 thrashing of Wolves at Molineux prompted one of the leading English football writers of the day, John Camkin – a man not given to hyperbole – to write in the *News Chronicle*, 'In my memory they will stand above Honved, Real Madrid and any other outstanding club team of post-war years.'

Wolves were technically and tactically wholly surpassed, even though they had an all-England half-back line in Clamp, Slater and Flowers, an England inside-right in Peter Broadbent, and the reputation of doing wonderfully well against strong Continental opposition at Molineux. Indeed, their much-vaunted defeats under floodlights of Honved and Moscow Dynamo in the early 1950s had galvanised English football, and raised great interest in future matches with teams from the Continent. Chauvinism had obscured the fact that these famous victories had been obtained in non-competitive matches.

The Barcelona team which won with such ease at Molineux, despite the heavy conditions which traditionally and allegedly favoured British teams, had Kocsis at inside-right, Martinez in superlative form at centre-forward, and Luisito Suarez, later to play for Internazionale and to manage Spain's international team, at inside-left. Barcelona had aready thrashed Wolves in Barcelona, but this win was still more convincing and humiliating, showing just how far British football had fallen behind the best of Europe.

The astonishing Kocsis, as elegant and deadly on the ground as he was when the ball was in the air, rattled off four goals despite the fact that he dislocated a shoulder and fainted in the dressing-room at half time. A pain-killing injection allowed him to take the field again for the second half. He had, of course, been a salient figure in Hungary's devastating 6–3 win over England at Wembley in 1953. Now, at 31, he seemed as incisive as ever.

Speaking to an English journalist at Birmingham Airport, Helenio

Herrera said, 'You in England are playing now in the style we Continentals used so many years ago, with much physical strength but no method, no technique.' Where Barcelona had used four defenders in line to counter Wolves' four attackers, the Wolves defence, despite the currency of 4–2–4, left Bill Slater on his own at centre-half, utterly vulnerable.

Not in the Barcelona team that evening was another great Hungarian forward, Ladislao Kubala, the treble-international who played for the Czechs, the Hungarians and the Spaniards. A few weeks before Kocsis and his fellow Hungarians destroyed England's record at Wembley, Kubala himself had scored twice for the FIFA XI which drew 4–4 with England, and would have won had it not been for a deeply doubtful late penalty against them. them.

Blond, thick-thighed, a magnificent striker of the ball and a superb strategist, Kubala had found his way to Barcelona after much wandering, but like the equally celebrated Di Stefano, he did not see eye to eye with Herrera and his flamboyant methods.

Before a European Cup match, Herrera was wont to impose an extraordinary ritual. First, in a huge bare room with a massive wood-clad pillar in its centre, Herrera put his players through an exhausting series of exercises, at the end of which he threw a ball at each in turn, first to head, then to foot, the player being expected to pounce on it like some bird of prey. 'A sort of fury seemed to possess the players,' wrote an astounded French observer, Jacques Ferran.

The team then went off to take a shower and came back for a still more bizarre ceremony. Now they formed a circle, with Herrera standing in the middle. To each of them he again threw the ball, shouting the while a series of questions: 'What do you think of the match? Why are we going to win? How are we going to play?' Evaristo, the Brazilian forward, answered, 'We'll win because we want to win!' Antonio Ramallets, a fine goalkeeper who had defied England in Rio in the 1950 World Cup, responded , 'We're one of the best teams in the world, that is why we'll win.'

A few more ecstatic sprints, then, thoroughly transported, the players would throw themselves into one another's arms, crying, 'We're going to play for one another. You can count on me. We have to win together!' Finally, Herrera produced a white football, like some kind of Holy Grail. Each player extended his hand towards it and chanted, 'It's the European Cup! We must have it! We shall have it! We shall have it! We shall have it! Ah! Ah! Ah!'

While Kubala stood sceptically by.

But Real Madrid were not Wolverhampton Wanderers, a team which had prospered for years in the backwater of English football, using a simple long-ball game which, amazingly, would return to fashion in England in the supposedly far more sophisticated 1980s. Stanley Cullis, once the Wolves captain and centre-half, then their much admired and applauded manager, seemed tactically ingenuous by comparison with the Continentals.

Munoz, Real's new manager, took advantage of what were then much more indulgent regulations on eligibility, and bought two new players for his team. Luis Del Sol, a tough little inside-right, came from Betis of Seville; Enrique Pachin, a full-back, arrived from Osasuna. Ironically and somewhat farcically, though both men could participate in the European Cup at once, neither could play for Real in the Spanish championship until the following season.

All smiles from Paco Gento (right), Barcelona skipper Ramallets and referee Arthur Ellis before the 1960/1 First Round first leg match at the Bernabeu stadium; but the tie would be dominated by controversy over refereeing decisions in both legs (Hulton Picture Company)

At Barcelona, Herrera quarrelled with Kubala and his fellow Hungarian Zoltan Czibor over bonuses, but it may well be that this was simply the tip of the iceberg, given the troubled relations between Kubala and Herrera. Kubala, like Munoz, would in due course become team manager of Spain. Both he and Czibor were left out of the team against Madrid, which displeased the Barcelona fans, who liked them both, especially Kubala. But too much emphasis should perhaps not be placed on the fact. Neither, after all, had been in the side which won so impressively at Wolves.

In the event, Di Stefano and Puskas, in transcendent form, proved too much for Barcelona's defence. Di Stefano bestrode the field at Chamartin, scoring twice. Puskas got the other, then added two more in Barcelona, where the building of the massive Nou Camp stadium had severely cut down the club's future options in the transfer market. Helenio Herrera was attacked outside the team's hotel by enraged Barcelona fans and was on his way before long: to Inter, two triumphs in the European Cup, and an enormously lucrative career in Italy.

Now, for Real, came Eintracht Frankfurt in the Final. Eintracht had no star to match the prowess of Puskas and Di Stefano, but their annihilation of Rangers had shown just how formidable a team they were. 'We were like the straight man to the comic,' said Willie Stevenson, Rangers' left-half, who would later play in the European Cup for Liverpool. Alfred Pfaff, a clever and inventive inside-forward, was the hub of the Eintracht team, Richard Kress a fast and penetrative right-winger, Erwin Stein a forceful young centre-forward, Stinka a wing-half who used the ball with great skill.

Real's team for the Final was almost as polyglot as Barcelona's. In goal was the Argentine Dominguez with Di Stefano, another Argentine, leading the attack. Santamaria of Uruguay was at centre-half, Puskas the Hungarian at inside-left, and a Brazilian newcomer, Canario, on the right wing. Quick and elusive, Canario was not in the class of the great Brazilian outside-rights, Julinho and Garrincha, but he was highly effective.

Under Munoz, the defence largely marked man to man. Marquitos, once the centre-half and scorer of the vital goal in the 1956 Final, was at right-back. In front of him was Vidal, an energetic and skilful young right-half. Del Sol was a busy, ubiquitous inside-forward; Di Stefano continued to be the grand puppeteer.

For some twenty odd minutes, the grand illusion endured that Eintracht might even win. It was on twenty minutes, in fact, that Kress had the temerity to close in and beat Dominguez to open the scoring. But the bull now was well and truly roused. Zarraga to Canario, a centre from the right, a pounce by Di Stefano and the equaliser was in. With half an hour played, Di Stefano swooped again, this time with a tremendous shot into the roof of the net when the German keeper Loy could only block a drive by Canario.

Plucky but outgunned, there was little Eintracht could do to resist the bombardment. With Di Stefano tireless, ubiquitous and magisterial, and Puskas his loyal and lethal henchman, Real commanded the field. Gento ran like an electric hare, Del Sol was as indefatigable as Di Stefano. A left-foot blast from an extraordinary angle by Puskas made it 3–1 at half-time.

Puskas, in the second half, was rampant. He scored from a controversial penalty; he even, most untypically, headed a goal. He smashed his fourth inside the post and just under the bar. No other living player could have even reached the ball.

The match had become a procession, an exhibition. Di Stefano was here, there and everywhere, always to the maximum effect. When Stein then scored for Eintracht he swiftly replied, taking a pass from Puskas and racing away to beat Loy again. Stein and Eintracht had the last word, for what it was worth, as a careless back pass led to a third goal for the Germans. So it was 7–3, and 127000 Scottish fans stayed to pay homage. Eintracht had been thrashed, but their sportsmanship had been impeccable.

The following season, Barcelona would have their revenge, knocking out Real in the First Round Proper. The writing was on the wall in the first leg when for the first time Real failed to win a home tie in the European Cup. There were two goals for Luis Suarez in the 2–2 draw, the second from the penalty spot when Kocsis, brought down, might have been offside. Arthur Ellis – Battle of Berne and 1956 Final – gave the penalty.

There was another English referee in the return leg, watched by 112000 at Nou Camp. He was Reg Leafe, and he disallowed three Real goals. Barcelona won 2–1: an own goal by Pachin, a header by Evaristo, a late and irrelevant response by Canario.

'No, no, no!' chanted the incensed Real players, Del Sol to the fore, surrounding Reg Leafe after the match banquet. Scenting trouble, Bob Ferrier, the Scottish journalist, shoved Leafe into a taxi and sent him speeding away from what could have been a painful encounter.

Santiago Bernabeu, President of Real Madrid for over 40 years and a father figure to the club and its players, celebrates with midfielder Amaro Amancio after Real had overcome Inter to reach the 1966 Final

(Farabolafoto)

Well beaten by Benfica in the 1962 European Cup Final in Amsterdam, Real would lose another Final in 1964 to a highly functional, counter-attacking Internazionale side in Vienna, as we shall see. Di Stefano and Puskas were still playing then, but by 1966, apart from the senatorial presence of Gento on the left wing, Real were a young and vigorous side. They reached the Final again and this time they won it, but their major triumph in the competition that season was the defeat of Inter in the semi-finals – thanks in no small measure to the courage and honesty of Gyorgy Vadas, the Hungarian referee, who so stoutly refused to be bribed. The experienced Pachin was still there too, at right-back, but the two major figures were Pirri and Amaro Amancio, an attacking right-half and a right-winger now playing at inside-right.

Both were technical players of great quality. Pirri, socks rolled down to his ankles, was the perfect wing-half; a strong tackler, dynamic, quick, and eager to come forward with the ball. Like a surprisingly large number of good Spanish players, he came from the little North African enclave of Ceuta. Later, he would qualify as a doctor.

Amancio, with his strong, thick legs, and impressive turn of speed, could avoid tackles with his ball control or withstand them. He was an excellent right-winger, and when he moved inside, where there was less space but the goal was nearer, he was just as effective. In fact when Real first signed him, as an 18-year-old from Deportivo Coruna of the 2nd Division, he was then an inside-right. Real converted him into a right-winger – then back again.

If he had a fault, it was perhaps the obverse of his virtues: he could tend, at times, to hold on to the ball too long. But he was certainly a player for the great occasions, not least in 1964, when he did so much not only to help Real to the European Cup Final, but to see that Spain won the European Nations Cup Final, too. When Real finally regained the European Cup two years later, he it was who equalised Partizan's opening goal.

In the semi-final second leg against Inter at San Siro, it was Amancio who gave Real the lead, putting the game beyond Inter, already a goal down from the game in Madrid. Gyorgy Vadas's defiantly honest refereeing did the rest.

Though Real won the Final in Brussels against Partizan Belgrade, any comparison with the great teams which won the first five trophies would be odious indeed. Vigour was the watchword of this team; but then how do you replace a Nijinski, a Garbo, an Olivier . . . a Di Stefano?

Partizan, who had eliminated a lustreless Manchester United in the semi-finals, had their own share of gifted players. Soskic was an agile and courageous goalkeeper; Vasovic, scorer of the opening goal, a powerful and resilient centre-back; Galic a strong, opportunist centre-forward; and Kovacevic a creative little midfielder, skilful on the ball and adept at making the through pass.

Real, their team made up solely of Spaniards, were neatly prompted in attack by their clever inside-left Velazquez, but were lucky not to go 2–0 down – Galic should have scored a second goal, after Vasovic headed Partizan in front from a corner. But Grosso gave Amancio the chance to equalise, and after 84 minutes the Spanish right winger Serena scored from outside the penalty box with his left foot, previously used almost wholly for standing on.

It took Real another fifteen years to reach their only European Cup Final since then, when they lost a deeply dull game 1–0 to Liverpool in Paris. Subsequently, despite the building of an often exciting team based on home-grown players, the semi-final has proved an impassable barrier. Indeed, in the 1989/90 competition, they foundered as early as the second round against the Milan team which had thrashed them at San Siro in the semis the previous season. The following season was still worse, the League was lost to Barcelona. John Toshack, the Welsh manager, was sacked and still Real faltered, even losing their precious inviolability at home, to Spartak Moscow in the quarter-finals.

Using 2nd Division Castilla as their nursery club, Real have, however, proved astonishingly successful in developing their own, fine players, a start contrast with the years of their European Cup dominion. Emilio Butragueño, though he found himself somewhat perversely excluded from the first team at the beginning, has been the salient example. A lithe, quick centre-forward of delightful touch and tremendous talent, his father registered him as a club member when he was one day old. One can scarcely be more 'local' than that.

Nicknamed El Buitre – The Vulture – Butragueño emerged with two other hugely talented young attackers: Michel, a well-built, elegant, creative player, used largely deep on the right flank, and Martin Vazquez, his skilful equivalent on the left, each capable of scoring as well as setting up goals.

But the tradition of acquiring foreign players continued in the shape of Hugo Sanchez, a little Mexican dentist. Tremendously quick and incisive around goal, able to nip in to score with his head as well as his feet, and famous for the joyful somersault he performs when he's done so, Sanchez was filched from the deadly rivals Atletico Madrid, who brought him across from Mexico only to lose him when Real made him an offer he wouldn't refuse, and Sanchez exploited a Spanish law which allowed him to buy himself out of his contract.

Sanchez's combination with Butragueño at times looked one of the most dangerous and productive in Europe; yet time after time, in the European Cup, something has gone wrong. Something which Alfredo Di Stefano, no doubt, would triumphantly have put right.

3

THE BENFICA
INTERLUDE

The Trattoria Romana, in Via Frattina, alas no longer exists. Located in one of the most fashionable areas of Rome, it was, in the mid-1950s, run as a waiters' co-operative, and was patronised by football fans and football people. I used to lunch there every day with Domenico Biti, who was then Lazio's youth coach; he would become Roma's in due course and would discover Bruno Conti, shining star of the 1982 World Cup.

One day early in 1955, Bela Guttmann turned up at lunchtime. Bald, suave, and courteous as ever, but a little subdued and for good reason. He had just been sacked by Milan, who were still leading the Italian Championship. But they had lost a couple of matches and in Italian football then, such things were not permitted. Bela must have been in his mid-fifties, a classical product of pre-war Austro-Hungarian football who had roamed the world and would continue to do so, as much at home in South America as in Europe.

'Next time I sign a contract,' he said, 'I'm going to have a clause in it: not to be dismissed when the club is top of the League.' Then he told us a wry little tale.

A few years ago, Lucchese, a little Tuscan club which played briefly in the 1st Division, was on its way up to Turin to play the mighty Juventus 'when their manager, poor fellow, died. What could an Italian team do without a manager? The directors phoned all over Italy, until at last they found one. He arrived just in time to sit on the bench, Lucchese drew 1–1, and their players carried the manager off on their shoulders.'

Enough said. Guttmann was a shrewd character – once a fine player, later a great survivor. He had begun his career in Budapest with the MTK club, making a large reputation as an attacking centre-half. Being Jewish, like so many of that team, he received and accepted an invitation to play for the all-Jewish club Hakoah of Vienna, which once, in the early 20s, beat a West Ham United reserve side 5–1 at Upton Park.

In Vienna, which would become his true home till well after the war, Guttmann gained the reputation of being a demanding dandy, a man who would allegedly sit in the dressing-room and refuse to play unless the club guaranteed him silk shirts. How, I once asked him, did he survive the ensuing war, the Nazi persecution? 'God helped me,' he replied simply.

When Benfica came to play Tottenham Hotspur in London in the European Cup in 1962, I remember a touching reunion between Guttmann and some of his ageing Hakoah colleagues, who had also survived the war. There was Katz, the famous inside-forward, now a quiet little grey-headed man, and two or three others besides. They came to see Guttmann at the Park Lane Hotel, where he and the Benfica team were staying.

What a team it was! And what a player it had in Eusebio, from Mozambique. He of the handsome, almost spiritual face; the lithe, flexible body; the long legs, so expert at conjuring the ball past tackles, so explosive both in movement and in the enormous power of his right-footed shot. But when Guttmann took over Benfica, Eusebio's coruscating presence lay in the immediate future. Benfica won first the Portuguese title, then their first European Cup, without him.

But without players from Africa, what would they have done at all? Without Mario Coluna, by turns inside-left and left-half, whose left-footed shooting was almost as ferocious as Eusebio's was with his right? Coluna, whose injury would cost Benfica, surely, a third successive victory in the European Cup Final of 1963 at Wembley when Milan's Pivatelli fouled him nastily, painfully and, as it transpired, decisively. There were no substitutes then, to replace an injured player; and who, in any case, could have replaced Coluna?

Coluna came from Mozambique, too. José Aguas, the centre-forward, came from Angola. No giant this, but so enormously quick in thought and movement, adept in playing with his back to the goal, a perfect point of reference for the whole attack. Another Angolan was the inside-right Joaquim Santana, a skilled and intelligent player. When Guttmann arrived in 1959, having inspired Porto to snatch the Championship from under Benfica's nose, he inherited the Lisbon club's policy of fielding players only from Portugal and its colonies. But with such talent at his disposal, Guttmann, who had put in a spell, and a successful one, with Sao Paolo in Brazil after leaving Italy, was none the less able to build a hugely successful – and attractive – team.

Guttmann's policy, as a coach – and he never ceased to go out on the field, even in his sixties – was essentially a progressive one. There are those who claim that he, rather than Fleitas Solich, initiated 4–2–4 in Brazil, though one doubts that. Certainly he used it, but he was also ready to throw up extra forwards, sometimes even five at once, and in defence adopt a zonal, English game.

Germano Figureido was another of his inspired acquisitions. The tall, prematurely bald, heavily moustached centre-half was bought from a smaller Lisbon club, Atletico. He would play in the first two, victorious, European Finals, but miss the third through injury. Alas, he was so often injured, and his career was ultimately cut short.

He had no greater admirer than the then manager of England, Walter Winterbottom. 'He bounces with energy!' Winterbottom once told me, and went on to describe how he had watched Germano catch an attacker who had passed him, win the ball with a superb sliding tackle, get up again, turn, and bring it into attack.

A ludicrous £2000 was all he cost when Guttmann signed him, and he was a 2nd Division player then, already in his mid-20s. In season 1964/5 he was back again in full fettle, though now 31 years old. He played for Benfica right the way through to a disappointing Final against Inter, when he showed his versatility by taking over in goal after the resilient keeper Costa Pereira was injured. Of all his Finals, however, none was more impressive than the first when he, more than anyone, frustrated the might of Barcelona's powerful team. Utterly cool and composed, he was capable of dribbling past opponents in his own penalty area. But cartilage operations brought his fine if curious career to a close.

Mario Coluna was, in his teens, an outstanding athlete, who one day opted for football. This did not prevent him, at the age of 17, becoming high-jump champion of Mozambique, with a leap of 1.83 metres. Athletics tugged at him again, but the strongest pull came in 1954 when he was signed by Benfica. Before the Guttmann Era, you will notice. A Brazilian, the celebrated Otto Gloria, who would later take over the Portuguese international team, was the club manager then. But Coluna was a centre-forward, and Benfica already had José Aguas.

What was to be done? Initially, Gloria gave Coluna the central position and shifted Aguas to the left wing. But it didn't work; Coluna was ill at ease. Gloria switched him to inside-left and restored Aguas to his proper position, the position which would one day be filled by his son. On tour in Portugal, Coluna was a colossal success, nicknamed 'The Portuguese Didi'.

When Eusebio arrived Bela Guttmann had a problem: an embarrassment of riches. He turned Coluna into a left-half, but had his doubts about him. Coluna, he said, 'cannot mark anybody. He has to run up and down the whole field.' But no one in the team, not even Germano, was ready to shoulder more responsibility than Coluna. It was one of his tremendous left-footed shots which flew past Ramallets in Berne to give Benfica victory against Barcelona in that astonishing Final. Then came another bullet in Amsterdam against Real the following year. Even in 1963, before he was injured, he let fly another of his howitzer shots which Ghezzi, the Milan goalkeeper, did wonderfully well to reach and turn away.

His private life had its difficulties. His wife was a passionate Mozambique nationalist who drew him, and his resources, into that ultimately successful campaign. But in 1966 he was at Wembley again, this time with Portugal to play splendidly against England in the semi-final; he was splendid again against Russia, when Portugal took third place. An inspired and inspirational captain.

The great Eusebio. A beautiful mover, with explosive pace and an equally explosive right foot which brought Benfica success in the 1962 Final (Allsport)

Benfica's progress to their first European Cup Final, in season 1960/61, was imposing. They did lose once, to Ujpest in Budapest, but only after thrashing them in the home leg 6–2. Hearts, in the so-called preliminary round, were no trouble; Benfica beat the Edinburgh team home and away. 'We were absolutely outclassed,' admitted the Hearts right-winger, that distinguished veteran international Gordon Smith, a member of the Hibernian team which competed in the initial European Cup.

Guttmann, who had once managed Ujpest, watched now as his Benfica team overwhelmed them in the massive Estadio da Luz, the Stadium of Light. The excellent, quick right-winger José Augusto, whom he had bought from Barreirense, scored yet again as he and Aguas had in both matches against Hearts. Aarhus, the Danes, were no great problem in the quarter-finals. Rapid Vienna, beaten 3–0 in Lisbon in the semi-final first leg, presented a particular and sinister kind of problem in the return leg at the Prater stadium.

By an odd chance, the referee was the Englishman Reg Leafe, just as it was in the turbulent first round game between Real Madrid and Barcelona. There were no goals till the 66th minute when Aguas made it 1–0, and 4–0 on aggregate. Rapid did manage to equalise but survival was clearly beyond them.

It must therefore have been an accumulation of resentment, rather than thwarted hope, which led Rapid and their fans to their excesses when Leafe refused them a penalty with only a couple of minutes left. But Rapid's players attacked Benfica's, fans rushed on to the field to join in and police had to quell the brawl, escorting Leafe and the Benfica team to safety. An especially distressing incident for Guttmann, of all people; Guttmann, who gave Vienna as his favourite city, the place where he wanted to – and would – spend his retirement, at open air café tables chatting with his old football friends. UEFA took stringent measures; Rapid were banned from Prater for three seasons.

For the Final in Berne, Barcelona were strong favourites; even for Guttmann, who looked with awe upon a team full of his fellow Hungarians. There was Kubala, Kocsis and Czibor, not to mention Evaristo of Brazil. Guttmann was, he would later admit, 'afraid of their forward-line', and who wouldn't have been? But on the day, Benfica fought as Guttmann hoped they would, and the sun played strange tricks on Barcelona's keeper Ramallets.

What Guttmann wanted his Benfica team to do was fight, and they did. Kocsis – back in Switzerland where he had played so superbly seven years earlier in the World Cup, emerging as the leading scorer – applied his Golden Head to a centre by Suarez in the 19th minute, with a dive this time, rather than a leap, to put Barcelona ahead. Costa Pereira thwarted Kocsis; Germano, a giant that day, kicked off the line from that other survivor of 1954, Czibor. All Guttmann's fears seemed horribly well founded. Even he could scarcely have hoped, let alone predicted, that Benfica would score twice in a minute.

Antonio Ramallets was the culprit, 11 long years after he had thwarted England in Rio. He was far too quick and rash in coming off his line to meet Cavem, then a left-winger, after Coluna had split the Barcelona defence. A squared ball, an easy goal for Aguas. Away again went Benfica from the kick-off. Neto lobbed in, Gensana could only back-head the ball and Ramallets, wrong-footed, pushed the ball desperately against the post, whence it dropped over the line; 2–1 to Benfica.

A goal from Coluna's right foot, of all unexpected things, made it 3–1, ten minutes after half-time. Coluna had found Cavem and carried on, then volleyed the ball when Cavem's cross was headed out, and Ramallets was beaten once more. An astonishing reversal, but it must have been a chilling moment for Kocsis and Czibor. It was on this very ground that Hungary, all those years ago, had lost the World Cup to West Germany. They'd had little luck that day, and still less now. The goalposts alone would save Benfica. From Kocsis's header, then from a shot by Kubala – a Kocsis header set him up for it – which struck each post in turn. A glorious movement and a fine shot by Czibor made it 3–2, but Benfica held out, held on. One Hungarian, at least, had found Berne benign. But it was Guttmann, not Kocsis, Kubala or Czibor.

A week later the marvellous Eusebio, then 19, made his debut for Benfica and inevitably scored. Benfica then took him to the Paris tournament where he scored three more, though Pele's Santos prevailed 6–3. It was Carlos Bauer, elegant right-half of the marvellous Brazilian World Cup team of

1950, who tipped off Guttmann about Eusebio. Bauer had been Guttmann's player at Sao Paolo. They met twice in a barber's shop in Lisbon, and on each occasion Bauer, who'd been taking a Brazilian team on tour through Africa, eulogised Eusebio. The second time, the penny dropped; Guttmann signed Eusebio for just $20 000.

The following September, Benfica flew to Montevideo to meet Penarol, the holders of the Libertadores Cup, in the second leg of the Intercontinental Cup, later known as the World Club Championship, a competition of dubious dimensions which had begun in 1960. A goal by Coluna gave Benfica the first leg in Lisbon, but in Montevideo, where Guttmann himself would later work, they crashed 5–0. That meant a play-off, again in Montevideo, and for this, Benfica flew out Eusebio.This time they lost only 2–1, Eusebio scoring their goal. From that moment, there was no displacing him. Indeed, he would win his first Portuguese cap after no more than 25 games in the 1st Division.

Another new face in the play-off match with Penarol was that of the immensely gifted little left-winger, Antonio Simoes, then but 17 years old. His presence enabled both Cavem and Coluna – who wasn't initially too pleased – to move back into midfield.

On, then, to the 1961/2 tournament, in which Benfica would have much trouble and a little luck, perhaps, against Spurs, but would triumphantly crush Real Madrid in an electrifying Final.

Tottenham Hotspur felt they had been maltreated in Katowice when they were beaten 4–2 by the Polish champions, Gornik. In consequence, the return leg at White Hart Lane was played in an atmosphere of seething aggression, both on and off the field. I can still remember that night; there was hatred in the air, and Gornik simply collapsed.

Spurs had a fine team which had just become the first to do the League and Cup double this century. Captained by the elegant, perceptive, inspirational Danny Blanchflower, right-half for Northern Ireland, it included John White, a Scottish inside-forward of exquisite talents and superb ability to pass and cross; Dave Mackay, a robust and commanding left-half; Cliff Jones, a very fast and immensely courageous left-winger, not least when it came to heading goals at knee height among the flailing boots; and Bobby Smith, the big centre-forward, who could be a formidable figure on his day, or night. Gornik, under the Tottenham floodlights, could do little or nothing with him as Spurs won 8–1, with three goals going to Jones.

Spurs, some of whose players had literally been bitten by fleas in their Polish hotel, had found all the determination which, according to their manager Bill Nicholson, they'd lacked in Katowice. To a fault, one might say. 'Heading is a skill,' remarked Nicholson succinctly, 'and so is crossing the ball accurately.' No one did that better than John White, pitifully to be killed by a bolt of lightning in 1964.

In November 1961, Jimmy Greaves arrived at Tottenham from Milan. There he had scored nine goals in ten games, a quite amazing record for a thoroughly homesick and unsettled player. Greaves, a quintessential Cockney, had made his name as boy wonder at Chelsea, a first-team player and a regular goalscorer at 17. Small, strong, immensely quick off the mark, a superb left-footed striker of the ball and wonderfully adept at finding space in a crowded penalty box, Greaves could also use his pace to cut through a square defence from halfway. Two rich Italian clubs wanted him in the spring of 1961: Roma and Milan. Milan won, but on England's subsequent

*Bela Guttmann at
White Hart Lane
before the return leg of
Benfica's semi-final tie
with Spurs, their
biggest test on the way
to retaining the trophy*
(Popperfoto)

tour of Europe, Greaves announced in mid-air between Rome and Vienna that he was staying with Chelsea.

'I don't see how he can,' rumbled Sir Stanley Rous, the large and imposing Football Association Secretary, dozing in his seat, and of course he was right; Greaves had signed the contract, Greaves had to go. But he had so many bitter disagreements with Milan that the club eventually let him go home, for £99 999, a nice profit on the £80 000 they'd paid Chelsea. (Spurs didn't want to be the first club to pay £100 000 in England). It was a fortune then, but Greaves still proved a bargain.

Benfica had trouble in their quarter-final against the West German champions, Nuremberg. Lacking Eusebio, who was injured, they were beaten 3–1 in the first leg; but with Eusebio back, they thrashed Nuremberg 6–0 in Lisbon. Bill Nicholson was able to watch that game. Strangely enough, clubs in the European Cup could at that time arrange their own dates, within a certain time span, rather than play them on the same nights.

Drawn against Benfica, so much more experienced in European football than they, Spurs made tactical mistakes in the first leg in Lisbon. Bill Nicholson imposed an overly defensive strategy, with Tony Marchi, usually a left half, as the spare man in defence. Alas, the defenders weren't good enough to implement it, especially the full-backs, whose errors cost the game. With Greaves now available, Tottenham would clearly have done better to have carried the game to Benfica, whose great strength – *pace* Germano – was after all in attack.

Those mistakes were exploited by Aguas and Augusto in the opening twenty minutes. Tottenham settled down in the second half, but though Bobby Smith headed a goal for them, Augusto headed another for Benfica who ran out winners by 3–1.

It was no greater a lead than Gornik had brought to London, but Guttmann was too wily a campaigner to let White Hart Lane become the cauldron it was that night. Tottenham, he believed, had watered their pitch, but he made light of it. Next he announced to the Press that he 'expected a bloodbath', in the hope of influencing the Danish referee, Poulsen. In the event, it seemed to work. Smith and Mackay, the Spurs players whose physical commitment Guttmann feared, were well watched by the referee. Finally, anxious to spare his players the tension of the atmosphere as long as possible, he let them take the field only at the last possible moment.

Spurs came at Benfica as Guttmann had expected. Greaves had the ball in the net, but the goal was ruled somewhat controversially offside. On the quarter hour came the decisive moment. José Aguas scored in a counter attack, and Spurs had a mountain to climb. But in a frenetic first half, Bobby Smith equalised and then Danny Blanchflower, always so precise from the spot, slid home a penalty.

That gave Spurs the whole of the second half to take the tie, but they couldn't. Their frantic attacks foundered on the goalkeeping of Costa Pereira, the commanding defensive play of Germano, and the woodwork, which they struck no fewer than three times. So Benfica again were in the Final – just. There they would meet Real Madrid, who had conquered Juventus in the other semi-final, an achievement marred by the brutal treatment handed out by Santamaria to Juve's majestic Welsh international centre-forward, 'King' John Charles, as he was known in Turin.

Before the match, at the Benfica team's hotel in Amsterdam, the old fox Bela Guttmann was in his element, smiling, joking, utterly relaxed. He was 62, but when anybody asked him his age the inevitable reply was, 'I'm 24.'

He was always good for an anecdote. He told a French journalist the tale behind Hungary's extraordinary defeat by Egypt in the 1924 Paris Olympic Games. 'After we had easily beaten Poland, we were eliminated, to the general surprise, 3–0 by Egypt. The thing was, we had been wretchedly treated by our delegation-chief who gave us little to eat and no pocket money, so we accepted the defeat without reacting and I joyfully took the road back to Vienna.' As indeed he would once more, when he retired.

Meanwhile, there was Real to face; a Real team which might be somewhat past its peak but still had the devastating pair of Puskas and Di Stefano in its ranks, not to mention Gento on the wing and Santamaria to shore up the defence, Real's answer to the mighty Germano.

One remembers that evening with delight. Nearly 30 years on, the game seems a marvellous anachronism, the product of an age of relative innocence in which defences and defensive tactics – such as Inter already deployed – were not yet strangling the sport. It was a night in which the shots simply flew into the net, whether from the left foot of Puskas or the right foot of Eusebio, with contributions of great class from Coluna and Cavem.

Puskas scored a hat-trick in the first half and what marvellous goals they were! Running half the pitch, put through by Di Stefano, to score one of them; coiling his left foot to hit a shot of pulverising power for another. Aguas and Cavem – his shot, too, a fulminating left footer – replied for Benfica. Then at half-time Guttmann put Cavem on the ageing Di Stefano, who no longer had the legs to evade a close marker. Now Puskas no longer had the same devastating service, and Benfica hit back with three goals.

When Puskas did drop deep for the ball, he lost it. Coluna seized his chance to strike a remarkable 30-yard drive past Araquistain, the Real keeper. The scores were level and now Eusebio ran wild; the long, lean powerful legs too quick for Real's defence, and the right-footed shot irresistible. Racing past Di Stefano, no longer the player of two years before, Eusebio was fouled by Pachin and banged in the penalty for 4–3. Then the *coup de grâce*: a free-kick slipped to him by Coluna, a drive which struck a Real player on the way, changed course and ended up in the net. Benfica had won their second Final, Real had lost their first. Puskas gave Eusebio his jersey. Guttmann was carried off the field.

He did not stay. He'd signed a contract which made no provision for bonuses if the European Cup were won, and Benfica's directors had foolishly kept him to it. There was, though, another factor. Scarred by what happened to him in Milan, Guttmann now never wanted to stay long – outstay his welcome – at any club. So he left, resumed his far flung travels and was replaced by the Chilean Fernando Riera. Benfica would reach the Final yet again the following year at Wembley, but Coluna was clobbered by Milan's Pivatelli, and Benfica lost to Altafini's two goals.

There was still tremendous life in the club and in the team. In 1965, there they were again in another Final, this time in Milan against Inter, Herrera's Inter, who were literally playing at home. Under a deluge, reduced to ten men with Germano in goal, Benfica lost to a single goal. By then, Cavem had retreated still further, to right-back. In these two Finals, Benfica played to a different pattern. No Aguas now, so subtle, skilful and mobile, but Torres, the Tower, immensely tall, prolific in the air, but a point of reference rather than a ubiquitous, dynamic all-rounder.

Still Benfica were not finished; in 1968 they were back at Wembley, five full years after they had lost there to Milan, this time to take on Manchester

United. They lost again; but United needed extra time and the brilliance of Best, despite some displeasingly rough treatment from the Benfica defence, to do it. This was the first season in which away goals counted double, but Benfica did not need such help when they conquered Juventus in the semi-finals, taking a 2–0 lead to Turin and winning there, too, 1–0.

Eusebio was decisive in both games even though his knee was giving him terrible trouble, so much so that Otto Gloria, the Brazilian manager now in charge after the sudden resignation of Riera, had almost to bully him into playing in the return leg. He could hardly run, but he did drive in a 35-yard free-kick. The first leg had seen him score, too.

Strangely, Benfica had had much more trouble with little Glentoran of Northern Ireland and they did, indeed, require the new 'away goals' dispensation to get past them. John Colrain, the tall, dark player-manager of the Belfast club, actually put them ahead when he scored from a penalty. It needed a goal from the inevitable Eusebio to level matters. At the Estadio da Luz, it was expected, the floodgates would open and Glentoran would be swamped. Not a bit of it. The Irish team held out superbly to draw 0–0 and Benfica slithered, embarrassed, into the next round.

There were more changes in the team, not least the arrival in midfield of the elegant Graça, a right-half who would score Benfica's equalising goal in the Final at Wembley. Not that that was a day on which Benfica wholly endeared themselves. In 1963 it was they, and Coluna, who had suffered, when Pivatelli did for him. Now it was Best who was chopped and obstructed time and again, notably by the abrasive Fernando Cruz. It was not Cruz's first experience at Wembley, nor the first time he had offended there.

Nearly seven years earlier when he was still a left-half – he returned now as a left-back – he had aimed a head-butt at England's genial right-back Jimmy Armfield. 'But I'm a coward' said Armfield. 'I ducked my head!' It was Cruz who came off the worse. Less typical, and an indication that even the most elegant footballers can show the cloven hoof, was Eusebio's brutal foul on United's Scottish right-half Pat Crerand. Humberto, a powerful centre-half, was a frequent transgressor.

Beaten 4–1 in extra time, after a seemingly shattered United team had triumphantly found its second wind, Benfica's famous team would now disintegrate, and not for another twenty years would the club reach the Final

Jose Torres (centre, dark shirt) and skipper Mario Coluna put pressure on the Inter defence in the 1965 Final at San Siro. Along with team-mates Jose Augusto and Fernando Cruz, Coluna played in all five European Cup Finals involving Benfica in the 1960s

(Farabolafoto)

again. When it did, it was with a team that raised no echoes of the exciting sides which had contested all those Finals in the sixties. Football by now was real – with a small R – and earnest, and in 1988 at Stuttgart, Benfica and PSV Eindhoven contested a Final of stifling boredom; though to be fair, one no more boring than most of those which had preceded it.

The words of Toni, once their propulsive right-half, for a time their manager, but usually in this period the club's assistant manager, were germane. 'I can't compare this team with the team of more than 20 years ago. Football changes and to stay at the top you have to change with it.'

Though not, ideally, in the way the 1988 Benfica team had changed, for they played a drab, dour, negative Final, intent it seemed merely on achieving what they did: a goalless draw after extra time, with the hope of winning on penalties. That hope was dashed. In the shoot-out, the defender Veloso missed and PSV won. European Cup Finals seem to have been jinxed for Veloso. Suspension prevented him even from playing against Milan in Vienna two years later.

Benfica, it is true, lacked one of their key attacking players in Stuttgart in the shape of big Diamantino. But their tactics were a travesty of what Benfica had once stood for. Oh, my Coluna and my Eusebio long ago! Rui Aguas, the son of the accomplished José, was chiefly remarkable for the endless trouble he seemed to have with his boots! He appeared to be marking Ronald Koeman, PSV's big, blond attacking sweeper, rather than the other way around. After 56 minutes, he was obliged to leave the field, pulling a hamstring after getting in the way of a free-kick. Still, he had had his moment of glory, scoring both goals in the 2–0 victory over Steaua Bucharest which enabled his team to win the semi-final.

No fewer than four Brazilians – Mozer, Chiquinho, Elzo and the substitute Vando – figured in Benfica's team in Stuttgart. Mozer, two years later, would play against them at centre-back in the semi-final for Marseille. There was also a Swede, the tall, blond Mats Magnusson, quite ineffectual that day. He and Mozer would be on opposite sides in 1990.

By then Sven-Goran Eriksson, the Swedish manager who had turned IFK Gothenburg into such a fine team, was in his second spell with Benfica after several years in Italy where he had managed Roma and Fiorentina. Another Swede, the gifted young midfield player Jonas Thern, had joined the team, and Brazilians were still much in evidence. In Portuguese football, they had contentiously, if conveniently, been classified as 'natives'. So much for the independence gained by Brazil from the Portuguese Empire, over a century before.

If Mozer had gone, there were now two current international Brazilian centre-backs in Ricardo and Aldair; and a mobile, clever midfield player in Valdo, converted from outside-right. Ricardo would score a spectacular third goal in the second leg of the quarter-finals away to the Russian champions Dnepr, beaten 3–0 on their own ground after going down only 1–0 in the Stadium of Light.

In Marseille in the semi-final first leg, Benfica's defence crumbled. Chris Waddle and Jean-Pierre Papin ran riot but Marseille's poor finishing and their own defensive lapses meant that their margin of victory was a bare and deceptive 2–1. Indeed, Adesvaldo Lima, scorer of two goals against Dnepr, actually put Benfica ahead after ten minutes with a header. After the game, Benfica's President fluttered the dovecotes with his claim that Marseille's players had been doped, such was the ferocity of their commitment. He adduced no proof.

It did, however, seem quite astonishing that after all those years, UEFA should still be imposing random rather than regular dope tests, thus leaving room for such doubts and accusations. These were well and truly laid to rest by Benfica's deeply displeasing victory in the return leg. If Maradona had scored against England in Mexico City with The Hand of God, how should one classify the goal with which Vata Garcia, the Angolan forward, sent Benfica into the 1990 European Cup Final?

This was another game in which defensive adequacy was at a premium, in both sides. Benfica lacked Ricardo who was suspended. Marseille, lacking Ettori, had had to call up the veteran French international keeper Castaneda, who looked utterly inept. The wonder of it was that there should not be half a dozen goals to either side, rather than the solitary goal steered in with his hand by Vata, just six minutes from the end. Valdo curled in a corner from the left. Magnusson got his blond head to it at the near post and Vata made contact with his hand. So Benfica went through to the Final in Vienna.

There, in a largely dull game, they did not disgrace themselves. Sven-Goran Eriksson had devised his tactics well. Benfica's defence – like Milan's – pushed up hard and fast, giving the forwards very little room and causing the offside whistle often to blow. True, such tactics may ultimately have cost them the game. Their defence broke down at least three times, and the third time, for Benfica, was unlucky. Franck Rijkaard, one of Milan's three splendid Dutch internationals, took Marco Van Basten's through pass and beat Silvino with a shot perfectly struck with the outside of the right foot.

When Ruud Gullit, playing his first full competitive game for the best part of a year after appalling knee trouble, was similarly put through by Van Basten he had wasted the chance, Silvino sprawling to save; while in the first half Van Basten, having lost his marker with an electric turn, shot far too close to Silvino.

Truth to tell, Benfica themselves hardly made a chance deserving the name throughout the match, cleverly though Brazil's Valdo and Sweden's Thern worked in midfield. Their best opportunity came in the first half when Thern, with surprising ease, split Milan's defence with a perfectly angled ball to the left. Hernani, all on his own, should have set up at least the chance for a shot at goal, but his cross was careless and inaccurate.

Thus Benfica lost another European Cup Final; one, this time, that they should scarcely have reached.

4

MANCHESTER UNITED: MATT BUSBY, MUNICH AND AFTER

Manchester United it was who, by so boldly defying the Football League, brought English football into the European Cup, with great distinction. And yet, by an horrific irony, it was the European Cup which less than two years later would bring about the Munich air crash, the pitiful destruction of a young team on its way back from a Cup match in Belgrade. Some fine players died; others, though they mercifully survived, would never play again. Matt Busby, the manager and inspiration of the club, struggled for his life. Frank Swift, one of England's most celebrated goalkeepers, was among the journalists who perished.

That United should pick themselves up, put themselves together, and still contest the European Cup semi-final was a small miracle. But they would have to wait ten long years before they won it for the first, and so far the only, time.

Busby came out of the Army to take control of Manchester United in February 1945. It was a club without a ground. Old Trafford had been bombed in the war, the stands destroyed, a crater left massively in the pitch. The team shared a ground with its neighbours and rivals Manchester City, and would do so for years to come.

Busby himself had played with distinction at wing-half for City, then for Liverpool. A wing-half in the Scottish style who captained his country during the war, he was unhurried, creative, steadily intelligent. The wartime years saw him playing mostly as a guest for Reading. What imbued him was the traditional spirit of Scottish football, even then withering away in favour of quicker, cruder, more combative methods. When United fell a goal behind to Blackpool in the FA Cup Final of 1948, the word was passed around by John Carey, the cool Irish captain, 'Keep on playing football.' They did, and they won. That summed up Busby's approach pretty well.

If he was, so far as the playing of the game was concerned, an idealist, if he could be the bland diplomat, he also possessed a typically Scottish shrewdness. A superb judge of a player, he had authority and no illusions. He lived and competed in the real world, where nice guys, in the words of American baseball's Leo Durocher, finished last.

So United made it their business to track down and acquire the best young talent. Other clubs were not always happy about their methods. Bobby Charlton, a Geordie from Ashington, County Northumberland, a nephew of Newcastle United's talismanic centre-forward Jackie Milburn, seemed sure to go to Newcastle. A job, Milburn once told me, had even been found for Bobby in Newcastle's Kemsley House, where the chief local newspapers were housed. But it was United who got him.

Another celebrated player, Duncan Edwards, who died in a Munich hospital after lingering for dreadful days on a kidney machine, might have been expected to go elsewhere. Born in the West Midlands at Dudley, West Bromwich Albion or Wolves would have seemed the natural home for his precocious power, his tremendous talents. But again, he went to United.

Busby, when he took over, may have had no stadium but he was not without playing resources. As well as Johnny Carey there was the big centre-back Allenby Chilton, who landed in France on D-Day. Stan Pearson was a locally born inside-left and Jack Rowley a centre-forward signed from Bournemouth, once with Wolves. These four had been there before the war and were still highly effective. So was Charlie Mitten, a well-balanced, elegant left-winger who would decamp to Bogota in the famous exodus of 1950, led by the England centre-half Neil Franklin. One of the last to go, Mitten would be the last back and would conclude his career with Fulham.

There was still more outstanding young talent. Henry Cockburn, a tiny, busy, skilful left-half, would almost at once gain a place in the England team, and would have his natural successor in another little wing-half, Eddie Colman, killed at Munich before he could win the England cap he deserved. Johnny Morris, another little player, was a quick, talented, inventive inside-right, who could make goals or score them; John Aston a powerful left-back whose son would help United win the European Cup Final of 1968.

In addition to all these gifted players already to be found at United, Busby boldly signed the Celtic and Scotland right-winger – or centre-forward – Jimmy Delaney, he of the famously 'brittle bones'. It was a risk, though the price was relatively low. But the risk proved wonderfully worth taking; Delaney's ebullient, intelligent play on the right wing once graced by Billy Meredith was a prime factor in United's success.

What should be emphasised was that until Busby's regime, United had for years played second fiddle to City in Manchester. Between the wars, United had done little more than run a shuttle service between the First and Second Divisions, and their days as great Cup fighters lay before the Great War. In the inter-war years, they never reached another Final, never challenged for the Championship. City, by contrast, won both Cup and League, even if they did immediately get relegated the reason after their Championship success.

When his splendid team of the late 1940s and early fifties began to disintegrate, Busby proved bold again. Like Major Frank Buckley at Wolverhampton Wanderers before the war, he went out for youth. The Buckley Babes had been in line for the Cup and League double in 1939, though in the event they won neither Cup nor League. When Busby began to deploy so many teenagers – Jeff Whitefoot at 16, Duncan Edwards at wing-half at 17 – it was perhaps natural that his team be known as the 'Busby Babes'.

Once at Chelsea, in the early 1950s, I asked him about it. His reply was simple, succinct and indicative. 'If you don't put them in,' he said, 'you can't know what you've got.' Some, inevitably, fell by the wayside but a remarkable number did not.

By 1956, Busby had laid the basis of an exceptional side. Two years later, at the time of the Munich crash, it had still not quite come to fruition, though it was already the most exciting and attractive in England. Had it been spared, who knows what heights it might have reached?

Brushing the Football League and its ill-conceived 'advice' aside, with Busby supported by his determined little Chairman, H P Hardman, United embarked on their European adventure. Hardman himself had been an amateur outside-left of renown, a full international and the winner of a Cup Final medal. If Busby became dominant in the club, Hardman's support and understanding remained important.

In the very first round, United showed their great quality, promise, and achievement. Two goals against the Belgian champions Anderlecht in Brussels preceded an astonishing ten against them, in the return at Maine Road. Little Dennis Viollet, a deceptively strong player at inside-left who had once supported Manchester City at this very ground, scored an important goal in the first leg after Jef Mermans, Anderlecht's illustrious centre-forward, missed a penalty; and he would score four more in the second.

Viollet, who would blessedly survive the Munich air crash, has said of his early period with United, 'It was a rare experience in my life.' Some English clubs have run their youth schemes like Army glasshouses. At United, though the late Jimmy Murphy – who would so impressively take over from Busby in 1958 – might curse at the players, they knew that he and Bert Whalley, the coach, were fundamentally on their side. Murphy himself had been a talented Welsh international wing half-back, renowned for making, in the 1935 Cup Final when he played for West Bromwich against Sheffield Wednesday, one of the most dramatic goal-line saves seen at Wembley.

Viollet was quick, incisive and sharp, combining fruitfully with Tommy Taylor, the tall centre-forward who had cost a curious £29 999 when Busby bought him from Barnsley. Busby had been reluctant to break the £30 000 barrier. Taylor was fast, strong, and powerful in the air. He would have led England's attack in the 1958 World Cup in Sweden had he, poor fellow, been spared.

Edwards, at left-half, was almost a force of nature. Indeed, his physical prowess tended at times to overshadow his many other qualities. He could brush off opponents like cobwebs, his left-footed shot – which brought him a remarkable goal against West Germany in Berlin – was formidable. Had he lived, who knows what heights he himself would have achieved, and what England might have done in that World Cup?

Jackie Blanchflower, younger brother of Northern Ireland's elegant and fluent captain Danny, was beginning to come into his own. Utterly versatile, he was by turns a skilled, progressive inside-right, an unusually mobile centre-half, and even a capable goalkeeper when Ray Wood was forced out of the game by Peter McParland's notorious charge in the FA Cup Final of 1957. How badly Northern Ireland missed Jackie's resilient presence the following year in Sweden. He survived the Munich crash but he would never play again.

Duncan Edwards – already a powerful figure in Manchester United's team at 17, soon to establish himself as an England star, cruelly lost at Munich

(Hulton Picture Company)

Roger Byrne, the left-back, was captain of the team and of England. He, too, would die at Munich and be denied to England in the 1958 World Cup. Once a left-winger, Byrne's era preceded that of the overlapping full-back, preceded that of 4–2–4, but how easily and successfully he would have adapted himself to such a role!

Of Colman we have spoken already. With his low centre of gravity, his accomplished ball-control and his eye for an opening, he was the perfect wing-half of his era; an attacking player in a team that loved to attack, in the image of Busby himself. I was lucky enough to cover what proved, alas, to be the last League game for Colman and so many other marvellous players: Arsenal 4 Manchester United 5, at Highbury. An extraordinary riot of goals, both teams casting caution to the winds in a way which seems sublimely obsolescent in these mean and meagre times.

United were, in fact, back playing at Old Trafford by the time of their European home debut against Anderlecht, but a lack of floodlights caused the match to be played at Maine Road, the perfect place for Viollet to get his four goals. Under continuous rain, they struggled to take hold of the game for fifteen minutes or so, but once the first goal had gone in, United simply ran riot, with a display of wonderfully adventurous and penetrative football.

It was strangely ironic that David Pegg, a fluent left-winger with speed and close control, should have an outstanding match, yet not score one of the ten goals. The right-wing pair of little Johnny Berry, an Aldershot player who had come to United via Birmingham City, and the skilful, inventive Irishman Liam Whelan, functioned splendidly too. Anderlecht, so dominant in Belgian football, a team packed with experienced internationals, were simply swept aside. An astonishing performance for a team without experience of Continental football, and for some of whose young players flying itself was a novel experience.

Borussia Dortmund, the West German champions, were less easy prey. In the first leg in Dortmund, Dennis Viollet bagged another couple of goals in the first half as United led 3–0 at the break; but they learned in the second half that in European football they could never relax, as Borussia pulled two of the goals back. The return leg at Maine Road ended 0–0 on a frozen field. No fewer than 75 598 spectators were at the game, a figure inconceivable in these post-Hillsborough days. And, indeed, long before that.

Next came a difficult game in Bilbao against Athletic, who had beaten Real Madrid to the title. The Spanish champions were without two of their key players, but in conditions as English as the club's name – a snowfall, a quagmire of a ground – they overran United, after nearly conceding a goal themselves almost from the kick-off. A sweeping movement ended with Viollet forcing his way through the mud. His shot beat the Spanish international keeper Carmelo, but the mud stopped the ball on the line. Away came the Basques; United's centre-half Mark Jones, forgetting the conditions, tried and failed to half-volley, lost his footing, and Arteche scored. Afterwards, Viollet was much aggrieved to be held responsible for the goal by Matt Busby!

United went into the dressing-room at half-time three goals down, to be harangued by Busby. It seemed to do the trick. Two goals in eight minutes by Viollet and Tommy Taylor, playing though not fully fit and giving the powerful stopper Garay a hard time, almost restored equality. But a most un-British deficiency in the air enabled Bilbao to score twice more for a 5–2 lead. Elimination loomed. Who could recover three goals, even at home?

Mercifully, it turned out to be just two. Liam Whelan, the skilful Irishman who had come from Home Farm, the Dublin club, scored a goal remarkable in any circumstances but almost incredible on such a pitch. Receiving the ball from Edwards in his own half, he beat two opponents, ran on from right to left leaving another Spaniard behind him, and turned past a fourth as he moved inside again. He had covered a good 40 yards and was some twenty-five yards out when Garay left Taylor to challenge him and Carmelo came off his line. Whelan drove the ball into the top left hand corner of the net.

In retrospect, what happened at Bilbao airport was a grim rehearsal of what would so tragically occur at Munich. Left out on the runway, United's Dakota aircraft was covered with ice and snow. Busby, mindful of the Football League's disingenuous objection to the European Cup on the grounds that it might interfere with League fixtures, insisted they take off.

With brooms and shovels, the United players chipped and brushed the ice from the plane. All but Whelan who, perhaps on the strength of his marvellous goal, stood aside, and took photographs; he sold them on his return to a Manchester newspaper. It was an alarming flight. Landing at Jersey to refuel, the aircraft swooped below a cliff as a gale blew, rose steeply above it, then bounced on the runway. Poor Mark Jones, one of those who would die at Munich, sat petrified, sweat coursing down his face.

Ferdinand Daucik, the former Czech international, now manager of Bilbao, announced that no team could beat his own by three goals. Under the lights of Maine Road, it looked for a long time as if he would be right. United missed good chances, and 41 minutes had gone when Garay kicked Edward's shot off the line and Viollet scored.

Twice in the second half Herr Deutsch, the big, dark West German referee, disallowed United goals for offside. With 20 minutes left, and Busby smoking nervously on the touchline, Taylor beat Garay and beat Carmelo in turn with a left-footed shot – and the ball bounced off the post.

Taylor tried again. Again he beat Garay, and this time the post did not save Carmelo. It was Taylor, a man inspired, who set up the third goal. Moving to the wing, eluding Garay yet again, he calmly pulled the ball back for little Johnny Berry to score. Now, in the semi-final, United would meet the other Spaniards, Real Madrid.

Athletic Bilbao's keeper Carmelo clears from Tommy Taylor and Dennis Viollet in the return leg of the 1957 quarter-final at Maine Road. United, two goals down from the first leg in Bilbao, recovered to win 3–0, with Taylor and Viollet both scoring (Popperfoto)

Matt Busby had a look at them and described Alfredo Di Stefano as the best player he had ever seen. For his own part, Di Stefano in a television interview was heard to remark that the reason European teams had systems was that they didn't possess the talent of the South Americans. Busby also raved to his young team about the tremendous speed of Gento, who indeed would be too fast for the United right-back Bill Foulkes. In later years Bobby Charlton, then a teenager on the fringe of the team, said, '[Matt Busby] was so enthusiastic it was almost unbelievable. I discovered I was building a defensive wall inside myself, for a player wants to see for himself. For instance, the Boss said Gento was the fastest man he'd ever seen. But what did that mean to Bill Foulkes, who had to mark him?'

Charlton himself, sitting high in the huge Bernabeu Stadium, admits that he was almost relieved not to be playing. It was a match in which both Di Stefano and Gento justified Busby's eulogies, and in which Real had most of the breaks from the well-known Dutch referee, Leo Horn. 'He let them get away with a lot,' said Johnny Berry. Di Stefano clearly disliked the marking of Eddie Colman, a late choice, and Jackie Blanchflower. He too, thought Berry, was 'a bit naughty at times'.

With David Pegg playing almost as well as Gento on United's left flank, there were no goals for an hour. Di Stefano, once lashing out in his frustration, might have been sent off by a more severe referee. If there was a real chance in the first half, in fact, it fell to Tommy Taylor but it wasn't taken. Then Foulkes committed a foul, United ingenuously waited for the free kick to be given, Horn played the advantage rule, Gento crossed and Hector Rial scored.

'These people just aren't human,' thought young Bobby Charlton, as he watched. *'It's not the sort of game I've been taught.'* But it would become the sort of game that he played.

Di Stefano scored a characteristically splendid second goal, accelerating past three opponents, seeing Ray Wood off his line and lobbing over him into the net. Taylor got a goal back, but the task became Gargantuan when Gento and Rial set up Mateos. As the United defence hung back, Mateos shot against Wood and then into the goal.

Bobby Charlton would play, at Old Trafford – there were floodlights now – against these superhuman beings. He was 18 years old, brother to the older Jackie, the Leeds United centre-half, nephew to the infinity of Milburns who had come out of the mining village of Ashington to play professional football. The lineage, in fact, went back even further. Jack Milburn, a formidably robust footballer, played for Northumberland in the 1880s.

That was on Charlton's mother's side; his father had little initial interest in football. Bobby's refulgent talent was obvious from the first. Perhaps a little too obvious, since there was a temptation for him in his earlier years to glide by on that alone, while he indulged his predilection for fishing – shared by his brother Jack – and the cinema.

Given the astounding power of some of his left-footed goals, it is a little hard to digest the fact that he was a just as naturally right-footed player. Indeed, when he made his debut for United at Charlton in season 1956/7 it was sheer necessity that led him to score twice with his left foot. Though his right ankle was swollen he had assured Matt Busby he was fit, when offered his chance to play.

So a stupendous shot in either foot was one of Charlton's great advantages. He had, in addition, with his low centre of gravity and sinuous movement, an elegant swerve which took him outside defenders, especially when he figured on the left wing, and precise ball-control to match. With this went the priceless asset of acceleration. Once past his man, he could seldom be caught.

Which was his best position? Inside-left, where he first became known and where he had that vital margin of space and time to line up his tremendous shots? Outside-left, where England used him so successfully in the World Cup in Chile when he glided so casually outside opponents to cross or shoot with that left foot? Which I must admit, when I watched him then, I thought was the stronger. Or deep centre-forward, where England deployed him so successfully in the 1966 World Cup, making him a major international star, bringing that spectacular long range goal against Mexico and the two in the semi-final against the Portuguese?

As a deep centre-forward he was in fact no Kopa, no Di Stefano – both rivals when Real came to Old Trafford. His prodigious 45-yard crossfield passes at Wembley, usually from right to left, would bring a great cry from the crowd but they were more spectacular than decisive. Charlton was a natural, an instinctive; what he did, he did superbly and off the cuff, but he was never a truly creative player. On the other hand, his ability to advance with the ball and beat people meant he could contribute to attack in other ways, making the man over.

Off the field, he was simple, straightforward and charming. The Munich crash would devastate him. He survived it, but for those of us who knew him during the subsequent World Cup in Sweden, he seemed a young man still in a kind of coma. This despite the fact that he would later say he wasn't hurt, nor even deeply troubled in his mind. 'I just couldn't take it in, and therefore it washed over me. I didn't want to accept what had happened.'

His plight was compounded when England, just before the World Cup, brought him back to Belgrade and picked him against Yugoslavia. In hot sunshine the whole team foundered, the Yugoslavs winning 5–0. Charlton went to Sweden, but wasn't picked for a single game. I remember him brightening just once – in the Park Avenue Hotel in central Gothenburg where England were staying. We were talking about North Eastern humour, and Charlton told a tale about a bus. A man was left in the queue and asked, 'How long will the next one be?'

'About as long as this one,' was the answer.

A decade or so later, when Charlton was a player of world renown, United were a less compact and harmonious group than in Charlton's early days when as Roger Byrne, the doomed captain, said, they were mostly a bunch of boys who had grown up together. Subsequently, though the team in itself largely functioned well, there was something of a dichotomy between what one might call the Denis Law and Bobby Charlton factions. Law, like Charlton, was an outstandingly gifted footballer. He had, especially among the Celts, his admirers in the team, just as Charlton had his own.

George Best, probably the most talented player to emerge in Britain since the war and certainly one of the most publicised, clearly saw Charlton as some kind of implicit rebuke, the white hen who never laid a stray. Doubtless he knew little or nothing of Charlton's earlier fishing and cinema-going days. Best has admitted that once, in a pub, he threw a whole clutch of raw eggs at a painting of Charlton which hung on the wall.

But both of them were, triumphantly, in the 1968 team which at long last won the European Cup for United, Charlton's head – once flaxen, now largely bald – so unexpectedly scoring one of the goals.

Charlton scored against Real, too, on his European debut, but it was not enough. Unlike Bilbao, Real did not come to defend in Manchester, though they had controversially managed to add a different right-back, Torres, merely on loan from Zaragoza, in place of Becerril whom Pegg had tormented. There was trouble before the game when Real turned up at Old Trafford, found the sprinklers on, and fiercely protested. With the prospect of the game being called off, United turned off the sprinklers.

It was a bruising match. Real, conceding 29 of the 51 fouls, were none too delicate in the methods with which they countered Tommy Taylor and Jackie Blanchflower in the air. Gento and Kopa on the wings were always threatening and it was the Frenchman, cleverly set up by Rial and Di Stefano, the two Argentines, who opened the scoring after 24 minutes. Then when Gento's shot was only blocked by Wood, Rial got a second and the tie was won and lost. Di Stefano bestrode the pitch, Taylor and Bobby Charlton scored for United, but Real were in the Final.

'A great, experienced team will always triumph over a great, inexperienced team,' said Matt Busby, who not long since had turned down the chance to become manager of Bilbao. As for Charlton, he felt that if United had played their 'normal' game, as they did in the second half despite all Real's cynical time-wasting, they might have come through.

Winning the Championship again, though losing the Cup Final after that appalling foul on Ray Wood by Aston Villa's Peter McParland, United approached the European Cup again at the start of the 1957/8 season. Their team, whose average age against Real was a mere 21, still clearly had its best years ahead of it.

Shamrock Rovers were thrashed 6–0 in Dublin, where Liam Whelan ran riot in his native city, though United won the return only 3–2. Dukla of Prague, the Army team, were beaten 3–0 at Old Trafford with Colin Webster, a young Welsh centre-forward, gifted but aggressive, scoring the first goal. Dukla largely outplayed United in Prague but with Eddie Colman, back in favour after a spell in the shadows, cleverly dictating the play, United lost only by a single goal.

Next, Red Star of Belgrade came to Old Trafford. There was a new United goalkeeper now – the big Ulsterman Harry Gregg, signed from Doncaster, a keeper who came thunderingly off his line to grab centres, and wore his torn old joiner's cap as a talisman. New wingers, too, with Ken Morgans, another Welshman, on the right and Albert Scanlon, replacing David Pegg, on the left. Dragoslav Sekularac, the wayward star of Red Star, a tough little gypsy who ran his team's midfield, was outplayed by Duncan Edwards.

When Gregg came off his line, Tasic beat him with an extraordinary shot which flew in off the underside of the crossbar. Charlton and Colman replied for United; and so, fatally, to Belgrade.

The match took place just four days after United's famous 5–4 win over Arsenal at Highbury, a match I reported and in which United prevailed after throwing away a 3–0 lead. The highlight of the game was Scanlon's sprint from one penalty area to the other to make a goal for Bobby Charlton, who called it the best solo he had ever seen. Charlton had yet to play abroad in the European Cup and, teased by his team mates about the food in Yugoslavia, he packed his case tight with sweets and biscuits, which he eventually gave to the chambermaid.

In Belgrade, United scored an odd early goal. A flick by Tommy Taylor after a rebound, a moment's inattention by Tasic, the scorer in Manchester, and Dennis Viollet nipped in to score. Sekularac gashed Morgans' thigh;

Charlton robbed Kostic, eluded two tackles, shot from far out, and it was 2–0. A botched free-kick by Edwards, an amazing intervention by Charlton, and the ball was in the net again. United led 3–0.

In the second half, Red Star saved face. First Kostic scored, then when Tasic and Foulkes tumbled in the box a penalty was given, and Tasic converted, though Gregg touched the shot. Gregg then handled outside the box, Kostic struck the free-kick with his famous left foot, the ball struck Viollet's head, and it ended 3–3.

Now it was back to England, via Munich, in an Elizabethan aircraft, a two-engined plane. In Munich, as in Bilbao the previous year, there was snow on the runway. After the plane had refuelled, at 2.30 in the afternoon, the pilot tried to take off but was not satisfied with the boost pressure on one of the engines. To be frank, this was not the first time such a thing had happened to an Elizabethan. Again the pilot tried, and again he gave up. Alas, he would try a third time. By now the view from the aircraft's windows was obscured by flurries of snow, and a great spurt of slush. All at once, horrifically, the plane lost momentum. Far from being airborne, it taxied on through landing lights, through a perimeter fence, covered another 250 yards and finally, fatally, smashed into a house, losing its tail and the port wing.

Seven players died almost immediately. They were Roger Byrne, Eddie Colman, Mark Jones, Liam Whelan, Tommy Taylor, full-back Geoff Bent, and David Pegg. They were not the only ones to die. Dead, too, were Walter Crickmer, for so long the club secretary; Tom Curry and Bert Whalley, its able coaches; an air steward, a travel agent, and one of the club's most influential fans. Eight journalists perished, among them Frank Swift and H D (Don) Davies, Old International of the *Manchester Guardian*, a man whose robust, evocative, carefully honed writing had been among the best the English game had ever known. 'Look at him, trying to dribble!' he once quoted a Mancunian fan. 'Why doesn't he learn, he's got nothing else to do?'

Later, the aircraft's co-pilot would die. Powerful young Duncan Edwards hung on, agonisingly, for another 15 days, placed on a kidney machine, before even his great strength ran out and he, too, succumbed. Twenty-one years old, already one of the foremost players of his day, one with what seemed an astonishing future.

There were many other casualties; and a hero, big Harry Gregg, who selflessly dragged a Yugoslav woman's child out of the wreckage. Matt Busby was gravely injured. So too was Johnny Berry, while Jackie Blanchflower, that paragon of versatility, had fractured an arm and his pelvis.

Busby, close to death, lay in the Munich hospital with a punctured lung, tubes down his throat, legs badly smashed. It would be three months before a remarkable specialist, Professor Maurer, told Busby he should leave and 'get some good air into your lungs'. Horrified by such carnage, Busby had at first decided to give up the game but his wife Jean encouraged him to go back. When at last he did visit Old Trafford, 'it was a haunting, nightmare experience.'

It was Jimmy Murphy, Busby's second-in-command and team manager of the Welsh World Cup side, who took over and, with splendid ebullience and resourcefulness, patched up the team with amazing speed.

Berry and Blanchflower might have survived but they had, alas, played their last game. It was Berry who, when Tommy Taylor joked about the

The team destroyed at Munich. Back row, left to right: Duncan Edwards, Bill Foulkes, Mark Jones, Ray Wood, Eddie Colman, David Pegg. Front: Johnny Berry, Liam Whelan, Roger Byrne, Tommy Taylor, Dennis Viollet (Popperfoto)

wheel going up, on the final run, replied, 'It's no laugh. We're all going to be killed.'

'If this is death,' said Liam Whelan, 'then I'm ready for it.' Another player to be struck down at the height of his powers. Among the others, Ray Wood, the keeper, was trapped agonisingly under the wheel of the undercarriage; Dennis Viollet's head had been split open yet he rose almost casually from the ground; Bobby Charlton was hurled out of the plane, strapped in his seat, some 60 yards into a field. Growing conscious again, he put his folded jacket under Busby. Of all the journalists, only Frank Taylor survived, cruelly injured – eventually to write his account of that dreadful February afternoon, *The Day a Team Died*.

Whose fault? Pilot error, that wonderfully convenient formula, was perhaps inevitably blamed. Heaven forbid that fault ever be found with the design of a commercial plane. So it was that the unfortunate pilot, Captain Thain, was made the culprit; 'guilty' of not checking whether there was ice on the wings, and for letting his co-pilot, the dead Captain Rayment, take the controls for the take-off.

For ten cruel years Thain battled to clear his reputation, insisting it was slush on the tarmac, not ice on the wings, which had caused the crash. Ultimately, he proved his point. Indeed, the Ministry of Aviation somewhat belatedly insisted that no take-off be made when slush was half-an-inch deep or more. But it could not bring back Thain's lost ten years, any more than it could bring back Manchester United's dead, or the careers of those who, though they lived, would never play again.

Murphy, who had missed Munich only because his other job had involved him with the Welsh team, burst out crying when he had to choose his first United side. He brought in players from the reserve and third teams and bought two: clever little Ernie Taylor from Blackpool, and Stan Crowther, a tough blond left-half from Aston Villa. It was Taylor's backheel at Wembley which had set up Bobby Charlton's uncle, Jackie Milburn, for the first of two spectacular goals for Newcastle against Blackpool themselves in the FA Cup Final of 1951.

The team sheet on the match programme for United's first game since Munich, an FA Cup tie at home to Sheffield Wednesday, was left blank – but more than adequately filled. Before a crowd of 65 000, in a vortex of passion, United won 3–0. 'Sheffield,' said a Munich survivor, Bill Foulkes, 'had no chance, and I felt sorry for them . . . The crowd was hysterical, and I was not far off being the same way.'

United would go all the way to the Final in the FA Cup, only to lose almost as controversially as the previous year, Nat Lofthouse charging Harry Gregg painfully into the back of the net, as the keeper caught the ball in mid-air, to score Bolton's second goal. In the European Cup, there was the semi-final and Milan to contend with.

It was a very strong Milan team, with the Uruguayan Juan Schiaffino and, in attack, the veteran Swede Nils Liedholm, Tito 'El Loco' Cucchiaroni and Ernesto Grillo, a strong, elegant inside-forward.

Yet United's patched-up team managed, somehow, to win the first leg at Old Trafford. England – these were strange, early European Cup days – took Bobby Charlton away from both legs, to play first against Portugal and then in the heavy defeat in Belgrade. He had skipped the first post-Munich game against Wednesday, then come back to play superbly in the rest of the run to the Cup Final.

The margin of United's first leg victory was narrow, 2–1. The subtle Schiaffino scored for Milan; Denis Viollet, with a shot, and Ernie Taylor, with a penalty kick, for United. The team, eschewing air travel, made the long haul overland to Milan. At the huge San Siro stadium, they had a sour reception, their coach being sullenly turned away from one gate after another – a ploy, the players felt, to upset them. There were only 25 minutes left to kick-off when the team at last managed to make its way into the ground. 'They were really a class above us,' said Harry Gregg, and the 4–0 score suggests he was right. United's patchwork team did its best, with young Ronnie Cope, not long since a third team centre-half, surpassing himself. United held out for three-quarters of an hour; then came a penalty by Liedholm, a couple more goals from Schiaffino, and they were out. Milan, as we have seen, went on to lose to Real Madrid in the Final.

By way of compensation for the crash, British European Airways paid Manchester United the sum of £35 000.

Still less sympathy was shown by the Football League, whose Secretary Alan Hardaker had a retentive memory. UEFA, with a generous gesture, invited Manchester United to compete in the ensuing European Cup tournament. The Football League forbade it, on the ludicrous grounds that UEFA were infringing their own rules – that only League Champions were eligible to play, together with the holders. United were neither. Quite apart from the fact that UEFA were presumably entitled to waive their own rules, they had, in the past, allowed teams which came into neither category to compete.

United appealed to the Football Association against this act of petty vengeance, and were upheld. But Hardaker and the League were not finished. They protested against the result of the appeal and insisted on a joint League–Association committee to pass final judgement. What precedent there was for this, who knows, but Hardaker got his way, the joint commission was convened, and it decided, shamefully, against United. So UEFA's kind gesture was virtually thrown back in their face.

Out of the horror of Munich there grew what amounted almost to a cult and a legend. The brilliant young team struck down as it began to reach the height of its powers. The swift, amazing resurrection. Manchester United had already, for some years, been the most popular team in the country, with its policy of playing attractive, enterprising football, but now its allure and prestige rose dramatically. Fans flocked to the team not just in Manchester and its environs but from all over the British Isles. Before a match you could find, in a pub near Old Trafford, Welshmen, Irishmen, Cockneys.

There was a darker side to this. As violence spread among young fans in the early 1960s, United's became known as perhaps the most violent. There was a long period in which they were feared and loathed wherever they went, attracting roughnecks whose commitment was to mayhem rather than to the club. Gradually, in the eighties, United managed, largely through control of tickets, to squeeze much of the hooliganism out.

Bobby Charlton is chaired around Old Trafford by team-mates Pat Crerand and David Herd. Also pictured are (left to right) Harry Gregg, Matt Busby, Noel Cantwell, Shay Brennan, Denis Law and Nobby Stiles (Hulton Picture Company)

Meanwhile, in those same, callous, nihilist eighties, there was a horrific reverse side to the Munich disaster, a grisly chorus sung by mindless fans from other clubs: *'Who's that lying on the runway? Who's that lying in the snow?'* I have heard it sung almost as a cheerful refrain by young football fans who were by no means hooligans or roughnecks, and it is true that much time had passed, that fans of that age would have no memory of the tragedy and the misery that it brought. Yet the song told one much about the times, and their moral vacuum.

Walking at first on two sticks, terrified of flying again, Matt Busby recovered to take over a team he knew must now be more thoroughly rebuilt. For

a couple of years, United would still not fly to any foreign fixture; then Busby decided that this phobia, too, must be faced and conquered.

Not till season 1964/5 did United win the Championship again. In the interim, they had competed in the Cup-Winners' and Fairs Cup. The 1965 title was won only on goal average from Leeds United, but it at long last put United back into the European Cup again. They had a hugely talented team.

Bobby Charlton was still there. So now were the Scots Denis Law and Pat Crerand, and the amazing young Ulsterman George Best. It was Law's second spell in Manchester. An Aberdonian, he had first come down to Huddersfield as a boy, tiny, ill-favoured, bespectacled. But his sight was corrected, he grew physically stronger, and of his refulgent talent there was never any doubt. Inside-forward or centre-forward, he was brave, acrobatic, inventive and tireless; remarkable in the air despite a relative lack of height, gymnastic in his mid-air shots and bicycle kicks.

He could cover acres of ground in midfield, he could battle it out with the toughest defenders as a spearhead. Manchester City bought him from Huddersfield but never gave him a decent team to play in. In 1961, when English and Scottish players were becoming fashionable again in Italy, City sold him profitably to Torino, at the same time as Joe Baker of Hibernian went there.

Neither enjoyed it. They detested – as did Jimmy Greaves, to their east with Milan – the rigorous discipline. On the field, Law was once so frustrated that at half-time in the dressing-room he tore off his jersey and hurled it into a corner. Baker got into trouble for hitting an importunate photographer by a canal in Venice. The two of them crashed their car, late in the season and early in the morning, in Turin itself.

Yet when I came to the city some months later to make a film about the England centre-forward, Gerry Hitchens, who had succeeded the pair at Torino, Law's name was still revered. Outside the club's training ground in Via Filadelfia, I met an old man who'd been supporting Torino for years. Law, he told me, was the finest inside-forward he had ever seen there. Even better than Valentino Mazzola, I asked him? Mazzola, the father of Sandrino, was the captain of the club, an heroic figure who perished in the Turin air crash at Superga in May 1949. 'Yes,' said the old man.

Crerand was not as quick or agile as Law, but he was a Scottish footballer in the classical school, a tough and studious right-half in love with the game, who came from Celtic and his native Glasgow to ply his long, shrewd, carefully conceived passes. Once I remember him telling me at United's training ground, almost plaintively, how he wished teams could just go out, put the ball down and get on with the game, rather than contend – implicitly – with all that now unappetisingly went with it.

He detested Leeds United in the days of their earlier success, when the team scratched and scrapped for its victories. Good football came later. Outside the Elland Road ground one windy spring day before a game, Crerand said how little he was looking forward to it; to Leeds' meagre football, with goals that seemed to come only from set pieces. Crerand could be a hard man both on and off the field, but he was an idealist, who once had sat and talked for hours with Celtic's famous manager Jock Stein, long before Stein took over the club.

George Best was something else again. Something unique, both in terms of talent and as a public – tremendously public – figure. At this time, he was still a shy, charming 18-year-old, his dark hair Beatle-cut, his eyes alert and blue. He was a winger still, where in time he would mature into a multi-talented forward, blessed with all the gifts of a Law or a Charlton, and much else besides.

He'd arrived from Belfast as a tiny, shy, homesick 15-year-old with another talented player, Eric McMordie. Both promply went home. Best, luckily for United, came back; McMordie didn't. Best was boarded out with a sympathetic landlady. Some years later, when he seemed to the club to be running out of control, he was put back with her again – a sentimental and a hopeless expedient.

'If I'd been born ugly,' he once remarked, 'you'd never have heard of Pelé.' That was half the truth and half the trouble. For where such glorious predecessors as Stanley Matthews and Tom Finney, to whom Best would inevitably be compared, had been, off the field, quite provincial figures, renowned and admired essentially as footballers, Best was handsome, dashing and magnetic, a 'sex symbol', to use the crass term of the times; able, moreover, now that the maximum wage was no more, to earn money and live in a style beyond the dreams of his predecessors.

The growing, unrelenting attention he received would surely have been too much for someone older and more resilient. It was the treatment more commonly associated with film stars and rock singers; but film stars and rock singers did not have to go out and run for ninety taxing minutes. His exploits on the field were the joy of his fans and the despair of his opponents. He even admitted he got a sexual charge when he beat an opponent. Off the field, his exploits were greedily followed by the Press. Once, when United were playing at Chelsea, he came down to London himself and spent the whole weekend in the Islington house of the actress Sinead Cusack, with reporters and photographers laying siege outside.

It could not, indefinitely, go on. No human being could drive himself so hard. For some years, Best played like an angel, making an art of the game. What couldn't he do? At five foot eight, he could jump and head like a Dixie Dean. His swerve was the equal of a Stanley Matthews. His pace was phenomenal, his flair extraordinary. Mark him tight and he could turn in a flash, as once, at Wembley, he turned away from his old club mate Nobby Stiles, that relentless marker, to score a marvellous goal for Northern Ireland against England.

As for his ball control, it was mesmeric. A football was almost too ludicrously large to test his skills. He could flip a coin off his foot into his top pocket. Yet, by a colossal irony, he would never play in the World Cup Finals; too young for Danny Blanchflower's gallant team in 1958, too early for the Northern Irish teams which contested two World Cups in the eighties.

He suddenly and impulsively retired, stayed out long enough to put on weight, then came back, but was never the same again; with United, with Fulham or in America. The dazzling pace had gone. I remember one Christmas, at Loftus Road, the Queens Park Rangers crowd cruelly and viciously booing him when a god seemed merely mortal. What envy builds up, in the mass psyche, of the brilliant maverick; and how much more so when to his professional success is added success with women. It was a sour afternoon.

But these were the early days, the days of dazzling promise. The European Cup was hugely important to United, and their fans. Bobby Charlton has said he realised that nothing else would do. United, though, would not win it this time.

It was no fault of Nobby Stiles, the wing-half who would be both hero and villain in the 1966 World Cup. I first saw Stiles play, appropriately, at Wembley, in a schoolboy international match. He was the best player on the field – lively, intelligent, mobile, progressive. He would never really fulfil such promise at Old Trafford, where any latent skills he may have had were overshadowed by his reputation as a tough marker and a hard – and sometimes, it must be said, a fearsome – competitor. As such, he precipitated a small crisis during the World Cup when an appalling foul on Jacky Simon of France – at Wembley, again – moved the Secretary of the English FA Denis Follows to demand that Stiles be dropped.

Alf Ramsey, a player's man through and through, and an idol to Stiles, responded that in such a case, he himself would resign as manager. Stiles stayed, and had perhaps his finest hour, or 90 minutes, when he marked Eusebio out of the game in the semi-final.

Stiles was for all his reputation a little fellow, stockings rolled down his thin legs, gap-toothed where he had taken out his dentures, and off the field he wore spectacles, too. The England players and the United players swore by him. You might call him a player's man. 'Remember you're from Salford!' he would cry to young Brian Kidd, the United striker who'd been born in the same Manchester suburb and who would have such a memorable birthday celebration when he helped United beat Benfica and Eusebio in the 1968 European Cup Final – at Wembley.

So, at last, to the European Cup again. HIJ Helsinki were no great trouble in the first round; the second leg saw the tall young left-winger John Aston, son of the former international left-back, make his European debut. George Best, given a game at inside-forward, scored twice in a 6–0 win. In the next round, who should return in goal after many a setback, many an injury, but Harry Gregg, who played exceptionally well on a bitter day in Berlin against the East Germans, Vorwaerts. Law, with a superb leaping header and a goal splendidly created for John Connelly, was the star.

Vorwaerts duly despatched, there was sterner opposition now: Benfica. Bela Guttmann was back again in charge, but this was an elderly, fading Bela Guttmann, and Benfica had not looked irresistible that season.

Nevertheless, it seemed after the first leg that United had thrown their chance away. Dominating the game, they eventually won only 3–2, with Eusebio cleverly making both Benfica's goals. In goal, Gregg had looked a little earth-bound. Who could survive in Lisbon, where Benfica had won every one of their 18 European Cup ties? In the event, Best ran riot, Benfica were ripped to ribbons and United won 5–1. It was one of the finest exhibitions given by a British team in European competition.

Benfica's mistake, on this occasion, was to fling themselves almost heedlessly into attack. They might even have got away with it had not two of their past heroes, Costa Pereira in goal and Germano at centre-half, been so shaky; but who, on that remarkable evening, could have subdued Best?

He scored his first goal after six minutes, a goal worthy of a Tommy Lawton rather than a Matthews or a Finney. A free-kick by Tony Dunne, the Irish left-back, a jump by Best, a header which flew past Costa Pereira. Six minutes more, and David Herd, the Scottish centre-forward whose father once played for Manchester City, headed back a long kick from Harry Gregg. Best pounced on it and, in a glorious slalom, went by three defenders before shooting home.

With a quarter-hour gone, Bobby Charlton, Denis Law and John Connelly, combining elegantly without benefit of Best, conjured another goal, scored by Connelly, the former Burnley winger, from close range. Even a farcical own goal, lobbed over Harry Gregg by Shay Brennan, failed to put Benfica back in the game. Nobby Stiles, eternal *bête noire* of Eusebio, was handling him comfortably. Denis Law sent his fellow Scot and fervent admirer Paddy Crerand through for a rare goal. The fifth United goal was scored, refulgently, by Bobby Charlton, beating three defenders on the way. Five-one, one of the finest footballing displays ever seen in the European Cup – to be followed by bleak anticlimax.

Partizan of Belgrade, who came next, were in no way as gifted a team as Benfica but they had such stars as the keeper Soskic; Vasovic, a versatile, adventurous centre-back; Galic, an opportunist; and the excellent attacking left-back Jusufi. Thrashed 4–1 in Prague by Sparta, they had recovered to win 5–0 in Belgrade.

Perhaps it would all have been quite different had George Best only been fit in Belgrade. But he wasn't, and Busby made a rare, if understandable, mistake by playing him. Not only did his injury cause him to hobble through the game – there were no substitutes then – but that very hobbling made him miss the return. In Belgrade, Partizan scored twice against a United defence weak in the air, an odd fault in a British team. Hasanagic exploited that debility with a headed goal; Becejac, exploiting a pass by Vasovic, scored another. United were on the ropes.

At Old Trafford, with no Best, Partizan shut up shop. The only goal was a strange one, scored by Nobby Stiles of all people, a narrow-angled shot which cannoned in off Soskic's body. But 1–0 was not enough to prevent Partizan progressing, to lose a dull Final to Real Madrid.

Alex Stepney, a humorous Mitcham man, replaced Gregg in goal. United regained the League title, and in 1967/8 set out again in their quest for the Holy Grail of European football. 'I don't think we would have won the Championship without Stepney,' said Busby. Tall, slim and agile, Stepney arrived after a fleeting stop at Chelsea, who had signed him from his first club, Millwall. 'You know where you are with him,' said Bill Foulkes, his centre-half. 'You can work something out with a fellow like that.' Matt Busby would later pick him ahead of Harry Gregg as the best goalkeeper he ever had at United.

The European Cup campaign built up to an extraordinary crescendo, with Real Madrid being overcome at last in the semi-finals, against all the odds, and Benfica defeated in the Final. It was a season in which a floating piece of bone in the knee largely deprived the team of Denis Law, in which Nobby Stiles dropped out for nine weeks with cartilage trouble, and in which the veteran Bill Foulkes, now in his middle thirties, tore fibres in his knee yet still came back to score a memorable goal in Madrid.

But the youth scheme came to the rescue. Two young Scots, midfielder or full-back Francis Burns and the rumbustious long-haired midfielder John Fitzpatrick, both battled doughtily. Brian Kidd, a teenager from the Manchester suburb of Collyhurst, where he'd perfected his football in the streets, began to score frequent goals. Strong, direct and fearless with a powerful left foot, and so forceful in the air, he would blossom at Wembley in the Final.

John Aston, lean left-winger and occasional centre-forward, came into his own this season, shrugging off the heartless baiting of the Old Trafford crowd. Neat, effective and productive rather than spectacular, an accurate crosser of the ball, his presence on the left wing enabled George Best to go back to the right, or wherever else he wanted.

An unexacting First Round tie against Hibernians of Malta was followed by a very rough passage, in Yugoslavia once more, against beginners in the competition, Sarajevo. Without the suspended Law and injured Stiles, United survived, but one could say little more. They even survived a 22nd-minute shot by the clever forward Musemic which almost everyone but Stepney and the referee thought had crossed the line. On the half hour, Sarajevo lost Prodanovic, their right-winger, after a hard tackle. He would be out for six months. Things grew rough. So often was United's trainer and former goalkeeper, Jack Crompton, called on to the pitch that, said Pat Crerand, 'I bet half the crowd thought he was playing!' Kidd almost won the match with a shot from the blue to the top corner, but the keeper, Mustic, splendidly reached it.

At Old Trafford things got rougher still. After 11 minutes Mustic saved a header from Burns, but Aston followed up to score. The second half was sheer turmoil. Prijaca was sent off for a savage foul on Best, while the Yugoslavs protested violently that United's second goal was illegal. The ball did, indeed, seem to have gone over the goal-line – a recurring theme in this tie – before it was pulled back by Burns for George Best to volley home. You could hardly call Delalic's header, three minutes from the end, any kind of consolation goal.

But United were through and next came Gornik, the experienced Poles, for whom Lubanski had emerged as a dazzling young inside-left, in the quarter-finals. At Old Trafford, Law was missing again – injured, this time. Gornik defended in depth, in front of a superbly powerful, agile goalkeeper in Kostka. One save, from a full-blooded shot by Aston, six yards out, defied credibility. But Gornik, though plainly short of match practice, were spasmodically very dangerous on the break and Lubanski should have scored in one such counter attack. But he did not get full force behind his shot and Stepney plunged to save it.

It was after half-time that Best conjured a goal out of nothing, chasing a pass from Crerand, squirming by two defenders, and forcing Florenski to boot desperately into his own goal. Crerand was at his finest as United continued to press, and Kostka to save. In the final minute, Kidd made contact with an angled shot from the right by Ryan, another youngster, and the ball rolled tantalisingly through a confusion of legs to end in the opposite corner of the goal. The softest of shots had got through where Kostka had stopped the hardest.

In Chorzow, the return took place on a frozen, unplayable surface. A blizzard blew. More than 90 000 impassioned Poles were there. United's defence stood up superbly with Fitzpatrick and Stiles indomitable, while the attack broke well. Lubanski, with a memorable shot, scored the only goal of the game, after a free-kick dubiously awarded against Stepney came back from the wall.

And now, at long last, it would be Real Madrid, and the chance of a belated and notional revenge. At least the one survivor of those far off clashes from the Real side had a large symbolic value. Francisco 'Paco' Gento had played in every one of Real's European Cup Finals.

In the United team, there were two players who had tackled Real before: Bill Foulkes, now 36, and Bobby Charlton. Eleven years had passed when the teams met, now, at Old Trafford.

Amancio and Pirri were the stars of that young Real team, and that night

Amancio was missing; he had been sent off the field in Prague playing Sparta, against whom he had scored three times at the Bernabeu. Pirri, with his poise, balance and consistent intelligence in midfield, went a long way towards making up for such a costly absence; but without Amancio, Real couldn't score.

United found it very hard themselves, though they attacked strongly from the first. Betancort, the Spanish keeper, made an excellent save from John Aston's header, full stretch at the foot of a post. From the resulting corner Pat Crerand would hit a post, but the one goal came when Aston's splendid run down the left flank ended with a cross pulled back to Best, whose fierce shot flew home.

The return was going to be difficult. Denis Law, who'd played in Manchester but was far from truly fit, went to Madrid but only for the ride. United's form had been haywire; six goals conceded to West Bromwich Albion, six scored against Newcastle. It was Manchester City, the deadly rivals, who would capture the League title after so many years.

There were times when it looked as if Real, too, would put half a dozen past United, in a packed Bernabeu Stadium. Amancio was back, and irresistible. Bill Foulkes and Nobby Stiles, operating as the centre-backs, struggled hard to resist the white hordes. A curving free-kick by Amancio was powerfully headed in by Pirri. Then Shay Brennan somehow missed a pass by Pirri which let Gento in to score. But in the course of the next couple of minutes, with half-time approaching, two more goals went home.

The freakish first was the one which perhaps saved United. Tony Dunne, the Irish left-back, lobbed into the box. Zoco, the big, blond left-half and a weathered Spanish international, swung at the ball and sliced it into his own net. The reprieve was brief. Back at once came Real, for Amancio somehow to find room to turn and crack a loose ball wide of Stepney.

It was a demoralised United team which trooped into the dressing-room at half-time, but there Matt Busby revived them. 'Look, we're losing,' said Busby, who had admitted he was not at his happiest, 'but it's still only 3–2 on aggregate. If we're going to go down, let's go down making a fight of it! We might as well lose 6–2 as 3–2!'

Ah, brave words from a vanished age! What manager of a major team would give such counsel to a losing team today? Ljubomir Petrovic, who planned to win the 1991 Final after extra time, on penalties, with Red Star Belgrade? Alf Ramsey, whose England team, trailing West Germany in the 1972 European Nations Cup quarter finals after losing at Wembley 3–1, went to Berlin for the return and played shamelessly for a 0–0 draw? United took Busby's words to heart, set about Real, and saved the game. Defying the 120 000 triumphant Madrid fans, they at last turned the tide, with a goal.

The scorer was David Sadler, some time centre-forward, now a midfielder, in the first leg a centre-half. Attacking consistently, taking the game to a surprised Real and especially dangerous on the break, United were finally rewarded 18 minutes from time. Crerand took one of his millimetric free kicks, George Best headed the ball on and Sadler materialised in the goalmouth to squeeze it in.

Five minutes more and the equaliser on the night, and aggregate winner, arrived, scored by a centre-half; and, of all people, by the old warhorse Bill Foulkes. George Best was intimately involved again. Beating his man, he turned the ball back and in ran Foulkes to score. United had become the first English team, the second British team, to reach the Final of the European Cup.

Perhaps their success, and the advice from Busby which encouraged it, should be no surprise. We had, after all, seen it before when United went a goal down to Blackpool in the 1948 FA Cup Final and the order which their captain, Johnny Carey, passed around the ranks was, 'Keep on playing football.' It had served United well in Madrid; it would do so again in the Final.

The Benfica side whom United, by good fortune, were to meet on English soil, at Wembley, was still ablaze with famous names; but the heroes seemed tired. It wasn't the same Eusebio, it wasn't the same Coluna that had been seen at Wembley less than two years earlier in the 1966 World Cup; though Eusebio, in the semi-finals against Juventus, had seemed to regain his old *élan*, scoring in both matches. For a while, at Wembley, it seemed he might repeat the dose.

The most significant event of the first half was a marvellous right-footed shot by Eusebio, a chance made out of nothing. Stepney hadn't a prayer of reaching the ball; he could only stand and watch as it flew past him . . . to rebound from the bar. So Eusebio had resumed his frustrating tattoo on the Wembley goalposts. Meanwhile David Sadler, still standing in for Denis Law in midfield – or, if you prefer, inside-forward – missed the kind of chance which Law would have put away in his sleep.

It was Brian Kidd, celebrating his 19th birthday in the most positive way, who sent him through the Benfica defence, with only the advancing keeper Henrique to pass. But Sadler could not make up his mind and when at last he did shoot, it was wide of the far post. He would miss again, after half-time; but after all, he had scored in Madrid.

The first half was also notable for some unpleasant fouls by Benfica on Best. Cruz was the chief offender, but it was Henrique who would be booked by the famous Sicilian referee, the Syracuse fire chief Concetto Lo Bello. Best himself most skilfully worked a chance for himself and shot hard, but the ball rebounded from Henrique.

Eight minutes into the second half, a most unexpected thing happened: Bobby Charlton scored with a header. Indeed the goal had a scarcity value which almost transcended its importance in the game. Tony Dunne, the United left-back, found Sadler on the left. Rising and twisting, Charlton met his cross on the near post and Henrique, himself perhaps amazed at so untoward an event, was stranded as the ball looped over him in a tantalising parabola to land in the opposite corner of the goal.

The game seemed to be in United's pocket, but instead, unexpectedly, they tired badly in the last quarter hour. Benfica, embracing the very English tactic of hitting high crosses to the head of a giant centre-forward, Torres, looked more and more dangerous. Eventually, with 11 minutes left, Torres headed down one of those crosses to the elegant right-midfielder Graça, whose excellent shot beat Stepney at last.

So United had cause to regret Sadler's second miss when, after good work by John Aston, always too quick and clever for the right-back Adolfo, Best turned the rest of the Benfica defence inside out, and Sadler was left alone in front of goal once more. This time his shot at least was on the target, but it struck Henrique's foot and spun over the bar.

By and large, Nobby Stiles had kept control of Eusebio, just as he had in the World Cup Final, but now, taking a pass from Graça, Eusebio was away at full pelt, with the United defence spreadeagled. On the bench, Matt Busby was saying to himself, 'Oh, no, not again.' But when Eusebio shot it was with his *left* foot, not his unforgiving right – a fact strangely ignored in subse-

A young Brian Kidd (centre, dark shirt) heads United's third goal in the 1968 Final at Wembley, as John Aston (11) looks on

(Popperfoto)

quent accounts. Still, the shot was so strong that Stepney, as he hurtled through the air, seemed to have no hope. But moving to his left he somehow, desperately, got a hand to the ball and kept it out.

Afterwards he would say modestly that to his surprise, the ball seemed softer in his grasp; had it been harder, he would never have saved it. For Pat Crerand, however, the save was 'quite fantastic, the turning point'.

Keep on playing football. That, 20 years after Johnny Carey's famous dictum, was the essence of Busby's advice. Simple, even simplistic, to a degree. Those who complicate football do it for their own self-aggrandisement. The Busbys of the game refine it down to its most basic principles. So all he said was, 'Just don't give the ball away. When you make a pass, make sure it reaches your team mate!'

Hardly the wisdom of the ages; but it worked. Busby, who had played at Wembley, knew how expensive it could be, on that huge, tiring pitch, to give the ball away. And if the object of any pass is, presumably, that it go to a colleague rather than an opponent, it was probably as well to advise due care.

So United went at it again; and won, rising from the ashes of what seemed a lost cause. Best and Kidd, now, were the heroes. Never would Brian Kidd play better. Never, surely, would he have a happier birthday. In the very first minute of extra time, Kidd headed on a clearance by Stepney to Best. Controlling it in a flash, Best, in an inside-left position, whipped past Jacinto, left the whole Benfica defence square and dead, converged on Henrique, dodged round him to the left, pivoted again and placed the ball in the net, just as Henrique rushed frantically back into the goalmouth.

That goal demoralised Benfica. Now they were easy prey. Charlton took a corner, Kidd got his head to it, the ball rebounded from Henrique and Kidd jumped again, headed again, the ball flying in off the crossbar. Finally, by way of variety, the left-footed Kidd went out to the right wing, held Cruz at bay, crossed the ball, and Bobby Charlton swept it home with his more powerful, less subtle, right foot. An English club had won the Cup at last.

5

MILAN AND INTER

Milan and Inter. Rivera and Mazzola. The *staffetta*, or relay, in the World Cup Final of 1970. The hooded authoritarianism of Helenio Herrera, in Inter's dominant days of the 1960s. The jiggery pokery of Moratti, Allodi and Solti, an inextinguishable blemish on Inter's triumphs, leading to the inevitable question, could they have won European Cups without it? That sordid story is recounted in the next chapter. Our concern now is largely with what Internazionale – and Milan – did on the field; and they did a great deal.

Milan might have won the European Cup as early as 1958, in Brussels, when their dazzling team of polyglots forced Real Madrid to extra time and the most breathless of victories. Inter, after their successes of the 60s, got to another Final only to be thrashed by Ajax in Rotterdam in 1972. But Milan, after two spells in *Serie B*, the Italian Second Division, took wing again under the presidency of Silvio Berlusconi and the managership of Arrigo Sacchi, played with a flat back four, and took the European Cup twice in succession, in 1989 and 1990.

Milan are the older of the two clubs. They were founded in 1899 as Milan Cricket and Football Club – note the order – chiefly by Englishmen, and won their first Italian Championship in 1901, eight years before Inter were born. Indeed their earliest star was an Englishman, the versatile Herbert Kilpin, who would remain celibate throughout the football season. Under Fascism, Milan were in fact made to change their name to Milano – and Internazionale, in an amalgamation, to Ambrosiana-Inter – but both changed back after the Second World War. Acquiring the Swedish inside-forward 'Grenoli' trio of Gunnar Gren, Gunnar Nordahl and Nils Liedholm in the late 1940s, Milan called the tune for a while. Then, in the early fifties, Inter began successfully to practise *catenaccio* defence, initiated in Switzerland, as we have seen, by the Austrian coach Karl Rappan.

The Inter team I used to watch in Italy at that time, though it used an extra defender to fill the gaps, was by no means negative. It scarcely could be with such dazzling attackers as the little blond Swedish inside-left or left-winger, Nacka Skoglund, and that accomplished centre or inside-forward Benito 'Poison' Lorenzi, a Tuscan with a fearful temperament but enormous skills.

When Helenio Herrera arrived at Inter from Barcelona in 1960, he was not renowned for cautious tactics, for a devotion to defence and the occasional breakaway. But now he would turn, with a vengeance, to that *catenaccio* which Inter had been applying less rigorously for years past. His rationalisation – it was hardly an explanation – was that he needed it to combat *less* gifted teams in the Italian Championship – whatever that was meant to mean.

Born in Buenos Aires, brought up in the slums of Casablanca, and a moderately successful footballer in France with Stade Francais of Paris, Herrera had enormous flair, a passionate love of publicity and money, and a tendency to treat his players like puppets. DEFENCE: LESS THAN 30 GOALS! screamed the notice on the dressing room wall. ATTACK: MORE THAN 100 GOALS! How sick Inter's English centre-forward Gerry Hitchens got of hearing Herrera, as the team coach headed towards the airport early in the morning after an away game, shouting, '*Pensa alla partita! Pensa alla partita!*' Think about the [next] game!

An authoritarian in an age when such figures seemed obsolescent, Herrera got away with what one might call his creative bullying because it brought results. Would Inter have got them without the cheating and finagling, the suborning of referees, which went on the background? Such a question must forever tarnish their achievements; nor was their style an endearing one. Yet the team bristled with fine players, and the irony of it is that they would surely have had success without a Solti in the shadows.

'Like coming out of the bloody army,' was how Gerry Hitchens described his sudden transfer, in the winter of 1962, from Inter to Torino, leaving Herrera free to sign the Brazilian greyhound, the right-winger, Jair. Hitchens had had an early taste of what discipline meant at Inter. He had taken immediately to the far more imaginative training practised under Herrera – speed and ball work, so much more enjoyable than the plodding routines he was used to in England.

He was, however, unprepared for what life would be like under such a disciplinarian. Lagging behind on a training run at Appia Gentile, before the season began, Hitchens, Luis Suarez and Marolino Corso, key men in the Inter midfield, had fallen behind the pack. As they drew close to the team coach, it drove off, leaving them to make their own way – all six miles – back to headquarters.

In March 1969, the death in the dressing-room at Cagliari of the young Roma player Giuliano Taccola would put a different, grimmer gloss on Herrera's intransigent methods. Taccola was a forward, who had been unwell for some time. An operation to remove his tonsils proved no palliative. He still felt unwell. Roma's doctors examined him and told the then President, Alvaro Marchini, that the boy had a heart murmur, product of a congenital weakness.

Herrera would have none of it. He had joined Roma on a massive salary, recouped by the club almost at once through increased season-ticket sales. Hardly endearing himself to the public by stating that Roma, champions just once in 1941, had won 'only because Mussolini was the manager', Herrera continued on his flamboyant way.

Poor Taccola played in Genoa against Sampdoria, lasted 45 minutes and fell ill again. Herrera, known to his infinity of admirers as *Il Mago*, the Magician, continued to insist there was nothing wrong with him. In mid-March he took him to Sardinia, where Roma were to play Cagliari, as a non-combatant. But he made him train in the morning with the rest, on a beach buffeted by icy winds. By the time the Roma doctor, Visalli, arrived, Taccola had a high fever. He watched the game from the stands, collapsed afterwards in the dressing-room, and died.

It should be said that the Inter team of those days was full not only of very good players but very pleasant ones, several of whom I knew well. There was the giant left-back Giacinto Facchetti, simple and straightforward to a fault, an eager attacker, proud of the fact that he frequently scored goals, often with his right foot.

Sandrino Mazzola, inside-forward who would turn centre-forward and surpass himself in the 1970 World Cup Final, had battled through harsh times to success. His father, Valentino, had been the inside-left and illustrious captain of Italy, and of the fine Torino team which perished in the appalling air disaster at Superga in 1949.

Torino had not looked after Sandrino, his brother Ferruccio, and their mother. It was Inter who eventually did so, spotting the promise of the two boys, taking both of them on as juniors, moving the family to Milan. Of the two, Sandro possessed by far the greater talent. Tall and slender but surprisingly strong, he was an accomplished ball-player with a powerful shot, probably at his best when playing just behind the attack, as he did so impressively in the 1970 World Cup Final. There, he had room to advance with the ball, take opponents on, and consummately beat them. His close control, quick football brain and ability to turn made him a great danger at centre-forward, even under tight marking, but he could exert more influence from a deeper role.

Helenio Herrera – domineering, authoritarian, flamboyant, controversial manager of Barcelona, then Inter. An Argentine, brought up in the slums of Casablanca, who played professionally in France

(Hulton Picture Company)

Almost inevitably, his name has been paired through the years with that of Gianni Rivera, the boy prodigy who was playing League football for his local Alessandria club at 15 and joined Milan at 16 for a record £65 000 fee. He dominated the team's midfield for years with his refined technique, superb passing, and surprisingly powerful shot. There were those Italian critics who damned him for not wanting to go into the penalty area and risk getting hurt, but his balance and skill were such that he was usually able to avoid injury.

In Mexico in 1970, Ferruccio Valcareggi, the amiable, long-suffering manager of Italy, had somehow to resolve his problem of finding room for both these superb players. The introduction of substitutes allowed him to find a solution – of a sort. This was the relay, or *staffetta*, in which Mazzola would begin the game and be relieved in the second half by Rivera.

It worked well enough when Mexico were thrashed and West Germany narrowly beaten in a goal-glutted semi-final. But in the Final, Mazzola was playing so well in an Italian team which had largely given up the ghost that there was no way he could be taken off. When Rivera did get on, it was for a mere, humiliating six minutes.

Both men were engaging and endearing figures. At 16, Rivera, the son of a railwayman, already spoke like a mature player; Mazzola had always been modest and forthcoming. It was Rivera's inspired defence-cutting passes which made the goals for José Altafini, himself once nicknamed 'Mazzola' in Brazil for his resemblance to Valentino, which won Milan the 1963 European Cup Final. The second of them might have been offside, but there was no gainsaying the quality of the passes.

In Inter's midfield, the general was Luis Suarez, the Spanish international with hair creamed down like an Argentine tango idol, who called the tune and the shots. With a right foot which could split defences or blast goals as required, and a combative temperament which could occasionally spill over into violence – as it did in the notorious 1964 European Cup semi-final in Milan – Suarez proved worth every lira of the massive fee Herrera paid to take him from Barcelona.

Armando Picchi, small, dark, mobile and compact, was the ideal sweeper in those days of defensive *catenaccio*. A Tuscan who had begun his career as a defender with Livorno, he was adept in marshalling his men and plugging all the holes. And what a competitor! Surprisingly and surely mistakenly, Italy did not pick him for the 1966 World Cup. So it was that, one Sunday summer morning in Battersea Park, I found myself playing alongside him in a pick-up game with a bunch of English Sunday players, like myself. The way Picchi played, it might well have been the World Cup Final.

He showed no patience with a plump little middle-aged friend he had brought with him, whom he nicknamed Pastasciutta and put out on the wing. '*Ah, Pastasciutta!*' he would cry when his friend made a mistake. '*Non é come dalla tribuna!*' It's not like being in the stand! Alas, Picchi died a sad, early death from cancer.

At deep outside-left was the long-legged Mariolino Corso, who always played with his socks around his ankles. Initially an inside-left, and always more of a midfield attacker than a true winger, Corso had joined Inter from his local club in Verona. He had a solid estimation of his own worth, and when he wasn't picked for the 1962 World Cup team he gestured his disapproval to the selectors in the course of a match at San Siro. Corso it was who would score the phantom, free-kick goal that never was, or never should have been, against Liverpool there in May 1965, a goal allowed by the ineffable Spanish referee Ortiz de Mendibil.

At right-back was the rugged Tarcisio Burgnich, a failure at Juventus but a success at Inter, later a centre-back above whom Pele soared to head Brazil's first goal in the 1970 World Cup Final. Bedin and Tagnin, at different times, were implacable markers in midfield. Aristide Guarneri was a centre-half who subdued most opposing strikers.

But just as they were founded first, so Milan were first to win the European Cup; and by a long way first to reach a European Cup Final. That was of course in 1958, with a team which, on the way to the Final, beat Rapid Vienna 4–1 in San Siro, lost 5–2 in Vienna, then won 4–2 in the play-off – yes, there were play-offs still in those innocent days before the penalty shoot-out.

Glasgow Rangers were far too naive – the familiar Scottish story – to withstand Milan at Ibrox. A goal up at half-time through Murray, they held on to that lead, and their illusions, till a very bad quarter of an hour. Much faster and more incisive, Milan equalised through the powerful Argentine inside-left Ernesto Grillo, took the lead through a young reserve left-winger Baruffi, scored again through Grillo, and rubbed it in with a fourth from the neat centre-forward Bean. Neither Bean nor Baruffi would figure in the Final, lost so narrowly to Real Madrid.

Three years later Jimmy Greaves arrived, reluctantly, from London, stayed a few months, scored no fewer than nine goals, then went home to join Spurs. 'He ruined my Championship,' rumbled Nereo Rocco, the bull mastiff of a manager, when I met him on a train from Cardiff to London. But it wasn't quite true. Greaves' blaze of goals in fact gave Milan a flying start, they picked up Dino Sani from Brazil – a 1958 World Cup right-half – and went on to take the title.

En route to the 1963 Final, Milan beat Ipswich Town, managed by Alf Ramsey, in the second round. I saw the first leg at a rain-soaked San Siro when Ipswich were made to look naive. Gerry Hitchens sat beside me; we had driven over from Turin. 'Must say hallo to Alf! Wish good luck to the lads!' he enthused. Ramsey had just agreed to leave Ipswich Town to become the England team manager. Hitchens had recently led England's attack in Chile in the World Cup.

To Hitchens's effusive greeting, in the dressing-room corridor, Ramsey replied, in his familiar 'Sarn't Major Posh', 'Oh yes! You're playin' in these parts!' Which had Hitchens fuming, imitating and expostulating throughout the game. He never won another cap for England.

Ipswich hardly competed that night; they seemed out of their depth. They were a side Ramsey had put together with consummate skill, rather as a man might produce a splendid artefact out of flotsam and jetsam. The whole was infinitely greater than the sum of its parts, with Ted Phillips and Ray Crawford raiding through the middle, and the elderly matchstick-legged Jimmy Leadbeater operating as a deep left-winger, confusing English opponents. That wet night in Milan, however, Phillips was absent, as was the big left-half, John Elsworthy.

'They were up to all the cynical stuff,' complained the Ipswich skipper and centre-half Andy Nelson, one of several players rejuvenated by Ramsey. 'Pulling your hair, spitting, treading on your toes.' Altafini, he said, was one of the worst, though he virtually vanished at Portman Road, where Ipswich won the return.

It was sad to hear that; because by and large, José Altafini's career was a long and distinguished one, its climax coming in Juventus' 1972/3 European Cup campaign when, at the age of 34, Altafini outwitted and penetrated the Derby defence in the semi-final in Turin; the day Brian Clough refused 'to talk to any cheating bastards.' Eventually dropped by Vicente Feola from his 1958 World Cup team because, the Brazilian coach said, Altafini – shades of Mazzola – confused his tactics, and because his expensive transfer to Milan from Palmeiras had allegedly gone to his head, he would mature over the years into a superbly complete centre-forward.

It was, however, the tall, strong left-winger Paolo Barison, sadly to die in a car crash at the age of 42, who was Ipswich's chief executioner at San Siro in the rain. He scored twice in the 3–0 win. He scored again at Portman Road where Ipswich played dashing football to win 2–1. It was not enough, any more than would be Dundee's 1–0 win in the return leg of the semi-final. In Milan, Dundee had gone down 5–1, complaining that their keeper Bert Slater was dazzled by the flash bulbs of the photographers as he went up for crosses.

Even if true, this hardly explained all five goals, no fewer than four of which came in the second half from the incisive wingers, Barison and Mora. Dundee had surpassed themselves to come so far, and it had been a marvellous Indian Summer for the 38-year-old Gordon Smith, once the boy wonder right-winger of Scottish football in the 1940s, yet never to excel in those many wartime internationals against England. Alan Gilzean, that superb header of the ball, later to score so many goals for Tottenham, got the only one in the return at Dens Park and then was sent off late in the game, retaliating to a foul.

It was a highly talented Milan side, with Dino Sani and Rivera to call the tune in midfield and Giovanni Trapattoni, later so successful a manager of Juventus, at left-half; though it was his misplaced short pass which led to

Milan skipper Cesare Maldini lifts the European Cup at Wembley in 1963, as manager Nereo Rocco celebrates. Two goals from Jose Altafini were enough to account for Benfica in the Final

(Hulton Picture Company)

Benfica going ahead in the Final at Wembley.

José Torres, the giant Benfica centre-forward, snapped up the ball and sent Eusebio through on a protracted run, Trapattoni faint yet pursuing. Ghezzi, the goalkeeper who had come from rivals Inter, stayed on his line; Eusebio shot in off the post.

But the determining factor in this game, alas, was a foul, by Pivatelli on Coluna. Cynicism ruled. Milan, under the managership of Gipo Viani, had decided they needed to contain Coluna. Had they decided that they needed to put him out of the game? Who can say. Suffice it that Barison, despite all his goals, was dropped, and Bruno Mora moved from the right to the left wing. Gino Pivatelli came in as number seven, with the brief to mark Coluna.

In early 1954 Pivatelli had been a highly promising inside-right with Bologna. On his home ground, on a frosty day, I saw him powerfully strike one of the goals whereby Italy won the first ever Under-23 match, 3–0 against England, who included a 17-year-old Duncan Edwards, Pivatelli's marker. But time had passed and Pivatelli now was a Milan reserve, exhumed that day to mark Coluna.

Just a minute after Rivera, the king of the midfield, had sent Altafini through to equalise, 13 minutes into the second half, Pivatelli tripped Coluna, who hobbled through the rest of the game. Soon afterwards there was confusion in Benfica's defence, a hasty attempted pass by Humberto, and an interception from – or a rebound off? – Rivera, sending Altafini away for the winner and his 14th goal of the tournament. Was he offside? I thought so at the time, but he may in fact have been just inside his own half when he started the run.

So Milan took their first European Cup, as Altafini, taking two bites at the cherry – Costa Pereira blocked the initial shot – made it 2–1. Hardly a glorious victory, against a Benfica team without Germano in defence and with an attack in which the replacement of Aguas by Torres necessitated a wholly different, less fluid, approach; one which involved the high cross and the frequent long ball.

Now came the time of Inter, and Herrera. Not to mention Allodi and Solti. They were, though, given a hard time in the preliminary round of the following season's competition, while Milan, as holders, were given a bye. Inter faced Everton, and at Goodison Park they packed their *catenaccio* defence. They seemed lucky to survive when what appeared to be a good goal by Roy Vernon, the Welsh international inside-left, was disallowed, but Everton's Young probably was in an offside position.

In the return game in Milan, the goal whereby Inter won was something of a freak, one of those crosses-cum-shots by the Brazilian Jair, which swerved its way home from a weird angle. Everton, in what was to become a familiar story all around Europe, complained they couldn't sleep in their hotel in Monza the previous night, as Italian fans drove round and round the hotel in their cars.

Next came the French champions Monaco, beaten 1–0 at San Siro and thrashed at Marseilles in the return, where Mazzola and Suarez were devastating and Inter proved Herrera right in his forecast that Monaco had run out of steam. Monaco's French international attacker, Yvon Douis, said that if he had to play against Tagnin every week he would retire from football.

Inter's machine was running strongly and smoothly. Next came another emphatic away win, 3–0 over Partizan in Belgrade, followed by a 2–1 win at home. Borussia Dortmund would be the semi-final opponents, and the second leg was the first match to engender deep suspicion of Inter's methods.

In Dortmund, in the first leg, they drew an exciting match 2–2. The prolific centre-forward Brungs scored twice in the first half for Dortmund, replying to a fourth-minute goal by Sandrino Mazzola; Mariolino Corso got the equaliser for Inter, four minutes before the interval. The hefty West German left-half Horst Szymaniak, bought as an extra foreigner to reinforce Inter's massed defence just in European Cup games, was now left out of the second leg; nor would he take part in the Final. Caution had been cast to the winds!

On 29 April 1964, at San Siro, Inter beat Borussia Dortmund 2–0. Mazzola went one better, scoring inside three minutes, and Luis Suarez kicked the opposing right-half in the stomach, putting him off the field, without let or hindrance. Reduced to ten men, Dortmund lost the game. The following summer, a Yugoslav tourist on an Adriatic coast holiday found the referee of that game, his fellow Yugoslav Tesanic, on holiday at the same resort. The trip had been paid for, he allegedly told the tourist ... by Inter.

There was much commotion in the West German Press, but no follow-up, either within UEFA – surprise, surprise – or, indeed, in the European Press at large. For which all of us, I think, must incur a measure of guilt. I remember reading the report at the time in a French magazine, raising an eyebrow, and doing no more. Which meant there would be all the more to do, belatedly, 10 years afterwards.

In the Final in Vienna, Inter came up against Real Madrid, who had eliminated Milan in the quarter-finals. A superlative performance in the first leg in Madrid enabled them to do that. Puskas was 36 now, and Di Stefano the best part of a year older, but each contrived to score in a 4–1 victory, Amancio and Gento getting the others. Milan won the return 2–0 with goals by the midfielder Lodetti, who had scored in Madrid, and Altafini, but it was too little, too late.

Real's defensive blunders signed their own death warrant in Vienna. A long range shot by Mazzola put Inter ahead before half-time, and 17 minutes into the second half a blunder by Real's keeper Vicente gave Milani, the Inter centre-forward, a second. When Felo headed in a corner for Real, the game looked open again, but another fearful defensive lapse, this time by the Uruguayan centre-back José Santamaria, let Mazzola score the decisive third. Lucien Muller, Real's French international right-half, poured scorn on Inter's beggarly methods. But they'd worked.

They worked again the following season, though again it needed help from a dubious referee in the semi-final second leg against Liverpool at San

RIGHT Club President Moratti leads the celebrations after Inter had defeated Real Madrid 3–1 in the 1964 Final at the Prater Stadium, Vienna. With him are (left to right) Facchetti, Guarneri, Mazzola and Suarez. Mazzola had clinched victory (TOP) with his second and Inter's third goal (Farabolafoto)

Siro. Peiró, the long-legged Spanish international inside-left or winger, was allowed to kick the ball out of goalkeeper Tommy Lawrence's hands to score, and of course there was that bizarre goal, from an indirect free kick, by Corso. Which made it 3–0 after Liverpool's brave 3–1 win at Anfield, just a few days after an exhausting FA Cup Final. Ortiz de Mendibil had proved a complaisant referee.

In the quarter-finals, Inter had emulated their rivals Milan by beating Glasgow Rangers, though they didn't win at Ibrox. Who knows what

Rangers might have achieved had the wonderfully gifted left-half Jim Baxter not broken his leg helping Rangers beat Rapid in Vienna in the previous round. As it was, Inter won 3–1 at San Siro, and could thus afford a 1–0 defeat – the goal scored by Jim Forrest – at Ibrox.

Luck favoured Inter against Benfica in the Final, as it was scheduled for San Siro itself. Played in an unrelenting deluge, it produced a victory by Inter which induced little applause or joy. It was the rain, the mud, which really gave Inter their goal – a shot by Jair, that specialist in strange goals, which slid under Costa Pereira's body. Benfica had actually threatened to boycott the Final or send their youth team rather than play it in Milan; but precedent existed, UEFA waved a big stick and the match, such as it was, took place.

Half an hour from the end, Costa Pereira injured his leg and came out of goal, replaced there by the big, bald centre-half Germano, who himself was already hobbling. Inter still couldn't score again, but they retained their tarnished Cup.

The following season, when the notorious semi-final second leg stage came round, referee Gyorgy Vadas wouldn't be bribed and Inter went out; a year later, in the Final in Lisbon and to the general delight, Celtic beat them. After the post-match banquet, according to Liverpool's idiosyncratic Scottish manager Bill Shankly, two of the Celtic coaching staff sat abusing Helenio Herrera. Why, I asked him. 'Because I told them to!'

Inter reached still another European Cup Final in 1972, in Rotterdam, but there, too, they were outplayed, by Ajax. It was Milan, in 1969, which would be the next Milanese club to win the European Cup, and Ajax whom they would outplay in Madrid in the Final.

Of the team which had won at Wembley six years earlier, only Giovanni Trapattoni and Gianni Rivera survived, but this was not a young Milan side. There were two veterans in attack, the big Brazilian centre-forward Sormani and Kurt Hamrin, the little Swedish outside-right who had been a star of the 1958 World Cup. Hamrin had joined Milan from Fiorentina, and still knew a trick or two. The blond, muscular West German Karl-Heinz Schnellinger played in defence.

Talking of veterans, Bill Foulkes, surprisingly enough, was still in the Manchester United squad, and he had a disastrous game at centre-half when United, winners of the competition the previous season, faced Milan in the first leg of the semi-final, at San Siro. That, and the selection of the inexperienced Jimmy Rimmer in goal, cost United the tie. Sormani, a dormant volcano for many a month, had his best game for ages against Foulkes, United lost 2–0, and an ill-natured, bruising, controversial game at Old Trafford brought only the mirage of a 1–0 victory.

Bobby Charlton scored that one, insufficient, goal; but Denis Law – accused after the match by Milan's President, Franco Carraro, of 'not being a gentleman' after an incident involving the visiting stopper – thought he had scored another for United when he met Crerand's cross, in the final minutes. Did the ball go over the line before Santin booted it away? United insisted that it did. But then, Kurt Hamrin too had a goal contentiously disallowed, for offside. And Fabio Cudicini, Milan's goalkeeper, was knocked out by a missile from the Stretford End. Matt Busby ducked and dived when I asked him about that.

In the Final, a young evolving Ajax team were given a lesson. But they had played some memorable matches on their way there, few as memorable as the series of three against Benfica in the quarter-finals.

Benfica, under their Brazilian coach, Otto Gloria, surprised Ajax on a frozen pitch in Amsterdam by going out for goals. And they scored them. Jacinto opened from the penalty spot, and Torres made it 2–0 after a mistake by Vasovic, three years earlier the Partizan centre-half and goalscorer against Real Madrid in the Final. Ajax looked better when they brought on their Swedish international centre-forward, Danielsson, for the second half. He got a goal, but Augusto got another for Benfica, and 3–1 looked a pretty safe lead for them to take to Lisbon.

But it wasn't. This time it was Ajax who went out looking for goals, and incredibly Danielsson and Johan Cruyff, already emerging as a marvellous centre-forward, had wiped out Benfica's advantage within 11 minutes. Cruyff then knocked in a third before half-time. Benfica recovered in the second half, Torres scoring the goal which gave them a play-off in Paris.

There, no fewer than 63 000 watched an extraordinary game, goalless till extra time then dominated by Ajax, with the Cruyff–Danielsson combination working incisively again. The Swede scored twice, Cruyff once, and Benfica had been dished, 3–0.

Milan were more difficult opponents. Piet Keizer, the clever, blond Ajax left-winger, would say afterwards that the pressures in Madrid were just too much for the then inexperienced Ajax side. Pierino Prati was their chief executioner, a tall, strong, 22-year-old left-winger or centre-forward who could operate effectively in either role. He had been with Milan since boyhood, and had twice been loaned out to lesser clubs. Not any more.

In the quarter finals it had been Prati, coolly exploiting a mistake by Billy McNeill and running on to score, who had got the only goal of the two ties against Celtic, at Parkhead. Now, in Madrid, he'd get a hat-trick. His first came after seven minutes, when he exploited a pass by Sormani, the old pachyderm, as a Milanese journalist called him. In vain Ajax dominated the play for a time; Milan never minded that, any more than Inter. Six minutes from half-time, the alert Prati shot home a pass pulled back to him by Gianni Rivera, and it was 2–0 to Milan.

When, after 71 minutes, Lodetti brought down Piet Keizer, Vasovic scored from the penalty and had thus scored for two different teams in a European Cup Final. But just when the game seemed up for grabs, Sormani scored in a counter attack; Pratti rubbed salt into the wound with a fourth, six minutes from the end, the pass once more coming from Rivera.

Soon we would be in the epoch of Total Football, dominated by the West Germans and the Dutch. Not till the late 1980s would a Milanese club put its name on the trophy again; and then, twice in a row, it would be Milan.

Milan under the Presidency of Silvio Berlusconi, and the remarkable managership of little Arrigo Sacchi.

Silvio Berlusconi remains an immensely controversial figure in Italy, and it is not my purpose here to go in any depth into his multifarious activities outside football. He played a decent level of amateur football himself – which, ironically, is more than could be said for Sacchi – and made huge sums of money in property. Still greater gains resulted when he became the proprietor of Channel 5 television, a highly commercialised station with no pretensions to enhancing the nation's cultural awareness. He was able to build the so-called 'Milano 2', a large extension to the city of Milan, and in 1990 he very nearly succeeded in gaining control of the immense Mondadori publishing empire, which included publications hostile to him such as the newspaper *La Repubblica* of Rome.

Bitter opposition sprang up in and out of Parliament, however, and in the event, Berlusconi for once was outmanoeuvred. He is known to have been a member of the notorious P2 Masonic lodge, presided over by the Fascist leader Licio Gelli. Berlusconi has always insisted that his involvement was merely peripheral. His detractors demur.

Rivalry with Juventus and the 'old money' of the Agnelli family, the patrons of that club and owners of FIAT, was perhaps inevitable, but it has always seemed unfair to me to compare Berlusconi unfavourably with Gianni Agnelli, the enormously powerful head of FIAT, at whose feet football journalists sit in reverence. The Agnellis are not aristocracy, though they may be treated as such. They have simply been rich for longer; and the family's behaviour during Fascist times does not bear much examination. Besides, Agnelli, when doing his unsuccessful best to suppress an unfavourable biography of him, hardly emerged as a benign democrat.

To the chagrin of Juventus and Agnelli, Milan, under Berlusconi, left them behind in the late 1980s. It wasn't that Berlusconi bought his way to success. He did indeed spend huge sums of money on his team, but he spent it with far more flair and shrewdness than did Juventus under the Presidency of their former captain, Giampiero Boniperti. The team 'Boni' put together after the departure of Michel Platini was a disastrous one, massive sums being spent on such players as Ian Rush, and others less known, to pitifully little avail.

Milan, by contrast, brought together the three marvellous Dutchmen, Marco Van Basten, Ruud Gullit and Franck Rijkaard; and enjoyed even greater success than when they had the three Swedes of the Grenoli trio. Besides, if Gullit cost more than £5 million when he came, Van Basten, by contrast, was out of contract and came for relative peanuts, when Ajax were obliged to sell him.

Then there was the inspired appointment of Arrigo Sacchi, for which Berlusconi must surely be given credit, even if Sacchi, then manager of Parma, was recommended to him. *La Sua Emittenza* – His Broadcastship, as opposed to *La Sua Eminenza*, His Eminence – at least had the foresight and courage to give Sacchi his chance. Tiny, bald, still little-known in the game, Sacchi sat in his office at Milan's headquarters in Via Turati and said he still couldn't quite believe he was there. But in no time at all, he would prove he was there on sheer merit.

Born and brought up in Fusignano, a town with 7000 inhabitants, in the Romagna, and the province of Ravenna, Sacchi loved football but couldn't play it. His father, who could, but gave it up early to concentrate on his shoe-manufacturing business, used his son as a salesman. At Arrigo's local club, little Baracca Luco, the general manager, asked him one day: 'My dear Sacchi, since you can't play, why don't you try to be a manager?'

It was an inspired suggestion. Sacchi began coaching the juniors, and went into orbit – a long one. Another small club came next, Bellaria. Then an actual League club, Cesena, where he joined the coaching staff. On he went to Rimini, and then came the breakthrough, as he moved to Fiorentina, where Italo Allodi – give the devil his due – wanted him to coach the youth team. It was his achievements there which got him the manager's job at Parma, whom he so nearly got into *Serie A*, the First Division, playing a vigorous four-in-line defence. Not *catenaccio*, note.

Parma played Milan in the Italian Cup and did so well that Berlusconi decided Sacchi was his man. 'I didn't know that a jockey had to be born a horse to ride one,' Sacchi says. His methods have been compared with those of Nils Liedholm, who first put Milan (and Roma) on to flat back-four tactics. Sacchi – who modestly conceded that while Liedholm has stories of the great Grenoli days to tell, his own concern tiny clubs and obscure players – says the two methods are different. Liedholm likes his teams to keep possession of the ball, he himself always wants to attack.

'Pressing' as the Italians call it, using the English word, is the essence of Sacchi's game. Pushing up hard to halfway. The tactic came under criticism during Milan's successful defence of the European Cup in 1990, after they had struggled desperately away to Mechelen. Moreover when two teams play such tactics, said the sceptics, a desperately impoverished spectacle results; this was certainly the case when Milan beat Benfica in the Final in Vienna that year.

When Sacchi got to Milan from Parma in 1987, he challenged his squad of famous, wealthy players: 'I come from Fusignano, but what have *you* won in your careers?' The response was predictably hostile, but in very little time Sacchi had brought about better, closer relations in the group. A man who gives as one of the chief influences in his life the librarian at Fusignano, Sacchi reads Hemingway, Faulkner and Cesare Pavese, and wishes he had more time for reading than he does.

Ruud Gullit, the powerful, skilful, superbly versatile Dutch international who played so large a part in Milan's success; as good with his head as with his feet.
(Farabolafoto)

To win the Italian championship in his very first season with Milan must have seemed as remote a dream as actually being made manager of the club. But it happened. Happened though Marco Van Basten, perhaps the best centre-forward in the world, played but 11 games, contributing three goals. Happened in large measure thanks to the prowess of the remarkable Ruud Gullit, second best player in the league – Maradona then came first – who made 29 appearances and scored nine times.

A massive man where Maradona is small and squat, a figure made still more striking by his dreadlocks, Gullit was still only 25 when he joined Milan. To his immense physical power he added almost every attribute imaginable. His great skill on the ball was remarkable in so large a man. He had a superbly powerful right foot, great authority in the air, sharp awareness of the play around him, and absolute versatility. He had already, in his Dutch days, played as 'fluidifying' sweeper – in the Beckenbauer style, though more dynamic – stopper, midfielder and striker. Play him where you wished, he was the very embodiment of Total Football, at a time when it had gone into abeyance.

Born in Amsterdam in 1962 of Surinamese parents, Gullit began his career with the local DWS club at barely sixteen years of age. Three seasons with Haarlem followed, the second in Division Two, followed by the move to Rotterdam and Feyenoord which gave him the chance to develop and display his great talents. In his three seasons there, he established himself as the most exciting player in the Dutch League; probably the best since Johan Cruyff, Marco Van Basten's idol.

But Gullit never played for Ajax. It was wealthy PSV of Eindhoven, backed by Philips electrical industry, which bought him in 1985. The following year Berlusconi, entranced by Gullit's talents, decided he must have him and set about courting him; even to the extent of playing and singing French songs to him, at the piano. Gullit has a great passion for music, not least for reggae, which he sings with his own band.

PSV had no wish to sell Gullit but Milan never ceased trying to prise him away. Eventually, early in 1987, when he was still under contract to PSV till 1990, they brought him, secretly they hoped, to Milan for a medical, having offered him the earth. PSV very properly cried foul and protested to UEFA, but Gullit was determined to go, seduced by the promises of Berlusconi; and, for over £5 million, Gullit duly moved to Milan the following season.

England's Ray Wilkins, whose place with Milan was now usurped, remarked, hurt but restrained, that Milan might have told him what was happening. He knew Gullit was a far better player, but surely he deserved better treatment. So he did.

With Gullit arrived Van Basten, for some £2 million. Growing up under the shadow and, in due course, under the aegis of Cruyff, he had become a formidable centre-forward in his own right, though of a somewhat different kind to his hero. Physically more powerful and almost as skilful on the ball, his magnificent technique was matched by pace, intelligence, strength in the air and a superb right foot, with which he scored a memorable, volleyed goal against Russia in the Final of the 1988 European Championship. An example of his marvellous, electric turn came in the first half of the 1990 European Cup Final, when he spun superbly to lose his tight marker, only to fail to get enough power behind his shot to beat Benfica's keeper.

But injury and an operation largely kept Van Basten out of the Milan team in his, Gullit and Sacchi's first season; though he did come back at last in the closing games. And did fight his way into a Dutch team from which Rinus Michels, in West Germany, at first inexplicably excluded him; only to reap the benefit of Van Basten's end-of-season freshness when he did have the sense to put him in the team.

Franck Rijkaard would not arrive in Milan until the following season, and then it was only after a protracted battle which told one much about the relationship between Berlusconi and Sacchi. For Berlusconi had got it into his head that the man Milan needed was not Rijkaard but Claudio Borghi, the young Argentine centre-forward bought after the 1986 World Cup – in which he scarcely played – and farmed out to Como.

There, he had a wretched time of it, kept out of the first team even in that little club by two different managers. His talent was beyond dispute, but he could not settle down in Italy. Berlusconi made it his crusade: Borghi had been underestimated, Borghi had been misunderstood. He brought him back to Milan and had him training with the team. A coruscating perform-ance in a friendly against Manchester United seemed to confirm his judge-ment: Borghi must be signed. But Sacchi insisted on Rijkaard, a dominant centre-half or thrusting midfield player, who had been floating between Portugal and Spain on loan after quarrelling irretrievably with Cruyff at Ajax.

Like Gullit, his exact contemporary, Rijkaard was born of Surinamese parents. Formidable both in the air and on the ground, a defender who always liked to sweep forward, a midfielder eminently capable of winning the ball – it seemed illogical to gamble on the fragile Borghi when such a paragon was at hand. But Berlusconi took a great deal of persuading and later, as a kind of vindication, would make Sacchi eat humble pie over Daniel Massaro, the attacking midfielder whom he allowed to go on loan for a season to Roma; and who did well, there.

The match which enabled Milan to take Napoli's title took place only two weeks before the end of the season, when Sacchi's team won 3–2 in Naples. Van Basten scored the third goal, having come on, as he did at that time, as a substitute, after the interval. The other two goals went to the 30-year-old Sardinian Pietro Paolo Virdis, hair grown distinctively grey in service; he had once bitterly resisted the call of Juventus when playing happily at home – or near enough to home, Sassari was in fact his birthplace – with Cagliari.

Virdis splendidly took up the slack when Van Basten dropped out, and was Milan's top scorer with 11 goals.

It had not been wholly plain sailing that season. In October 1987, Milan crashed out of the UEFA Cup in the second round to Espanol, very much the 'second team' in Barcelona. Espanol, astonishingly, beat them 2–0 in what for Milan was the 'home' leg, played down in the Deep South at Lecce since San Siro had been denied them after crowd troubles. In Barcelona, Milan could only draw 0–0. Now the other side of Berlusconi was to be seen. Next day, after the disaster of Lecce, he telephoned Sacchi at home.

'Sacchi, how are you?'

'Well in health, but in morale . . .'

'My dear Sacchi, go on as you are and you'll see in the end we'll both be proved right.' Which indeed they were. But by 1991, the romance was dead.

Quite the finest performance in Milan's passage to the 1989 European Cup Final was the glorious exhibition at San Siro against Real Madrid in the semi-final second leg, a match I was lucky enough to see. The Final, when Steaua lay down and died in Barcelona, looked somewhat better than it was. The way there was not always easy; least of all in Belgrade, when Red Star, winners themselves in 1991, were met in the second-round second leg.

The first leg had shown Milan were mortal. There were two goals, scored within a minute. That wonderfully elegant midfield-attacker Dragan Stojkovic scored for Red Star a couple of minutes into the second half. Milan equalised almost at once through Virdis and 1–1 was how it finished.

In Belgrade, fog oozed sullenly over the great, open Red Star stadium, putting a premature end to a torrid game, after 57 minutes. The following day, November 10, the teams tried again. Roberto Donadoni might have died; Ruud Gullit came on to replace him when he shouldn't have, and paid heavily for it; Milan had a perfectly good goal disallowed; and the tie was decided on penalties.

For the fact that they emerged victorious from the penalty shoot-out Milan had to thank their tall, sometimes erratic, keeper Giovanni Galli, who saved two of the Red Star kicks, taking his side through to the quarter-finals. Milan, though, had been denied what would have been the winning goal when Vasilijevic, the Red Star defender, deflected the ball over his own line; but both referee Pauly and his linesman were unsighted.

Gullit himself insisted he come on as substitute, despite the fact that his right knee was still very far from sound, after Donadoni had been mown down horrifically by Vasilijevic, who would later weep tears of remorse. For Donadoni might have died, as he lay senseless on the field; indeed he would have done had it not been for the resilience of Red Star's own physiotherapist, who had to break his jaw to open his clenched mouth, and let air down his throat. Poor Donadoni seemed always to be in the wars.

Most elegant of deep right-wingers, he had arrived at Milan from nearby Atalanta, his local club, as an all-round midfield player who called the shots. Milan restricted him to the flank, and that took time to digest. The previous season, playing against Wales in Brescia just before the European Championships, Donadoni had his head trodden on, when he fell, by Glyn Hodges, and emerged later wearing a heavy bandage, to the raucous amusement of the Welsh players. Though not, it should be said, of Hodges.

There were other talented Italian internationals in the team. Young Paolo Maldini, for example, an attacking left-back and a precocious star, son of Cesare, the club's former centre-half and veteran of the 1963 Final. Maldini, except on such rare occasions as when he had to face an inspired Chris Waddle, was defensively sound and dangerous going forward.

Franco Baresi was, alongside the three Dutchmen, one of the salient players in the team. It had taken him a surprisingly long time to win a regular place as sweeper in the Italian national side. The doomed Gaetano Scirea, who would perish in an horrific motor accident in Poland, kept him out for years; though Baresi surely should have figured in the 1986 World Cup finals in Mexico.

By an irony, it was his brother Giuseppe who'd be drafted in, somewhat cravenly, to mark Platini when Italy played France. The stratagem was a disaster, France won comfortably. Franco, who was turned down by Inter as a boy while his brother was turned down by Milan, developed into a complete fotballer, strong in the air, highly mobile, powerful and skilful on the ground, and always eager to burst into attack. Such chances tend to be limited when playing for Italy – so much the worse for the Italian attack. But when Milan went over to a flat back-four, Baresi found no trouble at all in becoming a straightforward, adventurous, centre-back.

Carlo Ancelotti, in midfield, had been bought from Roma, in whose 1983 championship success he had played so great a part that it was hard to understand why they ever let him go. Despite a pair of knees which had him forever on the operating table, he made a great contribution to Milan's success as well. A complete midfield player, hard in the tackle, clever in his use of the ball, he was also the possessor of a devastating shot, with which he scored a sensational goal, from long distance, in the semi-final drubbing of Real Madrid, 5–0 at San Siro.

The long, long winter-break over, Milan emerged from hibernation to knock out Werder Bremen in the quarter-finals, albeit with some difficulty. Werder had lost their star striker, Rudi Voller, to Roma, but had another of renown in Karlheinz Riedle, who himself would take the path to Rome in 1990, joining Lazio. The central defence was dominated by the big Norwegian Rune Bratseth, a hard man indeed to get by.

The tie produced nothing as violent as the match in Belgrade, but there was abundant controversy. In Bremen, no goals were scored, under pelting rain, but Milan once more felt they should have had one. On the half hour, not only did Bratseth seem to handle in the goalmouth, but Milan insisted that in any event the ball had crossed the line. They should have had a goal at best, a penalty at least; they got neither. Just before the interval, Galli went up for a corner and punched it into his own net. Bremen rejoiced. The referee decided Galli had been pushed. The Bremen manager, Otto Rehhagel, thought that was a goal, and also that Milan should have had a penalty when his own right-back Schaaf handled.

All set, then, for a jolly second leg in Milan, fittingly resolved by a controversial penalty, converted by Marco Van Basten on 32 minutes, after Gunnar Sauer had, according to the Scottish referee George Smith, fouled Donadoni in the box. Werder's players protested bitterly, ironically clapped Smith off the field at the end, and pushed him – or at least Oliver Reck did, after keeping goal for Bremen so well. Harsh accusations followed. Milan responded by saying they had been cheated of a goal in Bremen. But they were in the semi-final; and now they soared.

Though Real Madrid collaborated in their own doom, I have seen few finer European Cup performances than Milan gave in the second leg at San Siro. Tactical ingenuousness on the part of Real's Dutch manager, Leo Beenhakker, surely helped them. There was plenty of talent in Madrid's

Roberto Donadoni, a central midfielder turned right winger, elegant and inventive. A superb user of the ball who would miss the 1990 Final through suspension (Farabolafoto)

team. Three splendid young players had come up through the youth programme and the nursery club, Castilla: the centre-forward Emilio Butragueno, and midfielders Michel and Martin Vazquez.

The arrival from Barcelona of controversial Bernd Schuster meant Michel, a talented and penetrative midfielder, now had to play, reluctantly, deep on the right. Butragueno had a deadly combination with the sharp little Mexican striker Hugo Sanchez, he of the celebratory somersaults, up front. But for so many years now Real had been characterised as the Nearly Team, and so, for all their refulgence of stars, it would prove again.

In the first leg, in Madrid, Milan had the courage to attack. Van Basten, thwarted by Buyo, the Real keeper, might have scored twice; but so might Hugo Sanchez who did indeed score, four minutes from half-time and against the run of play, with a splendidly taken goal which Van Basten equalised, just as splendidly, 12 minutes from the end.

At San Siro, Real collapsed. Playing the fast, effective winger Paco Llorente – nephew of Gento, and so often an effective substitute – from the first threw the whole team out of balance. It weakened the midfield, in which Schuster hadn't the pace to compete with Milan's busy players, and forced Butragueno to spend much of the game fruitlessly on the right flank, rather than combining with Hugo Sanchez.

Carlo Ancelotti's devastating long shot, after 18 minutes, sent Real spinning, and they never recovered. Milan's performance was a compound of technical excellence, dynamic pace and inspired movement. Gullit, playing up front with Van Basten, can seldom have been better, seldom have shown such an irresistible compound of power, skill and opportunism; though the price would be high.

Real's *catenaccio* looked obsolescent and porous. Rijkaard, ebullient all evening, popped up in the goalmouth to head in a cross from Tassotti, the right-back, after a short corner from Donadoni. Gullit himself, just before half-time, potently headed in a centre by Donadoni himself, weaving his arabesques with consummate ability.

Real were down and out. It was a procession now as more goals, and further humiliation, followed in the second half. An all-Dutch goal arrived after just four minutes, cleverly fashioned by Rijkaard and Gullit for Van Basten. But not long afterwards Gullit was down, near the right-hand touchline. Irresistible he might have looked, but the right knee had not resisted. The cartilage had gone and he would need an operation, from which he would return much too soon.

Virdis replaced him; and almost at once, another goal arrived, Donadoni's this time. Buyo looked shell-shocked. Five–nil, and Steaua of Bucharest awaited Milan in the Final, in Barcelona.

It was Barcelona whom Steaua had beaten on penalties, in Seville, in 1986 to win one of the dullest, dreariest European Cup Finals yet. Since then they had acquired the brilliant Gheorghe Hagi from Sportul for their midfield, at the behest of the vicious Nicu Ceausescu, son of the dictator, their patron and the man who had Cup Final results overturned if they didn't go in his club's favour. Milan and Steaua already had close relations – Milan had provided kit.

Whatever the reason, Steaua lay down and died that night. They played pinball in their own goalmouth to give away the first goal. They stood back politely for Gullit – miraculously present – to wallop home another. In midfield, they hardly competed; in attack, they were nonexistent. It was said that their manager, Iordanescu, once their left-winger, was under such pressure that he hardly knew top from bottom. That evening Steaua touched the bottom. Milan were allowed to reach great heights. They well deserved the trophy, not least for their brilliance at San Siro against Real Madrid, but this was anticlimax.

Internazionale, under the managership of Giovanni Trapattoni, at last regained the Italian championship in 1989, but didn't last very long in the European Cup the following season. With three West German internationals in the side, one of them Lothar Matthaus who had captained Bayern Munich, Inter slid out of the competition to Malmo, a resilient Swedish team most shrewdly deployed by the English manager Roy Hodgson. Against all the odds, Malmo first beat Inter 1–0 in Sweden and then, after the West German striker Jurgen Klinsmann had put Inter ahead at San Siro, Leif Enqvist equalised, ten minutes from the end. Hardly the Inter of Herrera.

But Milan, forced to do without Gullit for almost the whole season, plugged doggedly away in defence of their European Cup. Gullit's would be a kind of Calvary. Forever traipsing off, after yet another operation, to his Belgian surgeon Professor Maertens, in doubt over whether he would ever play again.

Marco van Basten. Given a £1 million a year contract by Milan, he locked horns with Arrigo Sacchi in 1990– 91, a disappointing season for him
(Farabolafoto)

In the Second Round, who should be lurking in wait for Milan but Real Madrid? And Milan got through, again. This time the first leg was at San Siro, the second at the Bernabeu. Milan won 2–0 at San Siro where, again, a managerial error put Real in trouble. This time, however, the manager was not a Dutchman but a Welshman, none other than Liverpool's old hero John Toshack, who had arrived following his successes with Real Sociedad of San Sebastian, the Basque club, to accept the poisoned chalice. He ill-advisedly decided to risk Bernd Schuster at sweeper, though he well knew that the West German, who had missed the game against Malaga the previous Saturday, was unlikely to have recovered from injury.

So it proved. Schuster went off after 16 minutes, and Milan were two up in 13. After eight minutes, a Dutch combination undid Real again. This time the cross from the right was Marco Van Basten's and the header which flew inside the far post was Franck Rijkaard's. Just as he had headed a goal against Real the previous April.

The second goal gave rise to bitter controversy. Real, without the irreplaceable Butragueno who was injured, pegged away, plainly hoping to keep the score down and rise again in Madrid, as they had so often done over the years, sometimes against massive odds. But a hard challenge by Rijkaard on Sanchis led to the ball curving over the Real defence in a freakish parabola, leaving Van Basten free to advance on Buyo.

The keeper came rocketing out of his goal and brought the Dutchman down, a couple of feet outside the box. Herr Schmidhuber, the West German referee, decided it was inside and gave a penalty; Van Basten scored. As one who has so often criticised refereeing decisions in favour of Italian clubs in Europe in the past, I could not afford Real a grain of sympathy. It was a nasty, calculated foul, and it deserved all it got. Under the 'professional foul' rule so belatedly adopted by FIFA in 1990, it would have led to Buyo's proper expulsion. But Real were incensed.

The scene was set for storms in Madrid. They were violent ones. No fewer than eight names were taken by the French referee, M. Vautrot, who at that time – before his bizarre efforts in the 1990 World Cup – was in a state of grace, never prepared to be intimidated by the Ultras Sur, the young thugs behind the South goal, who had attacked fans outside the Bernabeu before the game.

Vautrot should, in fact, have sent Sanchis off for savagely hacking down Van Basten, when he moved on to a stray back pass. Van Basten was fouled time and again, just as John Charles had once been by Real's defenders when playing for Juventus. 'The kicks?' said Van Basten philosophically, afterwards. 'I expected them.'

Franco Baresi marshalled his defence magisterially; its use of the offside game time and again bewildered Real. In midfield Ancelotti, knowing he would soon undergo yet another knee operation, was in resplendent form, tackling, intercepting, prompting.

Butragueno was back and scored a strange goal, headed in when he was actually on the ground, but it was Hugo Sanchez who gave Milan most trouble. Butragueno's goal came in the third minute of first-half injury time, after Paco Llorente – who had committed the first, unpleasant foul on Van Basten, throwing the ball at him for good measure – hit the post, following a free kick. Butragueno and Sanchez might have been offside but the goal stood. Milan, however, held on.

Would Gullit ever be back? Endless bulletins appeared; hopes rose, only to subside, though he did some light training with the Dutch team in Rotterdam before they met Italy, early in 1990. The quarter-final against Malines, alias Mechelen, the Belgian champions, had to be faced without him, though, and very difficult it proved.

In the first leg, played to the dismay of Milan at the Heysel Stadium in Brussels, where five years earlier 38 fans had died and another had been fatally injured, Malines went for the jugular; and very nearly succeeded. With a little luck, they would surely have won a game they in any event largely controlled.

Arrigo Sacchi was characteristically frank. 'In the first half, that post saved us. And for the whole ninety minutes, the protagonist was Giovanni Galli.' Note that Sacchi used the word protagonist (there can be only one) correctly, which is more than most of our intelligentsia, let alone our football managers, can do!

'That post' was the post which Bruno Versavel hit after 18 minutes, having left Franco Baresi and Costacurta for dead. Galli was helpless, but the ball rebounded from the foot of the upright. With Van Basten played out of the game by the massive Albert, and Rijkaard reluctantly playing stopper at the other end rather than being allowed to surge forward, it was a flaccid Milan. Galli, and his saves, saved them.

At San Siro, Milan needed extra time to get through and Malines, with their harsh methods, made few friends. The greatest irony of the game was that Roberto Donadoni, who had played superbly throughout down both flanks, dancing his way past tackles and being fouled time and again, should himself ultimately be sent off, for a foolish retaliation.

Having lost recently both to Juventus and Inter, each of whom had scored three times, Milan were not in the best of form, or morale. But that night, they rose triumphantly from the ashes, with Van Basten as dazzling as Donadoni; they should not have needed extra time. Rijkaard initially played well upfield in support of Van Basten, but an injury to the ever vulnerable Ancelotti obliged him to drop back to midfield.

Milan should have won the game in ordinary time and they very nearly did so in the 90th minute, when Donadoni left Clijsters behind and was making for goal when Clijsters ruthlessly brought him down. It was his second bookable foul, and off he very properly went.

A goal came, at last, just at the end of the first period of extra time. Van Basten scored it, just four minutes after Donadoni had been sent off for a punch at Deferm, the latest Belgian to commit a foul on him. It was no worse than most of the others but in Donadoni something snapped, and he was sent off for the first time in his career. 'What a stupid thing,' he said. 'I wasn't smart.' So he, who had graced this game with his marvellous trickery, would miss both semi-final matches and the Final. Rough justice indeed.

As for Van Basten's goal, it came when Rijkaard drove a free-kick into the Belgian wall; Tassotti sent the rebound back into the goalmouth and Van Basten pounced. A second goal for Milan was scored by Marco Simone, a young centre-forward bought expensively from Como the previous summer and largely left wilting on the bench since then. Such has been the fate of so many gifted young Italian players, bought up by rich clubs which didn't really need them.

But this would be Simone's night. He was in excellent form from the moment he replaced Ancelotti after 25 minutes, dribbling, swerving, sprinting vertiginously, worrying the Malines defence almost as much as Van Basten and Donadoni. His goal came three minutes from the end. He saw an empty space and headed for it, ignoring Van Basten's plea for the ball. 'There was that phenomenon of a Belgian goalkeeper [Preud'homme]. I beat him, and when I saw the ball in the net, I cried. But it wasn't my best game. At times I have played even better.'

The next obstacle for Milan was Bayern Munich in the semi-final. Hardened warriors of the European Cup, now without Matthaus, they were still a formidable side. Milan beat them 1–0 at San Siro in the first leg, but this time Simone, starting the game, got nothing done against a massed German defence and was replaced 20 minutes from time – by another centre-forward bought from Como and put into cold storage, Borgonovo. Bayern were dismissed by one Italian critic as 'more like one of our provincial teams of the sixties than a great representative of European football', forever booting the ball away.

Another of Van Basten's penalties decided that game, 13 minutes from the end. Borgonovo it was who was hauled back by the left full-back, Pflugler. Van Basten put the kick away, for the one attempt which beat the admirable Aumann all night.

It was a better game in Munich; and though Milan lost it 2–1, they were the better team. Under heavy rain, Bayern now put their negativity behind them and came out to play, meeting a Milan team ready to do the same. Strange that Milan should have had one of their most impressive matches of the competition in defeat, but so it was. A goal by Thomas Strunz, on the hour, meant extra time had to be played; and now it was Borgonovo who would have his moment.

It came after 11 minutes of extra time. The centre-forward, who had come on after 68 minutes for another young reserve, the promising Under-21 international midfielder, Stroppa, exquisitely chipped the ball over Aumann for an 'away'; goal that was beyond price. Scotland's Alan McInally put Bayern back into the lead six minutes later, but it was not enough. 'We lost to a superb team,' said the Bayern manager Jupp Heynckes, outside-left for his country in the 1972 European Championship Finals. Arrigo Sacchi said, 'This is the third or fourth time we have won through after extra time, and that shows great physical and mental strengths.' Indeed.

The 'ideal' Final would have been Milan against Marseille, but Marseille had been cheated. An expensive, polyglot side, in which Chris Waddle, bought from Spurs for over £4 million in the summer, had been doing fine things, and in which his friend Jean-Pierre Papin had been scoring many goals, they had thrown their chance away in the home leg of the semi-final against Benfica. They had enough chances to have won by three or four goals. They ended by winning only 2–1.

So it was that in Lisbon, Vata Garcia's disgraceful, hand-scored goal, six minutes from the end, put Benfica in the Final in Vienna. A corner from the left by Brazil's Valdo, a headed flick-on by Sweden's Mats Magnusson, an intervening hand by Angola's Vata Garcia, and Marseille were out. Marseille had decided, against their natural instincts, to play defensively that night, and they suffered for it.

Sven-Goran Eriksson, Benfica's Swedish manager, knew all about four-in-line defence, all about 'pressing' and all about offside. All about Milan, come to that. Had he not, after all, been manager of both Roma and Fiorentina? Making his name impressively with IFK Gothenburg, who enjoyed an astonishingly long unbeaten run under his aegis, he had been vastly successful in his first stint with Benfica and then coached in Italy. Having agreed to go back to Lisbon, he had then changed his mind and tried to stay in Florence; but to no avail. So there, in Vienna, he was, in charge of a team which came up against a Milan side reinforced, at long last, by Ruud Gullit.

A few facts. On 1 December 1989 in Pellenburg, Belgium, Professor Maertens had operated on Gullit's right knee, 'cleaning up' the cartilage. As recently as April 22, Gullit had made his return to the Milan team, choosing, as it transpired, a violent and torrid match against Verona which Milan unexpectedly lost, thus virtually losing their chance of the Championship. Gullit played the last half-hour. A week later, in Bergamo – Milan had been suspended from San Siro – he played for an hour against Bari, and looked really good. On May 11, he played the whole of a friendly game in Reggio Emilio against Bologna, and looked the best player on the field. Now here he was in Vienna, to play against Benfica.

Milan's President Silvio Berlusconi celebrates with his players after Milan had beaten Benfica to retain the European Cup in 1990

(Farabolafoto)

Carlo Ancelotti, too, was able to play; but the match was a drab one. All things considered, Gullit did astonishingly well, though the old true Gullit would have snapped up the chance so neatly made for him early in the second half, when Van Basten beat Aldair, the Brazilian centre-back, and slipped Gullit through, all alone. Gullit advanced on Silvino, the Benfica keeper – and shot against him.

Rijkaard, after 67 minutes, showed him how it should be done, striking the ball with the outside of his right foot perfectly wide of Silvino and into the right-hand corner of the goal, to win the Cup again for Milan. Ten minutes from time Gullit had another chance when, after a splendid one-two with Van Basten, he was clear again, but this time he shot over the top.

Valdo of Brazil and the young Swede, Thern, gave Milan plenty to think about in midfield, and a glorious diagonal pass out to the left in the first half by Thern left Hernani free as air. Alas, he utterly wasted his cross, and that was really as close to a real chance as Benfica came throughout the sterile game.

Giovanni Galli, scarcely tested, played his last game in goal for Milan. It was already known he would be joining Naples, who were strangely accustomed to shedding their goalkeeper whenever they chanced to win the championship. You could hardly blame Galli, who had lost his place to

Pagliuca for much of the season yet, by Sacchi's own admission, had saved Milan at Heysel.

So Milan, who had failed to win the League and had lost the double-headed Cup Final to Juventus that season, emerged with their European Cup intact. It had been a long haul, sometimes a difficult one; but in the image of Gullit, they had finally prevailed.

Milan's second defence of the European Cup ended in shame and disaster; not only were the team eliminated at Marseille, but their disgraceful behaviour at the end of the game, when they used the partial failure of a floodlight pylon as an excuse to walk off the field when time was almost up, refusing to return, clearly hoping at least for a replay, had them banned from Europe the following season. Milan appealed against the ban, and had hopes – while others had fears – that the enormous power of Berlusconi could get them off the hook, just as Roma, some years earlier, had escaped with a large fine on appeal, having first been banned from Europe.

Altogether, it had been a most unhappy season for Milan; and for their manager, Arrigo Sacchi. In the past, his job had sometimes hung by a thread. Now, with success finally eluding him, the zonal and 'pressing' style proving less productive, Marco Van Basten locked in disagreement with him, and Gullit showing his old, great form only in flashes, Berlusconi seemed to turn the light of his countenance away from Sacchi; though the Italian Federation smiled on him. They let it be known they wanted him, sooner rather than later, as national team manager. Berlusconi, meanwhile, decreed that Fabio Capello, once a famous Milan inside-forward, would be the actual team manager, with Sacchi on a kind of roving commission.

Milan had made hard work of beating Bruges in the second round, though the shocking post-World Cup state of the San Siro pitch, conducive to Bruges' defensive tactics, had much to do with the goalless draw in the first leg. In the return in Bruges, Milan squeaked through 1–0, losing Van Basten for three matches in the process, suspended for lashing out with an elbow in retaliation, and breaking a bone in the face of the Bruges defender, Plovie. Van Basten had been the best player on the field, one of his few outstanding games for Milan all season; most of which saw him protesting that Sacchi's tactics left him a lone victim upfield, forbidding him to move about, join in the play, and elude his ruthless markers. The Milan goal was a fine, top-corner shot by the young, unsung midfielder, Carbone.

But in March, Marseille too drew at San Siro, then proved a tougher nut to crack, away from home. Taken over in mid-season by the veteran Belgian manager Raymond Goethals, after Franz Beckenbauer, on a £1.6 million salary, had signally failed to inspire the team, Marseille took wing. Chris Waddle found the best, most versatile form of his career, scoring goals and making them for Papin, while Pelé, the Ghanaian, given his chance in a free role, excelled. They would reach the final, only to lose in Bari to Belgrade's gifted Red Star on penalties, after a hugely disappointing match.

In the Marseille–Milan return leg, it was Waddle who scored the one, winning goal with a superb low volley, though he knew little about it, having been concussed by a blow to the back of the neck in a clash with Milan's left-back Maldini, whom Waddle had ridiculed in an international game at Wembley some eighteen months previously.

There followed Milan's squalid manoeuvre, for which two officials, Taveggi and Galliani, later took the blame. But the referee, Karlsson, was adamant; the players must return. Milan didn't, lost; and were banned.

6

THE YEARS OF THE
GOLDEN FIX

Two vignettes; each involving Juventus. First the Stadio Comunale in Turin, on a spring afternoon in 1973. Derby County have just lost 3–1 to Juventus in the first leg of the European Cup semi-final. Two of their players, centre-half Roy McFarland and inside-forward Archie Gemmill, both key men, have been booked, which means they will miss the second leg. Out of the dressing-room emerges Brian Clough, the Yorkshire-born manager of Derby County. Facing him is a throng of eager Italian journalists, waiting for his comments. I am among them. Clough speaks. 'No cheating bastards will I talk to. I will not talk to any cheating bastards.' Then he, together with the former Juventus hero and Wales centre-forward John Charles, disappears behind the dressing-room door.

'*Cos'ha detto, Glanville, cos'ha detto?*' cry the Italian reporters. What did he say? Diplomatically, I feign incomprehension. The dressing-room door opens again, and there is Clough. 'Tell 'em what I said, Brian!' I do. Alarm and consternation. Headlines the following day. *BASTARDI TRUFFATORI!* Cheating bastards! No real chapter and verse, though, on the why and wherefore, the scuffle in the dressing-room corridor when Peter Taylor, Clough's lieutenant, had tried to pull Helmut Haller, Juve's West German inside-forward, away from Schulenburg, the German referee.

Forward a year, to Turin again. This time the Presidential office of Juve's Giampiero Boniperti. Blond and blue-eyed, the eternal *jeune premier*, captain of Juventus and Italy in the years when I lived there, 'Boni' sits beneath two photographs. Each was taken when a FIFA XI played England at Wembley in October 1953 to celebrate the Football Association's 90th anniversary. One shows 'Boni' in the FIFA team's line-up, shaking hands before the game; the other shows him scoring one of his two goals in the 4–4 draw.

I was there because John Lovesey, the sports editor of the *Sunday Times*, had sent me. We had Juventus, in the vernacular, bang to rights. They had clearly sent the notorious Hungarian fixer, Dezso Solti, to Lisbon the previous year to try to suborn the Portuguese referee of the second leg against

Derby County, Francisco Marques Lobo. But Lobo was an honest man who had reported the attempt; an honourable act which had had a shabby sequel. By this time, the *Sunday Times* were ready to publish and be damned, but John Lovesey insisted I give 'Boni' his chance to vindicate, or at least explain, himself.

Boniperti heard me out in silence as I told him all we knew; which was almost everything. When I had finished, he replied, '*Brian, se ci sono questi pazzi in giro!*' Brian, if there are these madmen going about! Then he said, 'And what's happening in English football, now?' The conversation was closed.

Thus it was that the *Sunday Times*, a few weeks later, came out with a front page story on the Lobo–Solti Affair; on the failed attempt to bribe, the disgracefully inadequate inquiry by the European governing body UEFA, the astounding letter to Juventus which thanked and exculpated them. In time, we would dig up, in Holland, a letter which the 'madman', Solti, had actually signed in 1971 on behalf of Juventus. But UEFA did nothing then, and have done nothing since.

'Brian, if there are these madmen going about!' – Giampero Boniperti, President of Juventus at the time of the attempt to bribe referee Lobo (Farabolafoto)

So far as I was concerned, the saga had begun with a telephone call. I heard, from Budapest – which would become the fulcrum of our inquiry, a city where rogues and honest men were enmeshed in a strange network of intrigue and finagling – of the previous year's cover up in Zurich.

There, I discovered, UEFA had held an inquiry into the Lobo Case, of which no news had percolated into England. This despite the fact that Denis Follows, then Secretary of the Football Association, was also at that time head of the UEFA Disciplinary Committee. As an Englishman, he had stood down from the committee which passed judgement on Lobo–Solti but amazingly he had subsequently done nothing to inform the English news media of what had occurred. Indeed, when in subsequent years I had cause to turn to him for information, he had to search in his attic to discover the relevant papers. There were those in Budapest who believed he must himself be involved in the affair, but I am sure they were wrong. Continentals have so often mistaken English ingenuousness for deviousness.

I pursued the investigation as far as I could, but it was not far enough. That there had been dirty work at the crossroads was beyond dispute. That Solti, notorious for years as a fixer for Internazionale of Milan in their European Cup heyday, had offered Lobo a bribe, I was convinced. Just as I was sure that Lobo had sturdily refused it. That Solti had been 'run' by the general manager of Juventus, the notorious Italo Allodi who for years had used him while Secretary of Inter, I was equally sure. Just as I sure that Lobo had refereed the goalless second leg – which I also saw – impeccably. Derby had been awarded a penalty and missed it, while their centre-forward Roger Davies had been sent off for knocking Morini into the net with a punch.

To light the touchpaper, it was essential that someone speak to Lobo, get a statement, show what had happened. I couldn't do it; I had no Portuguese. And so I turned to Keith Botsford, a polyglot American journalist with an Italian mother and a father who'd played tennis for Belgium. His Portuguese was excellent. He also, like myself, spoke Italian, Spanish and French. German, too, and some Russian. He had worked for years in Mexico, and had acted as a secret agent in Budapest itself, just after the war, when the Russians interrogated him. He was also a passionate football fan, for many years a follower of Chelsea.

John Lovesey agreed to take him on, and sent him to Lisbon. There, he went to see Lobo, a telephone engineer when he was not refereeing, and with some difficulty and much diplomacy persuaded him to talk. Back to London he came with the whole story; of Solti's visit to Lisbon, of the car keys he dangled before Lobo's face in Room 142 of the Ritz Hotel, of the $5000 he offered besides – if Lobo would see to it that Juventus won their second leg game in Derby.

Lobo played Botsford a tape recording of a subsequent telephone call he received from Solti. Now it was my turn, to go to Milan and try to trace it. I began by visiting a private detective, one of the plump Ponzi brothers. Tom, the most notorious of them, was a known neo-Fascist, by turns buccaneer and unlikely hero. His brother was somewhat less enterprising. He could not, he said, do anything to help me trace the call from Solti to Lobo. He suggested that I could best try to do it myself. How? Simply by walking into the headquarters of the telephone service, and inquiring.

It seemed a very long shot, but it worked. I did as he suggested, went to the telephone headquarters, and asked a woman working there if she could find details of the call. She said she would try, and before very long, produced them. Solti had indeed called Lobo in Lisbon that day. As I continued to ask questions, a senior woman appeared, and looked at me suspiciously, saying that such information was not usually provided. But it was too late; I had it, and went home with it.

It should be said that though the revelations of the Lobo–Solti Affair came as a shock, they were not wholly a surprise. There had been dirty work at the crossroads before by Italian clubs, one well knew, even if nothing, so to speak, had stood up in court. Or ever got close to one. As long ago as 1964, as we have seen, there had been the Tesanic Case.

Reaching the semi-finals of the European Cup, Internazionale had to win the second leg at home to Borussia Dortmund to reach the Final. During the match, Luisito Suarez, the Spanish international inside-forward, brutally kicked the Dortmund right-half, who was obliged to leave the field. There were no substitutes then. Dortmund struggled on with ten men and lost; Inter went on to win the Final. Tesanic, the Yugoslav referee of that game, would later be found on holiday, allegedly at Inter's expense.

The following year, it was Liverpool's turn. They had gained a famous victory over Inter in the first leg of the European Cup semi-final, winning 3–1 at Anfield. In later years, Bill Shankly would tell one that afterwards he had met a large Italian journalist who shook his head and told him, sadly, 'You will never be allowed to win.' Nor was he.

The return leg in Milan was lost 3–0, with a couple of really strange goals. For one of them, Peiró, another Spanish international playing for Inter, ran back from behind Tommy Lawrence, the Liverpool keeper, who was preparing to clear the ball, kicked it out of his hands, and put it in the net. Corso scored an equally contentious goal. A free-kick was given to Inter, on the edge of the box. With his famous left foot, Corso struck it straight home. Though the referee, the Spaniard Ortiz de Mendibil, had clearly indicated that the kick was indirect, he allowed the goal.

Then, in 1973 itself, there was the vexed case of Leeds United's defeat by Milan in the Final of the European Cup-Winners' Cup in Salonika, where Michas, the Greek referee, gave a series of appallingly indulgent decisions in favour of Milan, who won 1–0. Michas would subsequently be suspended, but that was as far as it went.

Not that the Italian clubs had been the only suspected offenders. When

Panathinaikos of Athens most unexpectedly reached the Final of the European Cup in 1971, they were outrageously favoured by the French referee of their return home leg against Everton in the quarter-finals. During the first leg, Joe Royle, later to become an outstanding manager with Oldham, then the Everton centre-forward, remembers the Greek defenders hissing in his ear, 'Athens, Athens!' And in Athens, Everton got nothing from the referee.

Years later, Keith Botsford and I, after infinite attempts, would at last manage to obtain the full story of a Hungarian referee who did *not* comply with the blandishments of Inter and the pressures of his own Federation; but that is another story, and I shall tell it later.

Boniperti having stonewalled, the *Sunday Times* blew the whistle – an appropriate metaphor – on the Lobo–Solti Affair on 21 April 1974, under the headline THE $5000 FIX THAT DIDN'T WORK. No one appreciated better than Botsford and myself, Italophiles and *appassionati* of Italian football, the deep irony implicit in that headline and indeed in the story itself. For our exposure was wholly due to the fact that the 'fix' had failed, had gone off at half cock. So, indeed, it had in 1966, when Inter failed for once to bribe their man; but of that, at the time, we knew nothing.

Juventus, we would discover, had almost certainly tried before, with more success, in less exalted circumstances, when the referee was the familiar Ortiz de Mendibil. But we began by relating how Lobo was first approached, on 27 March 1973.

He was listening to a record in his home in a working-class suburb of Lisbon, when the telephone rang. 'An Italian gentleman' wanted to speak to him from the Ritz Hotel, in the city. The 'gentleman' told Lobo that he was a 'follower of football' who was in Lisbon to see an international match, the following day. He brought personal messages for Lobo from mutual

Mariolino Corso curls in a free-kick to open the scoring for Inter in the 1965 semi-final second leg against Liverpool at San Siro. The goal was allowed to stand even though referee Ortiz de Mendibil had clearly indicated that the kick was indirect (Farabolafoto)

acquaintances in Italy; he would like Lobo to come over to the Ritz to meet him.

Lobo was a simple, decent fellow, but he wasn't born yesterday. He had made it a practice never to meet people connected with football without the presence of a third party. He was, he said, just about to eat his dinner. Could he call back later? Or could the messages not be conveyed now, on the telephone.

No, said the mysterious caller, they were of a personal nature. He really did need to see Lobo at the Ritz. Lobo said he would call back after dinner. He put down the receiver, picked it up again, and called Sousa Loureiro, President of the Portuguese Referees' Association. Sousa Loureiro told him he could keep the appointment at the Ritz, but must confine himself to polite discussion, and make no comments of his own.

So off to the Ritz, on its high hill above the Avenida Liberdade, Lobo went, for an appointment which would prove fateful, whose reverberations would sound down the years. One might compare it with the turning over of some great stone, from beneath which crawled all manner of vile, slimy, secretive creatures.

The man Lobo met in Room 142, with its pretentious decor, was a Central European in his late fifties who, said Lobo, 'reeked of money'. With him was a much younger woman, blonde and attractive. Lobo wrongly took her to be Solti's wife; she was in fact his mistress. In time to come they would fall out, with sharp recriminations.

Solti began authentically enough by giving Lobo a message from a man who was indeed an Italian friend. He then congratulated him on his 'appointment as a World Cup referee'. This was news, though delightful news, to Lobo. How did Solti know this, he asked. From Dr Artemio Franchi, said Solti. Franchi at that time was President not only of the Italian Football Federation, but also of UEFA.

He had also heard from Franchi, Solti pursued, that Lobo had been chosen to control the second leg of the European Cup semi-final at Derby. Franchi, he said, had told him this as well. This astonished Lobo even more, but he reckoned that anyone who had such close contacts with Franchi must be an important figure indeed. 'Franchi,' pursued Solti, 'told me you were one of the best.' The unspoken message, Lobo realised, was that Solti was a close friend of Franchi and others who could promote his career as an international referee.

If Lobo were to referee that game at Derby to the best of his ability, Solti went on, it was important he attend the first leg, in Turin. Everyone in Europe recognised that the English played a tough kind of football. To illustrate his point, he produced a cutting from *Il Giorno*, the Milanese daily. If Lobo came to Turin, he could see for himself just how 'hard' English football was. Solti invited Lobo as his guest. While he was there, said Solti, he would see that he met people who could help him as a referee.

Solti announced that he'd already made travel arrangements for Lobo. He would fly from Lisbon to Madrid, thence to Milan. 'You will stay in my house there, and I want you to meet the President of Juventus and other club officials.'

Solti then made one of those gestures common in his career, at once flamboyant and insidious. He reached into his pocket, produced a car key, and dangled it in front of Lobo. 'The implication was,' said Lobo to Botsford, 'that when I left Italy, I would not have to fly back, but would have a car of my own to drive back in.'

Obeying his instructions, Lobo said nothing. Solti assumed this meant he agreed. 'Look, Lobo,' he now said. 'My friends and I are very interested in the return match. It's really nothing for me. I have to pay the players, anyway. There's no problem. I already have to carry 19 on my list, and it isn't difficult to put down 20. Anyway, I have a free hand to do what I want for the club. If I put down 20 instead of 19, nobody is going to say anything. The price is about $5000, and I can do this without any trouble.'

No doubt he could, since in his fixing days with Inter, Solti, in 1966, had unsuccessfully offered the Hungarian referee Gyorgy Vadas immensely more. Lobo, who had no more intention of accepting so repugnant an offer than Vadas, replied that he really could not go to Italy as he had conflicting obligations. Solti was at first insistent, then yielded, plainly believing that it was merely the trip to Italy which Lobo had refused. 'Well,' he said, 'it's all agreed, but I shall call you again at a later date to make the arrangements.'

Still following his instructions, Lobo replied, 'If you want to call me, that is all right with me.'

When he left, Lobo at once delivered a report to his referees' association President. They decided to set a trap for Solti. When his call to Lobo was eventually made, a representative of the association would be there, listening on another telephone.

Now came the contentious first leg between Juventus and Derby in Turin, culminating in those hot, strong words from Brian Clough. The curious thing about that game, which I watched, was that though strange and suspicious things may have happened, Juventus won it fairly and squarely on the field; if one accepts the amount of licence given by Herr Schulenburg, the referee, to the aggressive little Juve right-half Furino. José Altafini, once upon a time nicknamed Mazzola when he played for Brazil as a 19-year-old in the 1958 World Cup, had a superb game for Juventus, scoring two fine goals, and the 3–1 score was not unjust.

This was more than could be said for some other happenings. Peter Taylor, Clough's lieutenant, observed that when Schulenburg blew the half-time whistle, the West German international Helmut Haller, sitting on the Juventus bench, rose and went to him, 'talking earnestly in German' as the two walked on down the tunnel and into the dressing-room.

Taylor followed them and, he says, 'tried to intercept them' to show he knew what might be afoot, but his way was blocked, apparently on Haller's instructions, 'by a group of tough-looking Italians' and a scuffle ensued. Taylor had already been warned before the game, he said, by the old Juventus favourite John Charles, that 'Haller was in with the referee again.' There is, it should be said, no evidence that anything underhand was going on. 'Nothing can ever be proved,' said Taylor, 'but I believe it was corrupt and dirty. It brought us on a ton in learning about Europe and put us on our mettle for the future.' As it was, Gemmill and McFarland were booked and thus ruled out of the return, McFarland for no reason which was immediately evident.

On April 4, Solti did indeed ring Lobo and he, as an employee of the Portuguese telephone company, was able to have the call recorded. Botsford obtained and translated the transcript. Lobo spoke Portuguese, Solti an odd mixture of indifferent Italian and Spanish. The conversation went as follows:

SOLTI *So. How are you? Solti here.*
LOBO *I couldn't go to Turin. It wasn't my fault. I had my professional*

Peter Taylor – witness to some strange goings-on at the Juventus–Derby semi-final first leg in Turin (Allsport)

obligations to attend to, but I want you to know I do take your offer seriously.

SOLTI *Well, how do the possibilities look?*

LOBO *I couldn't go to Turin to see the match. I have received the notification to do the return match between Derby and Juventus, but I cannot go to Turin. How is Franchi?*

SOLTI *Very, very well, for a man of over fifty.*

LOBO *My compliments to Franchi.*

SOLTI *Fine. I shall do that.*

LOBO *I am pleased to hear that. Are you satisfied?*

SOLTI *Yes. Listen. Do you know who the linesmen are?*

LOBO *Fernando Leite and Caesar Correia.*

SOLTI *Is he an international referee or not?*

LOBO *He is on the UEFA list.*

SOLTI *I am not so sure.*

LOBO *He is a UEFA referee, and he has a UEFA badge. Solti, are you going to England?*

SOLTI *Before that, I will be back in Lisbon.*

LOBO *You're coming to Lisbon?*

SOLTI *I should know next week.*

LOBO *Then it is after that you will talk to me?*

SOLTI *Do you understand? Can you come through Paris?*

LOBO *Ah, I see. I go through Paris.*

SOLTI *Yes.*

LOBO *I see. We will make arrangements in Paris.*

SOLTI *Yes.*

LOBO *I will go earlier, and talk to you.*

SOLTI *We will talk next week in Lisbon. All right?*

LOBO *In Lisbon is fine. I will talk to you next week in Lisbon. Now . . .*

SOLTI *That is this week. Right?*

LOBO *You have my telephone number?*

SOLTI *I have it.*

LOBO *When you get here, call me.*

SOLTI *We will talk on the phone.*

LOBO *Yes. The arrangement we talked about at the Ritz Hotel was $5000, wasn't it?*

SOLTI *Yes.*

LOBO *Well, I haven't got anything more.*

SOLTI *I think we will discuss it personally.*

After listening to the tape, Lobo told Keith Botsford, ruefully, 'I am not a rich man. $5000 and a car is four years' work for me! I could have taken the money, and no one would have known. I'd be a richer man than today. But I didn't. I did my duty. And I didn't get to be on the World Cup list, which was the one thing I wanted. Why?'

Long before the end of our investigation, that became a pitifully rhetorical question. Gyorgy Vadas could have told Lobo why, had they ever met. Told him how, after his sturdy bravery, his defiance of all the temptation Inter put in his way and his impeccable refereeing of the Inter–Real Madrid semi-final in 1966, his reward was to be banished forever from international refereeing. You did not defy the European football 'mafia' with impunity.

Lobo sent the tape of the telephone call from Solti, with his own report, to his referees' association. From there it went on to the Portuguese Football Federation, and thence to UEFA in Berne. On April 24, the day before the return leg of the semi-final at Derby, a letter arrived from the UEFA Secretary, the Swiss, Hans Bangerter. It affirmed its faith in Lobo's skill and impartiality, and confirmed he'd still be refereeing at Derby. It made no mention of any possible investigation. For Lobo's protection, his referees' association sent an official observer, who gave him the highest possible marks.

He well deserved them. Again, I saw the match myself, and Lobo's refereeing was excellent. The game was a goalless draw, though Alan Hinton contrived to miss the penalty awarded to Derby by Lobo. There was also the ugly incident in the second half when, having been fouled by the blond Juventus centre-half Morini, Roger Davies knocked him flying into the goalmouth and was promptly and properly sent off.

On 20 June 1973, UEFA's disciplinary sub-committee met to consider the case at the Atlantis Hotel in Zurich. Its Italian President, Barbè, stood down, as did Denis Follows. When, the following year, I telephoned Barbè to ask him about the case, it was to receive the panic-stricken response, *'Io non ne so niente, io non ne so niente!'* I know nothing about it! Somewhat strange for the man who was President of the committee, even if he himself had not actually been present on the day.

And what a day! A fiasco, in this author's opinion. In the event, it was the Czech, Petra, who presided over the sub-committee. The other members were Wouters of Belgium, a lawyer who received a large retainer as an advisor to UEFA; Poroila of Finland; and the Maltese, Banisci. Lobo spoke of the meeting as follows: 'There were nine persons present . . . I repeated the substance of my report, and was listened to politely and asked no questions. Then, when I had finished, Franchi invited me to step with him into a neighbouring room. We went in alone, without any other member of the committee, and there I was shown a group of gentlemen and asked if I recognised any of them as the person who had offered me the bribe. No words were exchanged when I was in the room, nor could I put any questions. I quickly said that it was none of those present, and with that I was given permission to withdraw.'

The men in the room, it transpired, were directors of Juventus, though they did not include Giampiero Boniperti, the President; still less Solti.

Mystery was piled upon mystery. Artemio Franchi subsequently insisted that he was not present at the meeting of the sub-committee. This, he told us, was because the separation of executive and disciplinary functions was a matter of policy, even if, in his own words, 'I [can] think that in some specific situations, which involve not only disciplinary problems but perhaps matters of major international importance, this policy is too rigid, is wrong, and should be altered.' Yet were we to suppose that Franchi wasn't there at all, that Lobo didn't meet him in the Atlantis Hotel, that he mistook somebody else for Franchi? Not to mention his female companion, whom Lobo said he recognised.

Then there was the farcical 'identity parade' – a parade without the suspect! And Solti was in the Atlantis Hotel, because Lobo caught sight of him. Curiouser and curiouser. The disciplinary sub-committee did, however, decide that Solti be declared *persona non grata* in European football; a decision which would not, in the event, be implemented for another eighteen months.

Nine days later, meeting this time in Glasgow, the sub-committee decided that there was insufficient evidence to take such a step without fear of legal repercussions. Instead, it would circularise its clubs and members, warning them about Solti in more general terms. This, too, was not done. Franchi's explanation to us was that again, Solti might sue them. In December 1974, when Solti was at last made *persona non grata* in Budapest, such gossamer objections were simply brushed aside, or ignored. That the sub-committee, with a highly paid lawyer such as Wouters on it, should have thought for a moment that Solti could sue with any hope of success leaves one baffled.

More baffling still was the fact that on 5 July 1973, Hans Bangerter, the Secretary of UEFA, sent Juventus a letter, thanking them for their co-operation and telling them that they had been exonerated. It transpired that Franchi, the President of UEFA, knew nothing of that letter, with which such great play would subsequently be made by Juventus and the Italian sports Press.

A rank odour hung over the deliberations and actions of the sub-committee and indeed of UEFA itself. The only person initially to suffer was Lobo himself, and again, in puzzling circumstances. It emerged that the decision not to send out a circular, warning clubs about Solti, was taken on the advice of a Berne lawyer called Hodler, recommended by Bangerter. Yet it also transpired that when he gave this advice, Hodler had not even been given the chance to listen to the damning tape of Solti's telephone conversation with Lobo.

The reasons given for Lobo's exclusion from international refereeing were less ingenious than squalid. Never did he get another game, though at the time of the revelations in 1973, he was on the World Cup supplementary list. Behind this banishment was the Austrian Friedrich Seipelt, chairman of the UEFA Referees' Committee. He had personally decided, he told us, that since the Lobo–Solti Affair remained *sub judice*, it was best that Lobo be removed from circulation. No one in UEFA authorised such a move.

Artemio Franchi utterly rejected Solti's statement to Lobo that Franchi himself had informed Solti of Lobo's selection to referee the Derby–Juventus second leg, a month in advance. In that case, we wondered, who did tell Solti? Franchi did admit that Solti was well known to him by sight, from his presence at UEFA draws for the three European cup competitions. We had to presume that if Solti did not gain this information from Franchi, it was either leaked to him through UEFA, or through a club. No prizes for surmising which.

It is time, though, to present in greater detail the *dramatis personae* of this horrid affair. Who, in the first place, was Deszo Solti?

He was a notorious figure in European football long before the Lobo affair, but he had been associated chiefly with Internazionale of Milan. A man by then in his late sixties, a Hungarian Jew, he had survived the war, taken Argentine citizenship, lived in Vienna and eventually settled in Milan, in an expensive apartment. But Budapest still saw a great deal of him. There, he would sit in a café endlessly greeting and being greeted.

Before he moved to Vienna, Solti already had strong connections with Hungarian clubs. In Austria he promoted 'cabarets', living in a sleazy demi-monde and maintaining his café connections with people in the football world. He fell out with at least one partner, who claimed he had been cheated. By 1949 he was in Rome, using his acquaintance with Bela Guttmann, another Hungarian Jew, who had played before the war at centre-half for MTK Budapest and the Viennese Jewish club Hakoah. In later years, he would become a major manager, twice winning the European Cup itself, with Benfica of Lisbon, as we have seen.

In 1955, after Guttmann, to his chagrin, had lost his job with Milan, he and Solti were involved in a hit-and-run motor accident in which two children were killed. The investigating magistrates, however, did not press charges.

'I was full of ambition,' wrote Solti, in a memoir published in Budapest in the mid-1970s. 'I knew I wouldn't be able to play football well enough, but I decided to become an administrator.' The turning point came the year following the motor accident. 'In 1956,' wrote Solti, 'a very rich man became President of Inter. Signor Moratti was an oil millionaire and a typical Italian, very temperamental . . . Moratti took me into his confidence. He seemed to discuss football several hours a day.' Solti was hired; but not for long.

The first deal he did on behalf of Inter was to acquire, or so he thought, a Hungarian team manager, Kalmar. But Kalmar instead signed with Panathinaikos of Athens. An infuriated Moratti gave Solti the boot. 'As soon as that happened,' Solti wrote, 'Moratti chucked me out. My whole world collapsed. It was nearly the end of my career.'

Nearly, but not quite. Significantly, Solti now began 'helping Real Madrid with their European Cup games'; how, one can only surmise.

In the meanwhile, Solti became a kind of travel agent deluxe in Milan, assisting visiting foreign teams; an ideal opportunity to build up his network of connections in football.

In 1961, according at least to Solti's version of events, the flamboyant Helenio Herrera, an Argentine brought up in Casablanca and by then manager of Barcelona, 'asked me to help him get a job with one of the Italian clubs.' Solti said that he at once approached Moratti at Inter, and thus got back into his good graces. At Barcelona, Herrera, using methods at once authoritarian and incantatory, had built a powerful team, capable of challenging Real Madrid, and all but capable of winning the European Cup. Herrera joined Inter as their new manager, and Moratti, according to Solti, told him, 'I would like to employ you as "manager" of my club.'

The word 'manager' must be interpreted somewhat loosely. 'Fixer' would come a little nearer to Solti's subsequent functions. Public relations played a part in it. We may take with a grain of salt Solti's claim that he was sent to report on Inter's opponents in European tournaments. Though Keith Botsford and I would, poring through agency photographs in Vienna, turn up photographs of Solti, Italo Allodi, Herrera and Moratti exulting with the European Cup at Prater Stadium after the 1964 European Cup Final, Solti had no credentials as a football analyst.

Wheeling and dealing was more in his line. Thus he writes that in 1963 he went twice to Liverpool to obtain dates favourable to Inter for their two legs against Everton. On his first trip, he says, he failed. Moratti sacked him again, according to Solti. But then he was allowed to try again, and succeeded. So his job was restored to him.

The then chairman of Everton, John Moores, remembers meeting Solti in Milan; he was, in fact, the only official from Inter with whom there was any contact. Moores said that Solti made 'a very good job' of providing accommodation and facilities for training. But that was just the tip of the iceberg. 'What does the manager do for a big professional club?' asks Solti, plaintively, in his odd memoir. 'It is a hard question to answer, because it is a road full of obstacles and twists and turns.' Indeed.

There was none more familiar with the 'twists and turns' than Italo Allodi, in the late 1960s and through much of the 1970s probably the most powerful man in Italian football. Like Franchi, his origins were unexceptional. He was a professional footballer of modest accomplishments, who played for Mantova. Subsequently, he became club secretary, and played a major part in the brief rise of the team into the First Division, *Serie A*.

Angelo Moratti of Inter, known as *il gran petrolifero*, the great oil man, plucked him out of the chorus and made him Secretary of Inter. At Inter, Solti became Allodi's familiar, and his fixer. Wheeling, dealing and manipulating in the transfer market, Allodi became very rich. He acquired a splendid collection of paintings, which he often conferred in the shape of gifts. Gifts, indeed, were his stock in trade, from his early days in Mantua. He believed in liberally oiling the wheels, not least when it came to journalists and referees. From Inter, Allodi went, as general manager, to Juventus. Solti followed.

I met Allodi for the first time in May 1973, when we sat side by side at a roulette table in the Jugoslavia Hotel in Belgrade. He was playing, I wasn't. Juventus were about to meet Ajax in the Final of the European Cup. At that time, I knew nothing of what had gone on over Lobo. Allodi was genial and friendly, an elegant, affable man; who would instantly forget me.

The next time I met him, strangely enough, was again in a hotel just before a European Cup Final. It was at the Excelsior Hotel, in the Via Veneto, in Rome. Liverpool were to meet Borussia Monchengladbach that evening in the 1977 Final. Seeing me standing in the foyer, Allodi marched across, shook me by the hand and said, 'We don't know each other, but I am Italo Allodi. I should like to talk to you.'

When, outside the Olympic Stadium before the match, I reported the meeting to Enzo Bearzot, team manager of Italy and Allodi's mortal foe, he burst out laughing. 'You don't know what riches are about to drop upon you from the clouds!' he said. But Allodi and I never met again.

All this is the preamble to a strange interview Allodi gave the Milanese daily paper *Il Giornale*, some time later. Was he upset, the interviewer asked him, by Glanville's continuing campaign against him? Yes, said Allodi, especially because, when Glanville was ill, 'I was one of those who sent money so he could stay in Italy.'

This was bizarre. I had indeed been ill in Italy, and had had to return from Florence to London for operations on my back, early in 1954; some 19 years before I met Allodi, and 23 years before he approached me in Rome and said that we had never met before. Far from staying in Italy, I had had to leave. I wrote a letter to *Il Giornale*, which they published, pointing this out.

Allodi's reply was more bizarre still. Perhaps, he said, I had forgotten my friend Mauro Franceschini, the youth soccer coach who worked in Florence. Well, it was through him 'that I and others sent money'.

This was, in its perverse way, shrewd of Allodi, for he knew he could not be contradicted.

For Mauro Franceschini, a few years earlier, had disappeared in mysterious, even sinister, circumstances. His car, its doors open with his passport still below the dashboard, was found one day beside the river Arno. Of Mauro, not a sign. There never has been. Did he kill himself? Was he murdered? Did he simply – the least likely explanation – contrive to disappear? To this day, no one knows.

But Allodi, by then appointed as head of the Coverciano coaching centre, would have met several old, mutual friends of Mauro and myself, would have known of our own friendship, would have picked up the fact that I'd been ill in Florence all those years ago, and made his own odd concoction out of the ingredients.

Shortly after our revelations in the *Sunday Times*, Allodi was off to West Germany for the World Cup. He had, for reasons obscure to most people, been made General Manager of the Italian team – he and Juventus had already parted company – and the expedition was an utter disaster. The Italians took up their quarters at Ludwigsberg, in Bavaria, in a pleasant hotel. There, Gerry Harrison, of Anglia Television, and I repaired from Munich, a few days before the start of the tournament.

Nothing untoward happened. I glimpsed Allodi in the distance, but we did not speak. The following day, a short news item appeared on the sports page of the Milanese daily *Corriere Della Sera*, proving that not all Italian football journalists of that era, despite the hysterical response to the Solti revelations, lived comfortably in Allodi's pocket. Brian Glanville had come to Ludwigsberg, it said, and had been received by the players as though he were Father Christmas. 'But Allodi did a slalom to avoid him.'

Next day, when I was safely out of sight, Allodi roared and ranted. He had *not* done a slalom to avoid me, he informed a bewildered group of reporters, some not even Italian. If anything, it was I who had avoided him. But he'd bring me into court. *Magari* – even preferably – in England. Yes, in England! But it never happened.

Enzo Bearzot, a future World Cup winning manager, was assistant manager of the Italian team then, and it took him nearly 15 years to forgive Allodi for what happened in West Germany over the final group game against Poland. Defeat would mean Italy's elimination, after a stormy passage. In the opening game, in which it looked for a long time as if Haiti would beat them, Giorgio Chinaglia, once a Cardiff schoolboy and a Swansea centre-forward, was substituted. Infuriated, he made a lewd sign at the manager Ferruccio Valcareggi as he left the field, then went into the dressing-room and smashed a number of mineral water bottles. Full, said his critics. Empty, said Chinaglia.

In the event, Poland, whose fine team had already eliminated England in the qualifying rounds, beat Italy 2–1 in Stuttgart. Strange rumours were current at the time. Some months after the World Cup, Kazimierz Gorski, manager of the Polish team, gave an extraordinary interview to a Polish daily paper. In it, he said that 'wealthy Italian supporters' had come to the Polish training camp and offered money to the Poles to lose. They'd been refused. Later, clearly under pressure from his own Federation, perhaps because Poland were due to meet Italy again in the imminent European Championship qualifiers, he withdrew the allegation.

There were other rumours that bribes had been offered by Italian players to Polish players. These I myself followed up, obtaining statements from both Kazimierz Deyna, the Polish captain, when he played for Manchester City, and Jan Tomaszewski, the flamboyant goalkeeper, when he was playing for Beerschot in Antwerp. Both confirmed the story, but Bearzot, who was clearly anxious for the truth to come out, impatiently brushed this aside. Something had plainly happened, something grave enough to move Bearzot never to bring the Italian team to Coverciano, its former base, for training, so long as Allodi was in charge, but the case remains largely unproven.

With the World Cup over – very quickly – for Italy, violent criticisms descended on Allodi's head. He went, as did Valcareggi. A duo was installed,

Bearzot and the former international centre-half Fulvio Bernardini.

What would become of Allodi? There were various speculations. Then, surprisingly, he was asked by the Italian FA to prepare a report on the future of Coverciano. I was among those who heaped scorn on the idea, on the sinecure.

Strange that so many crucial meetings in this saga took place in 'official' hotels, on the occasion of a European Cup Final. So it was again in Paris in 1975, when Leeds United played Bayern Munich in what turned out to be another highly controversial game, strangely refereed. In the Hotel Crillon, Artemio Franchi took me aside and explained to me how Allodi had been neutralised.

Yes, he said, Allodi had been commissioned to draw up a plan for Coverciano. But who was to say that plan would ever be implemented? Who, indeed? But it was. All Franchi's ingenuity turned out, not for the first or last time, to be so much camouflage. Allodi not only drew up a grandiose plan. He was appointed, on an excellent salary, to run Coverciano himself.

Artemio Franchi, alas, is now dead; in a wretched motor accident outside his native Siena. Such are the undercurrents and labyrinthine conspiracies of Italian public life that it has even been suggested there that his death was not an accident. Franchi, a captain of one of the *contrade* in the historic Palio horse race, where each *contrada* runs a horse, ran head on into a lorry, when driving back from a *contrada* meeting. He was, the conspiracy theorists point out, an excellent driver, well used to the road between Siena and Florence.

On the occasions I have been asked to categorise Franchi, I have replied, 'A man who prefers to be honest.' Given the ambience of Italian business and football, and given the nature of Franchi's own career, it was sometimes a difficult ambition.

A Sienese, Franchi was the son of a chef who worked in the fashionable Sabatini's restaurant in Florence's Via Tornabuoni. Franchi was a bright, quick, subtle fellow, who got himself a university education, and eventually became secretary to Florence's chief football club, Fiorentina.

There he drew the attention of a Big Wheel, Dante Berretti, the top man in Tuscan football and a power broker. How well I still remember Berretti's massive, opulent presence in the Tribune of Honour – the directors' box – at Fiorentina's matches in the early 1950s. He was a huge, handsome man, with abundant, carefully brushed-back, grey hair. He it was who had Franchi made head of the so-called Semi-Professional League, which then had its headquarters in Florence. It was rather like being Secretary of the English Third and Fourth Divisions.

Thereafter, it was upwards all the way. In due course the able Franchi became President of the FIGC – the Italian FA – and then of UEFA, with a seat on the FIFA Council. He was a beguiling man, humorous, lively, immensely intelligent. In Italy, he was known as 'a diplomat', with all the ambiguity attached to such a word. If there was any general criticism of him, it was for his tendency to '*insabbiare*', a word which means to cover something over with sand. At this, he was adept. Problems tended to be obfuscated, rather than confronted.

There was no better example of this than the appointment of Italo Allodi to run the Coverciano coaching centre in 1975; a decision which enraged decent men in Italian football. Fulvio Bernardini acidly remarked that the only thing Allodi was qualified to teach was how to give gold watches to referees. But Allodi stayed, spending huge sums of money on so-called Super Courses for would-be managers, sending them all over the world to study the game. He even, in 1982 during the course of the World Cup finals, held a convention of managers and coaches at Coverciano, in the course of which one of his minions, the Tuscan manager Eugenio Fascetti, made a vicious assault on Enzo Bearzot. He accused him of disgracing Italian football with the tactics he was using in Spain. Bearzot and Italy went on to win the World Cup. Fascetti was fined.

Artemio Franchi, President of the Italian football federation and of UEFA – 'a man who prefers to be honest'
(Popperfoto)

But I am getting ahead of our story. Publication of it in the *Sunday Times* in April 1974 led at once to an almost hysterical closing of ranks by the Italian media, a despicable *omertà*. In the sense, at least, that though the clamour was great, there was dead silence on the subject of our specific accusations. The newspaper for which I myself had written for many years, the *Corriere Dello Sport* of Rome, was bold enough to publish a translation of the whole, long article on its back page. But in the editorials on its front page, it constantly attacked us.

'I had to do that,' Mario Gismondi, then its editor, explained to me. 'Otherwise they would have said I was playing Lazio's game against Juventus.' Lazio, the Roman club, at that time being a powerful challenger to Turin's Juventus in the Italian championship.

A senior correspondent of *Corriere Dello Sport* came over to London in May for a match at Wembley between England and Argentina, and told Botsford and me, during a reception at the Argentine Embassy, 'I'd have given a year of my life for a scoop like that.'

There were, and still are, plenty of decent, honest, upright men in Italian football, but their voices then were scarcely heard above the screams of outrage and denial. Why traduce Italian football, newspapers demanded. Why not investigate the way England manipulated its way to the World Cup in 1966? Had there ever been an atom of evidence, rather than supposition, on the subject, I am sure we would have been the first to investigate. But this was no more than a question of *tu quoque*, an attempt to avoid at all costs looking facts in the face.

Peculiarly shocking and disappointing to me was the behaviour of the supposed doyen of Italian sporting journalists, Gianni Brera: though I suppose it was pretty naive of me to have expected any better.

Brera, a sturdy little man who prided himself on not being an Italian but a Lombard, from Milan, was a quirky, idiosyncratic writer, with curiously bigoted and inflexible attitudes over race and geography. Italians, he insisted – and a surprising number of people in the game took him seriously – hadn't the strength and stamina to play the running game Anglo-Saxons played. He resented the emergence, at that period, of footballers from Italy's Deep South, though they were clearly enriching the sport. But I had expected him to be the first, rather than the last, to rise up in arms over the slimy stratagems which Botsford and I had exposed.

Instead, at first, not a word. Finally, I discovered that he had written something spiteful and malicious about me, a brief paragraph in *Guerin Sportivo*, then a weekly newspaper. Knowing nothing of it at the time, I greeted him cordially when I saw him during the 1974 World Cup.

Later, I took him up on his treachery, and there were violent exchanges in Italian magazines. The truth was, and he knew it, that he had not done his duty, that he had let down his readers, Italian football, and football at large. But goodness knows he was not alone.

Eight years later, immediately after Italy had won the World Cup in Spain, two young investigative journalists, Oliviero Beha and Roberto Chiodi, had the astonishing courage to allege that an early, drawn game against the Cameroons in Vigo, had been bought. The Camorra, it seems, were involved. I am quite sure Enzo Bearzot, manager of that Italian team, could not have been. True or not, it heralded a new era in Italian sports journalism; a new, incorruptible, kind of writer.

One curious defence mechanism employed against our discoveries was to accuse the English of mounting a campaign to undermine Italy's chances in the ensuing World Cup: conspiracy theory indeed! Needless to say it was Italo Allodi who propounded it. By contrast, Gian Paolo Ormezzano, the exuberant, ebullient young editor of the Turin daily, *Tuttosport*, made an honest and open response. 'The fact remains,' he wrote, 'that it's a nasty affair for our football; but to confront it is the only way to come out of it. And it's not to be excluded that in the end, the matter will reduce itself to the disappearance of a very dangerous personage, and to the umpteenth lesson in life-journalism given to us by the English.'

Giampiero Boniperti, Juventus' President, maintained his club were completely extraneous to the affair, and that its lawyers had been consulted with a view to taking legal action. They never did. Nobody did. How could they? There was nothing they could properly dispute.

Someone else did threaten to sue us. Not Boniperti, not Allodi, but an Englishman, Sir Harold Thompson.

Thompson might be described as a complex, perverse and gifted man. He was a celebrated scientist, specialising in Infra-Red Spectroscopy, a professor at St John's College, Oxford – a university where he had first arrived as an undergraduate from Yorkshire, winning a soccer Blue. He had been at once the creator and the destroyer of Pegasus football club, whose wonderfully romantic story began in Oxford in 1948. Composed of players from both universities, most of them initially war veterans, such as Ken Shearwood and Tony Pawson, it took wing with astonishing speed. In no time at all, the Pegasus club had delighted a packed Wembley stadium with a superlative win over Bishop Auckland, mightiest of Cup fighters, in the Amateur Final at Wembley. They won the Cup again, thrashing Harwich and Parkeston 6–0.

But as the years went by the Cambridge men tended to go off to join the Corinthian Casuals, and mature students gave way to beardless boys. Thompson now became a menace rather than an advantage. Younger undergraduates disliked being cajoled, even bullied. Nor could they stand up to Thompson as easily as men who had fought in the Western Desert or commanded little ships. John Tanner, centre-forward for Pegasus in their great days and later a club official, was once so exasperated by Thompson in the dressing-room before a game that he gave him a black eye. Thompson walked round the field saying, as he pointed to the eye, 'Look what Tanner did to me!'

Within the Football Association, he was a would-be *eminence grise*, a perpetual problem to the powerful secretary Sir Stanley Rous, who at times would swat him like a fly. But Thompson had his revenge. When, in 1962, the time came, after 28 largely remarkable years in office, for Rous to retire and become President of FIFA, he wanted his protégé, Walter Winterbottom, to succeed him.

Winterbottom seemed an ideal candidate. Since 1946, he had been both England team manager and Director of Coaching, a somewhat clerkly figure who had, in fact, once played for Manchester United. Thompson set about seeing that he did not get the job. In the event, an article in *The Observer* by Clement Freud played into his hands. It trumpeted the praises of Winterbottom, taking it for granted that he would be elected. Thompson took it doggedly to each member of the electing committee, asking them whether they meant to be manipulated by a single newspaper. So they chose the compromise candidate, the obscure treasurer Denis Follows.

Rous disliked Follows, and the antipathy was reciprocated. Follows, a former Secretary of the British Air Line Pilots Association (BALPA), was a small, somewhat pompous man, with no great presence; though in due course, he would stand up to the Government, in his future capacity as chief executive of the Olympic Committee, and insist Britain send a team to the Moscow Olympic Games, in the face of the American-led boycott.

So Thompson had his way and Follows was elected. That evening, I was asked to interview him for BBC radio. As we waited outside the studio, he said, 'The Secretary is the servant of the Association, and we all know what happened. The servant became the master.' Meaning Rous. And thank goodness Rous did become the master of an FA Council largely composed of pathetic, bumbling, insular old fossils.

Playing Mr Nice Guy to the FA did Follows little good. Thompson persecuted him. The genie was out of the bottle. He was a king-maker now, and a king-breaker, too. His constant bullying and pestering made Follows' life a misery. In the end, he succumbed to a heart attack. So Thompson, equally known to pester stewardesses on the England team's charter aircraft and the wives of fellow officials at banquets, set about making another king: Ted Croker. Again, he succeeded. Croker, once an heroic pilot, then a successful businessman and an ex-player for Charlton Athletic, became the new Secretary in due course. But he was made of sterner stuff than Follows, and wouldn't be bullied. Thompson was frustrated.

In 1974, not long before our investigation and its results were published, Thompson had been largely instrumental in getting rid of Sir Alf Ramsey, the England team manager, winner in 1966 of the World Cup. In this, I do not think Thompson was wrong. The decision was jointly arrived at by the Senior International Committee, alias the old selection committee, now deprived of any such function. The usual bunch of fence-sitters, they would probably have allowed Ramsey to carry on, though for at least two years it had been perfectly clear that he had lost his way.

In the Spring of 1972, his mistaken tactics had made a present of the home first leg of the European Nations Cup quarter-final to West Germany, who won the match 3–1. For the return leg, played in Berlin, he seemed to lose his nerve, and picked a ridiculously defensive side, full of harsh, physical players, which never had a chance of winning and eventually managed a useless 0–0 draw. 'The whole England team,' said the brilliant, blond German inside-left, Gunter Netzer, 'has autographed my leg.'

Technically, Thompson was quite justified in saying that he alone had not made the decision. But as the unquestioned moving spirit, it was Thompson who was seen as responsible, and his bitterness towards the Press was great. It was said that he'd never forgiven Ramsey for telling him, years earlier, not to blow cigar smoke in his young players' faces. It may even have been true. Thompson was not a man easily to forget a slight, real or imagined. But there were moments when paranoia appeared to set in; and soon we should see one of them.

Thompson had just been made a Vice-President of UEFA, and as such,

Botsford and I felt it our duty to give him a complete and regular briefing on the Solti–Lobo Affair, and its development. He seemed pleased enough at the time. But the following December in Budapest, of all places, where he attended his first meeting of the UEFA Executive Committee, he gave vent to an extraordinary outburst.

When Solti and his deeds were about to be discussed, Artemio Franchi, the UEFA President, volunteered to leave the room, since he was an Italian and an Italian club was involved. No, not a bit of it, said Thompson. There was no reason for him to go. He knew these journalists, and their fabrications. Why, they had recently and falsely accused him of getting rid of Alf Ramsey!

This bizarre explosion was faithfully reported to Botsford and myself by our Deep Throat in Budapest; and consequently reported by us in the *Sunday Times*. This produced, almost at once, a letter to me from Thompson, accusing us of 'printing quotations and statements about me which are false, and further, which reflect upon my integrity in football affairs. I am considering what further action should be taken.' I should not, he pursued, call upon his friendship or help in the future, 'for I cannot deal with people who write these cheap untruths.'

No action was taken, for our statements were not untrue. Indeed, we heard that Thompson's chief preoccupation, and that of certain members of UEFA, was to find out how we had received so accurate a report from the meeting. Apprised of what had happened, the Secretary of the Football League, Alan Hardaker, who detested Thompson and could show a nice, dry wit at times, remarked to me, 'They could take his braces off in those meetings, put them back on again, and he still wouldn't know what had happened.'

It was not much consolation, however, to know that the man who should have been our chief ally, the scourge of corruption in European football, defender of the English game, had effectively lined up with the opposition. For whatever perverse, tormented reasons.

One step, at least, was belatedly taken at the Budapest meeting. Solti was declared *persona non grata* in European football, a fairly empty gesture now that his cover had been 'blown', but an acknowledgement, at least, that dirty work had been afoot. Curiously enough, when Solti did go into a Hungarian gaol, it had nothing to do with football. He was stopped at the frontier and found to be in possession of a valuable Hebrew text, which he was trying to smuggle out of the country.

The Executive Committee also received the report of the two-man *ad hoc* committee which had been set up soon after the revelations by the *Sunday Times*, in an almost empty gesture. The members of this committee were a distinguished French lawyer, Jacques Georges – who would later become President of UEFA but hardly distinguish himself with his ill-timed, intemperate comments on the Hillsborough disaster – and a Swiss called Lucien Schmidlin. In the event, a mountain of seven months' labour produced a mere mouse of a report. Hardly astonishing, perhaps, given the fact that Georges and Schmidlin had no investigative arm, knew little or nothing other than what they had learned from Botsford and myself, and could hardly put their witnesses, such as Italo Allodi, on oath.

The *ad hoc* committee reported on the ludicrous identity parade at the Hotel Atlantis, the previous year. Louis Wouters, the Belgian lawyer, furnished them with some interesting rationalisations. 'Solti', he told them, 'is clearly guilty, and therefore why should the Disciplinary Committee bother with him?' Or, for that matter, interview officials of Juventus, since there was no evidence that any was implicated. None, after all, had visited Lisbon.

As for the extraordinary letter Hans Bangerter, the UEFA Secretary, rushed off to Juventus, exculpating them, the Disciplinary Committee had discussed two options. We know, of course, that these were either to declare Solti *persona non grata* or to circularise clubs about him, and we also know neither was embraced.

As for Juventus, the *ad hoc* committee had scarcely bothered with them. They listened to the tape, discussed its implications with Wouters, and took another opinion, allegedly of no assistance, from the Chairman of the Finnish FA, Poriola. That was that. The only evidence to appear in the committee's report consisted of internal UEFA documents, and even some of these were not given in full. The lack of will seriously to pursue so serious a case was evident. It was perfectly plain that had it not been for the publication of our *Sunday Times* report, sleeping dogs would have been left to lie.

In March 1975, we published in the newspaper a chart which showed how mysteriously often the Big Three of Italian football, Milan, Inter and Juventus, had their European matches controlled by the same small group of referees. Dienst of Switzerland, who had refereed the World Cup Final of 1966 at Wembley and the 1968 European Nations Cup Final in Rome (refusing a manifest penalty to Yugoslavia, who thus failed to beat Italy) came top of the list, with the Italian clubs winning six and drawing three of the games he refereed. Tschenscher, the West German, took half a dozen games; three wins, two draws, one loss.

Ortiz de Mendibil, who refereed the notorious Inter–Liverpool semi-final of 1965, and a highly controversial Twente Enschede–Juventus Fairs Cup quarter-final years later – Twente complained bitterly to me afterwards that they thought his refereeing in Turin had been shamefully biased – did not control a single game which was lost by an Italian team. Five wins out of five. Yet despite his controversial record Ortiz de Mendibil, who allegedly had a gravely sick child, requiring expensive medical attention, was actually on UEFA's Referees' Committee. The Austrian Seipelt, despite his long acquaintance with Solti being well known, was the committee's Chairman. Seipelt it was, of course, who had effectively disqualified Lobo.

As an exquisite envoi to the Budapest meeting, Lucien Schmidlin suggested that since Lobo had broken UEFA's rule of silence, he himself should be punished. A case of killing the messenger, indeed. Dr Franchi turned the idea down flat, but it showed clearly enough which way the wind was blowing. Lobo was regarded not as a hero, a very decent man, but an embarrassing nuisance.

As our investigation proceeded, other wretched cases came into the light. That, for example, of the Standard Liège–Inter European Cup quarter-final second leg in 1972, and the extraordinary behaviour of the referee, Gyula Emsberger, and a man called Istvan Zsolt.

Zsolt was a well-known former international referee, a known intimate of Solti, and in 'civilian' life once manager of the Hungarian State Theatre. Emsberger, on the line in 1966 at another notorious game, the Inter–Real Madrid European Cup semi-final when Vadas wouldn't be bought, refereed the Standard–Inter game, but there was a puzzle over his report, which had led to his suspension from two international games. He had not filled it in himself; he had inexplicably left it to Zsolt. Who, in completing the form, had equally inexplicably left out the fact that the Inter right-half, Bedin, had been cautioned; inexplicable too was Zsolt's very presence in Liège.

Once, when Zsolt came to London, the Hungarian actor and journalist, the late Leslie Vernon, brought him to my house, where I asked him about this curious event; and about a strange decision he once gave in a Switzerland–Italy game. It was hard to glean any cogent answer. He was a thoroughly evasive man. In Tatabanya, when Botsford and I were doing our December sweep through Europe on the Solti trail, from Vienna to Budapest to Switzerland to Milan, we had interviewed Emsberger. But the man who would pin down both him and Gyorgy Vadas was the talented Hungarian investigative journalist, Peter Borenich. He it was who would obtain from Vadas the full statement on the Inter–Real Madrid game which Botsford and I, subsequently, would try in vain to get him to make, in Budapest; at Budapest Radio, where all (football) roads meet. Borenich it was who would have Zsolt squirming, over the Liège affair.

Inter's Bedin had been booked once already in the European Cup that season. This meant that if he was booked again, he would automatically be suspended from the next tie. But why had Emsberger allowed Zsolt to fill in his report at all? Under questioning from Borenich, he gave an explanation. Of a sort.

'Because he had completed many reports and had seen the game,' said Emsberger. (Let me say, in passing, that the translation is the work of the admirable Charlie Coutts, a Scot from Aberdeen, once a Japanese prisoner-of-war, who had for years been settled in Hungary, broadcasting in English for Radio Budapest, working for Reuter.) 'On the plane going home, I asked him to fill it up for me in German. He did. I posted it when we arrived in Budapest. The next time we met, I asked Zsolt why he had not written in the names of both suspended players. To which he replied, "Was it not just one yellow card?"'

'No, two,' said Emsberger. Zsolt asked him when he had given it. Two minutes from time, was the reply. Then, said Zsolt, he had not seen it. He had already been on his way down from the stand to ask the UEFA observers what they had thought of the refereeing. A curious mission.

But why, Borenich asked Emsberger, ask Zsolt to complete the report at all? 'Because I do not write well in German,' was the answer. 'My son usually helped me, once I was back home. After this incident, I was suspended for two international games. If one is as stupid as I was, the punishment is deserved.'

Inter's Gianfranco Bedin – escaped a suspension when his second UEFA Cup caution was mysteriously not reported (Farabolafoto)

'Why was Zsolt at the game?' asked Borenich; the $64 000 question.

'I don't know. He never says much. A taciturn character.'

He did not say very much, at least of any relevance, when Borenich put him under pressure. A bold thing to do. Zsolt instantly called up senior people at Budapest Radio – senior figures in Hungarian football, too – to try to scare Borenich off the trail. But Borenich would not be scared.

Wriggling and squirming, as he did when he sat in my own house, Zsolt tried to evade hard questions behind a smokescreen of pompous verbiage. 'Your story is badly drafted. As a former referee, let me put you on the right lines. The story falls down, no matter how well it may sound, when it pictures the referee as not dictating the name of the player to whom he gave a yellow card. It falls down, because it was not drafted with expert knowledge. At the end of a game, if a referee, for any reason, asks someone to enter up the UEFA report sheet, then he tells that person what happens during the game, and details serious violations of the rules . . .'

Zsolt, clearly, was on the ropes; blocking, stonewalling and evading. The

difference, however, between Borenich's investigation and my own was that he virtually had to take his career in his hands, and face the prospect of Zsolt calling up the peculiar mafia of Hungarian football big-wigs who had important positions in radio. This Zsolt did, but to Borenich's enormous credit – Hungary then was a very different place indeed, under Communism, than Hungary now – he still persisted. All roads, as Botsford and I found in our inquiries, seemed to lead to Budapest, and winding, circuitous roads they were. Hard, at times, not to remember the old definition of a Hungarian as the only man who can go into a revolving door behind you and come out in front of you.

Borenich would eventually put the results of his fearless investigations into a short book called *Only The Ball Has A Skin*. Hungarian football in the 1980s was an absolute sink of iniquity. Infinite games had been bought, sold and fixed. Many of the leaders of the game were disgraced, but there was always a sufficient quorum of honest men to ensure a better future for football there. Men like Borenich himself – and Gyorgy Vadas.

Keith Botsford and I had known about Gyorgy Vadas, about the Inter–Real Madrid game, for a long time. That Vadas had been approached by the ineffable Solti, had refused to 'bend' the game in favour of Inter, and had suffered as a referee in consequence. That was one thing. Proving it, getting any kind of confirmation, was emphatically another.

We had been to Budapest, had tried and failed. What a vile visit that was! I was in one hotel, Keith, upon the hill above that splendid city, in another. Keith had been ill. I had waited endlessly in my hotel room for the call which would tell us that Vadas would see us. Cyril Connolly once wrote that the writer knows that he must always, in the end, return to the hotel room. But hotel rooms in those pre-war times were not the soulless, anonymous, debilitating rooms of an American hotel. I waited and waited. Keith continued to suffer. At long last, Vadas agreed that he would see us.

The meeting took place in the canteen of Radio Budapest; such a drab, dreary, sombre setting when one thought of the rogue millionaires, the great occasions, the grand conspiracies, which were implicated. Vadas was a large, good-natured, anxious man. He wouldn't talk. If we told him this and that, he might confirm it. He would go no further. Fear was in the air; he had suffered sufficiently. The walls could still close in on him. Perhaps he'd come to England; if we paid for the trip, he might talk to us there. We were willing to accommodate him but it never happened. It was Borenich, fellow employee at Radio Budapest, where all things led and all things seemed to happen, who eventually cracked it. After endless insistence.

And what creatures now crawled out from under stones! Solti, Allodi, Moratti. The ineffable Secretary of the Hungarian Football Federation.

Back to 1966. The semi-final second leg, at San Siro, as it had been for the past two years, years in which Solti, and Inter, had suborned the referee. Now they needed to do so again. Needed to win, to go forward to the Final. Under the steady pressure of Borenich's questioning, Vadas confirmed and elaborated on all the things we had already heard. It was a little late in the day, but yet another large, significant, repellent piece fitted into the arcane jigsaw. Let me quote the interview directly from Borenich's admirable book.

VADAS   *I was approached in Milan by Solti. He was with us from morning to night. The only time he was not around was when we were sleeping. He was making sure we did not encounter anyone from Real Madrid. On the one occasion I was left alone with* him in my room, he made a very serious proposition. Basically, I was to referee the game so as to ensure that Real did not go forward . . . I have never talked about this in public. The sum was enough to buy five, maybe six, Mercedes cars. [The going rate had certainly diminished by the time Solti approached Lobo.] *To be paid in dollars. Not negligible. Starting from an initial payment in the event of a straightforward win by Inter, doubled for a win by a penalty award at the end of the game, quintupled for a win during extra time, multiplied ten times for a win by a penalty during extra time . . .*

I told my two linesmen colleagues immediately. And we went out on to the pitch determined to control that game correctly and honestly. We may have made some wrong decisions, but of this I am certain: in our minds we were motivated by one aim, to control the game correctly.

BORENICH *I understand you met Angelo Moratti, the Inter President, in his house.*

VADAS *It was a pleasant meeting. At 11 o'clock on the morning of the match, Inter's General Secretary, Italo Allodi, accompanied by Dezso Solti, came to the hotel. They brought greetings from Signor Moratti, and an invitation to visit him at his villa. What a marvellous place it was! Name anything beautiful or wonderful, that place had it! . . . We lunched in a pleasant environment, and in an excellent mood . . . To start the lunch, Signor Moratti presented the three of us with a gold watch. Then, as the meal progressed, he told Solti that he should buy us this or that. We just ducked our heads in wonder . . . Colour television sets – very rare in Hungary in those days – tape recorders, record players, electric razors, radios and other electrical devices. We three Hungarians looked at each other in amazement.*

Solti showed great respect for Moratti. His behaviour was almost servile . . . At the same time, I knew that Solti was not employed by Inter, as such. Moratti and the Inter leadership commissioned him for successfully arranging this and that.

Amancio scores for Real Madrid against Inter in the 1966 semi-final second leg at San Siro. In the background is Gyorgy Vadas, the Hungarian referee who refused to be 'bought' (Farabolafoto)

BORENICH	*What was Solti's reaction at the end of the game, when Inter went out?*
VADAS	*His behaviour was not that of a sportsman. At half-time he had started bawling that I had refused three 'justified' penalties . . . I said to him, 'You must have been watching another game.'*
BORENICH	*And at the end, what did Solti say?*
VADAS	*Shouted and screamed that my refereeing had been a swindle. Threatened to spare no effort to have me struck off the FIFA list of referees. That was a threat he was able to make good. The screwing had been well done before I arrived home. At five o'clock in the morning after the game, Solti phoned the general secretary of the Hungarian Federation, Gyorgy Honti, to tell him that, in Solti's words, I had cheated them out of the game . . . Later, I was to learn that Solti told Honti, 'If you value my friendship, you must act to have him removed from both the FIFA and the Hungarian senior list of referees. I have never experienced such an example of unfair refereeing . . .' I am sure Solti held me responsible for a loss of $30 000. That was what he said he had lost through Inter failing to qualify.*

Translation, again, by Charlie Coutts.

On his return to Budapest, Vadas was confronted by an enraged Honti: 'Look at all the terrible things the Italian papers have been saying about you!' Vadas was withdrawn from all those UEFA games he had been chosen to referee, and removed from the FIFA list. He reported the attempted bribery, but no action was ever taken.

Nor was any taken when Botsford and I eventually dug up, in Holland, the document Solti – that 'madman going around' – had signed on behalf of Juventus in 1971. Damning evidence? Not a bit of it. UEFA's response was that 1971 was 1971. There was no indication that Solti was in any way connected with them in 1973, when he went to see and try to suborn Lobo in Lisbon.

A telephone call from a Dutch friend, then the general manager of Twente Enschede, had put us on the track. He remembered meeting Solti a few years earlier, he said, when he came to Enschede and tried to persuade Twente to swop the dates of their ties against Juventus in the Inter-Cities Fairs Cup. Keith, on a typical inspiration, surmised that a letter might have been signed, dropped in at Enschede on his way to Germany, and found his guess was right. A photograph of the letter was duly published in the *Sunday Times*, but there was no sequel. Hans Bangerter's deplorable letter had set the scene and the tone. There would always be reasons, good or bad, for doing nothing about Juventus, perhaps, with its FIAT backing, the most powerful club in Europe. Even in the world.

Not that any great zeal was shown in other quarters, England included. Harold Thompson, with his paranoiac outburst, had not exactly set the tone, but if we did not meet outright hostility, we met massive indifference. A senior official of the Football Association was heard to remark, 'I wish they hadn't started it, because they'll never finish it.' Nor did we.

There was much more that we heard in our investigations in Europe, above all in Budapest and Vienna, where the sweet, cosy, outdoor café life – of which Solti had been a part and Bela Guttmann still was – continued as it had for generations. How a certain official had protested violently because half the bribe he had been promised was pocketed by the go-between. How another was seen late at night in a Turkish hotel, having money counted into his hand.

And Allodi? He continued to flourish like the green bay tree, till illness overtook him in the late 1980s. It says much for the morality of Italian football that there was never any lack of major clubs panting for his services. Leaving Coverciano, he moved, so to speak, just down the road, to become General Manager of Fiorentina. Thence, when things did not go as well as the club hoped, he moved down South to Naples.

There were occasional displeasures. Enzo Bearzot, in his deep seriousness and integrity the very antithesis of all Allodi seemed to stand for, was slow to forgive. Nor would he, indeed, till 1989, when, meeting a clearly debilitated Allodi at Coverciano of all places, he made peace.

Relations were not as rosy in 1984, nearly ten years after whatever happened in West Germany during the World Cup. Once again, Allodi was threatening revenge; though once again, it was all huff and puff. He never succeeded; never sued.

Interviewed by the weekly magazine *L'Espresso*, Bearzot was asked whether he still had it in for Allodi. He replied somewhat opaquely, 'Not in that way.' But he considered Allodi 'an able but dangerous person.' He would say no more, for fear of 'poisoning the ambience.'

A furious Mr Fix-It protested. Bearzot's success in Spain, two years before, in the teeth of the opposition Allodi encouraged from Coverciano, had made Allodi's position there untenable. So he joined a complaisant Fiorentina; but he'd been planning, he said, to resign that job in 1985, in order to rejoin the Italian Federation. Now, he proclaimed, he was ready to resign straight away, so he could be free to sue Bearzot in the courts. Hopes that his case would be taken up by a Federation official, the grandly named Procurator of the Football Federation, had been disappointed. National team managers, it transpired, were too grand to be proceeded against in this way. Bearzot who'd made Allodi's removal from Coverciano a condition for renewing his contract, was inviolable.

Allodi, needless to say, did not resign, and he did not sue. His next little bit of bother came when he was in Naples. A strange anti-climax. The Italian Federation was carrying out an inquiry into the fixing of matches. Police investigating drug dealing had by chance stumbled on a network of corruption, run by gamblers. Allodi's name had been linked with a dubious character. Little more than that. It seemed the merest peccadillo by comparison with what had gone on, unpunished and largely undetected, in the Years of the Golden Fix.

But the prosecuting lawyer, acting on behalf of the Italian Federation, launched the most extraordinary attack on Allodi and his machinations. One agreed with almost every word, but wondered why this was happening now, in such a marginal context. The Freudian phenomenon of displacement seemed to be taking place. A great head of steam, a huge resentment, seemed to have been built up over the years, and here it was, finally being released.

Tearfully, Allodi protested that he was a pillar of rectitude, that he'd always kept himself respectable. When the tribunal gave its decision, it predictably exonerated him. How, after all, could it traduce a man who, when he did leave the Federation for Fiorentina, had the Italian sports Press beating a path to his door, dedicating to him whole pages of sycophantic flattery? The man of whom Bearzot had said, 'How can I work when I've a Brutus at my back?' and who'd replied, 'If I'm Brutus, then he must think he's Caesar,' had bounced back with a vengeance; and a fortune. Nor would he ever lose that pitifully misplaced respect,

History repeats itself, wrote Karl Marx, the first time as tragedy, the second as farce. Rome, then, was in his mind, I recall, but not Roma. Not the famous, passionately supported, endlessly storm-tossed football club. But in the case of Roma, its President, Senator Dino Viola, and the case of the bribe that never was, the dictum will still serve.

In the semi-finals of the European Cup of 1984, Dundee United, managed by the explosive but effective Jim McLean, surpassed themselves by reaching the semi-finals. There they were drawn against Roma, whom they beat 2–0 in the first leg, at Tannadice. McLean, bouncing up and down on the bench, was heard to utter the words 'Italian bastards'; words which would not be forgiven or forgotten by the Roma players. Indeed, at the end of the second leg at the Olympic Stadium, Roma's footballers surrounded him and angrily abused him.

It was before the second leg, however, that there was dirty work at the crossroads. One day, Viola was approached by two people. One was Spartaco Landini, once a centre-half who played for Internazionale and even in the Italian World Cup team of 1966. The other was called Giampaolo Cominato, who had previously been general manager of two clubs, Bolzano and Avellino. The two made Viola an offer he couldn't refuse; or at least, he didn't. They could 'fix' Michel Vautrot, the eminent French referee, who was deputed to handle the second leg. All it needed was 100 million lire; about £50 000 at the time.

Viola agreed. Had he temporised, had he made even the most superficial inquiries, he must have learned that Vautrot was the last referee to agree to be bought, that he was not only one of the best referees in Europe, but one of the most upright and honest. But conspiracy theory has been the name of the game – from chariot racing to football, through the Papal years – in Rome for a couple of thousand years now, and Viola clearly didn't need much convincing.

The two swindlers had made elaborate plans. The next stage in this *opera buffa* took place in a restaurant, the night before the game was due, where Viola's son and others took Vautrot out to dinner. It had been arranged, Landini and Cominato said, that a telephone call would be made to Vautrot during the meal. It duly was. Vautrot was called to the 'phone, and was baffled to be wished good luck by Cominato, calling himself Paolo. Be sure your sin will find you out! Had Cominato used any one of the multiplicity of Italian first names that exist, he, Landini and Viola might have got away with it. But when the fond and foolish old Senator Viola heard that 'Paolo' had called, he jumped to the conclusion that it must be the well-known Italian referee Paolo Bergamo. It would cost him – and Bergamo – dear.

The game took place; I saw it myself and Roma won comfortably and deservedly, wiping out the deficit and going on to the Final where they would lose on penalties against Liverpool. Viola was happy enough. Roma had come through; *ergo* it must have been money well spent. And Landini and Cominato went away to spend it. Vautrot, of course, was never even approached, let alone suborned.

That, doubtless, would have been that, had Viola, not long afterwards, run into Paolo Bergamo when they were both attending a refereeing course. The good old Senator blabbered on, ingenuously, about the 'fix', quite convinced that the astonished Bergamo had been a party to it. For thirteen

*Senator Dino Viola,
President of AS Roma,
talks to reporters after
revelation of his
attempt to 'buy' the
referee of his club's
European Cup semi-
final second leg against
Dundee United*

(Popperfoto)

months, Bergamo wrestled with his con-
science, before it finally won. Should he or
shouldn't he report what he knew, which was
his statutory duty, to the Italian Federation?
Finally he did. For delaying so long, he was
suspended; but the delay was long enough to
let Viola and Roma off the hook. For when
an inquiry was held by the disciplinary body,
the club and its President protested that it
had come too late to be valid, that the bizarre
statute of limitations in force at the time had
been infringed.

What the statute laid down, an indulgent
cheats' charter, was that any offence committed in a given season must be brought to trial
before the end of the year which followed
that season. To give the Italian Federation its
due, it did its absolute utmost to circumvent
the rule. Viola was brought to trial, but he slipped through the net. It was too
late. Nor did he seem to lose any prestige or respect on this account. The
rationalisation was that he was acting only to protect the interests of his
club, convinced that if he did not bribe the referee, then the opposition
would.

What he had wanted to do, Viola insisted, was to give Landini and
Cominato the money before the game, in order to disclose the identity of the
'Mr Big' whom he presumed to be behind them. Moreover, he pleaded that
extortion had taken place; that the two tricksters had told him, in effect, give
us the money, or your team will lose the match.

Landini, however, anxious to avoid being convicted for fraud by the State,
insisted that the money had been paid to him *after* the game. He had, he
claimed, the air tickets to prove as much; or at least to prove that he would
not have been in a position to collect, the day before the game took place.

UEFA, however, had no such statute of limitation. They, in turn, 'tried'
Viola, finding both him and Roma guilty of a serious offence. In consequence, Roma would be banned from the ensuing Cup Winners' Cup competition; a punishment which would cost them huge sums of money. Far
more than 100 million lire.

Roma appealed, and to the general horror – shared, it must be said, in
Italy itself, at least outside Rome – the sentence was commuted to a fine.
Roma could play in the Cup Winners' Cup, after all. 'A scandalous deci-
sion!' thundered the *Gazzetta Dello Sport*, of Milan.

Fond and foolish old Presidents, however, were a species to be found in
Milan, as well as in Rome. When the devious Angelo Moratti departed
Inter, and this world, his successor as President was Ivanoe Fraizzoli, a
pompous manufacturer of clothing with a wife, nicknamed Lady Fraizzoli,
who rejoiced in being in the public eye. By 1984, he was no longer President,
and seemed to resent the fact. It is a little hard otherwise to explain, except in
terms of his natural garrulity, why he did what he did at a banquet in Hamburg in 1984, held after Inter had played there in the UEFA Cup.

What he did, in brief, was to spill the beans about a notorious European
Cup match played 13 years earlier by Inter in Monchengladbach. At a
moment when Inter were losing 2–1, and a hail of beer and soft drink cans
came on to the field of play, Roberto Boninsegna, Inter's Italian inter-

national centre-forward and a star of the 1970 World Cup Final when he scored his country's goal, was hit on the back of the head, felled, and removed from the ground. Inter went on to lose 7–1. They appealed on the grounds of Boninsegna's injury; the appeal was upheld, the result annulled, and the game ordered to be replayed. Inter then comfortably won what became the first leg, at San Siro, and held Borussia to a 0–0 draw in Berlin, in the re-arranged second leg.

Well before the appeal was heard, there was much controversy about the match, not least in Italy itself. By chance, I was in Florence at the time, and went to visit Fiorentina's famous manager, the former Swedish international Nils Liedholm, later to manage Milan and Roma, at Florence's Stadio Comunale. 'Very strange,' he said, dourly and drily. 'A team loses its centre-forward; and is beaten 7–1!'

But there was more serious speculation than that. Above all, had Boninsegna been struck by a full Coca-Cola can – not, as at first reported, a beer can – or by an empty one? The Chairman of the UEFA Appeals Committee, a Swiss lawyer called Zorzi, whose name frequently crops up in the tormented annals of UEFA's disciplinary proceedings, accepted that the can was full. Hence the designated replay, hence Inter's passage to a European Cup Final which they would eventually and very emphatically lose to the great Ajax side of that era.

To give the talkative old Fraizzoli his due, the game had actually been given away the previous season by Sandrino Mazzola, elegant centre-forward of that Inter team and himself another Italian hero of the 1970 World Cup Final. The Coca-Cola can which had struck Boninsegna, he said, had been empty. The one he handed to the referee had been full. Devastating enough in itself.

But Fraizzoli, at that Hamburg banquet, went further. Before the appeals committee sat, he said, he had taken the precaution of sending a couple of representatives to Helsinki to put pressure on the Finnish member of the tribunal. Not only that, when the appeal was eventually heard in Zurich, the two hatchet men had gone into action again, this time to keep the Finn away from other members, who might influence him.

But then, Fraizzoli himself had had a very lucky escape over the Groningen Affair. Mere peanuts by comparison with the Years of the Golden Fix, when the prize was so much greater and Moratti, abetted by Allodi, was making referees offers they could so seldom refuse.

How had the mighty fallen! This time it was a mere UEFA Cup tie which was involved, and no Real Madrid, no Liverpool, but a little Dutch club, Groningen! In this shabby affair – needless to say quite unresolved by a UEFA Disciplinary Committee over which presided an old friend from the Solti era and its sub-committee, the Czech Vladimir Petra – the Fine Italian Hand of Moratti was missing, indeed.

Inter had lost the first leg of their second round UEFA Cup tie against Groningen, 2–0. A week later, on October 26, said the manager of the Dutch side, Hans Berger, he had been offered £55 000 to see that his team lost the return leg, by sufficient goals to let Inter go through. The intermediary, Berger would reveal after his team had in fact lost the second leg 5–1 in Bari – Inter were at the time suspended from playing at San Siro – was himself a Dutchman; an agent, the grandly-named Apollonius Konijnenburg. Four days after Berger was approached, Renzo De Vries, the President of Groningen, passed the complaint on to the Dutch Federation. Two days before the return leg, the Federation conveyed it to UEFA.

It was only after his team's defeat in Bari that Berger spoke out to the Press. 'Inter wanted to win at all costs,' he said. 'One of their representatives offered me £55 000 to throw the game.' To this, Fraizzoli rather clumsily responded, 'It's all a pack of lies. Anyway, how could you hope to buy an entire team for such a small amount?'

At the eventual UEFA enquiry, De Vries said that he himself had been illicitly approached in Bari, the day before the second leg game. Berger, for his part, testified that he'd been told that, were Groningen to let Inter win through, Fraizzoli would pay for the club to have a new grandstand, and see that Berger himself was offered the managership of Pisa or Verona.

There was further testimony from Theo Huizinga, General Manager of Groningen. He had, he said, heard at least one of Konijnenburg's damning conversations with Berger, in the course of which he had said that he was acting on behalf of Fraizzoli. But then, as we knew, Solti had said to Lobo that day in Lisbon that he was acting on behalf of Juventus, and Juventus escaped scot-free. So would Inter.

Curiously and ironically enough, UEFA's more permissive rules allowed, in such cases, the big Italian clubs to escape the consequences of their chicanery. In Italy itself, where realism, if not cynicism, ruled the day, the actions of such an intermediary implicitly involved the club for which he purported to be acting, which was thus held guilty until proved innocent. With UEFA, it was comfortably and comfortingly the other way around.

Who, meanwhile, was Apollonius, what was he? An increasingly significant Italo-Dutch agent, was the answer to that one. Fifty years old, he had opened an agency known grandly as International Football Management at Imperia, to sell players from the Low Countries to Italy. It had prospered sufficiently for him to transfer his base to Milan, where he enlisted the help of his son Ricky. So did Groningen themselves in Bari, where he was their interpreter.

The Disciplinary Committee was the usual fiasco. Apollonius didn't even turn up. At least you could say that Solti was present at the Atlantis Hotel, a decade earlier, even if he was never confronted with Lobo. A double room had been booked in the Dutchman's name at the Zurich Hilton, but he sent a message by special delivery claiming that he was ill. So the committee was adjourned to December 15, which meant that FK Austria were obliged to play their Third Round matches with Inter knowing that they might have to play them again against Groningen. But being pretty sure, I'll wager, that they wouldn't.

And they didn't. When at last the committee did meet again, cosiness ruled once more. The impression of UEFA as an affable gentlemen's club, in which first-class hotels, splendid meals, limousines and jet travel were regularly enjoyed, in which the undeclared motto was Don't Make Waves, persisted. Groningen, the committee concluded, had produced no evidence to connect Apollonius with Inter, no evidence that Inter had been behind the approach. The committee could establish only that Apollonius 'had sought to have a talk with Berger with a view to manipulating the game'. In other words, 'If there are these madmen going about'.

All these years away from the Solti scandal, UEFA had still set up no investigating arm; and this time there was no *Sunday Times* investigation to embarrass them, and force them to set up the sop of an *ad hoc* committee. One which would shuffle papers to and fro across a desk at irregular intervals, but do no more, largely because, even had it wanted to, it hadn't the means.

There is only so much a journalist can do, however popular or seemingly powerful the paper he works for. He can bring scandals to light, but however irrefutable his evidence, nothing will happen if the relevant body has no will to act. UEFA have never evinced that will. Their attitude is enshrined in the abject letter – a letter with no apparent authorisation – which the Secretary Hans Bangerter sent so speedily to Juventus. Exonerating them.

When the journalists themselves, even the decent, honest ones, have no will to investigate, then there is less chance than ever of justice being done, the game made straight. It would be shockingly unfair to say that the majority of Italian football journalists during these years were corrupt, even if many did undoubtedly receive handsome gifts and privileges from the major clubs. But my thoughts go back to a train journey to Turin which I made with one of the best Italian football journalists of his time, Pier Cesare Baretti, pitifully killed in an aircraft accident early in 1988.

By that time, he was actually President of Fiorentina. Not the classical, moneyed President, but essentially an administrator, a nominee. Earlier, he worked for the Turin paper *Tuttosport*, of which he became the Editor. When I spoke to him in that railway compartment about the Juventus–Lobo–Solti business, it was as though feet had walked over his grave. He became suddenly quiet, almost evasive, and said, '*Non mi interesso del costume*. I'm not interested in background.'

What an appalling, significant admission that was. For if the good guys, the Barettis of this journalistic world, were going to behave like the Three Wise Monkeys, what chance had Italian football got? And how could they square such a stance with their consciences? How could they go out seriously to report games when they sensed that they might be bought, fixed, manipulated? Only the season before the Groningen Affair, Inter had been accused of throwing, or trying to throw, a match away to Genoa, to bring off a coup on fixed odds. But Bini and Bagni scored goals – for which not a single colleague congratulated them – and Inter won 3–2.

The Brazilian right winger, Juary, who would later splendidly win a European Cup medal in Vienna with Porto, alleged that afterwards in the dressing-room both players were beaten up, though he later withdrew his story. There was plainly no involvement, then, of the club itself. But the incidents, not to mention the massively greater fixed-odds betting scandal which led to the suspension of so many star players in 1980, was surely the consequence of the general atmosphere of chicanery and cynicism seeping through to the players themselves, so that when the two major tricksters, Trinca and Crociani, approached any *ritiro* – training camp hotel – they were welcomed by the players where any other outsider would have been taboo.

What kind of an example, after all, were the club directors setting? Vittorio Pozzo, the grand old man of Italian football who had learned his tactics in England before the Great War and won two World Cups, in 1934 and 1938, with his *azzurri*, had lamented the post-war decline many years before. A new kind of director had emerged, he said, to replace the Old Guard. He had made a lot of money, very quickly. He had no background in the game, and not much real love for it. Above all, he wanted success quickly, and at almost any price.

He was unquestionably right, though whatever the affection of the Old Guard for football, they were seriously compromised by their acquiescence in Fascism. Pozzo's own militaristic approach to football was itself somewhat questionable. He was certainly an honest, decent man, but he shamelessly made use of the bombastic nationalism of the times to enforce discipline and invoke nationalism. Sometimes he could be comically hoist with his own petard, as he was over the case of the *oriundi*, the name given to players of South American birth and upbringing who held double passports as Italian citizens, and thus became eligible to play for Italy, not least in World Cups.

'If they can die for Italy,' said Pozzo dramatically, 'they can play for Italy.' Referring to the fact that *oriundi* were liable for military service. But playing was one thing, dying another. When the Abyssinian War broke out in 1936, Guaita, one of three Argentines in the Italian team which had won the World Cup two years earlier, was caught trying to sneak across the Swiss border.

Some of the old footballing dynasties remained, notably that of the powerful Agnelli family, the bosses of the FIAT motor company, and patrons of Juventus. They had held out as long as possible against the machinations of Fascism, but the end of it was that they and the newspaper they controlled, *La Stampa* of Turin, had fallen into line.

Gianni Agnelli would become one of the most powerful men in Europe, let alone Italy, after the Second World War. His love for Juventus was beyond dispute, and there was a certain feudalism in his assertion that football was a game which could 'be shared with everybody else.' Just as there was sound sense in his remark, when once I interviewed him in Turin, in 1962 for a BBC television documentary, 'If it's a business, it's a losing business.'

Sometimes President, always patron, sometimes mischievous, always committed, Agnelli was a figure of a very different stamp from the new era of *nouveaux riches* which Pozzo so deplored. All the more sad and deplorable then that his Juventus, however little he may have known about it, should allow themselves to become embroiled in the kind of chicanery practised by a relative upstart like Moratti.

But what strange Presidential figures emerged from the shadows in the post-war years! There was one, the chairman of a major Northern club, who had made his fortune in the wartime blackmarket on the Ligurian coast, chiefly in cigarettes; so much so that cigarettes themselves were endowed with his own name, so that you were asked not whether you wanted cigarettes but, 'Will you have an X?' The name of the future President.

Milan had an extraordinary Presidential succession, after the substantial publisher and film maker, Rizzoli, stood down. There was the fair-haired Riva, the son of a street sweeper who had married his rich boss's daughter. Riva's factories went bust in the 1960s, putting thousands out of work, and he fled to Lebanon, which was then a place of refuge. Then there was Felice Colombo, who was responsible for the bribery coup in a home match with Lazio which brought the whole house tumbling down about the ears of Italian football in 1980.

He it was who agreed to pay some of the Lazio players a bribe to lose a match which they would probably have lost, anyway. Unfortunately for him, when he got the cash out of a Lombard bank he did not bother to remove the wrappings, and it could not have been more easily traced. He was suspended from football, but continued blatantly to run the club for some time, just the same. After all, it was he who had the money.

'Giussy' Farina, a businessman who had transformed Lanerossi Vicenza into a major power for a short time, and then ruined them by vaingloriously outbidding mighty Juventus for their half share in Paolo Rossi, also came to

Milan. The consequences were severe. Years later, in late 1989, he and a string of Milan players were brought to trial for tax evasion. Almost all of them were heavily fined, and given suspended gaol sentences.

To pretend, however, that Italian clubs alone were involved in dubious incidents across the European years would be preposterous. The Greeks had a word for it – probably several – while in November 1984, perhaps the Viennese had one, too.

The case is interesting, in its depressing way, demonstrating once again the bizarre ineptitude of UEFA's disciplinary procedures and their extraordinary inconsistencies. The Swiss, Herr Zorzi, Chairman of the Disciplinary Committee which upheld Inter's protest against Borussia Monchengladbach in 1971, was, these 13 long seasons later, Chairman of the Appeals Committee which would rule so bizarrely in favour of Rapid Vienna. *Plus ça change*. There has been a wonderful durability about UEFA's disciplinary figures. If only durability were all!

Celtic had lost the first leg of a UEFA Cup tie, 3–1 to Rapid in Vienna. In the second leg, Rapid emerged at Celtic Park with a thoroughly aggressive stance. Tommy Burns was the chief victim, hit in the back of the head by an opposing defender, brutally kicked by the goalkeeper as he ran through. Celtic eventually came out winners by 3–0, but there was a 14-minute stoppage, when two bottles were thrown on to the field from the crowd and the Rapid left-back collapsed to the ground.

There, the mystery began. What hit him? What had happened to him? The claim was initially that a bottle had struck him. Television showed that it hadn't. The appeals committee, bizarrely, would refuse to look at the televised recording. Rapid then quickly changed their story. Indeed, the aggrieved Celtic Chairman, Desmond White, pointed out that they were permitted to change their deposition no fewer than three times. Now they asserted that their man had been hit . . . by something. Something: but what?

A coin? They can do nasty damage. A missile from a catapult, such as that which, by an irony, had apparently laid out poor Ronnie Simpson, Celtic's goalkeeper, before the start of the Intercontinental Cup game in Buenos Aires in 1967? Who could say? What *was* beyond doubt was that the injured man left Celtic Park in a bandage so huge that, in the words of Celtic's manager and former full-back, David Hay, 'It looked as if his head had been chopped off.'

Hay told me, himself, that ambulancemen who went to the left-back when he collapsed could detect no wound at all, though later Rapid would assert that he needed three stitches in his cut. This evidence was given solely by Rapid Vienna's own club doctor. True or false, it was uncorroborated evidence given by an interested party; such as would never have been accepted in any properly constituted court.

Piling Pelion upon Ossa, Herr Zorzi's appeals committee then ordered the second leg to be replayed – in Manchester. To decree a replay at all was a most dubious decision. To have it played at Old Trafford, Manchester United's ground, where police had none of the experience of their Glaswegian equivalents of dealing with the volatile Glasgow fans, was dicing with death. And so it proved.

I went to that game, and travelled on a bus full of aggressive Celtic fans rubbing finger and thumb together to indicate corruption, banging and stamping, threatening that there would be trouble if their team didn't win again.

It didn't. Alas, it played ineptly, succumbing to the only goal, scored resourcefully on the break by Peter Pacult, the centre-forward, after eighteen minutes. Three-quarters of an hour later, the police allowed a vicious Celtic fan to run on to the field and attack the Rapid goalkeeper, Herbert Feurer.

At the end of the game, another thug ran on and assaulted Pacult. Glasgow police, whose habit, as David Hay remarked, is to move round and round the ground throughout a game, rather than waiting for something to happen, wouldn't have allowed that. Manchester's finest, perfectly capable of dealing with their own kind of trouble, were taken unawares. Not only were Celtic thus eliminated from a competition in which they had previously and legitimately progressed, they were also now fined £17 000 and ordered to play their next home European game behind locked doors.

Nothing exonerates the brutal behaviour of those two fans, but if there was an accessory before the fact, it was surely UEFA.

But it wasn't the end of this horrid affair. Or unending sequence of affairs. The fact that UEFA had so often dealt so cravenly and ineffectively with suspected cases of corruption provided a kind of Cheats' Charter. Inter, after all, had got away with murder, or its metaphorical equivalent, right through the sixties. Juventus were never brought to book. The wells had been poisoned. The police often say that it isn't punishment but the possibility of detection which deters criminals. By that criterion, clubs which intended to bribe and cheat in the European competitions had little to dissuade them. And the clear corollary of that was the spread of cynicism. Matches became suspect to the knowing, or the cynical, when there may have been nothing the matter at all. As late as the 1989 European Cup Final in Barcelona, when Milan thrashed Steaua, there were whispers about the Rumanians' supposed passivity, while 1975 had of course seen a deeply contentious Final in Paris between Bayern Munich and Leeds United. Leeds had a Lorimer goal ruled out through a most debatable offside decision against Billy Bremner. They were refused a penalty when it was perfectly clear, as television and photographs would show, that Allan Clarke had been tripped by the usually immaculate Beckenbauer.

I remember Artemio Franchi – by now a man made rich by his involvement in the oil business, a bonus owed to his friends in football – telling me after the match that UEFA had awarded the French referee, Kitabdjian, only two marks out of a possible twenty. But that was where it ended. No attempt was made to dig deeper.

But then where was the spade, let alone the diggers? Botsford and I had done our best to dig, and that Football Association official had expressed the wish that we had never started. Don't make waves. Don't rock the boat. Have another drink, eat another meal, catch another jet, enjoy another good hotel. What could be done, after all, if there were these madmen going about?

$$7$$

THE CELTIC DAYLIGHT

'Jock,' cried Bill Shankly with typical hyperbole, 'you're immortal!' The place was Lisbon in May 1967, and Glasgow Celtic, managed by big Jock Stein, had just beaten Internazionale in the Final of the European Cup, the first British club to have taken the trophy.

Stein's was an extraordinary, romantic story. A centre-half of modest attainments, he spent seven unexceptional years with little Albion Rovers, 'and then I wanted away, I was discontented, I went down non-League to Wales.' To Llanelly, where he seemed to have dealt himself out of the game once and for all.

What was it that inspired Celtic to bring him back to Scotland? 'I think it was just that I had asked to get back home. They were stuck at the time for someone to see them through a sticky period. The initial thought was that I'd play among the reserves, then I managed to slip into the first team.'

To some purpose. In his third season at Parkhead, 1953/4, Stein, now captain – a role that came naturally to him – took Celtic out of the twilight, out of Rangers' shadow, to the League and Cup double. A Protestant, he had become a hero of that deeply Catholic club.

He played another three years, then an ankle injury finished his career. Now he took over Celtic's reserves, again to some purpose. Pat Crerand, who spent long hours listening to him, and Billy McNeill, a future centre-half, skipper and manager of Celtic, were among his protégés. Next Stein managed Dunfermline, and then went on to Edinburgh and Hibernian, whence he sold the veteran goalkeeper Ronnie Simpson to Celtic.

Simpson, son of a Rangers and Scotland centre-half, had actually been a 14-year-old prodigy, keeping goal for the amateurs Queens Park. Later he would be a star with Newcastle United and a star again in his late thirties with Celtic, under Stein. When Stein got to Parkhead as manager, Simpson was in the reserves. Stein put him in the first team; 'I think he takes all the credit, himself.'

Stein was an inspired Resurrection Man. Joe McBride was another player whom he rehabilitated; a failure in England at Wolves and Luton, purchased by Stein for £22 000 from Motherwell, scorer of over 40 goals a season. Bertie Auld was brought back to Celtic Park after a dull time with Birmingham as a left-winger, just before Stein himself returned. Stein made him inside-left and inspiration of the midfield. 'I think it would probably be true to say he'd been ordinary with Birmingham,' Stein said, 'but I don't think he *was* an ordinary player; even as a boy here, he wanted to play *his* way. He's a provider with us. He was bought about a month or six weeks before I came home. We went on the American tour with this in mind, and it came off. This was the purpose of the tour.' To turn Auld into a provider.

Stein's tactics could be '4–2–4, 4–3–3, but attacks coming from different positions. Any formation we play, we play with attack in mind, not defence in mind – when your forwards come through and score goals.'

In training, where Stein was always present, 'we do everything with the ball. Every function, we try to do something that'll happen in a game. We went to Milan *(this was four months before they beat Inter)* to watch Inter training, not to pick up anything tactical from them, because their game wouldn't go with us. Our players themselves take every opportunity to see every type of play. They don't just play it, they think it a bit, too. We don't do anything at all that the players don't fancy doing. They work out everything on the practice field; if anybody doesn't fancy it, we drop it.'

The obverse of that was that once anything had been decided, it must be stuck to. Thus the little, red-haired right-winger Jimmy Johnstone, a player with superb acceleration, a wonderful, classic swerve outside his full-back and fine ball control – admired by Stein 'especially against Continentals' – was dropped because, in the words of Stein, 'He was doing things he wasn't supposed to.' Once, when visiting his mother, it's said she told Stein, 'I think you're very hard on that wee fellow.'

The Celtic team played at an almost terrifying pace. It had technical skill, in the Scottish tradition, but the sheer breathtaking speed of the team showed how far the old, gradual, measured build-up of the classical Scots game had been left behind. Scottish football had been hectic for many years and would become more hectic still, but Celtic had intelligence and skill to complement their speed.

Bobby Murdoch, converted by Stein from an inside-right into a right-half – such terms were still lingeringly in use, then – was a superb passer of the ball. Billy McNeill had developed into an inspiring captain and centre-half, Tommy Gemmell was an attacking left-back with a ferocious shot. Sadly, an injury put McBride out of Celtic's team midway through the 1966/7 season, and out of their first ever attempt on the European Cup. Stein bought Willie Wallace from Hearts. There was also John Hughes, a big attacker nicknamed Yogi Bear, who could play either through the middle or on the left wing.

Zurich were Celtic's first opponents. Gemmell scored three in the two ties, one a penalty. Ladislao Kubala, the treble international, once such a great centre or inside-

Jock Stein . . . a remarkable captain, a still more remarkable manager, of Celtic, the first British side to win the European Cup
(Hulton Picture Company)

forward and now manager of the Swiss team, decided at the age of 39 that he would play in Zurich. He accomplished as little, alas, as he did when playing in the American professional soccer league the following summer.

Jimmy Johnstone proved to be in irresistible form in Nantes, when Celtic played there in the first leg of the second round; the French Press called him The Flying Flea. Two more victories, then a very tough quarter-final against Vojvodina, the Yugoslavs. Celtic lost 1–0 in Novi Sad. At Parkhead, without Auld, Stein told his team to keep pressing in the second half, for the equaliser. It came through Steve Chalmers after an hour, but it wasn't till the last minute that McNeill headed the goal which made it 2–0, following a corner.

'For me,' said John Clark, Celtic's left-half, 'that game was the hardest of the European Cup season.'

Dukla, the experienced Army team from Prague, full of battle-hardened internationals and skippered by that famous half-back Josef Masopust, were the opponents in the semi-final. Willie Wallace, playing his first European Cup game, scored twice at Parkhead in a 3–1 win, but in Prague, Stein made one of his rare tactical mistakes. He decided that defence was the order of the day, and Celtic nearly suffered for it. It was a difficult 0–0 draw, which prompted Clark to say, 'Jock asked us to play a game that was foreign to us, and I think it was the worst thing we ever did.'

Internazionale would now be met in Lisbon. It wasn't the old Inter, though a new centre-forward, Renato Cappellini, had given some life to a jaded attack. The heroes were tired. It had taken a play-off in Bologna and a goal by Cappellini, a 23-year-old Inter junior who had spent a season on loan with Genoa, to prevail against the ever stubborn CSKA Sofia. Another new face in the Inter side was that of Angelo Domenghini, the dark little right-winger – and occasional centre-forward – signed from nearby Atalanta of Bergamo, a player with a fearsome right foot.

Moreover, Inter would not even be at full strength in the Final. Luis Suarez, still the irreplaceable midfield strategist, was injured; Sandrino Mazzola wasn't fully fit. But Inter, playing their third Final in four years, impressive conquerors of Real Madrid in the quarter finals – 1–0 at San Siro, 2–0 in the Bernabeu – started as favourites.

They scored the first goal. Barely eight minutes had been played when Jim Craig, a qualified dentist who had made a solid, reliable right-back, chased a long pass by Mazzola with Cappellini and brought the centre-forward down. Simpson moved the wrong way to Mazzola's penalty.

Celtic did not repine. As Stein would say, this was an adventure for them. They'd everything to gain and nothing to lose and had, in Stein's view, the advantage of meeting Inter in a one-off game, rather than home and away. Stein was also convinced that Celtic had far the greater stamina. Inter, having scored, unwisely scuttled back into defence. Stein's tactics began to work admirably.

He had told his wingers, Lennox and Johnstone – who soon turned Tarcisio Burgnich inside-out – to move into the middle, leaving the flanks to the attacking full-backs. Mariolino Corso was playing so deep on the left flank for Inter that Bobby Murdoch had all the room and time he wanted to dictate the game.

At half-time, Stein told his men to pull the ball back across the Inter defence. Celtic resumed the second half as they had ended the first: constantly attacking. Giuliano Sarti had to make a difficult save from the explosive Tommy Gemmell, but could do nothing about the full-back's superb

Jock Stein's dream of Celtic being crowned champions of the world ended with four of his players being dismissed in a violent encounter in Montevideo against Racing Club of Argentina. Police were needed more than once to escort players from the pitch (Hulton Picture Company)

half-volley after 63 minutes. Gemmell had started the attack, Murdoch found Craig on the opposite flank, Craig gave his fellow full-back the perfect ball to run on to. A superlative goal; or an illegal one? Two Celtic men were in an offside position, but the referee decided, evidently, that they were not interfering with the play.

Sarti made a glorious one-handed save from Murdoch's close-range header, changing direction to reach the ball. 'I promise you, he'll be a great goalkeeper!' Fulvio Bernardini, once a famous centre-half, then manager of Fiorentina, had told me in Rome's Olympic Stadium 12 years earlier, after the young Sarti had played a patchy game. He was probably right.

But that hot day, there was no denying Celtic, even though they had to wait till five minutes from time for the winner. Gemmell and Murdoch were involved again; and so was a pass pulled back. Gemmell made it, Murdoch shot, Chalmers deflected the ball past Sarti. Celtic were champions.

'We had Scotsmen falling out of cupboards for weeks afterwards,' said a diplomat from the British Embassy in Lisbon, drily. By hook or by crook, thousands of Glaswegians had made their way to Portugal. Perhaps the most bizarre story concerns the two who spent a glorious evening at the match, a memorable *nuit blanche*, and flew back to Glasgow the next day; only when they reached the airport did they remember that they had driven to Lisbon by car.

It was unfortunate that five months later, Celtic should find themselves involved in a repugnant series of matches with Racing Club of Buenos Aires for the so-called world club championship. A goal headed by Billy McNeill gave Celtic the victory at Hampden. Before the return in Buenos Aires, Ronnie Simpson was knocked out by a missile from the terraces. Fearing the consequences had they withdrawn – as they had every right to do – from the game, Celtic put Fallon in goal, played it, and lost 2–1 to vicious opponents.

The ludicrous rules of the competition enacted that when each team had won a game, the play-off should take place on the territory of the one which played at home in the second leg. In fact the match was moved across the River Plate to Montevideo where Celtic, exposed to the same brutal methods, lost 1–0. Four Celtic and two Racing players were sent off. Hughes and Gemmell, provoked beyond endurance, kicked opponents; Gemmell did so behind the back of the referee when play had been stopped, but in the sight of millions of television viewers. Each Celtic player was fined £250. Each Racing player was given a new car.

It would be three years before Celtic reached the European Cup Final again. 1967/8 proved an anticlimax, as they went out in the first round to Dynamo Kiev, who beat them 2–1 in Glasgow, thanks largely to a fine performance by Bychevetz, the forward who, after the 1990 World Cup, would become Russia's team manager. His was the second goal, scored when McNeill drove the ball against him. Celtic dominated the second half, but the only goal came from Lennox, and they lost, 2–1.

In Kiev, Murdoch was sent off soon after half-time. Lennox still managed to put Celtic ahead, but away goals that season now counted as double, and there was a steep hill to climb. In the event, Bychevetz made it 1–1 in the last minute, after a brawl had erupted among the players. Celtic were eliminated. Manchester United would succeed them as champions.

Beaten 2–0 by Saint Etienne in the first leg of their first-round tie the following season, Celtic then thrashed the French champions 4–0 in Glasgow. After overcoming Red Star of Belgrade, they faced Milan in the quarterfinals and drew the first leg 0–0 at San Siro. But another error by McNeill, this time at a throw-in, enabled the predatory Pierino Prati to glide through and score the only goal of the game in Glasgow.

Season 1969/70 was more successful – till the Final itself, when Celtic would be bewilderingly inept. They did not begin the season well, and in their opening European Cup match were held to a goalless draw in Basle. The return was won 2–0; now came Benfica, and a schizophrenic tie.

In Glasgow, Celtic won 3–0. Eusebio, who forced Fallon to make two saves, was later hurt, retiring at half-time. A tremendous free-kick by Tommy Gemmell, whom Celtic had just put on the transfer list, gave Celtic the lead inside two minutes. Wallace and Harry Hood scored in the second half. It was another of Jimmy Johnstone's inspired evenings.

That should have been that; but it wasn't. In Lisbon it was Benfica who won 3–0, and Celtic prevailed on the spin of a disc. Again, Eusebio had to leave the field at half-time; otherwise Benfica might well have gone through. Eusebio had already scored a fine headed goal, and only a magnificent save by Fallon from his half-volley robbed him of another.

The elegant Graça, taking a return pass from Artur Jorge, made it 2–0, and despite the stalwart defence of McNeill and Fallon, Diamantino dived in to head a third. The disc decided.

The quarter-finals brought Italian opposition in Fiorentina. In Glasgow, the Florentine team cravenly shut up shop, though it should long since have been clear to all that the time and place to attack was in away legs, when more space would be afforded. Big John Hughes, 6ft 2in, 14 stone, the right-footed centre-forward whom Stein had converted into a left-winger, was so maltreated that he'd have to give way at half-time to Harry Hood. Not, however, before he had made a goal for Bertie Auld. Four minutes after the break, Carpenetti diverted Auld's cross past his own keeper, and when Fiorentina at last came out to play, Celtic scored from a last-minute counter-attack, from Wallace's header. Fiorentina won the return 1–0; Celtic marched on.

Now came the great British clash between Celtic and Leeds United. It was not a good moment for Leeds who, embroiled in the FA Cup, League and European Cup, had begun to look a weary team. The Saturday before they played the first leg at home to Celtic, they had fielded half their reserve team; and the whole of it when obliged, absurdly, to play a League match at Derby. Yet they would still look tired, and would gravely miss the forceful presence of their left-half, Norman Hunter.

The match at Elland Road was a triumph for one young Celtic midfielder, the tall, powerful George Connelly, who not only mastered Leeds' chief engineer, Johnny Giles, but proved highly dangerous in attack. He would score in the second minute. Big Paul Madeley, deputising for Hunter, took much of the blame. He grievously missed a ball out on the right. Connelly met the resultant cross, and the ball was deflected past Gary Sprake.

It was another dazzling game for Jimmy Johnstone, whom Leeds could never subdue. Johnstone was the perfect modern winger, using the whole of his touchline, often dropping deep to collect the ball, giving Terry Cooper, Leeds' left-back, such a torrid time that he could hardly think about overlapping. His run and pass, just after the interval, gave Connelly the chance to beat Sprake again, but the goal was contentiously refused for offside. Midway through this half, Billy Bremner, a subdued figure that evening, had to go off with concussion. Celtic's 1–0 win flattered Leeds.

Stein had the return leg moved to Hampden Park, where an incredible crowd of 136 000 watched the game. Leeds were fresh, or stale, from a drawn Cup Final against Chelsea at Wembley but they surprisingly took the lead, against the play, after 14 minutes. A fine, long drive by Billy Bremner flew in high off the post.

But with Johnstone again irrepressible, Celtic needed only a couple of minutes to equalise. David Hay, the talented right-back, pushed a short corner to Auld. 'Yogi Bear' Hughes flung himself at the cross to head a spectacular goal.

When Hughes collided with Sprake, the Leeds keeper had to leave the field, giving way to David Harvey. He had been on the field only five minutes when Celtic, playing with splendid flair and invention, got the winner. Johnstone was again the architect, making himself space with his speed and flair, pulling back a ball which Bobby Murdoch struck into the near corner. Auld, Murdoch and Connelly had dominated midfield. Celtic were strong favourites to beat Feyenoord in the Final at San Siro.

But they didn't. Might they have done so if Stein, mysteriously, had not decided to drop the excellent young Connelly and deploy a four-man attack, instead of sticking to the 4–3–3 which worked so magnificently well against Leeds? Connelly would come on only as a late substitute, for another midfield player in Auld, thus leaving the 4–2–4 formation untouched. None of this might have mattered had Jimmy Johnstone, the inspiration of the team in both matches against Leeds, not had an inexplicably subdued and ineffectual evening. With his alchemist's skill at turning the dross of an ordinary situation into the gold of a goal, Johnstone could turn any game. But though he was not up against an especially good left-back – even if Feyenoord's was a 'sweeper' defence – Johnstone remained obstinately anonymous. The virtue had mysteriously gone out of Celtic.

From the Celtic Daylight of 1967 to the Celtic Twilight, as alas it would prove, of 1970. A myth or two lay irretrievably in pieces. That of Johnstone as an irresistible destroyer, who could take apart any defence in the world – Leeds', England's. That of Celtic as the Real Madrid of the 1970s. Invincible.

Well, hardly invincible; they had lost 3–1 to Aberdeen in the Scottish Cup Final. Beforehand, Jock Stein had categorised Feyenoord's big, imposing, dominating inside-left, Wim Van Hanagem, as 'a slow Jim Baxter'. Fast Van Hanagem never was, but his superb strategy, his magnificent left foot, would make him a key player in the great Dutch Total Football teams of the 1970s, probably the best man on the field when Holland lost the 1974 World Cup Final in Munich. Van Hanagem, in the second round, had scored the goal which gave Feyenoord a 2–1 aggregate edge over Milan.

Tommy Gemmell scored first for Celtic in the 1970 Final against Feyenoord in Milan, following his equalising strike against Inter in 1967 (Hulton Picture Company)

After half an hour of a dull first half, Celtic, flattering to deceive, took the lead. Murdoch backheeled a free-kick, Gemmell smashed it home. Lo Bello, the referee, had whimsically stationed himself between the Celtic players and the Dutch wall. Only a couple of minutes later, however, Feyenoord exploited a free-kick of their own. Celtic's defence was statuesque as it was nodded back across goal and headed in by the Dutch sweeper Israel, who would have a marvellous second half.

Feyenoord, indeed, emerged as a whole team, with Hasil, the Austrian international, eclipsing even Van Hanagem in midfield. Three minutes after half-time, he hit the post. Jansen was breaking vigorously from defence; once he put through Wery, the right-winger, who should have scored. He didn't, and Celtic survived into extra time.

Football being the perverse game it is, John Hughes might have given them the lead back after just thirty seconds when he robbed an opponent, tore through in his characteristic way, and all but scored. Feyenoord, with Israel rampant, then took over again. Evan Williams, Celtic's keeper, preserved them with a fine double save early in the second period, saving Ove Kindvall's shot with his feet, and gallantly reaching Wery's drive from the rebound.

But Celtic were only hanging on. Four minutes from the end, poor Billy McNeill, so often a bulwark, was fated to err again. Moving to a long pass down the left he slipped, and handled. Kindvall ran on with the ball, as referee Tschenscher played the advantage, and beat Williams. There was still time for Hasil to strike the underside of the bar. Celtic had been well and truly overcome.

'The better team won,' said Stein, at the dressing-room door. 'We didn't play well, but that's taking something away from another team; they played well, they deserved to win. We had too many bad players, too many players off form . . . I'm not going to tear my team to bits. I know the reason we didn't play well, but I'm not going to tell you. I'll tell my players, not you.'

Poor Jock Stein. An horrific car crash in 1975, on the way back from Renfrew Airport, would cruelly sap his strength. There was an unhappy 44-day period with Leeds United, before he went back to manage Scotland, and he would die at last, pitifully, from a heart attack, sitting on the bench – where he should surely not have been – when Wales played his Scotland team in a World Cup qualifier at Cardiff.

Scotland has produced many fine managers, but Stein must rank among the very best. First as a player, then as manager and coach, he transformed the Celtic club. Where English clubs had failed in the European Cup, Celtic, in 1967, succeeded; and showed them that it could be done.

8
———

TOTAL FOOTBALL

Total Football is just a memory now; but a marvellous one. 'Football has its fashions,' a well-known French soccer journalist observed to me, happily, in Rotterdam, the day after Ajax had played Inter off the pitch, 'but this is the new reality.'

So it was. The trouble being that it didn't last for long. Cruyff and Beckenbauer. Ajax and Bayern Munich. Holland and West Germany. The 'Shoot Out at the OK Corral' coming in July 1974, in Munich's Olympic Stadium, when Cruyff and the Dutch should have crushed the West Germans out of sight after a paralysing early goal; but somehow didn't.

Franz Beckenbauer and Bayern still had a couple of European Cups to pick up after that, but by 1978, when the so-called Kaiser Franz had opted for the lush green plastic pastures of the Giants Stadium in New Jersey – where the money was real but the football wasn't – the virtue had somehow gone out of Total Football. It has left its mark, but we have sadly to realise now that those exciting, dazzling years of the early 1970s were an epoch rather than a harbinger. The New Reality was great and glorious while it lasted, but in the end, it seemed, it was the old, old story; the tactics were as good as the players you had to use them. Beckenbauer, Cruyff and co. were great footballers, with other great players around them. When they went – and Cruyff too went, refusing to play in the 1978 World Cup – who could replace them?

The true begetter of Total Football was Johan Cruyff rather than Franz Beckenbauer, but its precursor was Willy Meisl in his 1955 book, *Soccer Revolution*. A lovable, didactic, voluble Viennese, brother of Hugo Meisl the creator of the illustrious pre-war Austrian Wunderteam, Willy wrote of something he called The Whirl. Though a protégé of his at the time, I confess I was not sufficiently advanced to comprehend its possibilities. The essence of The Whirl, as it would briefly but brilliantly be of Total Football, was that anybody could do anything.

Full-backs and centre-backs would turn into attackers, surging forward with the ball, to be replaced by attackers who would effortlessly become defenders. The narrow, limited, specialised footballer would be no more. Consummate technique, unusual fitness, an alert intelligence would make the player of the future a polymath. Alas, Willy had died well before he could see his ideas put so impressively into practice.

Franz Beckenbauer, the young, precocious Bavarian, had not, I am sure, read a word of Willy's when he virtually invented the idea of the attacking sweeper. He had scarcely got into the first team of Bayern Munich – a club which would surge ahead in the 1960s, overtaking the much older and better established Munich 1860 – when he was implementing his radical ideas. Ideas which would take years to be accepted by Helmut Schoen, manager of West Germany, much as he liked and admired Beckenbauer.

Beckenbauer's inspiration was Giacinto Facchetti. On television, he had often watched the giant Facchetti thundering upfield from his position of full-back, unleashing powerful shots at goal. If a full-back could do it, Franz reasoned, then why not a sweeper, a *libero*? Heresy, almost, in those days, when the sweeper did exactly that; he swept. Stayed behind the three or four tight markers in defence, and dealt with anything which got past them.

Beckenbauer's technique, and his own elegant, adventurous play, were an immediate success at Bayern. In Amsterdam, Cruyff began moving Ajax in the same direction. Like Beckenbauer, he had been with his club since boyhood. Indeed, by giving his widowed mother a charwoman's job, Ajax had enabled his family to survive. Wiry, slender, perfectly balanced, and immensely fast over the vital first few yards, Cruyff had as forceful, dominating a personality as Beckenbauer, and a shorter fuse. Retaliation and expulsion after making his international debut against Czechoslovakia led to a long exile from the Dutch international team, but when he got back, he stayed – and transformed Holland, just as he transfored Ajax.

Cruyff was a greyhound, though he was wont to deny it. He once told me that he was no quicker than anybody else; his anticipation was such that he simply started before them. How he whirled! How he turned! How quickly he saw, sized up and exploited situations! Beckenbauer of course was a different breed of cat; advancing unexpected from his lair at the back, employing, in his earlier days, a sudden and surprising burst of speed as he approached the opposing penalty area.

That was his undoing when he played for West Germany against Italy in the semi-final of the 1970 World Cup. He was in full, glorious flight when an Italian defender chopped him down. He wasn't sent off, and Italy got away with a mere fruitless free kick. Beckenbauer hobbled through the rest of the game with his arm in a sling. That was why Italy, in extra time, won.

Cruyff could drop deep like a Hidegkuti, move out to the wings, beat defenders with ease, and serve his teammates the most delectable passes. The most brilliant goal I ever saw him score was in the World Cup game of 1974 against Brazil in Dortmund. On a rainy surface, he played the ball out to his ideal partner Johan Neeskens, Total Football incarnate, raced on to a perfect return, and scooped it into the goal without breaking stride.

The odd thing is that if you examine the half-dozen European Cup Finals the two clubs won between them, three in a row by Ajax beween 1971 and 1973, three for Bayern between 1974 and 1976, none but Ajax's victory of 1972 in Rotterdam was won with much to spare. True, Bayern did eventually annihilate Atletico Madrid in the 1974 Final, but that was in a replay, after the initial match had been drawn. Ajax's first Final, at Wembley in 1971, was a dull affair, in which they made quite a meal of despatching a mediocre Panathinaikos team, whose path to the Final had been a controversial one; not least when a French referee let them do virtually anything they pleased at home to Everton.

Bayern's victory over Saint Etienne in Glasgow in 1976 was the narrowest

Johan Cruyff, centre forward and moving spirit of the great Dutch and Ajax teams of the early 1970s, later a player and manager of Barcelona

(Hulton Picture Company)

of triumphs, and one which nearly escaped them when Dominique Rocheteau came on to play a coruscating last eight minutes for the French side. While in 1975 in Paris, Bayern beat Leeds United in the most controversial and torrid circumstances. A trip by Beckenbauer on Allan Clarke which went unpunished, a goal by Lorimer dubiously disallowed as Billy Bremner ran back from an offside position.

Yet this cannot detract from the brilliance of much of the football which was played, not least when Ajax and Bayern met each other.

Ajax were not the first Dutch club to win the European Cup. Their Rotterdam rivals, Feyenoord, had impressively accomplished that feat the previous year, 1970, when, at San Siro, they deservedly beat a Celtic team doubtfully deployed and finally outwitted, thanks not least to superb performances by the Dutch sweeper Rinus Israel and the Swedish international centre-forward Ove Kindvall. Surprisingly, Feyenoord went out in the first round of the 1970/1 competition to the little-known Rumanian team, U.T. Arad, only a few weeks after winning the World Club Championship against the ruthless Argentines, Estudiantes de la Plata. Both games against Arad were drawn, but the Rumanians won on away goals.

Managed by the very father figure of Dutch football, the authoritative and somewhat remote Rinus Michels, Ajax were that season reaching towards their zenith, but they had not reached it yet. Aarie Haan and Johan Neeskens, the propulsive force in the midfield in later seasons, were still winning their spurs. In the eventual Final at Wembley, Neeskens would play as a full-back and Haan would come on only as a substitute, though he would proceed to score a goal. Also used as a substitute in that game was the blond West German Horst Blankenburg, who would become the exciting, adventurous sweeper of the team. Vasovic, the powerful Yugoslav, was still a first-choice central defender. Beside him played the muscular Hulshoff, always a dominating figure. Swart, a clever outside-right, was still in the team, as was the striker Van Dijk.

Injury kept Johan Cruyff out of several games, but Ajax showed they could survive without him. When they drew 2–2 in the first round first leg match in Tirana against the Albanians, Nenduri, both their goals were, significantly, scored by their attacking right-back Wim Suurbier. Ruud Krol, the left-back, was just as powerful and adventurous. He would, in the latter seventies, have a new lease of life as a formidably versatile sweeper, outstanding in the 1978 World Cup tournament.

Piet Keizer, a left-winger of high skills and intelligence, ran the packed Basle defence ragged in the next round, scoring the first of three goals in the first leg in Amsterdam. In Basle itself, Cruyff at last returned, and Ajax won again. Now it was Celtic, and another three goals in Amsterdam; Cruyff got the first and Keizer the third, sandwiching one by Hulshoff straight from a free-kick after McNeill brought down Cruyff.

There was little a defensive Celtic could do with Cruyff that evening. David Hay followed him around as best he could, but it was a futile assignment. Celtic, looking the parody of a great team, did hold out till a quarter of an hour from the end. Then Neeskens knocked on a long clearance from goalkeeper Stuy, and Cruyff streaked through to score with a low drive.

By the end, he was playing ducks and drakes with Celtic, and in the last minute, dribbling by two defenders on the greasy surface, he gave Keizer an easy goal, scored with a sharp turn and a rising shot.

But this was not the great Ajax, the real Ajax, the Ajax which believed so firmly in itself and its Total Football. Now in Madrid, against Atletico, they dourly shut up shop, lost to a goal by Irureta, and could have lost by more. Cruyff and Keizer were left largely to their own devices throughout the whole match, though Cruyff did make Keizer a fine chance, which he wasted. So Ajax lost 1–0 as indeed they had to Celtic in Glasgow, a game in which their defence committed many a foul, one of which eventually led to little Jimmy Johnstone scoring the only goal of the match.

In Amsterdam, Ajax went all out to attack Atletico, the 19-year-old Johan Neeskens forceful and inspirational in midfield. Neeskens, who had joined Ajax from the Haarlem club, was an all-round athlete who excelled at baseball, enjoyed tennis, but perhaps was the most complete of all Total Footballers; one of the few who could call himself a genuine midfielder, as opposed to a wing-half or an inside-forward.

For Neeskens, as he proved time and again, not least in the 1978 World Cup when he could change in a single match from implacable stopper into incisive striker, was a complete player. Very strong, very fast, very combative, a hard tackler, a good ball player, an intelligent passer of the ball, with a dynamic right-footed shot.

Neeskens it was, surging out of defence in his characteristic way, who scored the third goal for Ajax against Atletico Madrid in Amsterdam. Piet Keizer, early on, had wiped out the deficit, but it was not until 14 minutes from time that Suurbier finally put Ajax in an overall lead.

Panathinaikos, meanwhile, had surpassed themselves, recovering from a 4-1 deficit in Belgrade against Red Star with a 3–0 victory in Athens. This was unquestionably their finest performance in the tournament, and a special satisfaction for their manager, none other than that hero of the European Cup, Ferenc Puskas. He had said, before the first game against Red Star, that Central European was still far ahead of Greek football. But dropping his experienced goalkeeper Oeconomopoulos, in favour of the young Konstantinou, he saw his team gallop home in the return. Antoniadis, the big centre-forward, scored twice and inside-left Domazos showed what an elegant, intelligent general he was.

There was plentiful passion when the Final came to Wembley, but not much football to applaud or enjoy. Panathinaikos weren't good enough seriously to challenge Ajax, and Ajax, deplorably, shut up shop in the second half. Perhaps it would have been a better game had Ajax not scored after only five minutes. Oeconomopoulos, restored to favour, would have an excellent game, but he was shaky at the start, and a statuesque defence didn't help him. Keizer made the goal, though he was carrying an injury. Boring in from the left, he crossed to the near post and Van Dijk's head flicked the ball nicely into the opposite corner.

Kapsis did his best to close-mark Johan Cruyff, and Kamaras was intermittently a sweeper, but Cruyff was for long irrepressible. Running superbly, indulging in short, deadly bursts of speed, well abetted by Van Dijk and Keizer, Cruyff was a host in himself. The sharp, diagonal ball caught Panathinaikos out time after time, and Oeconomopoulos alone kept the score down with four fine saves, two of them from Cruyff.

The music changed after half-time; very much for the worse, though matters might have been different had Kamaras taken a good chance to equalise, shortly before the break. Vlahos was the provider. Domazos never stopped prompting his team, flicking, back-heeling, but finding himself, in the second half, reduced to hopeful long balls against an Ajax defence which had little difficulty with them as they floated into the penalty box.

With two substitutions made and Van Dijk dropping virtually into

midfield, Ajax were sitting on their advantage. Rijnders, who had been so lively in midfield – and who had not long to go in the team – was one of those who went off. Haan, one of those who came on, scored, just three minutes from time, when a goal seemed most unlikely. A glorious run by Cruyff laid the basis. Haan's shot hit a defender, and was deflected past an unlucky keeper. Panathinaikos' men thus lost a bonus of £100 000 each.

Now Stefan Kovacs, the little Rumanian, took over the managership of Ajax, and the players got more of their own way; flexibility was the watchword. There was a rearguard action against Arsenal, the English champions, at Highbury, but by and large, Ajax went out excitingly for goals. The team had settled, now, into the formation we tend to remember. Haan and Neeskens playing alongside the clever, left-footed Gerrie Muhren, brother of Arnold, in midfield; Blankenburg sweeping behind Hulshoff, in defence; Van Dijk and, occasionally, the young Johnny Rep lining up in attack beside Johan Cruyff. Krol, recovered from the broken leg which made him miss the 1971 Final, resumed at left-back.

Dynamo Dresden were beaten without conceding a goal. Marseille were defeated 2–1 in France and 4–1 in Amsterdam, Cruyff scoring in both matches. Then came Arsenal, winners of the English League and Cup double. A team without frills, the Gunners had a big double spearhead in Ray Kennedy and John Radford, with a maverick star in the Londoner, Charlie George, behind them; and a strong defence with a good, brave goalkeeper in Bob Wilson.

In Amsterdam in the quarter-final first leg, Ajax overwhelmed Arsenal, yet came out with no more than a 2–1 victory. The North London side looked clumsy and naive by comparison, yet they actually went into the lead after 14 minutes. Piet Keizer, of all people, was responsible, trying to head a free-kick by the Scottish international stopper, Frank McLintock, to his own goalkeeper. The ball fell short, and Ray Kennedy scored.

Thereafter, it was the flying Bob Wilson against Cruyff and the Ajax attack. Wilson was beaten twice, each time unluckily. After 27 minutes one of his best defenders, the other centre-back Peter Simpson, deflected Muhren's shot past him. Eighteen minutes from time, when Van Dijk was

brought down, a penalty hardly seemed called for. But it was given, and Gerrie Muhren scored from it.

Arsenal had signed Alan Ball, perhaps England's salient star in the 1966 World Cup Final, but not in time for him to qualify for the European Cup. Moreover, a suspension on John Radford, incurred in a reserve game of all things, kept him and his powerful presence out of the second leg. Arsenal gambled by choosing, for the first time for six months, the expensive little Scottish right-winger Peter Marinello, so gifted, so elusive, but so fragile; and he should have scored in the first minute.

A serious mistake by Blankenburg made a glorious chance for Marinello, but Stuy was able to repel his shot, and Ajax had escaped. Now, after a quarter of an hour, George Graham, later to be Arsenal's manager, reciprocated Keizer's first-leg gift. A foolish header, intended for Bob Wilson, did not even need the intervention of an Ajax man, as it dropped tantalisingly into the net.

Ajax shut up shop. Cruyff, who had an injured foot and had needed several injections, confined his contributions to the left wing but still looked dangerous, making two fine chances on the break.

Benfica, the eternal Benfica, who had won that fabulous European Cup Final in Amsterdam ten years earlier, would be Ajax's opponents in the semi-finals. The new Benfica had a superb pair of wingers: Nene on the right; the sparkling, 18-year-old Angolan Jordao, all pace and clever footwork, on the left. In the 5–1 thrashing in Lisbon of Ajax's fellow-Dutchmen, Feyenoord, in the quarter-finals, Nene had got three of the goals; and another had gone to the indestructible Eusebio, who would now be revisiting the ground on which he had won his spurs and Puskas' shirt. The manager of Benfica was none other than Jimmy Hagan, a memorable inside-left in the refulgent England forward-line of the war years, which put so many goals past Scotland. Stanley Matthews, Raich Carter, Tommy Lawton and the polymath Denis Compton were the other four. Later Hagan, a Sheffield United player, managed West Bromwich Albion, but was largely not honoured in his own country.

Im Amsterdam, his Benfica team deployed a solid four-in-line defence,

A mistake by Arsenal's George Graham leaves his keeper Bob Wilson stranded, and Arie Haan watches the ball heading for the net. Ajax, a goal up from the first leg, won this quarter-final second leg at Highbury 1–0, and went on to retain the Cup, beating Inter in the Final (Hulton Picture Company)

kept Ajax out for most of the game, and succumbed in the event to a single goal by the right-winger Swart, headed from a free kick. In Lisbon, neither team could score. Thus it was Ajax who went on to meet Inter in the Final in Rotterdam.

It was an Inter team as fearful as that which met Celtic five years earlier in Lisbon. Oriali, the solidly built defender, had shadowed Jimmy Johnstone with success in the semi-final in Glasgow, where Inter had dished Celtic only on penalty kicks after two 0–0 draws. Now he had to mark Cruyff. Ajax flowed beautifully up to the penalty area. Thereafter, it wasn't easy to score.

Perhaps Ajax would not have scored at all had Vieri been fit to play in goal, rather than the young Bordon, who was suspect on both the crosses which eventually brought goals. In the first half, Ajax switched with fluent, practised ease, with Ruud Krol, nominally the left-back, just as likely to pop up at outside-right – whence he struck a post in the first half. Inter kept Mazzola doggedly deep, left Roberto Boninsegna up front on his own – two heroes, these, of the World Cup Final a couple of years earlier – and simply hung on. A task made all the more difficult when after only 12 minutes Mario Giubertoni, victim of a displeasing foul, had to go off, giving way to the squat Bertini, and thus depriving the Inter defence of much-needed height.

A most agile save by Bordon, from a deflected shot, kept Inter in the match, but after half-time, goals came for Ajax. The crucial first was a disaster for Bordon and Oriali, who collided as both went for a cross from the right by the ever-overlapping Wim Suurbier. The ball ran loose and Cruyff scored the easiest goal he would ever get in the European Cup.

Inter still showed signs of life, notably when one rousing move, begun by Frustalupi and carried on by the lively substitute Pellizzaro, ended when Stuy dived at Mazzola's advancing feet. But Cruyff rose powerfully and untypically to head the second Ajax goal from Keizer's free-kick. Three splendid saves by Bordon kept it to 2–0. Total Football had totally eclipsed *catenaccio*.

The 1973 Final would again see Ajax overcoming bleak Italian opposition, though this time it would be Juventus in Belgrade.

That was a thoroughly forgettable Final. Johnny Rep headed the only goal early on, from a long high centre from the left by Horst Blankenburg. The rest was largely tedium. The 'real' Final, you might say, took place in the quarter-finals, when Ajax met Bayern Munich. The two exhilarating Total Football teams locked in battle, and Ajax had immensely the better of the argument, thrashing Bayern 4–0 in Amsterdam, losing only 2–1 in Munich. It was to be Johan Cruyff's last European Cup tournament with Ajax, and he played superbly; his loss, when he followed his old manager Rinus Michels to Barcelona the following season, proved quite irreplaceable.

There could scarcely have been a greater compliment to Total Football and the clubs which played it than the fact that a group of English team managers actually chartered an aeroplane to watch the first leg in Amsterdam; men who usually would not be seen dead even at a World Cup. Cruyff, in particular, did not disappoint them. He was on one of his most inspired and irresistible days – wholly overshadowing Franz Beckenbauer – and was the true inspiration of Ajax's easy success.

Bayern did, in fact, manage to resist for the best part of an hour but Gerd Muller, their prolific centre-forward, was not wholly fit, and it was a day on which their usually secure goalkeeper, Sepp Maier, with his big gloves, proved fallible. Aarie Haan, of the ferocious right foot, scored twice; Gerrie

Muhren and Cruyff himself added further goals, and the second leg became a formality.

Ajax did not even need Cruyff to survive it. He had an injured knee at the time, but he was at odds with the club – a recurrent theme in his brilliant but turbulent career – and there were those in the team who thought he could have played had he wanted to. Piet Keizer scored an early goal to put the tie far out of Bayern's reach, and although Gerd Muller replied twice for Bayern, it was irrelevant. Ajax were the champions of Total Football.

Next they accounted for Real Madrid, though neither game was as one-sided as the home quarter-final against Bayern. Ajax won first in Amsterdam by only 2-1, with their defenders Barry Hulshoff and Ruud Krol scoring; Real's reply came, as it so often did, from the indomitable Pirri. Ajax then won in Madrid with a goal by Gerrie Muhren, who like a famous left-half before him, Jim Baxter of Scotland, rubbed in his team's superiority by playing 'keepy-uppy' with the ball at one late stage of the game.

Cruyff now took off for further fame and fortune in Barcelona, a club to which he would eventually return as manager, while Franz Beckenbauer was guiding West Germany to the World Cup. When the cat's away, the mice do play. Large, combative mice, in the case of Beckenbauer's Bayern, but unlikely to have flourished as they did had Johan Cruyff stayed with Ajax.

We may safely say, I think, with hindsight to guide us, that Bayern were second best to Ajax even if in 1974 Beckenbauer had his massive revenge on Cruyff when West Germany, after falling behind in the World Cup Final in barely a minute, recovered to win it 2-1. In Munich, mind you.

In the Bayern side, tremendous talent flowed and surged around its maestro Beckenbauer. There was Paul Breitner, for example, who disliked him. The old, traditionalist Germany confronting the new and rebellious. Beckenbauer was to the Right in his politics, an admirer of the bombastic Franz Josef Strauss. Breitner, woolly-haired, moustached, the very embodiment of youthful dissidence, was at times described as a Maoist, which was almost certainly inaccurate. But he was unquestionably at that time well to the Left, with ambitions, when he retired, to set up a home for disadvantaged children from all over the world. I do not think this ambition was ever fulfilled, but Paul Breitner did adopt a Vietnamese orphan, and remained to the last – in journalism as on the football field – an unrepentant maverick. He is said to have walked out of the celebrations which followed the national side's great victory in the 1974 World Cup Final, insisting he did not want to play for such a *scheiss verein*, which might politely be translated as 'crap team'.

As an attacking left-back, he was wonderfully well adapted to Total Football, whizzing down the flank with force and speed, unleashing tremendous shots. One such gave West Germany a difficult victory over Chile in their opening game of the 1974 World Cup in Berlin, and another broke the deadlock in a second-round match against Yugoslavia. It was Breitner, too, who equalised from the penalty spot against Holland in the Final. Later, joining Real Madrid, he would become a midfield player, and would score the West German goal in Madrid itself in the World Cup Final of 1982, though by then he had long since returned to Germany to play first for Eintracht Brunswick and then once more for Bayern. He had sworn in 1974 never to play for his country again, but he was persuaded to change his mind.

Gerd Muller, Der Bomber, was an astonishing centre-forward. At a time

Six Bayern Munich players starred in Total Football's showdown, the West Germany–Holland World Cup Final in 1974. From left: Bayern's Uli Hoeness, Paul Breitner, Franz Beckenbauer and Gerd Muller are joined by Berti Vogts (2) and Wolfgang Overath (far right) as they celebrate Muller's winning goal (Allsport)

when defences were supposed to have never been so hard to crack, he simply could not stop scoring. Sixty-nine goals in 62 games for West Germany was a record to defy belief. He, too, swore to retire – and did retire – from international football after the World Cup Final, in which of course he scored the winning goal.

Squat, dark, heavy in the thighs, Muller was underrated almost from the first. Two clubs turned him down when he was playing for his local team, Noerdlingen, and the then president of Bayern had to overrule his manager, the former Yugoslav star Zlatko Cjaicowski, to make him sign Muller. So much for directors being amateurs who know nothing about football.

Muller showed at once that he could make goals out of nothing, take chances where none appeared to exist. His goals were remarkable; volleyed in from close range, flicked in with a twist of the head from an unpromising position, swept home as low crosses came into the box which defenders might be favoured to reach. Left foot, right foot, head, it made no difference. In the ball went.

Little, blond Uli Hoeness, who would later become Bayern's general manager, was a richly gifted right-winger with pace, flair and ball control, who would develop into a midfield man. Georg Schwarzenbeck was a big blond centre-half ready to come forward, at times like some great cannon, to fire shots, one of which scored the vital nail-biting equaliser in the European Cup Final of 1974. Sepp Maier authoritatively kept goal.

Ajax without Cruyff now waned. George Knobel, the new manager, eventually lost patience with an intransigent team, and was sacked. CSKA Sofia, well beaten by Ajax the previous season, put them out in the second round, though things might have been different had that clever little centre-forward, Jan Mulder, bought from Belgium to replace Cruyff, not missed a penalty in Amsterdam. So Ajax won by only 1–0, and in Sofia they succumbed in extra time.

Bayern's path to the 1974 Final was quite a thorny one; not least in the very first round when the Swedes, Atvidaberg, gave them a nasty fright. A worse one still for the unlucky Paul Breitner, whose leg was broken in the away game by a missile flung from the crowd. Bayern had won 3–1 in

◄ A proud moment for Manchester United and their manager Matt Busby (front row, centre) as the European Cup is displayed at Old Trafford in 1968. Beaten semi-finalists three times under Busby, United finally captured the trophy at the fourth attempt (Hulton)

▼ Tommy Gemmell's free-kick puts Celtic in front against Feyenoord in the 1970 Final at Milan's San Siro stadium, but the Dutch champions came back to win in extra time (Syndication International)

▲ *Ajax were comfortable winners in the 1972 Final, 2–0 against Inter in Rotterdam. Here Arie Haan skips past a challenge from the grounded Sandro Mazzola watched by (left to right) his team-mate Johan Neeskens and Inter's Bedin and Facchetti (Syndication International)*

▶ *Franz Beckenbauer – Der Kaiser – looks typically at ease as he starts to move forward for Bayern Munich in the 1976 Final at Hampden Park. Bayern completed a hat-trick of European Cup triumphs with a 1–0 win over the French champions Saint Etienne (Syndication International)*

◄ *Ian Bowyer's header in Cologne completes a remarkable comeback for Nottingham Forest in their 1979 semi-final tie (Bob Thomas)*

▶ *In the first leg, on a muddy pitch at the City Ground, Forest had quickly found themselves two goals down to the German champions, but fought back to draw 3–3, despite losing the inspirational Archie Gemmill, pictured here, through injury (Syndication International)*

▼ *Trevor Francis celebrates after heading what proved to be the only goal of the 1979 Final between Forest and Malmo (Bob Thomas)*

▲ *John Robertson, whose cross from the left wing had set up the winning goal in 1979, strikes a right-foot shot from the edge of the area to give Forest the lead in the 1980 Final in Madrid. The holders survived a second-half onslaught from Hamburg and Kevin Keegan (far left) to retain the Cup (ASP)*

▲ *Aston Villa line up before the 1982 Final in Rotterdam. Few expected them to prevail against their much-fancied opponents, Bayern Munich (ASP)*

▲ *Villa's dangerman Tony Morley is brought down by Bayern's Wolfgang Kraus (Bob Thomas)*

▶ *Karl-Heinz Rummenigge volleys towards goal despite the attentions of Villa's Des Bremner (Bob Thomas)*

▲ *Jubilant Villa players celebrate Peter Withe's winning goal, scored from close range after a fine run by Morley (Bob Thomas)*

▼ *Heroes of Rotterdam . . . goalscorer Peter Withe and substitute keeper Nigel Spink, a first-half replacement for the injured Jimmy Rimmer (ASP)*

▼ *Dennis Mortimer holds the European Cup aloft. Villa's was the sixth consecutive English success (ASP)*

Jimmy Case, Emlyn Hughes and Phil Neal (above, left to right) celebrate Liverpool's thrilling 3–1 victory over Borussia Mönchengladbach in the 1977 Final in Rome. Neal scored Liverpool's third goal, a penalty (Bob Thomas)

Seven years later, Neal and Liverpool were back at the Olympic Stadium for their fourth European Cup Final, against Roma, and another goal from Neal (above) gave Liverpool an early lead (ASP)

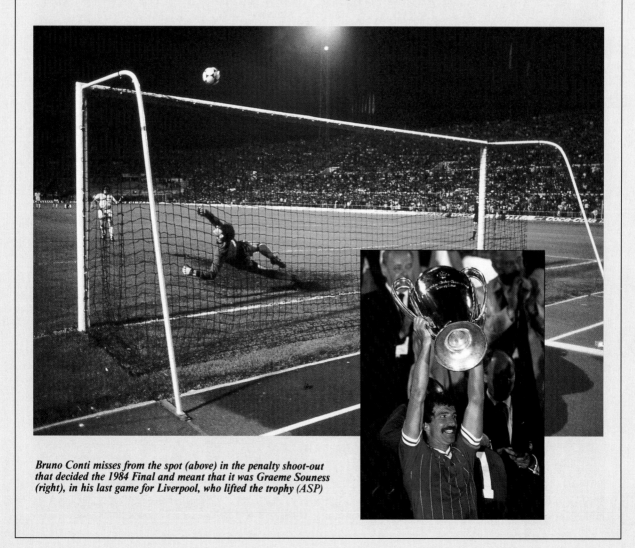

Bruno Conti misses from the spot (above) in the penalty shoot-out that decided the 1984 Final and meant that it was Graeme Souness (right), in his last game for Liverpool, who lifted the trophy (ASP)

▼ *Milan's reign as Champions of Europe ended in shame and confusion at Marseille. A T-shirted Gullit leads the protests after the partial floodlight failure at the Stade Velodrome (Allsport/Simon Bruty)*

◄ *Milan's Dutch trio, the spearhead of their European Cup success in the late 1980s. Left to right: Marco Van Basten, Franck Rijkaard, Ruud Gullit (Allsport/Simon Bruty)*

▼ *Gullit opens the scoring for Milan in the 1989 Final against Steaua Bucharest. He and Van Basten shared the goals in a 4–0 win that was as convincing as the scoreline suggests (Allsport/Simon Bruty)*

▶ *Benfica have twice reached the European Cup Final in recent years without ever living up to the standards set by the great Benfica sides of the past. Here Rui Águas (red shirt) challenges PSV Eindhoven's Ronald Koeman during the uninspiring 1988 Final in Stuttgart, won on penalties by the Dutch champions after a goalless match*
(Bob Thomas)

◀ *Real Madrid's European Cup campaigns in the eighties were a constant source of frustration to the club. The last of three successive semi-final defeats came against Milan in 1989, with the first leg in Madrid drawn 1–1. Here Milan's Rijkaard is shadowed by Real's highly effective striking partnership of Hugo Sanchez (9) and Emilio Butragueño*
(Bob Thomas)

Munich, but now they lost 3–1, two of the goals going to the lively Swedish attacker, Torstensson.

Bayern, prevailing on penalty kicks, proceeded to sign him and, the rules of the tournament being what they then were, deployed him with great success from the quarter-finals onwards. He scored twice in Munich in the 4–1 defeat of CSKA – a game in which Beckenbauer got one of his rare goals – and was a decisive factor in the conquest of Ujpest in the semi-finals. He scored for Bayern in a 1–1 draw in Budapest, then got the first in a 3–1 win in Munich, the other two going to Muller.

The Final, in Brussels, would be against Atletico Madrid, managed by the ever-controversial Juan Carlos Lorenzo. Eight years earlier Lorenzo, who had played as an inside-right in France and Italy, had taken an abrasive Argentina to the quarter-finals of the World Cup at Wembley, eliciting Alf Ramsey's famous 'act as animals' phrase. When Arsenal's team were attacked by Lazio players in Rome, Lorenzo, then Lazio's manager, was greatly involved.

But in the European Cup, Atletico kept surprising people, when they were not kicking them. Their away form was formidable, not least in the Balkans. They beat Dynamo 2–0 in Bucharest, then drew 2–2 with them at home. They beat the powerful Red Star team, conquerors of Liverpool, 2–0 in Belgrade, although without their most dangerous attacker, the long-haired, thick-thighed, explosively quick Argentine, Ruben Ayala. In Belgrade, the first goal was scored for them by Luis Aragones, an inside-right of great intelligence and quality, who would later become their manager. Once more, a draw in Madrid followed.

Then came a visit to Glasgow to meet Celtic, a team rebuilding at the time, though it included the young Kenny Dalglish. Atletico disgraced themselves, had three men sent off, yet survived to a 0–0 draw. Ayala was one of the three, a mere hatchet man for the evening. Diaz and Quique were the other two, Babacan the courageous Turkish referee who expelled them all. One of the three players even attacked Jimmy Johnstone, Celtic's outside-right, as he came off at the final whistle. Not only these three but also three who were cautioned were suspended from the next game.

Jock Stein, Celtic's manager, was incensed when UEFA decided the second leg should go ahead in Madrid, though at least Johnstone would not have to come up against Diaz yet a third time. The first was when Celtic played their ferocious series of Intercontinental Cup matches against Racing Club of Buenos Aires. Johnstone, at half-time in the play-off in Montevideo, had had to wash the spittle out of his hair.

Fierce hostility was in the air, both inside and outside the stadium, in Madrid; and Celtic seemed, perhaps predictably, a prey to it. In the closing minutes, Garate drove in a cross from Irureta; Adelardo cleverly lobbed a second.

Even now, the first Final in Brussels is hard to reconcile with the replay. A 1–1 draw, in which Schwarzenbeck just managed to pull Bayern's chestnuts out of the fire, was followed by four Bayern goals and a veritable cakewalk.

Schizophrenia of a sort; as was the behaviour, impeccable in the first Final, of the Atletico team. They showed they'd no need to resort to skulduggery to contain an attack even as formidable as Bayern's, though perhaps they paid the penalty for having two men watch Muller; Hoeness had rather too much room in consequence.

The match went to extra time, when it looked as if Bayern's superior stamina might be decisive. But with only six minutes left, Luis curled an inspired free-kick past Maier, and suddenly Bayern were fighting for their lives. It was with almost the last kick of the match that Schwarzenbeck, thundering upfield, shot from 30 yards, beat Reina, and equalised.

Two days, later the teams met again. Bayern decided to be bolder, and found the Atletico defence porous to a degree. Hoeness and Muller did much as they pleased. Hoeness should have scored when Muller – who said he only scored goals, never made them? – skilfully put him through, but the shot flew high over. Muller headed against the bar, but a goal could not be long delayed. It came when Breitner, his shin quite healed, sent Hoeness through alone a second time, and this time the blond striker shot neatly through Reina's legs.

With Adelardo hurt and substituted, Atletico collapsed in the second half. Muller crashed home Kappelmann's centre from the left; then, perceiving Zobel's pass, he beat the keeper with a perfect lob. Hoeness, when Melo slipped, raced by him, evaded a tackle, took the ball wide of Reina, and put the ball in the net. Over the victory Franz Beckenbauer had presided with tremendous aplomb, strategy and skill.

The 1975 Final, at the Parc des Princes, would be far more controversial, and provoke the violence off the field, at least, which did not occur in Brussels. Leeds United would be Bayern's opponents in Paris and both clubs changed managers that season. Leeds were first, after Brian Clough's disastrous 44 days in charge, of which there is more, elsewhere. Jimmy Armfield, the calm, pipe-smoking former Blackpool and England right-back, ex-manager of Bolton Wanderers, succeeded him. He was criticised by some for his alleged indecisiveness, but he got Leeds to the Final at the expense of Cruyff and Barcelona. Don Revie, the true builder of the Leeds team, had never done as much, though Leeds, in 1973, had reached the Cup Winners' Cup Final in Salonika – to be cheated by abominable refereeing. To some, it looked as if they were cheated in Paris, too.

Udo Lattek, a shrewd, urbane, resourceful manager, had guided Bayern to their recent triumphs, but now he left to his successor a disintegrating, weary team. Paul Breitner took off for Madrid; the other heroes were tired. Too many hard games for club and country, with the addition of friendlies which should not have been arranged.

To take Lattek's place, the tiny Dettmar Cramer was recalled from America, to the fury of the Americans, whose national coach he was. Cramer had been West Germany's assistant team manager in the 1970 World Cup, and previously had travelled the world for FIFA, being much respected in Japan.

Leeds, under Don Revie's inspirational, driven, obsessional leadership, had soared from the depths of the Second Division to the height of the First. Initially their functional kind of football had made few friends. They chivvied referees, they put it about, as the saying goes, and while they did not exactly bend the rules, they tended to stretch them as far as they could go. But as time went by the team matured; they had a remarkable midfield duo of little men in Billy Bremner of Scotland and Johnny Giles of Ireland, and passed the ball about with supreme skill, turning into far and away the most successful side a previously mediocre club had ever had.

There was Peter Lorimer, the Scottish right-winger with the hardest right-footed shot in the game; Eddie Gray, a gloriously fluent and graceful left-winger; his younger brother Frankie, whom Armfield perceptively turned from a reserve left-winger into an exciting, attacking left-back. Jackie Charlton had been persuaded by Revie to take the game more seriously, and in consequence had developed into a dominating centre-half, winning a World Cup medal with England, no longer overshadowed by his own younger brother, the incomparable Bobby, 'Our Kid'.

Barcelona, whom Cruyff had taken to their first championship for many years in 1974, found life harder now. Cruyff was getting less respectful treatment from rough Spanish defenders. Johan Neeskens arrived from Ajax but didn't make the difference which was expected. His inclusion meant that the Peruvian forward Sotil, with whom Cruyff had played so successfully the previous season, had to drop out. Neither did finding most dubious Spanish nationality for Heredia from Argentina and the little stopper Marinho from Brazil do the trick.

Leeds accounted for Barcelona in the semi-final, after reaching it in impressive style. Zurich, Ujpest and Anderlecht were beaten, with the big, blond Scottish international centre-half Gordon McQueen turning up time and again to score decisive goals. In the first leg of the semi-final, at Elland Road, Leeds won a tight game 2–1. Jimmy Armfield surely gambled by leaving out two of his most talented attackers, Peter Lorimer and Duncan McKenzie, a highly talented centre-forward who'd matured with Nottingham Forest but had never fully been accepted by the compact Leeds team.

After 10 minutes, Leeds worked a free-kick to score. Johnny Giles took it from the left, Joe Jordan, the big Scottish centre-forward, flicked it on and his fellow Scot Billy Bremner found himself strangely unmarked, with all the time he needed to line up his shot and score. When Eddie Gray left De La Cruz standing and crossed, Jordan's shot was gloriously saved by Sarduni. So Barcelona were able to equalise, 19 minutes into the second half. Cruyff rolled a free kick to the diligent midfielder Asensi, who shot low through the wall.

Leeds, who should have had the game won by then, had run out of steam. But after 77 minutes, Paul Reaney, always an adventurous right-back, flew down the wing, crossed after beating a man, and Allan Clarke – nicknamed Sniffer for his prowess in the penalty area – made it 2–1.

Would it be enough? It was, thanks above all to a seventh-minute goal by Peter Lorimer, properly back in the side. A long clearance by the keeper Stewart, a back header by Jordan, a fulminating drive from Lorimer's famous right foot, and Leeds were ahead. Until half-time, they were calmly in control of the game.

Afterwards, things changed, partly because Barcelona began, in the vernacular, to dish it out, and partly because the Catalans made tactical changes. Marinho, who had been wasting his time at sweeper, was pushed up, and Rife was brought on for Asensi. Barcelona now abandoned their tactic of high, hopeful crosses, of little use against such a dominating figure as McQueen – though he was not destined to finish the match.

Brutally elbowed by the centre-back Migueli, Joe Jordan had to have four stitches in his cheek; Neeskens was at his most aggressive, Gallego was booked for a savage foul on Bremner, the Scottish terrier. Heredia, just before Barcelona equalised, kicked the Welsh international Terry Yorath with impunity.

After 68 minutes, Gallego took a free-kick from the right, and Clares neatly headed the equaliser. Glorious saves by Stewart from Heredia and Cruyff – twice – preserved the draw, and ultimate qualification, for Leeds. For the last 25 minutes, they had to play without McQueen who, in a moment of wild aberration, felled Clares and was properly sent off.

The scene in the Press interview room afterwards resembled that on the field in chaos and animosity. Not often do you see the correspondent of *L'Equipe* being led away in chains by police, but that was what happened to Robert Vergne after he lost his temper with a provocative Spanish radio reporter as wildly as had McQueen.

Bayern awaited them in the Final. The holders had reached it without ever showing the majestic form of previous seasons. The second round found them drawn against the East German champions, Magdeburg, who the previous season had become the first team from their country to win a major European trophy – the Cup Winners' Cup, in whose Final they had beaten the 1973 winners, Milan.

Jurgen Sparwasser, the East Germans' inside-right, was the man who had scored a spectacular goal which had beaten West Germany in Hamburg in the 1974 World Cup, just four months previously. He would score in both legs, but only once. Muller, in all, got five, and Bayern went through.

In the quarter-finals, Bayern knocked out Ararat Erevan, the Soviet champions from Armenia, winning 2–0 at home, losing 1–0 away. Saint Etienne, the French champions, whom they'd meet in the 1976 Final, came next; a goalless draw in France, a 2–0 win in Munich which looked better on paper than it did in actuality. So to the Final, and Leeds.

Bayern won again, but in highly contentious circumstances. The Leeds United fans' notoriety had gone before them. The Parc des Princes, with its deceptively green, appalling pitch, was ringed by French riot police in blue tracksuits. When the Leeds fans, exasperated by the refereeing decisions against them, found a new use for their seats by tearing them up and throwing missiles, the special police had no answer. They did, however, converge bravely in large numbers on a solitary Leeds fan who got over the barrier, dragging him painfully and sadistically across the ground, before carting him away.

Bayern showed little initiative and Beckenbauer himself might well have given away a couple of penalties in the first half. Neither was awarded by an inept referee, the Frenchman Kitabdjian; perhaps he felt to penalise Der Kaiser would be a matter of *lèse-majesté*. First, the Bayern captain handled the ball to stop Peter Lorimer breaking through. Later, he palpably tripped up Allan Clarke, as the striker moved in on goal. No penalties.

Leeds lost friends early in the game when, after M. Kitabdjian had blown for a foul against Frankie Gray, Terry Yorath severely fouled Andersson, Bayern's defender, who had to leave the field. Uli Hoeness was hurt, too, tackling Frankie Gray, and also had to be substituted. It took Bayern half an hour, said Dettmar Cramer afterwards, to digest these changes.

Bayern owed much that night to the inspired goalkeeping of Sepp Maier. Diving to catch Joe Jordan's right-foot shot in the first half, stopping Bremner's point-blank drive in the second, he kept Bayern in the game. And so did M. Kitabdjian, after 67 minutes. A free-kick by Giles, a header by the versatile, powerful Paul Madeley, a header out, a fulminating volley home by Lorimer. The referee disallowed the goal; for offside, he said, 'against three players'. In fact the only Leeds man in an offside position was Billy Bremner, haring back out of the box to put himself onside. Could it truly be said that he was interfering with play?

Now the Leeds fans behind that goal went berserk, breaking up the seats, bombarding quite innocent people. A ball boy and a policeman were knocked out, a photographer blinded in one eye, Sepp Maier was put under siege.

Five minutes later, Bayern scored the first of two excellent goals. The muscular Roth, only just restored to the team, got the first, a low left-foot shot into the right-hand corner, after Muller and a previously anonymous Torstensson had done the spade-work. Muller, the inevitable Muller, then swept the ball in for Bayern's second with a typical right-footed shot, after Kappelmann's clever work on the goal line.

UEFA gave Kitabdjian 2 marks out of a possible 20 but did nothing more. Leeds United had a three-year ban imposed on them.

Coming into the dressing-room at the end, the Leeds players bitterly tossed their runners-up medals aside. Jimmy Armfield started trying to console them, then stopped, realising there was nothing useful to say. Leeds had been cheated again, just as they had been two years earlier in Salonika, and they knew it.

The following season's European Cup would be still richer in contro-

A jubilant Franz Beckenbauer lifts the European Cup after Bayern, defending for much of the game, had overcome Leeds United at Parc des Princes, Paris, in 1975 (Hulton Picture Company)

versy. Malmo, the Swedish champions, protested to UEFA, enraged by two bizarre goals scored against them by Bayern in Munich, in the second round. They insisted that Stanev, the Bulgarian referee, had received expensive gifts before the game. UEFA, doing their familiar Three Wise Monkeys act, reported that Stanev had been given only a banner and a beer mug. Plainly he was not one of those referees inside whose beer mug nestled an expensive gold watch; a well-established stratagem.

Bayern had been finding it hard to break through the Malmo defence till, in the second half, the winger Kappelmann, pursuing a pass from Beckenbauer, came down in theatrical style to gain what looked like a non-existent penalty. Deprived of both Gerd Muller, who had needed an operation on his torn muscle, and Uli Hoeness, with knee problems, Bayern were struggling to score goals. By way of compensation, the blond young winger Karl-Heinz Rummenigge, intensively coached and cajoled by Dettmar Cramer, was impressively making his mark.

Real Madrid, who now had the talented West German inside-left Gunter Netzer, with his flowing blond mane, in their team, were also under suspicion. Odd and sometimes vicious things went on that season at the Bernabeu, not least when West German teams were playing there. The refereeing of the Dutchman Van der Kroft provoked an angry protest by Borussia Mönchengladbach who thought with some justification that they had two perfectly good goals disallowed in Madrid. The result was a 1–1 draw, and since Real had drawn the away leg 2–2, they survived.

Bayern, who had come imposingly back to form in the second leg of the quarter-finals, when Benfica were thrashed 5–1 in Munich – two each for Muller and the incisive Durnberger – were seriously maltreated at the Bernabeu in the first leg of the semi-final. They drew it 1–1 and Gerd Muller, their scorer, was knocked out when Real's fans attacked both him and the

Austrian referee Herr Linnemayr, at the end.

Paul Breitner, who had missed the first leg, played against his old club in the return and was predictably barracked. Gerd Muller scored twice and Bayern were through to the Glaswegian Final, to play the attractive French team Saint Etienne.

Though the greatly gifted right-winger Dominique Rocheteau was still recovering from a thigh injury, Saint Etienne had abundant talent. Osvaldo Piazza, the Argentine centre-half, was adept at joining the attack – though Liverpool's captain Emlyn Hughes would subsequently dismiss him as 'just a big bully, in to kick Toshy', meaning John Toshack. Dominique Bathenay was an exuberant midfielder, Hervé Revelli a resourceful and incisive centre-forward. Bayern had two of their own men under par; Franz Roth was suffering from a skin rash, winger Jupp Kappelmann had an abscess on a tooth.

It was an exciting Final, full of lively incident, which might have gone either way, and was notable for the electric brilliance of Rocheteau when Saint Etienne at last put him on, for the concluding eight minutes. Twice in the first half the French team hit the bar, once with a drive by Bathenay, bursting through the German defence, once through a header by Jacques Santini.

Bayern themselves were often dangerous, and Yvan Curkovic, the Yugo-slav keeper, had to make a remarkable save from Rummenigge, set up by the ever-adventurous centre-back Georg Schwarzenbeck, who went outside two men before he crossed. There was Total Football for you.

After 57 minutes, Bayern scored; and it was Franz Roth, so often their marksman, who got it. A free-kick just outside the box, Roth moving in, a ferocious right-footed shot, and the ball had flashed past Curkovic. Even when Rocheteau had come on to torment the Bayern defence, Roth broke away to run half the length of the field, only for his shot to be kept out by another remarkable save by Curkovic. Rocheteau struck again, Sepp Maier dived to save from Patrick Revelli, Hervé's younger brother, and Bayern had won the European Cup for the third successive time.

Now the pendulum would swing. Now, at last, it would be Liverpool's turn.

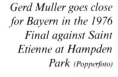

Gerd Muller goes close for Bayern in the 1976 Final against Saint Etienne at Hampden Park (Popperfoto)

9

LIVERPOOL – AND HEYSEL

Bill Shankly made Liverpool what they were, and what they are. There is no gainsaying that. When that extraordinary, ebullient, cantankerous Scotsman arrived at Anfield, the club had subsided into mediocrity. It had won the long-drawn-out Championship of 1947, the first post-war Championship, with the impressive likes of Billy Liddell, Bert Stubbins, Jack Balmer. It had contested and lost the 1950 FA Cup Final to Arsenal, and might have won it had Billy Liddell not been harshly fouled. But by the time the extraordinary 'Shanks' arrived from Huddersfield Town, such times were but a memory. His appointment was, as they say, inspired. With his sublime eccentricities and his inspired tunnel-vision, he would turn Liverpool into a great team, a great club. Which they still, emphatically, are.

Something about Shankly. A fine player first, a right-half of true quality, long before he ever was a manager. He played in the first professional match I ever saw, England v Scotland at Wembley in January 1942. A frosted ground, Mrs Churchill inspecting the teams, then rushing off to meet her husband, just returned from seeing Stalin in Moscow. Stalin then as hero, not as mass murderer. At left-half for Scotland was Matt Busby. But Scotland subsided; England walked all over them, 3–0.

Shankly began with the Glenbuck Cherrypickers, or rather – to kill the legend – he had a trial with them when he was 16, whereupon they went into extinction. A team called Cronberry was his first, then it was across the border to Carlisle United. Stocky and blond, a great loser of money at cards, Shankly was a Preston North End star by the time the war came. The incomparable Peter Doherty, greatest of Irish inside-lefts, remembers playing against him with deep frustration while Shankly kept muttering, throughout, 'Great wee team, North End, great wee team!' He won an FA Cup medal with them in 1938, the match won by a last-minute penalty from George Mutch, in off the crossbar.

Tom Finney was his idol. 'He could wriggle out through the eye of a needle.' After the war, and service in the RAF, rather than down the mines where he'd been working, Shankly resumed with Preston. At 35, still playing, he became manager of another of his clubs, Carlisle United, at £14 a week. Then on to Huddersfield.

Anecdotes about Shankly, some apocryphal, abound. At Huddersfield one day, coming back from a training session to the stadium, he detailed nine players to come with him. 'Right! You five, white shirts: England! Us five, blue shirts: Scotland!' The flower in Huddersfield's buttonhole at that time was the very young left-winger, Mike O'Grady. Shanks played for 'Scotland'. O'Grady glided past him twice, and scored. The third time it happened, Shankly hacked him down. 'Do that again, and I'll break yer bloody leg!'

Chestnuts, now, some of his aphorisms. 'Some people think football's a matter of life and death. But it's more important than that.' Sublime mono-maniac! Once at Anfield, he hustled a tabloid reporter who had been critical of Liverpool into the lavatory. What would happen next? 'We should have beaten Arsenal ten!' said Shanks.

To the same reporter, Frank McGhee, he once said of his centre-half, 'Ron Yeats! He's a colossus! Six foot two, 14 stone, and there's no' an ounce of superfluous flesh on him! You can see for yourself! You can see *noo*! He'll be stripped!'

On the bus, the team bus, up to Hampden, on the way to the 1966 European Cup Winners' Cup Final against Borussia Dortmund. I am sitting behind Shanks. He is trying to persuade me that Liverpool have not lost a game all season. 'We've won the League: so we've no' lost a game in the League! And we're in the Cup Winners' Cup Final: so we've no' lost a game in that!' Alas, they would lose that evening, when their only goal came after Roger Hunt had clearly pulled the ball back from behind the goal line. Better things would happen: yet Liverpool's domination of the European Cup itself would occur only when Shanks, in a fit of perversity and strange anxiety, had resigned his managership, and his number two, Bob Paisley, had taken over.

Shanks in the Liverpool directors' room. 'That So-and-So,' – an Everton director – 'he's an idiot. He came to watch one of our games the other day. He said, "I don't think much of that Leishman." Leishman was no' even playing!'

'Bill! Bill!'

'What?'

'Back there. It's So-and-So!'

Shanks looks over his shoulder. 'Aye, that's him! He's an idiot!'

My happiest memory of him takes us to Belgrade in 1973; just weeks away from the famous Boot Room meeting when Shankly and his lieutenants boldly and bravely decided that Liverpool's methods wouldn't work, at least in Europe. The team, due to play and lose to Red Star, was staying in the Jugoslavia Hotel, on the banks of the Danube. The large, pleasant dining-room overlooked the river through its picture windows. Shanks was at breakfast. 'Sit down, Brian! Have a cup of tea!'

And then, the marvellous anecdotes. An hour or so of them; quite irresist-ible. On a tour of Europe in 1938 with Preston, after winning the Cup. 'We went to Paris. They took us to the brothel. Where Edward VII used to go. They still had this chair they used to put him in, and swing him about. The girls were naked. They sat on the edge of the baths! I was slapping their bot-toms!' And in Hungary, later on, 'A man came up to me. He offered me his sister!'

Shanks was not, of course, all sweetness and light. What successful manager ever could be? 'He can treat you like dirt at times,' one Liverpool player told me, gloomily. It was true. Expensive players who didn't fill the bill were left to rot in the reserves, till they were sold. That, as they say, is football. Or, as the French revolutionary Saint-Just used to put it, 'You can't govern without blood on your hands.'

Shanks pulled Liverpool out of the Second Division, out of the mire, and made them a marvellous team. Down in the Boot Room, he and his cronies plotted the team's destiny. There was Bob Paisley from the North East, once the team's competent left-half, dropped at the last moment from the 1950 Cup Final; Joe Fagan, who'd played centre-half for Manchester City; and Ronnie Moran, trainer *par excellence*, once Liverpool's left-back.

A benign Board of Directors allowed Shankly his way – though when he so unexpectedly resigned, they did not co-opt him. There were fears, one heard, that he would dominate any board meeting.

Peter Robinson, an exemplary secretary, later to become Chief Executive, showed from the first a pleasing breadth of European vision. It was significant that even after the appalling events of Heysel, his and Liverpool's relations with Juventus remained excellent. In 1984, when Liverpool reached the European Cup Final in Rome for the second time, against Roma themselves, the club found itself with a large number of unsold tickets. Afraid they might fall into the hands of Roma supporters and provoke violence, Robinson paid for them but hung on to them. For which Liverpool were fined by UEFA.

Had Robinson had any say in the matter, the Heysel tragedy would surely have become impossible. He of all people would have seen to it that tickets would not be allowed – with almost criminal negligence – to fall into the hands of Italian supporters on those Z terraces next to the sections for Liverpool fans. Once, though, it had been ludicrously decided that tickets on the Z sector could be sold to Italian fans, the presence of so many Italian immigrants in Brussels, not to mention the operation of the black market, made such an eventuality inevitable. The worst of it was that those Italian fans who did get tickets for that section were by and large gentle people rather than hard-core Juventus fans. Those were stationed at the other end.

But enough of Heysel for the moment. Liverpool's first, intimate involvement with Italian football in the European Cup came when they were virtually cheated out of it by Inter and the Solti connection in 1965. That they should reach the second leg of that semi-final with any chance at all was almost a miracle, given that they had taken part in an exhausting Cup Final at Wembley, decided in their favour after extra time, just three days before the first leg at Anfield.

Greek met Greek that night at Anfield; Shankly versus Herrera, whom Shanks described as 'a remarkable little fellow, a cut-throat man who wanted to win'. But of course behind one Greek was a Hungarian, in Solti, and that combination was to prove unbeatable. Still, Shanks enjoyed a major and a minor victory at Anfield, the minor one being that he eventually persuaded the Inter players to go out first, then sent Gerry Byrne, who'd gallantly played through the Cup Final with a broken collar bone, and the injured, clever right-half Gordon Milne round the ground with the Cup.

The famous Kop, then renowned for its inspired improvisation, sang 'Go Back to Italy' to the tune of *Santa Lucia*, followed by bizarre choruses of 'Ee-ay-addio, Mussolini's dead.'

On the way to the semi-final, Liverpool had eliminated Anderlecht and Cologne. Shankly had shown tremendous flair in the transfer market, acquiring first-rate players for relatively modest fees. There were Scots in Ian St John, such a lively and intelligent centre-forward, 'Massive Ron' Yeats, and the clever left-half Willie Stevenson, who had European experience with Glasgow Rangers, but left them to play for a while in Australia. Gordon Milne and Peter Thompson came from Shankly's own old club, Preston. Thompson's ball control was superb and he had speed and strength to go with it. Yet somehow he never quite achieved what such natural talents made possible; he and the other Liverpool winger, the highly effective Ian Callaghan, would both be dropped by Alf Ramsey on England's way to the 1966 World Cup.

Young Tommy Smith was only nominally the inside-left. Very much a Liverpudlian, forceful, down to earth, a fierce tackler, he was used against Anderlecht to mark their renowned centre-forward Paul Van Himst, and did so well that he remained in defence beside Ron Yeats.

The story went, apocryphal or otherwise, that when a poster went up in the city, *'WHAT WOULD YOU DO IF CHRIST CAME TO LIVERPOOL?'* the words appeared, *'Play St John at inside-left'.* Long years in the shadow of the eternal rivals, Everton, were being compensated. 'There are two great teams in Liverpool,' ran a typical Shanklyism. 'Liverpool and Liverpool reserves.' Is it true that he was once seen on a freezing winter's night in the directors' box at Crewe Alexandra, watching a Fourth Division game side by side with his devoted wife, Nessy? That when taxed with it, he replied, 'It's her birthday,' then answered, when the tale was told him, 'No, no; it was our anniversary'? Probably not, but the man's fanatical involvement is reflected in the story.

Anderlecht were impressively overcome, Cologne were beaten only on the toss of a coin. Goalless draws at home and away meant Liverpool had to play off in Rotterdam. Two of Cologne's talented side would play in the World Cup Final the following year at Wembley, as would Roger Hunt for England. Wolfgang Overath at inside-left was the general of the team. Wolfgang Weber, who was destined to score that breathless last-minute equaliser against England when he moved up from defence, alas broke his leg in a tackle with Gordon Milne. No substitutes, so Weber bravely limped about at centre-forward.

Things looked good for Liverpool. Twice Roger Hunt was involved in goals, first when he pulled the ball back for Ian St John to score, then when his header from a centre by Callaghan hit the bar and fell behind the goal line, Milne running it in to be sure. No Russian linesman was thus needed.

Commendably, Wolfgang Overath brought the diminished Cologne back into a game which seemed lost. A free-kick by Hornig, a header by Thielen, and it was 2–1. Then Lohr beat the resourceful Scottish keeper Tommy Lawrence with a long, low drive. No more goals; Cologne thought they'd got one in the last minute through Lohr, but Lawrence had been fouled. So at the end of extra time there was a toss-up; the vexed stratagem of penalties, simulating justice, had yet to be adopted. The referee tossed up a red and white disc, which promptly stuck on its side in the mud. He tried again, and it came down Liverpool red. Liverpool were in the semi-final.

How well they played that evening against Inter, despite the strenuous efforts at Wembley the previous Saturday! They scored within three minutes, when Roger Hunt drove in Ian Callaghan's centre, leaving Inter's elegant goalkeeper, Giuliano Sarti, once a Fiorentina player, helpless. But an

The end of Liverpool's first European Cup adventure as Giacinto Facchetti fires a shot past Tommy Lawrence for Inter's third goal in the semi-final second leg at San Siro

(Farabolafoto)

untypical mistake by Ron Yeats, muffing a long ball from Giacinto Facchetti, allowed Inter a rather soft equaliser. Peiro, the Spaniard, beat Yeats, drew Lawrence, and squared for Mazzola to score.

Liverpool took that in their stride. A free-kick on the edge of the box. Callaghan dummied over the ball, Stevenson rolled it to Hunt. Hunt now played it into the path of the sprinting Callaghan, and Sarti was beaten again. The third goal came in the second half, following a sustained move – Thompson to Callaghan to Smith to Hunt, a save by Sarti, final execution by St John. 'We have been beaten before but never defeated,' Helenio Herrera told Bill Shankly. 'Tonight, we were defeated.'

Sarti and the referee, Ortiz de Mendibil, would see to it that Liverpool were beaten, rather than defeated, in Milan. Corso scored directly from an indirect free kick, Peiro kicked the ball out of Tommy Lawrence's hands for Inter's second. Both these 'goals' were put to shame by Facchetti's marvellous third, after a 70-yard dash. Not for another twelve years would Liverpool reach a European Cup Final.

In season 1966/7, in December, Liverpool were thrashed 5–1 in Amsterdam by an Ajax team galvanised by Johan Cruyff. Shankly's response was wonderfully perverse. It was a terrible thing, he declared, to see a home team playing defensively. As well in the circumstances, no doubt, if Ajax actually did. In the return leg, there were two goals for Hunt and two for Cruyff, and Liverpool, defensive or otherwise, were out.

The real watershed came in 1973, after Red Star had beaten Liverpool home and away in the European Cup. It was immensely to the credit of Shankly and his Boot Room brains' trust that they had the courage and initiative to admit to themselves that their traditional, often long-ball, English tactics were never going to gain them what they wanted in Europe, that changes must be made to a more Continental style, with more emphasis on a patient build-up, and on ball control.

Four years later, the European Cup came to Anfield in consequence, but Shankly was not there to enjoy it. That strange, emotional, impulsive little man had suddenly resigned in 1974, soon after Liverpool had won the Cup Final against Newcastle. It's still hard to know what made him do it. What was there in his life but football? He was tired, he said, but retirement was a penance. He was embittered by the fact that Liverpool didn't invite him to their away games, but in essence it was a situation he had created himself. He walked his dog, accepted invitations from clubs whom Liverpool played, smouldered and suffered. He needed to retire; but retire to what?

Bob Paisley succeeded him. A Geordie who'd played amateur football for Bishop Auckland till he joined Liverpool just before the Second World War, Paisley had none of the idiosyncrasies, the sublime intransigence, of Shankly. He was a quiet man who wore baggy suits and took any criticism of Liverpool to heart. He didn't want the job, he said, at first, but was finally persuaded to take it. He did it uncommonly well, a natural heir to Shankly in all but temperament. The UEFA Cup was won, and then the European Cup itself.

'Bob Paisley took on a big job when he became manager of Liverpool,' wrote Shankly in his autobiography, 'but I felt he had the necessary qualities to be capable of doing it . . . Perhaps some of my psychology has rubbed off on Bob.'

Beyond doubt, Paisley did the job well. He had good players to deal with. Two had come from Scunthorpe, for modest prices: Ray Clemence, the elegant, left-footed but right-handed goalkeeper (Shanks did not like left-handed keepers), and Kevin Keegan, self-made but all the better for it, a dynamic little outside-right who would become an all-around attacker of the highest quality, European Footballer of the Year, a star not only with Liverpool and England but also with Hamburg. Few players can have worked so assiduously on their game to greater purpose.

Phil Neal was an elegant, attacking right-back, successor to the polished Chris Lawler; lacking perhaps in defensive qualities, but deeply fortunate in the presence first of the 'Scouser' Jimmy Case, then of Sammy Lee, who would play in front of him devotedly and do his tackling for him. Emlyn Hughes, son of a Welsh Rugby League player, was a propulsive left-half, an England left-back, signed from Blackpool.

The remarkable Steve Heighway had broken into the team, a centre-forward-cum-left-winger, straight from senior amateur football with Skelmersdale, thus giving the lie to many a dearly-held nostrum. Shankly brought Heighway to Anfield in 1970, at the same time as another university graduate, the little inside-forward Brian Hall. Heighway was a spectacular success from the first, with his pace and wonderfully graceful movement. Exploiting a space left between Bob Wilson and the near post, he scored Liverpool's goal in the FA Cup Final they lost to Arsenal in 1971.

In the dressing-room afterwards, a crestfallen Emlyn Hughes went up to Shankly and, in his familiar high voice, apologised for an error: 'That last goal was down to me, boss. I was knackered.'

'Hey-er,' said Shankly, with that strange, prefatory noise of his. 'Don't worry, son. Everybody makes mistakes.' And then, when Hughes was out of earshot: 'And that's the —— who cost us the Cup Final!'

'Oh, Liverpool, we love you!' sang their fans, when they were not singing their adopted anthem, 'You'll Never Walk Alone'. Not everybody loved them. Under the captaincy of Hughes, they were famous for the money they made in ancillary ways, not least through an exclusive deal with a local photographer. It was this, perhaps, which caused their team group to break up so precipitately, immediately after they'd been presented with the European Cup in Rome.

There was no doubt, though, that they won it well. I myself did not expect them to get past Saint Etienne in the quarter-final, still less when Kevin Keegan had to drop out of the first leg. Spurned as a boy by Doncaster, his local club, he had matured from an exuberant outside-right to a thoroughly mature, intelligent and versatile striker, making an excellent double spearhead with Heighway.

Seven years now with Liverpool, Heighway had settled down to be a thoroughly professional player. It was said that when he missed an easy chance in a game at Anfield, he was given a fearful dressing-down by Tommy Smith, who informed him that on such things depended his bonus. Initially, Hall and Heighway had, like their wives, adopted a slightly superior attitude to the unlettered rest of the team, recounting once in a newspaper interview how the other players had been surprised because once, on an away trip, the two of them had wanted to see the film *Cromwell*. (A poor choice, in fact, if the critics were to be believed.)

In another interview, one of the wives expressed her surprise at the way the other players' wives, dressed to the nines on a Saturday afternoon, would look at them when they turned up casually in slacks. 'Until we realised, this was their great day!' Such attitudes did not persist. Hall moved on, and Heighway's bosom companion became the modest, likeable, ultra-Scouse footballer Phil Boersma.

Saint Etienne had been most unlucky losers in the previous season's Final. True, in the image of Dominique Rocheteau they had not been at their best in the 1976/7 season, but they seemed to hold a few too many cards for Liverpool. A second-half goal by Dominique Bathenay won them the first leg, though Phil Thompson missed an easy heading chance and Heighway hit a post.

At Anfield, Keegan returned but Thompson, who had ripped a cartilage, was out. This was another proud Liverpudlian, one who had even stood rapturous with his brother on the Kop when Inter had been beaten in 1965, contributing to the wall of noise which, he felt sure, had demoralised the Italians. So lean as to be almost ectomorph, Thompson began as a right-half, but developed into one of the best, most mobile central defenders in the League. His injury let Tommy Smith back into the team – to score his unexpected goal in Rome.

A famous night of European Cup football at Anfield begins with a cross-shot from Kevin Keegan (out of picture) curling over the Saint Etienne keeper, Curkovic, as Tommy Smith follows in (Popperfoto)

But we are getting ahead of the story. First Saint Etienne had to be overcome. Bob Paisley, who had done so much, so shrewdly, to give Liverpool success in Europe, and had so fruitfully used five-a-side training games to instil a more gradual, less hectic approach, accused me of not favouring Liverpool to survive. Without 'Super-Sub', the tall, pale, red-haired David Fairclough, his electric turn of pace and his pulverising right-footed shot, perhaps they would not have done.

Breasting down a lob from Ray Kennedy – the former Arsenal striker whom Bob Paisley had boldly and percipiently converted into a midfield player – Fairclough had left Lopez, the squat French sweeper, standing, and gone on to smash the ball past Curkovic. The Yugoslav keeper had no hope with that one, but this was not what you might call one of his Hampden nights. He should have had Keegan's shot-cum-centre from the left, which found its way in within three minutes.

A 30-yard shot from Bathenay wiped that goal out after half-time. With the Kop going through frenzies of zeal, Ray Kennedy put Liverpool ahead again, but they still needed to score again to avoid being eliminated on away goals. Then Fairclough got his goal.

Although Paisley had undoubtedly honed and polished the team's style, there was still some way to go before it could be compared with the very best of Europe. Zurich, the opposition in the semi-final, certainly did not enter this category. Liverpool scored three against them away, another three at home. But Borussia Mönchengladbach, who would now be met in the Final, were another thing again. And if Liverpool had Keegan, Borussia had the brilliant, tiny Danish centre-forward, Allan Simonsen.

Of Liverpool, I wrote at the time:

> Tactically speaking, you might vary the words of Pliny and say, 'Out of Anfield, never anything new.' Liverpool plug away with their unfashionable 4–3–3, their three competent, unimaginative, one-paced midfield men – perm any three from Callaghan, McDermott, Case and Kennedy – but get results just the same.
>
> They get them, let it be noted, not simply because they have superb morale and physical condition, but because they have, up front, several strikers capable of doing remarkable things. In France, for instance, the glorious individual goal with which the red-haired David Fairclough extinguished the hopes of Saint Etienne is still being breathlessly spoken of . . .
>
> It was, by any standards, an outstanding technical feat, of which any striker in the world would have been proud. By the same token, both Keegan, when he has the sense to stay up front rather than confuse the midfield, and Heighway, who has never run so fluently and to such good purpose, are forwards of the highest quality, always capable of pulling something spectacular out of the bag. Given the limitations of the three men behind them, this is just as well.
>
> It has been said that Liverpool are a team of ordinary players whose whole is infinitely greater than its parts. This seems to me quite unfair. It is true that the full-backs are of substantially poorer quality than their predecessors, but, besides their gifted strikers, Liverpool also have one of the game's best goalkeepers in Clemence, one of Britain's most resilient defenders in Hughes.
>
> The fact seems to be that conventional methods can and will prevail over more modern ones unless the modernists are at their very best.

Thus, if your goalkeeper plays like a clown, as did Curkovic at Liverpool, or your unique opportunist drops out, as did Muller from Bayern, you will be in difficulty and danger. *(Sunday Times, 22 May 1977)*

Liverpool already had an edge over Borussia Mönchengladbach; they had beaten them in the two-legged UEFA Cup Final of 1973. Since then, Borussia had lost Gunter Netzer to Madrid, and though Simonsen was shining, another fine Danish attacker, Jensen, was no longer with them. Uli Stielike, however, was an international sweeper of high quality, and a biting tackle. I gave Liverpool, before that Final, 'a good even chance'.

And how well they took their chance! If on the night Borussia looked a weary side, that was hardly Liverpool's fault. In style and with panache, they became only the second English and third British team to take the trophy.

When Liverpool arrived at Rome airport, an Italian journalist asked Kevin Keegan what he thought of Cuccureddu, the Sardinian defender who played for Juventus and had close-marked him out of the game when England lost to Italy in Rome earlier in the season. Keegan replied, with a somewhat wry smile, that as Cuccureddu had dominated him that day, he had to admit he was a good player, but playing for Liverpool, with so much understanding and support, was very different from playing for England. He would like to play against Cuccureddu, and Juventus, in the European Cup.

In the event, Keegan, who had announced that this would be his last season with Liverpool before going to Europe, found himself man-marked by Berti Vogts, the player who'd been given charge of Cruyff in the 1974 World Cup Final, and who after the 1990 tournament became team manager of West Germany. Udo Lattek, the former manager of Bayern Munich, now in charge at Mönchengladbach, had in fact stated that Vogts would not be marking Keegan, and Vogts had allegedly exchanged angry words with him when he discovered that he would be. Lattek, still more surprisingly, had said that Keegan would be marked by Rainer Bonhof, the powerful, dynamic midfielder whose inclusion had made all the difference to West Germany in the 1974 World Cup Final.

Vogts found himself utterly dominated by Keegan, who virtually played cat and mouse with him, twisting and turning away from him, exploiting his own pace, strength and poise, while an inspired Steve Heighway did much the same with his own marker, Klinkhammer. Borussia's attempt at Total Football was a feeble one. There were too many men out of form, too many tactical mistakes, too little spirit of adventure. It was as though the team's defeat by Liverpool in the UEFA Cup Final still weighed upon it. Even the gift of an equaliser to Simonsen – beautifully taken as it was, when Case mis-hit a back pass – wasn't enough to revive them.

Making light of the heat and humidity of the Roman evening, Liverpool had gone ahead with a spectacular goal. Heighway's glorious pass, picking up Terry McDermott's inspired run from midfield, cracked a Borussia defence which never looked watertight. The use of the ponderous Wittkamp rather than Stielike as sweeper seemed almost perverse, while Jimmy Case kept drawing Bonhof to the flank, where he was on his weaker left foot. There was an anxious moment when Borussia, in the only 10 purple minutes that they played, after Simonsen's equaliser, split the Liverpool defence and sent Stielike through alone. But Clemence dealt superbly with the shot, allowing Liverpool to regain the lead, 20 minutes into the second half.

Just as Keegan's clever run had taken Vogts out of the middle when McDermott got the first goal – Bob Paisley observed, 'Vogts might as well

have been selling programmes when the goal went in' – so two defenders followed Keegan at Heighway's corner. Into the space ran Tommy Smith, to head his team's second goal.

Desperation entered Borussia's play. They could well have conceded a penalty when Bonhof, who did once put a shot against the post, brought down Steve Heighway from behind. They did give one away when Vogts brought down Kevin Keegan; the final humiliation for that famous but, on this occasion, toothless German bulldog. Keegan had yet again lost Vogts and had negotiated Wittkamp when Vogts tripped him. Phil Neal, always such an expert penalty-taker, scorer of one against Zurich in the semi-finals, chose the opposite corner this time and the goalkeeper went the wrong way. Ian Callaghan the while stood on the edge of the box, his hands clasped in silent prayer.

Liverpool kept the European Cup in 1978 – without Kevin Keegan. Shrewdly and sensibly, they bought Kenny Dalglish from Glasgow Celtic. Not only would he serve them wonderfully well as a player, he would meta-morphose with the speed of light into a remarkable player-manager. A very different kind of footballer from Keegan, he unquestionably had more sheer natural talent, could operate in midfield as successfully as up front – where Liverpool could use him – spun splendidly on the ball, passed superbly, and hit his right-footed shots with great power.

He was already deeply experienced in international and European club football. He had played in the 1974 World Cup and would take part in two more. The strange thing is that for all his ebullient talent, he never really gained the Blue Riband of a player who excels in the World Cup Finals. Nor, for that matter, did Keegan; for England were eliminated by Poland before the 1974 Finals, failed to qualify in 1978, and in 1982 Keegan was injured and should never have made his one, disastrous, appearance in the Finals, against Spain.

Though mourning the loss of Keegan, Liverpool's men soon found it easy to play with Dalglish. He was the ideal back-to-the-goal player, who could receive the ball to feet under the severest pressure, and lay it off at once with precision. Six goals in his first seven games showed that he was an oppor-tunist, too.

Another gifted Scot to arrive was Alan Hansen, from Partick Thistle, a tall, strong, immensely elegant centre-back with fine ball control, always ready and eager to join in attacks. Impeccable in the air, his one defect was the obverse of his virtues – a tendency to give second chances by playing too much football in defence. Dalglish was known to be incensed when Alex Ferguson, the Scottish manager, did not pick Hansen for the 1986 World Cup Finals in Mexico. It may even have influenced his decision – he was injured at the time – not to go himself. His last chance of distinguishing himself in a World Cup.

Exempted till the second round of the European Cup, Liverpool crushed the East Germans Dynamo Dresden 5–1 at Anfield, Hansen scoring one of the goals. They lost 2–1 in the return leg, their performance once again improving with the arrival, as substitute, of David Fairclough, who had not played in the Rome Final. This, alas, was to be his fate; a Super Sub indeed who would never quite graduate to an acknowledged first-team place. But the new tendency, under Paisley, would in any case now be to go for ready-made players rather than to tap the deep sources of talent in the city of Liverpool itself. The youth scheme withered and wilted; Dalglish divined as much when he took over as manager. Paisley's reasoning was that when there was such pressure on a club for results, so many hard fixtures, there was no time to develop home-grown talent. Perhaps.

Hamburg were played in that two-legged, ersatz tournament, the Super Cup. Kevin Keegan had joined them. At Anfield, he and Hamburg were annihilated 6–0, with three of the goals for Terry McDermott. During the protracted winter break, Liverpool signed yet another gifted Scotsman, whose future influence on the team would be immense: Graeme Souness.

Souness, an Edinburgh man, had had a sticky beginning at Tottenham where, as a teenager, he had constantly clashed with the club coach Eddie Baily, himself once an outstanding inside-left for Spurs and England. In later years, Souness tended to blame himself, but the upshot of it was that Tottenham sold him to Middlesbrough, and thus lost one of the salient British players of his generation.

Strongly built, sometimes abrasive on the field, an enforcer as well as a creator, Souness began as an inside-forward, but in due course showed most of the qualities of an all-round midfield player. He could win tackles, and when he had the ball, would use it with consistent flair and intelligence. His shot was fearsome. He had great authority. Later, like Dalglish, he would make the transition to player-manager – at Glasgow Rangers – with astonishing speed, and when Dalglish suddenly resigned in 1991, Souness would succeed him as manager at Anfield. £325 000 brought him from Ayresome Park.

Souness made his European Cup debut as a substitute against Borussia Mönchengladbach – fate pitted them against Liverpool again – in the semi-final first leg in Dusseldorf. To reach that stage, Liverpool had had to dispose of Benfica, now managed by John Mortimore, the old Chelsea centre-half whose headed goal against Liverpool in a semi-final at Villa Park had been ruled out for obscure motives.

With his centre-forward Batista suspended and his clever young left-winger Chalana hurt, Mortimore's team for the first leg in Lisbon was lacking in punch. Nene, the Portuguese international striker, did give Benfica the lead, under a deluge of rain, but a goal scored by Case's potent right foot from a free-kick, and a curving shot from the left by Emlyn Hughes, gave Liverpool victory. Benfica, said Hughes, had 'a false reputation'.

At Anfield, a bizarre early own-goal by their keeper Bento sent Benfica still further down the slope; a strange error for a player who, in his manager's view, had been 'brilliant all season'. Dalglish, McDermott and Phil Neal also scored; Nene got one for Benfica. Now it was Borussia again.

Stielike, like Netzer before him, had now joined Real Madrid. Simonsen was injured. In Dusseldorf, Liverpool ran few risks. Hannes scored for Borussia, David Johnson, a centre-forward best known for his exploits with Everton and Ipswich, himself a Liverpudlian, equalised minutes from the end, only for one of Bonhof's extraordinary right-footed free-kicks, whizzing in off Ray Clemence's shoulder, to regain the lead for Borussia.

'It will be a great return game,' prophesied Bob Paisley; and Liverpool won it. Berti Vogts himself admitted afterwards that several of his teammates had been intimidated by the very idea of playing at Anfield. Ray Kennedy was unmarked when he headed in a centre from Kenny Dalglish after just seven minutes. Dalglish and Case added goals, while Souness, on for 90 minutes this time in place of Ian Callaghan, kept the wheels turning smoothly.

The opposition in the Final, surprisingly, would be the Belgian champions Bruges, under the knowing management of Ernst Happel. As an Austrian defender of renown, Happel had played in 1951 at Wembley with a splendid Austrian team which deserved to smash England's unbeaten home record against foreign teams, but drew 2–2. Now he brought Bruges to Wembley, the first Belgian side ever to play a European Cup Final, and one which in 1976 had lost in the UEFA Cup Final to Liverpool, just as Borussia Mönchengladbach had done. Bruges' most remarkable feat had been to eliminate Juventus in the semi-finals, though Happel himself admitted how lucky they were, after losing 1–0 in Turin, to win the home leg 2–0.

Bastijns, the Bruges full-back, had caught Juventus cold with a remarkable solo goal after a mere three minutes. Juventus had then outplayed Bruges without scoring, faltering only when their notorious defender Gentile was sent off for a second bookable offence – only, on this occasion, a handball. So, in extra time, after 116 minutes, Rene Vandereycken scored the goal which put Bruges in the Final.

It would not be the full Bruges team. Above all, Raoul Lambert, the experienced centre-forward, was missing. So was the midfielder, Courant. So Bruges came to Wembley, shut up shop, and were largely to blame for a dismally dull match. For David Fairclough, however, there was at least the satisfaction of starting the game in preference to Heighway, who would come on only as substitute for Jimmy Case.

Kenny Dalglish chips the ball over Bruges keeper Birger Jensen for the winning goal of the 1978 Final at Wembley (Hulton Picture Company)

Soon after that, Heighway began the move which gave Liverpool the solitary goal. It became a deadly one when Souness characteristically split the Bruges defence, and Dalglish, on the right of the goal, cleverly and coolly lofted the ball over the diving Danish keeper, Jensen. Phil Thompson, fit to play in this Final, preserved the lead close to the end, squeezing the ball off the line after one of those strangely casual errors which littered the otherwise distinguished career of Alan Hansen.

As Bob Paisley said, patience had paid. The celebrated Boot Room meeting of 1973 continued to pay its dividends. 'Careless passing,' thought Paisley, 'is the most common cause of injury.' Thus Liverpool's approach was the very antithesis of the fatuous new orthodoxy which would emerge in the 1980s, not least at Lancaster Gate from the Football Association's degenerating coaching scheme. It would be a while before Liverpool won the European Cup again; meanwhile, they had triumphantly shown the way.

For the moment it was Nottingham's turn. The extraordinary side Brian Clough and Peter Taylor had built soared ahead of Liverpool in the 1977/8 Championship, and proceeded to knock them out in the first round of the European Cup the following season, then to go on to win it themselves. Twice in succession; just like Liverpool.

The following season saw Liverpool once more expire in the first round. This time it was to a marvellously talented Georgian team, Dynamo Tbilisi, who lost 2–1 at Anfield but played Liverpool off the pitch in the return, winning 3–0. Chivadze, the superbly versatile sweeper, scored in both ties, though his goal in Tbilisi was from the penalty spot. Dynamo turned out in the end to be something of a nine days' wonder; but what a wonder they were, while they lasted!

Shengelia, the winger, was a splendid compound of pace, strength and evasive skill; he and the excellent centre-forward, Gutsaev, scored the other goals in Tbilisi. Some of the virtue, however, went out of Tbilisi when a vicious foul by a player inaptly named Angel broke the leg of their midfield inspiration, David Kipiani, in one of those savage Spanish pre-season tournaments, and put him out of the game for good. In Georgia, Liverpool looked an outmoded team, but in the next round their old favourite Kevin Keegan, now comfortably settled in at Hamburg after a turbulent beginning, scored home and away for Hamburg against Dynamo, who lost both games.

Bitterly distressed by the defeat in Tbilisi, by the way his team had been outclassed, Bob Paisley gave way to an uncharacteristic outburst. Individually, he said, his team were worth little. With such as Souness, Dalglish, Clemence and Hansen? Things were duly put to rights the following season when Liverpool, qualifying as champions of England once more, regained their European Cup, despite some hiccoughs during the domestic season.

These were due in large measure to the protracted absence of both the international centre-backs, Hansen and Thompson. But when Liverpool were drawn against the much-lauded Scottish champions Aberdeen, they beat them by a single goal at Pittodrie; then, in the return – though their first half hour, as Paisley admitted, was not impressive – they swept Aberdeen aside, 4–0. Paisley, surprisingly, thought his team might have been nervous. After so much European Cup experience? Unlikely. With Dalglish showing remarkable opportunism and no outstanding team left in the field, Liverpool's chances looked good.

Even though they were drawn in the quarter-finals against the surprising Bulgarians, CSKA Sofia, who'd had little trouble with the holders Nottingham Forest. At Anfield, in the event, CSKA proved sitting ducks for the stupendous shooting of Graeme Souness. Three times he scored, in a 5–1 victory. True, he had scored three at Anfield in the first round, but that was in a 10-goal rout of Oulun Palloseura of Finland, which was more of a training canter.

The talented Swiss international attacker Raimondo Ponte, who had played for Nottingham Forest against CSKA in Sofia, was astonished. 'Everybody says Liverpool are in a state of crisis. I don't believe it . . . Liverpool can easily get to the semi-finals of the European Cup, and then win it, again. Even so, I don't understand their 5–1 result against CSKA; a very fine win, but I don't think Souness will often produce three shots like that in one game!'

New faces continued to appear in the Liverpool ranks, though one was by no means so new to loyal Liverpool supporters. Fresh and boyish, it belonged to little, blond Sammy Lee, who from about the age of 16 had been delighting supporters with his fine displays at inside-forward for the reserve team. A native Scouser at a time when so few could find a place in the team – though Jimmy Case, another, had come from South Liverpool FC – Lee was a devotedly hard-working and unselfish player. Over the years, I could not help thinking that perhaps it would have been better for him had he left early to join another club, one where he might have been less deeply respectful to his elders, the players he had worshipped as an apprentice and as a fan. There were those Liverpool players who said that Phil Neal should have given his medals to Lee – or to Case – each of whom worked so doggedly in front of him to seal up Liverpool's defensive right flank.

At left-back, the popular Welsh international Joey Jones (*NOW JOEY'S MUNCHING GLADBACH!* read a banner in the Olympic Stadium before the 1977 Final) had given way to Alan Kennedy, a powerful overlapping full-back who had played in the Newcastle team which Liverpool overwhelmed in the Cup Final of 1974. He would have his moment of glory in the European Cup Final to come.

In Sofia, Liverpool beat CSKA again for good measure, with a goal by David Johnson. Now, in the semi-finals, came a Bayern Munich team which was described by Ponte as being not yet mature: 'They still have players who are not quite there. They're only at the beginning of finding a team at the level they had some years ago. Perhaps in a year or two, they'll reach a higher level.'

Paul Breitner was hardly of the same opinion. Ten years after his salad days as an overlapping full-back, he was back again in Munich, as a thoughtful, creative – though inevitably much slower – midfielder. After a dour, dull game at Anfield, in which Liverpool badly missed the injured Souness from midfield and not a goal was scored, Breitner unleashed one of his typical broadsides. English football, he said, was 'stupid'. There was no subtlety about it. It relied solely on pressure to break down an opposing defence. But in Munich, where Souness returned and Liverpool were given some bruising treatment, Bayern and Breitner were left embarrassed. Ray Kennedy's late goal gave Liverpool the lead, and though Karl-Heinz Rummenigge equalised, Liverpool once again were in the European Cup Final.

Their opponents were a much-diminished Real Madrid, who had overcome an equally disappointing Internazionale; no comparison, here, with the matches between these teams in the 1960s. Helenio Herrera, Inter's manager in those turbulent days, tipped Real to win the Final. 'Not necessarily because they are the better team,' he said. 'Over two games, home and away, they would probably lose to Liverpool or Bayern Munich. But for a one-off match, it's remarkable how they can raise their game.'

In the event, it was remarkable how little they did so. Liverpool encountered an old foe in Uli Stielike, and a familiar face in that of the black winger Laurie Cunningham, who had made his name with Orient and West Bromwich Albion before going to Madrid; a city, alas, where he would die pitifully young, in a motor accident.

The fourth rotten European Cup Final in a row, I called it at the time, and so in retrospect it was. Perhaps it would have been livelier had the talented, fiery Spanish right-winger Juanito, who faded out after Real initially forced the pace, stayed farther upfield. His Yugoslav manager, Boskov, said afterwards that this was what he had wanted him to do; in which case, one wondered, why didn't Boskov make him? Phil Thompson had a magnificent game in the centre of Liverpool's defence, well abetted by Alan Hansen, but both were unusually cautious. Afterwards Bob Paisley, oddly tetchy and, well, defensive, said his defenders had instructions on defensive play, but themselves chose when to attack.

Just when it looked as if the game – despised by those great figures from the Real past, Puskas and Di Stefano – must drift on to extra time and penalties, an error by the Spanish right-back Cortes let Alan Kennedy in, and from a sharp angle, he drove his shot past the tall Agustin.

To a German journalist who asked him how he reconciled Liverpool's victory that night with their fifth position in the League, Paisley responded, 'If somebody broke your legs, you'd be last out of this room.' He went on to lament the fact – lamentation was in the air – that so many of his players had missed more than six weeks of the season. Meanwhile, Dynamo Tbilisi and Ipswich Town were winning the Cup Winners' Cup and UEFA Cup respectively in far greater style. 'Chloroform football' was the pungent dismissal by a French journalist of what happened at the Parc des Princes. Still, at least no one broke up and threw any seats.

Season 1981/2 brought Bruce Grobbelaar, and a new dimension of goalkeeping. Ray Clemence, after years of serene service, had gone to Spurs. Grobbelaar, a muscular Rhodesian who had fought African guerrillas in the bush, arrived from Vancouver, via Crewe Alexandra. Spectacular but unpredictable, a superb athlete, and totally fearless, he was a grasper of difficult crosses and, too often, a dropper of easy ones. He would remain for over a decade to thrill, delight and appal the Kop; now hero, now culprit.

After Liverpool had played scintillating football at Anfield but won only 3–2 against the Dutch champions, AZ Alkmaar, thus qualifying, the Dutch manager George Kessler sounded the familiar theme. Liverpool weren't as good as they had been, and would not win the Cup. In fact Liverpool should have won by a street, the two goals against them were freakish, and, as I wrote:

> Grobbelaar, Clemence's successor, is the trouble, and Liverpool know it. 'I think we're just missing the understanding at the back,' said Ray Kennedy, 'because of the new goalkeeper. It's not down to him, it's a question of getting used to him.'

It's debatable whether they ever did. Grobbelaar has always been unique,

Bruce Grobbelaar
(Allsport)

adventurous, sometimes to a fault – though no Higuita of Chile when it came to leaving his penalty box to use his feet – gymnastic, idiosyncratic. Some felt that after his experiences in the Rhodesian bush, football could never be taken wholly seriously by him; if it came to matters of life and death, he had experienced real ones. It was Grobbelaar who almost decided to retire after the horrors of Heysel, Grobbelaar who persuaded a policewoman to open the gate and save lives at the Leppings Lane End during the Hillsborough disaster, Grobbelaar who did his best to comfort survivors.

Other remarkable players were gradually drafted into the Liverpool team by Bob Paisley that season, giving the lie to anyone who thought of the side as standing still or disintegrating. There was Ian Rush, for example, the shy young centre-forward from Flint, in North Wales, where he lived a quiet life among his family and intimate friends. Liverpool had paid what did seem a fortune for him – £300 000 to Fourth Division Chester – then stuck him, for an unhappy period, in the reserves.

At the end of the previous season, Rush had played seven times for the first team, without scoring. Paisley told him to be more selfish, and the advice seemed to work. Rush now started scoring goals, and hasn't stopped since.

Blistering pace, superb anticipation, and, in due course, clever movement were his greatest assets. He was not a back-to-the-goal player – that was Kenny Dalglish, who would understand his needs perfectly and slip him the through balls which he pursued with such ferret-like effectiveness, often banging them in with his powerful right foot. He was not a great header of the ball in the tradition of a Dean or a Lawton, but he could head goals, too, when the crosses came in. He was also adept at pulling out to the wing, negotiating defenders, and cunningly making himself the angle from which to score. In the European Cup, he'd prove prolific.

Ronnie Whelan, the young Irish midfielder – inside-forward, one would have called him in earlier times – had arrived from the famous Dublin club Home Farm, a player with splendid control, a fine distributor of the ball, with a strong right foot of his own. Later he would prove an impressive captain.

Mark Lawrenson was another Irish international, but only by virtue of the bizarre new dispensation which counted ancestry as a qualification. He was in fact a Preston man who had developed with North End then gone on to Brighton. England had approached him too late. Centre-back, midfield, full-back; he could play with strength, poise and elegance in any of those roles.

From Middlesbrough, where Graeme Souness had played, came Craig Johnston, an Australian with South African roots and Scottish background, a right-winger of great pace, good control, and lively initiative, with a breadth of interest beyond that of the average footballer. He would retire sadly early from the game, and turn up at the 1990 World Cup as a photographer, for UNICEF.

The team, then, was rebuilding, and perhaps it was not surprising that the European Cup was not retained, though it was very surprising indeed that CSKA Sofia should be the team to knock Liverpool out, in the quarter-finals. A season earlier, Liverpool had swallowed them whole. Now, they squeezed out no better than a 1–0 win at Anfield – Whelan scored – where they'd got five the season before.

In Sofia, where the refereeing was bizarre, and far from fair to Liverpool, the clever, experienced Bulgarian international winger Mladenov scored twice, once in extra time, and Liverpool against all logic, were out. Aston Villa won the Cup.

The following season saw Liverpool crash again, 2–0 in the quarter-finals in Eastern Europe, and Bruce Grobbelaar's fallibility was largely why. Widzew, the Polish champions, whom Liverpool met in Lodz, hadn't played a competitive game for nearly four months, and Liverpool comfortably survived the first half. Then came disaster.

Greboscz crossed from the left wing, and Grobbelaar, moving to collect it, succeeded only in pushing the ball backwards into his own goalmouth, where Tlokinski scored. Liverpool shrugged off the goal manfully and played some excellent football, but conceded a second in a breakaway to Wraga. A 3–2 win at Anfield – Liverpool's third and winning goal coming only in the final minute – was not nearly good enough.

Aston Villa succumbed, too, losing twice to Juventus, and Bob Paisley was displeased when I suggested in the *Sunday Times* that the recent successes of English clubs in the European Cup betokened a declining standard. It is a little ironic that, some years later, he himself should castigate the English First Division as 'the worst in living memory'! I had, he claimed, 'insulted' Nottingham Forest and Villa, by which he plainly meant Liverpool as well. In fact, especially.

At the time, and even now, I was unrepentant. *Qui s'excuse, s'accuse*, I replied. A string of wretched European Cup Finals in the last few years, all of them involving English clubs, seemed abundantly to prove my point. The technical gulf between our football and the best in Europe still seemed to me to remain immense. English clubs had surely prevailed through organisation, stamina, pace and morale in a way they never could when Real Madrid, Ajax and Bayern Munich were at their peak.

In March 1983, after Liverpool had yet again won the League Cup, at Wembley, Graeme Souness broke with tradition by insisting that Paisley climb the steps to the Royal Box to receive the trophy. It was a well-merited accolade. Paisley had stepped splendidly into the breach left by Shankly, had retained all that was best in Liverpool's tradition, had kept the team trying always to play progressive, creative football, and had dealt cleverly in the transfer market. All without the sleazy flamboyance of the sharp-suited, gold-chain-bedecked managers who were becoming the wearisome vogue.

In his place another long, loyal servant of the club, Joe Fagan, took over; a kindly, affable, sympathetic man, who would find, however, the immense pressures of publicity more than he bargained for. Yet Liverpool, under Fagan, went on to further, coruscating success.

The European Cup was regained in his first season, and Ian Rush's opportunism had an immense amount to do with that. Odense of Denmark were beaten home and away; Athletic Bilbao gallantly held Liverpool 0–0 at Anfield, but lost to a goal by Rush in the return leg. In March, Benfica, those weathered warriors of the European Cup, came to Anfield for the quarter-final first leg and went down only 1–0, to a goal scored by Rush. Liverpool at that time were strangely vulnerable and inconsistent in the domestic cup tournaments, their defence sometimes shipping water in the centre – Hansen especially – and the full-backs defensively suspect.

In the FA Cup, Liverpool had even lost to modest Brighton. They needed two bites at the cherry to overcome their eternal city rivals Everton in the Final of the League Cup, a 0–0 draw at Wembley being followed by a narrow 1–0 win in the replay at Maine Road. But in Lisbon, they walked all over a

Benfica team managed by the experienced and knowing Swede, Sven-Goran Eriksson. Ronnie Whelan and Craig Johnston – who had been asking for a transfer, frustrated by the few appearances he was making in the team – scored in the first half; Rush and Whelan again added goals late in the game. Benfica could manage only a goal by Nene, which briefly made it 1–2, only for Rush to score the third for a rampant Liverpool four minutes later.

Next came Dinamo Bucharest. They came to Anfield and they kicked, prompting Joe Fagan to remark, 'I thought that at this stage the European Cup is supposed to be about ability and skill.' The most serious casualty of this ill-natured evening, however, was a Rumanian, Movila, who left the field with what seemed a fractured jaw, after Graeme Souness had retaliated to a foul. Four Rumanians were booked by a feebly inadequate referee. Sammy Lee, of all people, headed the one goal of the game, from a cross by Alan Kennedy, not long after Augustin had broken through the Liverpool defence, run half the length of the field, and shot against a post.

Dinamo played bruisingly again in Bucharest, but the opportunism of Ian Rush saw Liverpool through. After 11 minutes, he scored when Sammy Lee took a corner which Souness played out to the left. Orac equalised from a free-kick but six minutes from the end, with the Rumanians now resigned to elimination, Ian Rush scored the winner for Liverpool. Now in the Final they'd meet Roma . . . in Rome.

'We've no worries about going to Rome for the Final,' said Souness. 'In fact, looking at our home form, it's probably the best we could hope for. When you're under pressure, it puts you on your toes.'

Roma, under the clever guidance of the old Milan and Sweden star Nils Liedholm, had ditched the traditional, deadening Italian *catenaccio* style, dispensed with the sweeper, and deployed a flat back four. It was a bold initiative, for which Liedholm was also responsible at Milan. The team was full of football. In midfield, there were the two superbly talented Brazilians, Toninho Cerezo and Paolo Falcao, members of the splendid Brazilian team which had been squeezed out by Italy in the 1982 World Cup. Each was a magnificent ball player, each a superb passer of the ball. Beside them played the powerful Di Bartolomei, with his excellent right foot, and his ability to hit long, searching passes.

Bruno Conti, the cheeky little winger chosen by Pelé as the best player of the 1982 World Cup, was a threat on either flank; Roberto Pruzzo was a neat opportunist of a centre-forward, surprisingly good in the air, as he would prove in the Final, despite a lack of height. The tall, forceful Francesco Graziani had been a member of the Italian attack when England lost a vital World Cup eliminator at the same Olympic Stadium in 1976.

In the semi-finals, Roma had shown themselves far from invincible when losing 2–0 at Tannadice to Dundee United, but they won the return 3–0 – a match I saw – and at the end surrounded United's fiery manager, Jim McLean, to abuse him. They'd not taken kindly to the cries of 'Italian bastards!' rising from United's bench in the first leg.

It would later transpire, as we have seen, that Roma's president, Senator Dino Viola, had been party to a 'plan' to bribe the referee of the second leg, Michel Vautrot. Discovery came too late for the Italian Federation to punish Roma. UEFA, who *were* in a position to do so, feebly commuted their initial punishment – suspension from European competition for a season – to a fine. *La Gazzetta dello Sport* of Milan called it 'a scandalous decision'.

For Roma, the 'scandalous decision' would involve the goal Liverpool scored against them in the Final. Did Ronnie Whelan foul Franco Tancredi, Roma's goalkeeper, when he jumped with him after 13 minutes for Craig Johnston's right-wing cross? Tancredi lost the ball, Phil Neal put it in, and the Swedish referee Fredriksson, right under the boiling Curva Sud where Roma's most passionate fans stood, gave the goal. Clearly he believed that Whelan had simply preceded Tancredi to the ball.

With Souness utterly eclipsing both Falcao and Cerezo in midfield, and Liverpool simply tormenting Roma with their clever possession football, Bruno Conti was his team's chief hope of success. Three minutes before half-time, he centred after picking up a rebound from the Liverpool

Liverpool's inspirational midfielder Graeme Souness challenges Roma's Bruno Conti in the 1984 Final in Rome. Souness orchestrated the Merseyside club's 'possession game' which so demoralised the Italian champions (Allsport)

defence, playing in a short ball to which Pruzzo delicately and skilfully got his head, looping the ball backwards over Grobbelaar and into the net.

It was a dramatic rather than a distinguished game, with attempts on goal at a premium. Craig Johnston, after an excellent first half, eventually ran out of steam and was substituted, as was Kenny Dalglish, curiously anonymous that evening. But Joe Fagan's instructions that 'whoever was close to Falcao should close him down' worked well. Roma never controlled the midfield. In the second half, Grobbelaar leaped to save from Falcao; Tancredi saved from Dalglish, diving to the far post. Pruzzo, who had been suffering from stomach pains, was less in evidence.

Extra time. Grobbelaar whips the ball off Falcao's toes, saves at his right-hand post from Conti. No more goals. The decision, alas, will rest on penalties.

Steve Nicol, the versatile young Scot who has replaced Johnston, bangs the first of them over the bar. It's Souness, deputed by Fagan, who has decided on the spot-kickers, Falcao who's decided he won't take one for Roma. Di Bartolomei scores for Roma; Phil Neal, who'd got that penalty in Rome seven years earlier, replies for Liverpool. Grobbelaar, told by Fagan that all he can do now is 'try to put them off', shakes and shimmies on his line. Conti shoots over the bar.

Now Souness himself converts his penalty. So does Righetti; then Ian Rush. The veteran 'Ciccio' Graziani runs up to the ball – and boots it over the bar. Can Alan Kennedy, Liverpool's left-back, scorer of the winning goal against Real Madrid in Paris but no great penalty taker, succeed? He does. The Cup is Liverpool's.

'They knew how to keep the ball, which we usually do,' said Nils Liedholm. Cerezo endorsed that; substituted in extra time, he wept tears at the end. 'The English showed themselves to be a great team, an almost unbeatable team. When they passed the ball to one another, which is undoubtedly their speciality, I seemed to go mad. There was a moment when I felt like the bull in the arena. I couldn't do anything to block their style of play, their passing.'

Grobbelaar, who had dropped one cross – studiously nodded back into his hands by Mark Lawrenson – but otherwise distinguished himself, had his admirers. One Roman paper described him as 'histrionic and formidable'. Roberto Pruzzo said, 'That crazy Grobbelaar, the monkey goalkeeper.' 'He's mad!' exclaimed Conti. 'I shot right-footed, the ball hit the line in front of him, and he got it.'

Modest, self-deprecatory, Joe Fagan could scarcely have presented a greater contrast with Liverpool's true begetter, Bill Shankly. Who could grudge him his triumph? 'You see,' he said, 'we're rather coming to the stage where I'm talking simple, and it's a simple game. We closed the space down on them.'

In the streets, alas, the aftermath was savage, and would bear bitter fruit in Brussels. As horrified Roman newspapers described, young thugs of the Roman *ultras* rushed to their cars to grab knives and iron bars which had been left there; then they set about the Liverpool fans. There were vicious assaults, and the extraordinary sight of fans of Lazio, Roma's bitter rivals, pressing weapons into the hands of Liverpool supporters, urging them to defend themselves.

Italy is still less a country than a collection of mutually suspicious city-states, but it would be of little use to tell a Scouser how much difference there was between a plebeian Roman and a supercilious *Torinese*, from Turin. All were simply 'Italians', and I am convinced this misconception played a part in what so tragically happened at Heysel, a year later.

For Liverpool were destined to reach the Final once again. 'What do they say?' enquired Joe Fagan, after Liverpool had thrashed the Poles of Lech Poznan 4–0 at Anfield in the first round. 'One robin doesn't make a summer?' And one player, he might have added, doesn't make a Liverpool. For Souness, like Keegan, had gone in his glory, taken off for the Continent, though for Genoa rather than Hamburg, to play for Sampdoria, right after a victory in a European Cup Final in Rome. The new incumbent was a very different figure, the marauding half-back John Wark, a Scot from Ipswich Town, who had been Cup-tied the previous season. Against Lech, Wark scored three goals. 'The manager told me before the game where I was playing,' he said, 'and I really enjoyed it. I've not been playing there lately. I've been playing behind the front two. I was able to lay back and come in late. I think I get more space in Europe, and people don't know about me coming in late and getting goals.'

Wark, in fact, had also scored the only goal of the game in Poland, a typically well-judged late run to the far post, on to a clever chip by Kenny Dalglish. Old foes came next in Benfica. A hat-trick by Ian Rush brought a 3–1 win at Anfield; there were protests that one of the goals was blemished by two Liverpool men running offside, another by a preceding handball by Whelan. In Lisbon, Liverpool did not run riot this time. They lost 1–0 to a fifth-minute penalty by Manniche, and had to hold out with 10 men after Kenny Dalglish was sent off a minute before half-time.

This meant a two-match suspension and a chance for the blond, sturdy, mobile Paul Walsh to come into the attack in the quarter-final against FK Austria. Walsh, a Londoner, began with Charlton, and had been bought from Luton. Austria's own highly promising young centre-forward, Toni Polster, who'd find his way to Italy and Spain, beat two Liverpool defenders and drove past Grobbelaar midway through the first half in Vienna. Steve Nicol, playing in midfield with Wark, Whelan and another new man, the left-footed Kevin MacDonald from Leicester City, equalised five minutes from time, after two of his shots had been blocked.

Parits, Austria's manager, gave them little chance at Anfield, and he was proved right. Prohaska, in such fine midfield form in Vienna, missed an excellent chance before Liverpool took the lead, and later scored his team's only goal, but it was Liverpool's night. They won 4–1 with two for Walsh, who missed a penalty near the end, and thus a hat-trick. Joe Fagan was uncharacteristically vexed with his players who, egged on by the Kop, let Walsh take the kick.

Now came Panathinaikos, and problems. The progress of the Athenian club to the semi-finals had been, if not suspect, then unusual. Penalties had played a curiously large part. Liverpool, alarmed, received puzzling, unsubstantiated allegations from Greece itself. Panathinaikos were now the property of a very rich, or *nouveau riche*, man, the ship owner and oil magnate Vardinoyannis. He and his family had made their fortune breaking the half-hearted sanctions placed on trade with Rhodesia, in the days of UDI and Ian Smith.

Panathinaikos had had no fewer than four penalties given them on their way to the semi-final. Linfield, the Belfast club, were actually a goal ahead in Athens when Panathinaikos were given a penalty from which they equalised, going on to win 2–1. In Belfast, each side was given a penalty. The Greeks' spot-kick came when Linfield had gone into a remarkable 3–0 lead. Saravakos, a fast, clever winger, scored. Linfield collapsed, Panathinaikos drew 3–3 and qualified.

Most controversial of all were the penalties received in the two quarter-final ties against Sweden's Gothenburg. The only goal in Sweden, where the Greeks played a bruising, breakaway game, came after 51 minutes. Wernersson, the Swedish goalkeeper, dived at the feet of Dimopoulos. To the general astonishment, the Scottish referee, McGinlay, awarded a penalty, from which Panathinaikos scored.

In Athens, the Swedes were 2–1 ahead with 14 minutes left and on the verge of eliminating Panathinaikos on away goals. Saravakos was tackled, fairly it seemed, and demanded a penalty. The referee, a West German called Roth, had already given the Greeks a goal which looked offside. Now, when Schiller challenged Saravakos a couple of minutes later, Roth did give a penalty, from which Saravakos equalised, enabling Panathinaikos to get through. According to the highly respected French sports paper *L'Equipe*, Roth, 'seeming to indulge himself in the detestable game of compensation', gave what was 'without doubt a non-existent foul'. An ill augury for the games with Liverpool.

Then, as I reported in the *Sunday Times* three days before the first leg at Anfield, there was the matter of the referee, Jan Keizer of Holland. A year earlier, he had been plunged into controversy. Manchester United had been drawn against Juventus in the semi-finals of the Cup Winners' Cup, Keizer being designated to take the first game at Old Trafford.

By a strange coincidence, Ron Atkinson, then the United manager, found himself at Schiphol Airport, Amsterdam, to discuss a transfer. Looking across the airport lounge, the Ajax club official with whom he was talking noticed Jan Keizer, in conversation with Barattini, a Juventus employee concerned with 'foreign relations', and Peter Stephan, the former general manager of the Feyenoord club.

Manchester United reported all this to UEFA. Keizer insisted he was speaking only to Stephan, who had brought him various presents from Rumania. No one explained what Barattini was doing there. Keizer was not removed from the first-leg game, which was refereed quite adequately. 'So, one hopes, it will be at Anfield,' I wrote.

My *Sunday Times* article, and the controversial circumstances surrounding the semi-final – semi-anonymous warnings and the like – produced a tempest of controversy in Athens. Panathinaikos' president arrived in Liverpool breathing fire and slaughter. He would report Liverpool to UEFA, he would close down the *Sunday Times*, etcetera.

I had pointed out that among the various possessions of the Vardinoyannis brothers was a splendid hotel, the Meridian, where visiting referees were well looked after. The Hungarian referee, Nemeth, had been a guest there before the home tie against Linfield, as had Roth before the match against Gothenburg. He had been met on arrival at Athens airport by a certain Kalogeras, notionally assistant to the Polish manager Gmoch, formerly in charge of his national team.

The hospitable Kalogeras, and a Greek referee called Christos Kolokithas, took Roth and his linesmen round Athens the night before the Gothenburg match. According to a local sporting daily paper, they went to the Myptia Taverna to eat, then took in a Bouzouki music club, till an exhausted Kolokithas left them, saying that he couldn't stay up all night.

The match at Anfield turned out to be a rather odd one. Liverpool won it 4–0, but neither Gmoch nor his president was pleased. At the end, Gmoch went hurtling down the dressing-room corridor. 'Stupid, effing . . .' he cried, showing a command of English obscenity to be reckoned with. 'I am sorry. I am very excited. I do not like this . . .' We were not told quite what. The refereeing, perhaps? 'My best opinion,' promised Gmoch, 'I give you after the second game. That is all I have to say. We make revenge in Athens. We see who is better. And who make football.' He was also quoted by Greek journalists as having cried, as he departed, 'Whores! We will screw you in Athens!' Hardly the pleasant, smiling, Anglophile Gmoch we had known and loved. 'It was hard,' I wrote at the time, 'not to see it as the petulant outburst of a spoiled child, deprived for once of unmerited privileges.'

In the event, Keizer refereed the game well, though he seemed averse almost in principle to awarding penalties. Not that Liverpool, 4–0 winners, really needed them. In the first half, a shot by Dalglish seemed to be handled in the box. A minute later, he was impeded there, but got only an indirect free-kick. Twice, Saravakos was brought down in the Liverpool penalty area. The first time, after being brought down by Mark Lawrenson, he threshed about like a landed fish. On the second occasion, he lay prone as a dead man, ignored by his colleagues, till at last Grobbelaar booted the ball out of play. Keizer was unmoved on each occasion.

Rocha, Panathinaikos' elegant, clever, incisive Argentine midfielder, gave Liverpool's defence trouble at times, but what really undid the Greeks was the abysmal goalkeeping of Laftsis. He fumbled Macdonald's shot on to the post for the first goal, stayed rooted to his line for the second. Karoulias ineptly surrendered the ball for Sammy Lee to set up the third. Lee played only because Nicol was injured.

'It was like starting all over again,' he said, ever the cherubic tyro. 'I was very nervous. Thankfully, the crowd gave me a great lift, a great boost. I'm nervous before every game, but I couldn't eat today, and that's usually no problem for me.'

Rush, with typical honesty, admitted he might have had four or five goals rather than the two he did get, and it was true; his finishing was oddly wayward.

What would happen in Athens? There was reason for alarm, but in fact, all passed off smoothly, though poor Saravakos, that talented, tumbling winger, was refused yet another penalty when Beglin brought him down. Inside the box, it seemed; outside, decreed the referee. On the hour, a fine, sustained Liverpool move ended with Mark Lawrenson exchanging passes with Whelan and running on to score. Liverpool would now play Juventus in Brussels. It would be their last European Cup game for many years to come.

That Juventus eventually beat Liverpool 1–0 through a penalty scored by Michel Platini, awarded for a foul by Gary Gillespie which was clearly committed outside the penalty box, was the least important thing that happened that evening. That terrible evening. Before even the game started, Liverpool fans broke out of the X and Y terraces and chased Juventus supporters, in section Z, into a wall which collapsed. Thirty-eight died, the great majority Italians. Another would later die in hospital.

I have already adumbrated several of the factors which would lead to disaster: inadequate inspection of an inadequate stadium, the acquisition of tickets on the 'neutral' Z terrace by Italian fans. To these one may add the incompetence and lack of courage of the police and gendarmerie. None of which exonerates the Liverpool fans. As Mrs Thatcher would remark in 10 Downing Street, a couple of days after the horrors, it was an appalling thing that one set of supporters could not stand beside another without being attacked.

As a club, Liverpool, alas, were not remotely matched by their notorious supporters. Among these there was beyond doubt a core of decent, largely middle-aged, peaceful, pleasant fans, who would share the mature, sensible attitudes of the club itself. There were also, as fans from other clubs all over the country knew all too well, thousands of brutalised, violent toughs, whose excesses had been known for many years.

Liverpool's, in the 1960s, were really the first of the hooligans, though their chant, 'We're The Best-Behaved Supporters in the Land', sought to belie it. They'd be surpassed in due time by Manchester United's fans, who included thugs from all over the country. Liverpool's at least were home grown. Such roughnecks not only attacked fans of opposing clubs at home, but sometimes ventured abroad with the club to commit robberies.

Some weeks before the European Cup Final, when the detested Manchester United visited Anfield on a Sunday, the city had seemed awash with hatred. Coaches and trains of United's supporters were stoned. Mechanics would run out of the very garages to scream abuse at the coaches as they went by. When United, just a few weeks later, came once more to Merseyside to play Liverpool, this time in the FA Cup semi-final at Goodison Park, Liverpool's supporters were firing flares into the Manchester fans' sections. Quite where Liverpool's following had gained its spurious reputation for good conduct with a blinkered press was obscure. But then, journalists see little or nothing from the Press Box, nothing of what goes on, often sinister and violent, in the surrounding streets and alleys, at railway stations. Unless they are privy to good, first-hand information, journalists accept the public, distorted image; in this case, a misleadingly benign one.

Nor would it be enough to say that violence among Liverpool fans could be explained by unemployment, the crumbling and deliquescence of a doomed city. The behaviour of Everton's fans, in Rotterdam for the Cup Winners' Cup Final two weeks before, had been exemplary.

But long before the match at Heysel, scores of Liverpool fans lay around, manifestly drunk, in the sunshine, on grass around the stadium. Drunkenness would play a sombre part in what happened; but so would the almost unbelievable laxity of the local police. There was no attempt to search fans for weapons as they passed into the stadium, no attempt to stop them bringing in drink. The ineffable Count Nothomb, Minister of the Interior, whose obdurate refusal to resign would eventually bring down the Belgian government, said that Belgian policemen had been sent to England before the match to study the problems of violence, but had been astonished that violence should occur at Heysel *prior to the kick-off*. It was rather as though one should be astonished that night followed day. The pattern of violence in English grounds had been known for years.

A dangerous situation was compounded by the decrepit stadium itself. It was only too easy for Liverpool fans, once inside, to hand their tickets over the wire to others outside, and for still other fans to wriggle in under the wire. The problem of *lebensraum* played its ugly part; squashed and crowded on the X and Y terraces, with the influx of ticketless fans, the Liverpool supporters would eventually storm the flimsy barrier, to chase the Italians in the adjacent Z section from 'their' end of the ground.

The Liverpool fans – some of whom had been herded by the police into the Z terracing, and been maltreated by Italian fans – drove the Italians into a fatal triangle, formed by two walls. Of these, the vertical wall collapsed, with horrific consequences. Many of the Italians died where they stood. Others were trampled to death. Eight Belgian policemen – just eight of them – watched from the track; and attacked those trying to escape the carnage, with their batons.

English police, one felt, would have intervened far earlier, wading in with their usual courage when the first signs of trouble had been seen, a good half an hour earlier. For the final, fatal charge was in fact the *third*.

'The first attack by the Liverpool fans came at 6.30 pm,' said an Italian witness, Marco Fornelli, director of a machine tool company in Turin. 'It consisted of rocks and rockets. At least twenty rockets were fired into the middle of the Juventus supporters, who were obviously terrified. They withdrew in what seemed an orderly fashion, about five metres back. There was a lull of about half an hour. Then the second assault began. The English began to break down the fence and pelted the Italians with rocks, beer cans, bottles and fireworks. The fence was broken and a few Englishmen climbed over it, but by then the Italians had moved back about sixty yards. There was a pause of about a quarter of an hour.'

Still no action by the police.

'Then the third assault began,' said Fornelli, 'with the English moving over the broken fence, and then charging into the Italians with broken bottles, tin cans, rocks and fists. I didn't see any of them armed with knives or pistols, but about ten or fifteen belted into the crowd, who began to panic.'

Liverpool fans confront police at the Heysel Stadium before the 1985 Final. The lack of effective police action was notable as the tragedy unfolded
(Allsport/Dave Cannon)

Yet when all is said and done, one has to take account of the particular circumstances, the dreadful death trap constituted by the two walls, each topped with wire, too high for anyone to climb. Such charges, 'running' opposing fans, were all too common at the time in English stadiums. Only with improved police control, through closed-circuit television, would they become largely a thing of the past. They were not, in their intent, murderous, however violent. Nor can one believe that those rampaging Liverpool fans, however drunk, vicious and xenophobe, intended that anyone should die.

For over an hour, at the opposite end of the ground, young 'Juve' fans taunted the passive police. The Italians themselves would view the disaster with amazing objectivity and comprehension. There, blame was chiefly reserved for the shockingly inept Belgian authorities, for Nothomb himself, for the pitiful police.

Long after the charge and the deaths, in fact, one remembers the absurd sight of a pompous officer marching his policemen into the stadium, lining them up in the centre circle – and inspecting them!

John Smith, the chairman of Liverpool, gave an interview in which he said he had been approached by half a dozen London members of the National Front, claiming they had started the brawl. 'They seemed,' wrote the *Sunday Times*, 'lame excuses, bred of football's familiar malaise: a refusal to face up to its own responsibilities.' Though Liverpool, in fact, had faced those responsibilities with a determination which, alas, was not emulated by UEFA.

When, after a long examination by the Liverpool police of television footage of the riot, the presumed culprits were brought to trial in Brussels, the great preponderance of them were, in fact, Liverpudlians. Hardly a surprise to those who had seen the drunkenness outside the stadium, or were aware of the ways of Liverpool fans.

Two days after the events, Margaret Thatcher, Prime Minister of Britain, summoned a group of seven football journalists to Downing Street. I was among them. She said she wanted to hear *our* views, but she clearly had strong views of her own, which had been formulating since the appalling riots by Millwall fans at a Cup replay at Luton the previous March, shown on television.

'I *don't* like to speak about informing,' she told us, 'but I think we ought to get the *decent* fans to express their *disapproval*.' But if football journalists knew so little about hooliganism, why should Prime Ministers know more? Mrs Thatcher spoke about registering supporters and giving them identity cards. A misbegotten scheme had been born.

Not till the devastating Taylor Report on the Hillsborough disaster of 1989 had contemptuously dismissed the ID card plan were football clubs at last free from it. Lord Justice Taylor had seen what was plain from the start to almost all but Mrs Thatcher and her minions: that such a scheme would provoke more trouble than it would resolve. Her Minister of Sport, Colin Moynihan, small but imperfectly informed, pushed the plan with febrile, mistaken energy for five shrill years.

The Football Association, after Heysel, withdrew the English clubs from European competition. UEFA banned them indefinitely, with an extra three-year ban for Liverpool. The final irony. Liverpool, who had warned UEFA about the Heysel stadium, who had always done everything in their power to prevent conflict and violence, who had set a marvellous example to English clubs, on the field, were out of Europe for who knew how long? Victims of their own supporters.

10

THE MIDLANDS
IN EUROPE

For a few brief, remarkable years, the East and West Midlands played a victorious part in the European Cup. Manchester United and Liverpool were great, rich clubs which might be expected to spread their wings in Europe. Nottingham Forest and Aston Villa, though steeped in history, had spent years in the doldrums – from which they would emerge in glory.

There could scarcely have been a greater contrast between the winning managers. For Forest, Brian Clough, best described perhaps as a sacred monster; bombastic, dictatorial, overbearing – and inspirational. A manager who first transformed and galvanised nearby Derby County, in a famous partnership with the late Peter Taylor which had begun in their days as Middlesbrough players, Clough would do better still with Nottingham Forest. Tony Barton, Villa's manager, was, by contrast, a quiet, modest, charming man, once a footballer of limited achievement, where Clough had been a prolific centre-forward.

Taylor was one of the very first to descry Clough's potential. Arriving at Middlesbrough as reserve goalkeeper, he found Clough, a local boy, not long out of the Royal Air Force where he'd served two years' conscription. Taylor's estimate of Clough's potential as a centre-forward was even higher than that of Clough himself; which was saying much. As a player, Clough became renowned for his single-minded, some would have said greedy, pursuit of goals, not to say his penchant for giving advice to the rest of the team. The Middlesbrough manager could scarcely handle him. Taylor, who said he admired him as a player but did not much like him as a person, spent endless hours with him; sometimes in Taylor's house, sometimes at football grounds all over the North East, watching football and footballers.

For Taylor, Clough was an incomparable goalscorer; a devastating shot, with scarcely any backlift, a sublime snapper-up of unconsidered trifles. It is hard to know, in retrospect, how good Clough was, for most of his abundance of goals was scored in the Second Division, and he was picked only a couple of times for England before a cruel injury, as a Sunderland player, put him out of the game.

When George Hardwick, former captain and full-back of Middlesbrough and England, then Sunderland manager, gave Clough the job of coach to the juniors, which he did impressively, Sunderland's directors insisted he be thrown out. Hardwick felt bitter about that for many years to come. It was surely Sunderland's loss.

Football utterly obsessed both Clough and Taylor. As managers, a double act, they cut their teeth on the run-down little Hartlepools club, in the North East. 'People said you could drop off the edge of the world if you went to Hartlepool,' said Clough. But he and Taylor put the club on the map.

Clough had become a disenchanted and unhappy figure. 'He was a no-hoper,' said Taylor – which is hard to imagine. 'Jobless, boozing heavily, and on his way out.'

Suddenly Clough was offered the Hartlepool job. He told Taylor, nicely ensconced as manager of the non-League club Burton Albion, that he'd reluctantly accept – if Taylor would join him. Though it meant a financial loss, Taylor did.

No less a figure than Len Shackleton, the great maverick inside-forward of his times, had recommended Clough to Hartlepool, which showed he was as perceptive off the field as on it. Later, it would be 'Shack' who recommended Clough and Taylor to Derby County; though Derby, when he brought them together, didn't even pay for his lunch.

The long, largely productive relationship between Clough and Taylor is as mysterious as a marriage. Who did what? Who owed exactly what to whom? Within a limited context, they were splendidly successful at Hartlepool, after battles with a five-foot, millionaire chairman. At Derby, they worked wonders. At Brighton, they failed pitifully. At Leeds, without Taylor, Clough was humiliated. At Nottingham Forest, subdued and demoralised, Clough did not really begin to perform his small miracles till Taylor rejoined him from Brighton. Taylor could galvanise him, joke and jolly him out of his depressions, complement Clough's particular inspirational talents with his own.

Now and again, feeling unappreciated, not least in their Derby days when the chairman, Sam Longson, gave every credit and every present to Clough, Taylor would erupt in bitter resentment. Clough, he implied, could never succeed without him. Yet when the split between them eventually came, and Clough was left on his own at Forest, he remained impressively afloat. Was it that he'd matured, that he'd learned enough from Taylor, had enough support from Taylor, to be able at last to swim on his own? Had Taylor exaggerated his own contribution? Who knows? Perhaps a partnership so intense – the kind of managerial partnership virtually unknown in English football beforehand – could never have lasted indefinitely. But it may be significant that Taylor, on his own, never achieved the success which he and Clough had together.

They took over at Derby County in 1967, and stayed for six remarkable, often turbulent, years. They took Derby out of the Second Division to win the First Division Championship, just as they would later do with their neighbours, Nottingham Forest. They reached the semi-finals of the European Cup.

Their transfer policy was remarkable. Clough always had his favourite, almost talismanic, players. One was the slender midfielder John McGovern, whom he had persuaded as a 16-year-old to give up his studies and sign for Hartlepools. Another was John O'Hare, whom he had coached as a Sunderland junior, persuading him to turn from a right-half into a centre-forward; he would play for Scotland. Roy McFarland, a future England centre-half, arrived from Tranmere Rovers, though he had no real interest in playing for anyone but his local Liverpool. Obtaining his signature involved the most extraordinary machinations from Clough and Taylor.

First, pretending to phone his chairman from the office of Dave Russell, the Tranmere manager, Clough agreed on a fee of £24 000, insisting that was his limit, when in fact he had £49 000 to spend. Then he and Taylor drove in the middle of the night to McFarland's house and refused to leave until he agreed to sign for Derby. Eventually, at his father's instigation, he did, and initially thought he'd 'made the biggest mistake of his life'.

Later, Clough would bring off a very different but equally successful transfer, buying the experienced Scottish international left-half, Dave Mackay, from Tottenham. Mackay was slowing down and putting on weight. Clough told him, to his surprise, that he wanted him not in his old, propulsive role, but as a defender, strolling about and sweeping up. Mackay joined Derby, and flourished.

The volatile relations between Derby's chairman Sam Longson – another self-made millionaire – and Clough and Taylor finally led to the end of the regime. Longson, at first bedazzled by Clough, whom he treated almost as a favourite son, then, by his own admission, became jealous of the kudos he was gaining. This in turn was exacerbated by the problems Clough's outspoken statements on television and in the Press caused with the Football League. When, early in 1973, Clough and Taylor in turn fell out, after Taylor discovered Clough had received a pay increase of £5000, there was anarchy. Twice, Longson offered Clough's job to Taylor, according to Taylor himself, though Longson denied it.

In the autumn, the balloon went up. Longson instructed the club secretary, Stuart Webb, to lock the drinks cabinet. Bitter ultimatums were exchanged. Clough and Taylor submitted their resignations. After great turmoil, they were accepted. Longson subsequently issued a statement which cost him a £25 000 libel settlement out of court, with Clough. The Derby players 'sat in' at the Baseball Ground in protest. Clough himself was ready to return. But instead, the directors made Dave Mackay the manager. A Protest Movement waxed, and waned. In November, the players signed a letter to say they would strike; then didn't send it, after their plans became known.

Two and a half years later, under a new chairman, the inevitable self-made millionaire, George Hardy, Derby tried to bring Clough and Taylor back, from Nottingham Forest. Taylor was eager to agree, but Clough eventually refused.

Nottingham Forest's Stuart Dryden, a committee member then, and a future chairman, had wanted Clough to take over at Forest after the resignation from Derby, but it was Mike Bamber, a millionaire of course, who moved in and persuaded both Clough and Taylor to take over at Brighton and Hove Albion, then only a Third Division club.

They were hardly an instant success. An overawed team was thrashed at home in the FA Cup 4–0 by the amateurs of Walton and Hersham, then lost 8–2, again at the Goldstone Ground, to Bristol Rovers. Clough stayed for eight months, then accepted a surprising offer to manage Leeds United. Surprising, because he had publicly accused Leeds of cheating their way to success. It was doubtful whether his customary methods, hard and soft detective in one, would work with the seasoned, tough professionals of Leeds; nor did they. After 44 days, he was out, demoralised. Taylor had not gone with him; he preferred to stay at Brighton.

At Leeds, Clough bought three new players: his old stand-bys, John O'Hare and John McGovern, plus the highly-talented Nottingham Forest centre-forward, Duncan McKenzie. The Leeds team which had grown up under Don Revie rejected them, as they rejected Clough, like a body rejecting a transplant. Clough had also brought with him as coach Jimmy Gordon, a Scot who once played left-half for Middlesbrough and had stayed there as a trainer. He never liked Clough, but had been persuaded to join him at Derby. Precisely, said Clough, because at Ayresome Park, Gordon always argued with him. He would follow Clough to Nottingham Forest, too; and still didn't like him.

So it was that in January 1975 Clough, still without Taylor – Laurel without Hardy, Morecambe without Wise – became at last manager of Nottingham Forest, a Second Division team.

It was not, for a while, the same exuberant, domineering Clough. The experience at Leeds had been a traumatising one. This time, Clough's chairman would not be the usual, unlettered, self-made millionaire but a successful QC in criminal law, the highly educated Brian Appleby, a man whose intellectual and educational superiority were hardly likely to reassure Clough's feelings of cultural inadequacy. Nor – though Appleby brought him to the club to avoid 'disaster' – would he ever warm to Clough as Longson once had.

John McGovern inevitably arrived, and found a deflated, diminished Clough. John O'Hare arrived too, as of course did Jimmy Gordon. Peter Taylor did not join Forest for another 18 sterile months, when Clough came to Canossa – or rather, Mallorca –to persuade him to leave Brighton and rejoin him. Once at the City Ground, Taylor began hiring and firing, and Clough became a different man.

Brian Clough, twice winner of the European Cup with Nottingham Forest, semi-finalist with Derby County. Endlessly controversial; and resourceful (Allsport)

John Robertson, a Scottish left-sided midfielder, was perhaps the key to the Forest revival. Taylor found him overweight and unambitious, discerned his qualities as a deep outside-left, made him into one, and reaped enormous benefit. With his clever control and fine distribution, Robertson became the fulcrum of Forest's attacks, while the equally left-sided Tony Woodcock, a largely disregarded striker, moved out into the spaces Robertson left on the flank, with devastating effect.

Robertson would later deny that Clough 'ruled by fear'. He wanted to play for him, he says, and his tactical advice was always precious. Clough, in fact, has always done things in his own way. He could be outrageous, could criticise Woodcock publicly on television, could stay away from the training ground for much of the week. But when do you meet a famous player who will say a word against him? When Clough turned up at the training ground, said Peter Shilton, whom Clough would make the game's most expensive goalkeeper, what you'd see was 'attitude training'. He and Taylor had their own extraordinary way of doing things. Sometimes, before an important European Cup match, they would simply sit the team down and ply them with drink, to relax them. It was they who initiated the midseason break in the sunshine, abroad.

Clough would buy the first million-pound player in the history of British football, in Trevor Francis, and Francis' header would win Forest the European Cup Final against Malmo. He would also spend more than a million pounds on strikers such as Ian Wallace and Justin Fashanu; money down the drain.

The revitalised Forest got out of the Second Division, won the First Division title, and found themselves faced, in the first round of the European

Cup in September 1978 – as an unseeded team – with mighty Liverpool, the holders. This was going to be the new, rationalised Forest, European edition. Entertainment and adventure, Clough and Taylor decided, had now to give way to the *realpolitik* of dour defence and counter-attack; though when the team did go forward, it would be in numbers.

In one of those surprising, inspired or impulsive – have it as you wish – transfers for which they were renowned, Forest suddenly sold their big centre-forward, Peter Withe, to Newcastle, at the start of the new season. They replaced him with the young Steve Elliott, unsuccessfully. So the third choice Garry Birtles got his chance; the stuff of fairy tales.

I was among those who felt the sale of Withe had been mistaken and premature, not least when Elliott failed to flourish. But then there was Birtles: Garry Birtles, whom Clough had first watched playing non-League football for the nearby Long Eaton. 'Even the Oxo was better than Garry Birtles,' said Clough, who signed him only because Taylor looked at him and thought there might be potential. Now Birtles got his chance, and took it remarkably.

Against Liverpool, in the first leg at Nottingham, Birtles was a swift if inelegant menace to Liverpool's defence, now striking from the right, now from the left. Woodcock was just as effective and dangerous. Liverpool's back four never liked the opposition to run at them without respect, and this was just what Forest did. Liverpool's midfield four, even with Graeme Souness, who had played superbly in the World Cup for Scotland against

Peter Shilton (Allsport)

Holland that year, was pedestrian, which meant equally that the potentially explosive Kenny Dalglish found himself isolated in attack. Getting through a Forest defence commanded by as mobile, versatile and decisive a centre-half as Kenny Burns was no easy matter.

Clough and Taylor had worked the oracle again, buying Kenny Burns from Birmingham City, when Forest went up to Division 1, a player renowned as much for his indiscipline, his eruptive episodes, as for his all-round ability; but he was a fine centre-forward. Taylor, pursuing his policy of softening up 'hard' cases, decided it could be done with Burns, too; and so it was. He would give one of his most immaculate performances in the European Cup Final against Kevin Keegan and Hamburg.

Another Scot, a more familiar face, arrived at the same time: the tireless, clever little inside-forward Archie Gemmill, who in that same 1978 World Cup in Argentina was thought to have scored the best goal of the tournament, against Holland. Gemmill had come from Preston to join Clough and Taylor at Derby, recommended by Stuart Webb, who had been secretary at North End. Now, after being one of the most loyal supporters of Clough and Taylor during the protest movement, here he was in Nottingham. Ironically Taylor, a Nottingham man, would still have preferred to be in the more passionate environs of Derby. As for

Gemmill, he once said of Clough, 'I hate the bastard, but I'd give him my last half-crown.'

Emlyn Hughes, the Liverpool skipper, lamented after their 2–0 defeat at the City Ground that they hadn't taken it seriously, specially enough; hadn't treated it as a European occasion, rather than as just another League game. Liverpool, thought Hughes, attacked too much, which certainly suited Forest's new, more realistic, style.

In the first half, Birtles shot home a pass from Tony Woodcock. Three minutes from the end, he snapped up a careless pass on the left, beat Phil Thompson as he came across, and centred. Woodcock headed the ball for Colin Barrett, the left-back, who had come steaming out of defence, to smash it home.

Anfield held no terrors for Forest, who had drawn their final match of the previous season there, 0–0. Now Clough and Taylor devised elaborate schemes to trap Liverpool in their web. Gemmill played on the right of midfield to stop big Ray Kennedy breaking forward, a little man against a giant; McGovern marked Souness, Robertson dropped deeper than ever to take care of Case; Bowyer looked after McDermott.

Another 0–0 draw was the consequence, even if Viv Anderson, the right-back who'd be the first black player to play for England, had to kick off the line from Dalglish, who also forced two excellent saves by Peter Shilton. Like the first leg at the City Ground, it was hardly a distinguished game. 'There was too much frenzy,' said Bill Shankly, who was watching, 'no composure. There's a difference between playing it quick and doing it in a hurry. Tonight, Liverpool were doing it in a hurry.' Bob Paisley, please let it be noted, expressed the view that Continental opposition was so poor that English clubs would win all three European cups. Shankly was in large agreement. 'Forest will go on and win it because they have a goalkeeper,' he said; 'they have Shilton. European keepers are inept.'

He called Anderson the best right-back in Europe, and I myself was greatly impressed by the inspired bursts of Tony Woodcock, the sometimes breathtaking feats of ball control by John Robertson, far more than a mere spoiler that night. Raymond Goethals, Belgium's team manager, was an enthusiastic spectator at Anfield. 'Only the British can unleash such a battle on a football field without falling into excess. And that crowd! What community, what force, what an example! I don't believe Liverpool are in decline. I think their team is better than Nottingham Forest.'

But it was Forest who went on to play AEK Athens, managed by none other than the Galloping Major, Ferenc Puskas, back in Athens again. Before the first leg, played in Greece, Puskas fell out with the veteran inside-left Domazos, such a star of the 1971 Panathinaikos team, and dropped him. Forest won 2–1 with their own veteran, left-back Frank Clark, rejuvenated at Forest after leaving Newcastle, an ebullient attacker.

The 35-year-old Clark began the move which led to Woodcock beating his man and making the first goal for McGovern; Clark himself then beat the offside trap and ran half the field before giving a goal to Birtles. AEK, who had Domazos' replacement, the Uruguayan Viera, sent off for punching Burns, replied from a penalty. At Nottingham, Birtles scored twice and Forest won comfortably.

Encouraging their midfield players to run with the ball, as they had at Derby, Taylor and Clough brought Forest through the quarter-finals against Grasshoppers of Zurich. Forest won 4–1 at home but the score was a little flattering. Sulser, the gifted Swiss centre-forward, scored after 10 minutes, beating Larry Lloyd, the big centre-back, another player Taylor and Clough had brought out of limbo. Sulser might have had another, after 75 minutes, when he again broke clear, but this time Peter Shilton made a memorable save.

Woodcock made a goal for Birtles just before half-time, Robertson converted a penalty for hands, just afterwards. The ever-active Gemmill got a third, created by Lloyd, three minutes from the end, and Lloyd himself – who had some epic confrontations with Clough while with Forest – headed in from a corner. In Zurich, Sulser scored again but that clever, right-sided midfield player Martin O'Neill, a university graduate and a Northern Ireland international, equalised the Swiss penalty. Cologne would be the opposition in the semi-final, with the first leg at home.

FOREST SUNK BY JAPANESE SUB read the inspired headline in a daily paper, the morning after Forest had been pegged to a 3–3 draw by a goal from Yasuhiko Okudera, a Japanese substitute, nine minutes from time. It was an immensely eventful game, played on a mudheap, in which Forest for once forgot their cautious posture – and could have paid for it.

Forest were two goals down in less than 20 minutes. Two of their key defenders were missing – Anderson suspended, Burns injured – and the *ersatz* back four had shaky moments, compounded by the fact that, for once, the usually immaculate Shilton was off form. In six minutes the Belgian Van Gool, whom Bruges badly missed in their European Cup Final against Liverpool, having transferred him, had scored. The shot was a low, angled one, to which Shilton got his right hand, but no more. The ball hit one post, then the other, and finished in the net. Not the kind of shot which usually beat Peter Shilton.

Though they lacked their key midfielder, Heinz Flohe, Cologne continued to look dangerous whenever they attacked. Another clever midfielder, the blond Neumann, combined with Van Gool to outwit the defence again and Dieter Muller, Cologne's free-scoring centre-forward, took the easiest of chances. A misplaced pass by John McGovern had been admirably exploited.

Red-haired Ian Bowyer, once a young Manchester City left-winger, now playing at left-back for Forest, hit the wood of the Cologne goal, as the reserve centre-half Dave Needham had done earlier on. Then the ever-persistent Birtles forced a corner, Robertson took it, Lloyd flicked on, and Birtles headed past the formidable German goalkeeper Harald Schumacher.

When Archie Gemmill had to withdraw, injured, Bowyer moved up into midfield, and got the equaliser, eight minutes after the break, having been replaced in defence by the evergreen Frank Clark. Robertson cut in, beating Konopka, panic ensued in the Cologne defence, and Bowyer exploited it. Cologne were rocking. Schumacher had to make a dazzling save from McGovern, but when Birtles crossed from the right, Robertson, quite untypically, launched himself at the ball to head a brave goal.

Cologne seemed down and out, when another mistake by Shilton threw them a lifeline. Okudera had barely been on the field a minute when Hennes Weisweiler, Cologne's renowned manager, gained an unexpected reward for the move. There was nothing very special about Okudera's shot; again, it was one which Shilton, the usual Shilton, would have gobbled up with ease. But on the sticky pitch, he was deceived when the ball bounced in front of him, 'stayed low, and went under my hands. It was possibly the first major error I had made since joining Forest.'

Forest players celebrate Trevor Francis' winning goal in Munich. From left: Tony Woodcock, John McGovern, Garry Birtles, John Robertson and Larry Lloyd

(Allsport)

With three away goals under their belt, whatever the way they had been scored, Cologne could only be favourites on their own ground. No English team had ever gone abroad, after failing to win the first leg at home, and survived. The bookmakers were laying 4 to 1 against Forest. 'Bite their hands off,' Taylor told the fans. For his own, complex reasons, he'd decided that Cologne would not score and Forest would win. His niece's husband, who had studied under Weisweiler, had told him the Cologne coach was 'deeply conservative' and would not take chances.

And lo, it came to pass that Forest did win, by the only goal. Scored, again, by Ian Bowyer, still standing in for Gemmill. The defence, meanwhile, had been reinforced by the return of Burns and Anderson. When Dieter Muller went off injured, before half-time, the game was already going Forest's way. After 65 minutes, the old corner-kick ploy worked. Robertson sent the ball over, Larry Lloyd flicked on, Bowyer stooped to conquer. A fine save by Shilton from Konopka, in the 90th minute, preserved the lead.

The opposition in the Final would be the Swedish champions Malmo, coached by a young Londoner called Bob Houghton. They'd beaten FK Austria in the semi-finals, a solitary home goal deciding it. Taylor looked at them and couldn't believe how bad they were. Moreover, Nottingham Forest could at last call on their million-pound attacker, Trevor Francis, signed the previous February but ineligible in the European Cup till now.

The fee was huge, but if anyone commanded it, it was Francis. Still only 24, he had been a first-team player with Birmingham City – who discovered him in his native Plymouth – since he was 16. Of his coruscating talents there was no doubt; grace, pace, exquisite ball control, a thundering right foot, a flair for knowing where to run and when. There was equally little dispute about his personality: quiet, modest, shy, disciplined. His physical condition, his vulnerability, was the problem. Whether or not it was true, as has been suggested, that an excess of uric acid was responsible, who can say, but he was forever pulling muscles and tendons.

Clough and Taylor now used him, against his will – and against the grain – as an outside-right, clearly a waste of a player who longed to break through the middle, using his control, anticipation and pace. Ironically, it would lead to his scoring the only goal of a deeply dull match against Malmo – with his head. A rarity indeed for a player 'whose heading,' in Taylor's words, 'was something we tried to improve from the day he signed.'

A spectacular goal it was, too. John Robertson went by the Malmo defence on the outside, crossed hard and fast with his left foot, and Francis, racing in from the right, met the ball full pelt to head it just inside the right-hand upright. The goal was scored, moreover, at the delicate psychological moment of injury time in the first half. It won a tired Forest team the Cup, against a tediously defensive Malmo.

Now the Cup had to be kept. Gemmill wasn't. The exuberant little Scot who had done so much for Clough at Derby and Forest, who had said, 'A player can never feel too sure of himself with Clough, that's his secret,' proved all too right. He was sold in the summer to Birmingham. The blond Scot, Asa Hartford, arrived from Manchester City – and was sold to Everton in August. Clough and Taylor discovered, belatedly, that he couldn't, or wouldn't, switch the play. In December, when Forest were comfortably in the quarter-finals, they took a still greater risk: they paid Queens Park Rangers £250 000 for their inside-left, Stan Bowles, a player Taylor, at Derby, could have picked up from Carlisle United for £90 000.

Bowles was one of the most marvellous English talents of his day, but like so many of the truly gifted English players of his generation, he was his own worst enemy off the field. Gambling was his crucial problem; it was said he could never pass a betting shop without going in.

So it was that, in his early days, he drifted from club to club, despite his astonishing gifts, his feathery elusiveness, his delicately accurate left foot, his flair for making the unexpected pass. Finally he settled down, after a fashion, at Shepherd's Bush, though the White City dog track seemed temptingly close. He inspired a fine Queens Park Rangers team which so nearly won the Championship, and no doubt Taylor wanted him because he felt that here was another unruly talent he could tame. Alas, it was too late. Bowles would walk out on the club, when a European Cup medal was within his grasp.

Forest also bought Frank Gray, an attacking Scottish left-back, from Leeds, but found themselves, again, without an ineligible Francis. An ante-cedent contract with an ephemeral American club in Detroit kept him in the States too long to be registered in time for the opening round of the European Cup. A £2.5-million new stand – which would prove the usual albatross – was being built, Clough was challenging his directors. At Forest, there was never a dull moment.

Swedes had to be met again, in the first round, in the shape of Osters Vaxjo. Faithful Ian Bowyer scored both goals against them in Nottingham. The away leg was drawn 1–1; a remarkably precocious 17-year-old right-winger, Gary Mills, made the equaliser for Tony Woodcock. Arges Pitesti, the Rumanian champions, were beaten home and away, their defender Zamfir being sent off in Nottingham. Dynamo Berlin, the quarter-final opponents, would be a tougher nut to crack.

Tony Woodcock had gone, the previous November – to Cologne, Forest's victims in the previous campaign's semi-finals. Had Forest kept him till the end of the season, UEFA rules would have cut his price substantially. At Nottingham, Dynamo's trump card Hans-Jurgen Riediger unexpectedly played. He scored, and won the game for Dynamo.

The strong, quick, thrusting Riediger, jewel in Dynamo's crown, had had an operation on his ankle the previous December, and was not expected to be fit. He took his goal, 17 minutes from the end, superbly, dashing on to a fine crossfield pass from Frank Terletzki, leaving Gray and Burns in his wake, then beating Shilton. So Forest went to Germany, in the wake of losing the League Cup Final to a farcical goal, with a still higher mountain to climb than in Cologne.

They climbed it. Looking at the Dynamo players before the game, a euphoric Peter Taylor told Forest's players that they looked like zombies; victory was there for the taking. Indeed Dynamo, without their most creative player, Lauck, seemed bemused by the implicit need to attack. The tie was sewn up for Forest before half-time, with Trevor Francis getting the first two goals. Needham nodded on Lloyd's free kick to set up the first, the second was struck off the underside of the bar from a pass by Martin O'Neill. Three minutes later, Robertson made it 3–0 from a penalty when Noack tripped him. He in turn tripped Noack in the second half, to give Terletzki a penalty goal. At half-time in the dressing-room Clough, forever unpredictable, simply requested silence.

Next, Ajax, who had thrashed Strasbourg. They had Ruud Krol at sweeper – sole survivor from the great days – the clever Danes, Frank Arnesen and Soren Lerby, in midfield, and gifted 'new' Dutchmen in La Ling and Tahamata up front. 'There is little doubt that Ajax are much the more thoroughly prepared, tactically alert team,' I wrote beforehand, 'but this does not mean they will have the better of the argument.'

Nor did they. Forest, indeed, won the first leg at Nottingham with so much to spare that overconfidence in the return seemed the only real danger. Trevor Francis, less stringently marked than he had been in the home leg against Dynamo Berlin, was irrepressible. Krol – what price the old Total Football? – didn't cross the half-way line till six minutes into the second half. With his wonderful turn and outstanding acceleration, Francis ridiculed his marker, Bove, scoring the first goal, setting up the second. Taking a pass from Stan Bowles, who had a pleasing second half, he sent over a cross which was foolishly handled by Zwaborn. Another penalty for John Robertson, and it finished 2–0.

Ajax won the return, in Amsterdam, 1–0; but had it not been for a couple of majestic saves by Peter Shilton, they might well have put Forest out. As it was, their only goal, headed by Lerby after 65 minutes, came from a corner which Clough insisted should never have been given away. Ajax, as one had anticipated, were a very different proposition at home, and Forest, who had cautiously left Bowles out of their midfield, owed much to their centre-backs, Lloyd and Burns, as well as to Peter Shilton.

The Final would be in Madrid against Hamburg, but with no Trevor Francis. Playing at the City Ground against Crystal Palace, he ripped his Achilles tendon. Taylor showed his usual optimism before the Final; Clough, it has been said, disguised his pessimism. Beaten 2–0 at the Bernabeu by Real Madrid, Hamburg had waltzed through the semi-final return, 5–1. Del Bosque was sent off for punching the rampant Keegan. Manny Kaltz, the attacking right-back, scored twice, one a penalty; another two went to the giant centre-forward Horst Hrubesch, both from his formidable head. But an injured ankle meant he couldn't start the Final.

It was a dreadful game, a sustained rearguard action by Forest, after John Robertson had scored the vital goal. Would Bowles have made a difference? Alas, he had, not untypically, gone AWOL after being left out of John Robertson's testimonial match against Leicester: 'I can't stick it here. I'm off.'

Picking the teenager, Gary Mills, who rewarded them with an admirable performance, Forest strung five men across the midfield and hoped for the best. And after 20 minutes, hope proved justified, when Robertson ran at

Kaltz, shot, and the ball flew in off the far post. 'Hamburg,' Peter Taylor had told his team, 'are there to be taken, especially if we get at Kaltz. He's their strength, but he doesn't look good when attacked.' So it proved.

Peter Shilton had pulled a calf muscle – a secret well kept by Forest – and he needed an injection to play, which made his superlative performance all the more astonishing. 'The team, the tactics,' I wrote, 'essentially gambled on the brilliance of Shilton, and the gamble succeeded.'

Yet why should Forest have gambled at all? Clough himself insisted that his team were exhausted, yet they dominated the quarter-hour before half-time against a Hamburg team which looked as poor as Taylor had promised it would be. Mills, playing so well, would be needlessly substituted. Forest, deeply defensive now, conceded their initiative, left Birtles to run himself ragged up front alone – where he once would have scored had he not been so weary – and nearly succumbed.

Birtles, after a splendid, sustained run, allowed himself to be tackled, telling Taylor afterwards that he wasn't aware of the defender coming in. 'I was thinking only that it was a certain goal if I could take the ball round the keeper.'

'You didn't need those sort of trimmings,' retorted Taylor. 'All it required was a simple, left-foot shot.'

Which Forest's misbegotten tactics had rendered Birtles too tired to produce. This though the veteran John O'Hare, mistakenly brought on for Mills, the player half his age, said that he'd never learnt so much as he did, sitting on the bench beside Clough, about tactics.

Hrubesch got on at half-time but was plainly unfit. Forest held on to their lead. 'Having saluted their unquestionably superb achievement in winning the European title twice in a row,' I wrote, 'having acknowledged the excellence of Shilton, the prowess of Lloyd, Burns, O'Neill, Birtles and Robertson, it must still be said that their second-half strategy was a craven one, worthy of Juventus at their worst.'

Forest have yet to win another European Cup. Defending the trophy the following season, they went out at once, to the always formidable CSKA Sofia, who won both games 1–0. Yonchev got the only goal in Sofia,

Tired but elated, Forest celebrate their victory over Hamburg in the 1980 Final in Madrid

(Popperfoto)

Kerimov the only goal in Nottingham. 'The temptation to dismiss Brian Clough and Peter Taylor as humourless, arrogant and greedy is not always easily resisted,' I wrote at the time, when Taylor published his book, *With Clough by Taylor*. 'They themselves can make it very difficult . . . Like them or loathe them, the story of Taylor and Clough is an irresistibly dramatic and successful one.' It would last another couple of years before Taylor walked out, and the two parted in bitter enmity; exacerbated when Taylor, just six months later, took over at Derby County. Later, at a transfer tribunal in London, Clough would turn his back on Taylor; the ultimate, symbolic action. Taylor was devastated. So much for the perfect partnership, corroded by time, envy and ultimate incompatibility.

The next Midland club to win the European Cup would be from the West rather than the East: Aston Villa. Villa had been somewhat controversial champions; the first time they'd achieved the title in living memory. A once mighty club, still the first in Birmingham, they had in modern times won only – among principal tournaments – the FA Cup in 1957; and that was largely because a foul by Peter McParland deprived Manchester United of their goalkeeper, Ray Wood.

Ron Saunders, a hard-driving manager who believed in '105 per cent effort', had built up the team, which had seemed rather fortunate to pip Ipswich Town for the title. Ipswich, under the managership of Bobby Robson, had played much pleasing football, and had won easily at Villa Park late in the season, but in the end they had succumbed under a plethora of fixtures.

Hard and soft detectives. When Saunders had gone, the much gentler and less demanding Tony Barton, once a Fulham right-winger, then a chief scout, took over, and it soon became clear that the team were prepared to play for him. A talented team they were, too. Gordon Cowans, nicknamed El Sid, son of the club kit man, was a busily inventive little figure in midfield, with a fine left foot, often keeping Tony Morley on the move.

Villa's left-winger, who had made his name at Preston, had tremendous speed and superb control, but had never quite fulfilled his promise. In the European Cup, he would score one stupendous goal, and make another.

Allan Evans, a powerful, uncompromising Scottish stopper, was the lynchpin of the four-in-line defence, Jimmy Rimmer an experienced goalkeeper, once with Manchester United and Arsenal, the blond Gary Shaw a young striker with great acceleration and incisiveness. Villa's European experience was negligible, but it proved no more of a handicap to them than it had to Forest. It seemed that just as the breaking of the four-minute-mile barrier by Roger Bannister had opened the floodgates to milers who followed, so the domination of the European Cup by English clubs encouraged any which won the Football League to believe it, too, could succeed. For Peter Withe, the hefty centre-forward, strong in the air, good at making space for his colleagues, it was a welcome chance to make up for the disappointment of being sold by Forest, just before he could play for them in Europe.

So, as mighty Liverpool themselves dropped out of contention, Villa astonished European football, and perhaps even themselves, by going from strength to strength. In the first round, the Icelanders of Valur Reykjavik provided a gentle introduction, a kind of *hors d'oeuvre*. Villa beat them 5–0 in Birmingham, 2–0 away, where Gary Shaw got both their goals. Then it got harder. Dynamo Berlin, with the formidable Riediger, came next. He scored

Flying winger Tony Morley – Aston Villa's outstanding player in their European Cup triumph. Morley scored some outstanding goals and set up Peter Withe's winner in the Final (Allsport/Duncan Raban)

in Berlin, but so did Tony Morley, twice, five minutes from the beginning and five minutes from the end, one goal coming from an astounding, sustained, 80-yard run, a small miracle of pace, control and composure.

Dynamo, always resilient, came to Villa Park and won by the only goal of the game, scored on the quarter-hour by the ever-alert Frank Terletzki, but Morley's away goals were enough to take Villa into the quarter-finals to face another Dynamo, this time from Kiev, a team packed with internationals and rich in experience. Oleg Blokhin, that superbly talented blond left-winger, was still in his prime. Villa were unimpressed. They went to the Soviet Union and drew, then took a surprisingly flaccid, demoralised Dynamo Kiev apart in Birmingham, with Gary Shaw and another strong Scottish centre-half, Ken McNaught, an excellent lieutenant to Allan Evans, scoring the goals.

That gave Villa plenty of confidence to take on another team deeply experienced in Europe, Anderlecht of Brussels. Robust and well integrated, cleverly prompted in midfield by the young Spaniard Lozano, dangerous in the forays of the left-footed Vercauteren, Anderlecht came to Villa Park and lost 1–0 to a goal by Tony Morley. The return in Brussels was a 0–0 draw; Villa would meet Bayern Munich, finalists yet again, in Rotterdam.

And again Villa prevailed; even though Jimmy Rimmer, their keeper, on whom so much seemed to depend, had to go off the field, hurt, early in the game. So a large, blond young goalkeeper called Nigel Spink, who had played only one game for the first team, came on – and played like a hero. After one marvellous, blocking save from the formidable Karl-Heinz Rummenigge, irrepressible in the Bayern attack, the German, in Spink's words, 'just kept looking at me, after that. He kept looking back up the pitch at me.' Later Rummenigge, whom the Villa defence never mastered, would generously congratulate Spink. Evans stuck splendidly to his difficult task against Rummenigge, and it was perhaps as well that Rummenigge did not drift out to his old stamping ground on the wings, to take on Villa's full-backs. One of them, Kenny Swain, made a glorious save on the line from the West German sweeper Klaus Augenthaler, who eight years later would win himself a World Cup medal in Rome. 'Was it amazing?' asked Swain, afterwards. 'At the end of the day, it's instinctive, isn't it?'

An intelligent analyst of a game, he felt that Villa, in the early stages, were lulled into a false sense of security. 'For the first twenty minutes, they didn't want to know. All of a sudden, we think we'll compete with them in the passing stakes, and this is not our game. We *buzz*.'

In the Bayern midfield lurked Paul Breitner, who would soon be captaining West Germany to the World Cup Final. Villa were not without talent in midfield – Cowans, the accomplished Dennis Mortimer, the vigorous Des Bremner – but Swain was right. Buzzing was Villa's game.

And how Tony Morley buzzed, when he set up the only goal! A true winger's piece of virtuosity, a masterpiece of cheek, beating Hans Weiner once, making it a double sidestep, taking it to the line whence he pulled back a ball which Withe – strangely fallible that evening – managed to knock in off the post.

It had been a difficult game, Morley said later; the great heat, the long grass, the two men he knew would be detailed to mark him. Running with the ball had been hard. 'I felt the lads were only giving three-quarters. Bayern without any doubt were there for the taking. But you can't complain.'

Indeed.

RESULTS APPENDIX:
THE EUROPEAN CUP 1955–91

1955–56

First Round
Sporting Lisbon 3–3 Partizan Belgrade
Partizan Belgrade 5–2 Sporting Lisbon
Voros Logobo 6–3 Anderlecht
Anderlecht 1–4 Voros Logobo
Servette Geneva 0–2 Real Madrid
Real Madrid 5–0 Servette Geneva
Rot Weiss Essen 0–4 Hibernian
Hibernian 1–1 Rot Weiss Essen
Aarhus 0–2 Reims
Reims 2–2 Aarhus
Rapid Vienna 6–1 PSV Eindhoven
PSV Eindhoven 1–0 Rapid Vienna
Djurgarden 0–0 Gwardia Warsaw
Gwardia Warsaw 1–4 Djurgarden
Milan 3–4 Saarbrucken
Saarbrucken 1–4 Milan

Quarter-finals
Hibernian 3–1 Djurgarden
Djurgarden 0–1 Hibernian (*in Edinburgh*)
Reims 4–2 Voros Logobo
Voros Logobo 4–4 Reims
Real Madrid 4–0 Partizan Belgrade
Partizan Belgrade 3–0 Real Madrid
Rapid Vienna 1–1 Milan
Milan 7–2 Rapid Vienna

Semi-finals
Reims 2–0 Hibernian
Hibernian 0–1 Reims
Real Madrid 4–2 Milan
Milan 2–1 Real Madrid

Final
13 June 1956, PARIS, 38 000
REAL MADRID (2) 4, REIMS (2) 3
Real: Alonso; Atienza, Lesmes; Munoz,
  Marquitos, Zarraga; Joseito; Marchal,
  Di Stefano, Rial, Gento.
Reims: Jacquet; Zimny, Giraudo;
  Leblond, Jonquet, Siatka; Hidalgo,
  Glovacki, Kopa, Bliard, Templin.
Scorers: Leblond, Templin, Hidalgo for
  Reims; Di Stefano, Rial (2), Marquitos
  for Real.

1956–57

First Round (Preliminary)
Borussia Dortmund 4–3 Spora
  Luxembourg
Spora Luxembourg 2–1 Borussia
  Dortmund

Borussia Dortmund 7–0 Spora
  Luxembourg
Dinamo Bucharest 3–1 Galatasaray
Galatasaray 2–1 Dinamo Bucharest
Slovan Bratislava 4–0 CWKS Warsaw
CWKS Warsaw 2–0 Slovan Bratislava
Anderlecht 0–2 Manchester United
Manchester United 10–0 Anderlecht
Aarhus 1–1 Nice
Nice 5–1 Aarhus
Porto 1–2 Athletic Bilbao
Athletic Bilbao 3–2 Porto
Byes: *Real Madrid, CDNA Sofia,
  Grasshoppers, Rangers, Rapid Vienna,
  Rapid Heerlen, Red Star Belgrade,
  Fiorentina, Norrköping, Honved.*

First Round Proper
Manchester United 3–2 Borussia
  Dortmund
Borussia Dortmund 0–0 Manchester
  United
CDNA Sofia 8–1 Dinamo Bucharest
Dinamo Bucharest 3–2 CDNA Sofia
Slovan Bratislava 1–0 Grasshoppers
Grasshoppers 2–0 Slovan Bratislava
Rangers 2–1 Nice
Nice 2–1 Rangers
Rangers 1–3 Nice
Real Madrid 4–2 Rapid Vienna
Rapid Vienna 3–1 Real Madrid
Real Madrid 2–0 Rapid Vienna
Rapid Heerlen 3–4 Red Star Belgrade
Red Star Belgrade 2–0 Rapid Heerlen
Fiorentina 1–1 Norrköping
Norrköping 0–1 Fiorentina
Athletic Bilbao 3–2 Honved
Honved 3–3 Athletic Bilbao

Quarter-finals
Athletic Bilbao 5–3 Manchester United
Manchester United 3–0 Athletic Bilbao
Fiorentina 3–1 Grasshoppers
Grasshoppers 2–2 Fiorentina
Red Star Belgrade 3–1 CDNA Sofia
CDNA Sofia 2–1 Red Star Belgrade
Real Madrid 3–0 Nice
Nice 2–3 Real Madrid

Semi-finals
Red Star Belgrade 0–1 Fiorentina
Fiorentina 0–0 Red Star Belgrade
Real Madrid 3–1 Manchester United
Manchester United 2–2 Real Madrid

Final
30 May 1957, MADRID, 124 000

REAL MADRID (0) 2, FIORENTINA (0) 0
Real: Alonso; Torres. Lesmes; Munoz,
  Marquitos, Zarraga; Kopa, Mateos, Di
  Stefano, Rial, Gento.
Fiorentina: Sarti; Magnini, Cervato;
  Scaramucci, Orzan, Segato; Julinho,
  Gratton, Virgili, Montuori, Bizzarri.
Scorers: Di Stefano (pen), Gento.

1957–58

First Round (Preliminary)
Rangers 3–1 Saint Etienne
Saint Etienne 2–1 Rangers
CDNA Sofia 2–1 Vasas
Vasas 6–1 CDNA Sofia
Red Star Belgrade 5–0 Stade Dudelange
Stade Dudelange 1–9 Red Star Belgrade
Aarhus 0–0 Glenavon
Glenavon 0–3 Aarhus
Gwardia Warsaw 3–1 Wismut Karl-Marx-
  Stadt
Wismut Karl-Marx-Stadt 2–0 Gwardia
  Warsaw (*Wismut won on toss of a coin*)
Seville 3–1 Benfica
Benfica 0–0 Seville
Shamrock Rovers 0–6 Manchester United
Manchester United 3–2 Shamrock Rovers
Milan 4–1 Rapid Vienna
Rapid Vienna 5–2 Milan
Milan 4–2 Rapid Vienna
Byes: *Antwerp, Real Madrid, Norrköping,
  Ajax, Dukla Prague, Young Boys Berne,
  Borussia Dortmund, CCA Bucharest.*

First Round Proper
Antwerp 1–2 Real Madrid
Real Madrid 6–0 Antwerp
Norrköping 2–2 Red Star Belgrade
Red Star Belgrade 2–1 Norrköping
Wismut Karl-Marx-Stadt 1–3 Ajax
Ajax 1–0 Wismut Karl-Marx-Stadt
Manchester United 3–0 Dukla Prague
Dukla Prague 1–0 Manchester United
Young Boys Berne 1–1 Vasas
Vasas 2–1 Young Boys Berne
Rangers 1–4 Milan
Milan 2–0 Rangers
Seville 4–0 Aarhus
Aarhus 2–0 Seville
Borussia Dortmund 4–2 CCA Bucharest
CCA Bucharest 3–1 Borussia Dortmund
Borussia Dortmund 3–1 CCA Bucharest

Quarter-finals
Manchester United 2–1 Red Star Belgrade

Red Star Belgrade 3–3 Manchester United
Real Madrid 8–0 Seville
Seville 2–2 Real Madrid
Ajax 2–2 Vasas
Vasas 4–0 Ajax
Borussia Dortmund 1–1 Milan
Milan 4–1 Borussia Dortmund

Semi-finals
Real Madrid 4–0 Vasas
Vasas 2–0 Real Madrid
Manchester United 2–1 Milan
Milan 4–0 Manchester United

Final
28 May 1958, BRUSSELS, 67 000
REAL MADRID (0) 3, MILAN (0) 2
(after extra time, 2–2 at 90 mins)
Real Madrid: Alonso; Atienza, Lesmes; Santisteban, Santamaria, Zarraga; Kopa, Joseito, Di Stefano, Rial, Gento.
Milan: Soldan; Fontana, Beraldo; Bergamaschi, Maldini, Radice; Danova, Liedholm, Schiaffino, Grillo, Cucchiaroni.
Scorers: Schiaffino, Grillo for Milan; Di Stefano, Rial, Gento for Real.

1958–59

First Round (Preliminary)
Boldklub Copenhagen 3–0 Schalke 04
Schalke 04 5–2 Boldklub Copenhagen
Schalke 04 3–1 Boldklub Copenhagen
Standard Liège 5–1 Hearts
Hearts 2–1 Standard Liège
Dynamo Zagreb 2–2 Dukla Prague
Dukla Prague 2–1 Dynamo Zagreb
Jeunesse Esch 1–2 IFK Gothenburg
IFK Gothenburg 0–1 Jeunesse Esch
IFK Gothenburg 5–1 Jeunesse Esch
Wismut Karl-Marx-Stadt 4–2 Petrolul Ploesti
Petrolul Ploesti 2–0 Wismut Karl-Marx-Stadt
Wismut Karl-Marx-Stadt 4–0 Petrolul Ploesti
Polonia Bytom 0–3 MTK Budapest
MTK Budapest 3–0 Polonia Bytom
Atlético Madrid 8–0 Drumcondra
Drumcondra 1–5 Atlético Madrid
DSO Utrecht 3–4 Sporting Lisbon
Sporting Lisbon 2–1 DSO Utrecht
Ards 1–4 Reims
Reims 6–2 Ards
Juventus 3–1 Wiener SK
Wiener SK 7–0 Juventus
Walkovers: *Young Boys Berne (v Manchester United); Besiktas (v Olympiakos).*
Byes: *Real Madrid, CDNA Sofia, Wolverhampton Wanderers, Palloseura Helsinki*

First Round Proper
Sporting Lisbon 2–3 Standard Liège
Standard Liège 2–0 Sporting Lisbon
MTK Budapest 1–2 Young Boys Berne
Young Boys Berne 4–1 MTK Budapest
Wiener SK 3–1 Dukla Prague
Dukla Prague 1–0 Wiener SK
Atlético Madrid 2–1 CDNA Sofia
CDNA Sofia 1–0 Atlético Madrid
Atlético Madrid 3–1 CDNA Sofia
IFK Gothenburg 2–2 Wismut Karl-Marx-Stadt
Wismut Karl-Marx-Stadt 4–0 IFK Gothenburg
Wolverhampton Wanderers 2–2 Schalke 04
Schalke 04 2–1 Wolverhampton Wanderers
Real Madrid 2–0 Besiktas
Besiktas 1–1 Real Madrid
Reims 4–0 Palloseura Helsinki
Palloseura Helsinki 0–3 Reims
(at Rouen)

Quarter-finals
Standard Liège 2–0 Reims
Reims 3–0 Standard Liège
Atlético Madrid 3–0 Schalke 04
Schalke 04 1–1 Atlético Madrid
Wiener SK 0–0 Real Madrid
Real Madrid 7–1 Wiener SK
Young Boys Berne 2–2 Wismut Karl-Marx-Stadt
Wismut Karl-Marx-Stadt 0–0 Young Boys Berne
Young Boys Berne 2–1 Wismut Karl-Marx-Stadt

Semi-finals
Young Boys Berne 1–0 Reims
Reims 3–0 Young Boys Berne
Real Madrid 2–1 Atlético Madrid
Atlético Madrid 1–0 Real Madrid
Real Madrid 2–1 Atlético Madrid

Final
2 June 1959, STUTTGART, 80 000
REAL MADRID (1) 2, REIMS (0) 0
Real Madrid: Dominguez; Marquitos, Zarraga; Santisteban, Santamaria, Ruiz; Kopa, Mateos, Di Stefano, Rial, Gento.
Reims: Colonna; Rodzik, Giraudo; Penverne, Jonquet, Leblond; Lamartine, Bliard, Fontaine, Piantoni, Vincent.
Scorers: Mateos, Di Stefano.

1959–60

Preliminary Round
Nice 3–2 Shamrock Rovers
Shamrock Rovers 1–1 Nice
CDNA Sofia 2–2 Barcelona
Barcelona 6–2 CDNA Sofia
Linfield 2–1 IFK Gothenburg

IFK Gothenburg 6–1 Linfield
Jeunesse Esch 5–1 LKS Lodz
LKS Lodz 2–1 Jeunesse Esch
Wiener SK 0–0 Petrolul Ploesti
Petrolul Ploesti 1–2 Wiener SK
Olympiakos 2–2 Milan
Milan 3–1 Olympiakos
Fenerbahce 1–1 Csepel
Csepel 2–3 Fenerbahce
Rangers 5–2 Anderlecht
Anderlecht 0–2 Rangers
Red Star Bratislava 2–1 Porto
Porto 0–2 Red Star Bratislava
Vorwaerts Berlin 2–1 Wolverhampton Wanderers
Wolverhampton Wanderers 2–0 Vorwaerts Berlin
Walkover: *Eintracht Frankfurt (v Kuopion Palloseura)*
Byes: *Real Madrid, Odense BK 09, Young Boys Berne, Sparta Rotterdam, Red Star Belgrade.*

First Round
Real Madrid 7–0 Jeunesse Esch
Jeunesse Esch 2–5 Real Madrid
Odense BK 09 0–3 Wiener SK
Wiener SK 2–2 Odense BK 09
Sparta Rotterdam 3–1 IFK Gothenburg
IFK Gothenburg 3–1 Sparta Rotterdam
Sparta Rotterdam 3–1 IFK Gothenburg
Milan 0–2 Barcelona
Barcelona 5–1 Milan
Young Boys Berne 1–4 Eintracht Frankfurt
Eintracht Frankfurt 1–1 Young Boys Berne
Red Star Belgrade 1–1 Wolverhampton Wanderers
Wolverhampton Wanderers 3–0 Red Star Belgrade
Rangers 4–3 Red Star Bratislava
Red Star Bratislava 1–1 Rangers
Fenerbahce 2–1 Nice
Nice 2–1 Fenerbahce
Nice 5–1 Fenerbahce

Quarter-finals
Nice 3–2 Real Madrid
Real Madrid 4–0 Nice
Barcelona 4–0 Wolverhampton Wanderers
Wolverhampton Wanderers 2–5 Barcelona
Eintracht Frankfurt 2–1 Wiener SK
Wiener SK 1–1 Eintracht Frankfurt
Rangers 3–2 Sparta Rotterdam
Sparta Rotterdam 1–0 Rangers
Rangers 3–2 Sparta Rotterdam

Semi-finals
Eintracht Frankfurt 6–1 Rangers
Rangers 3–6 Eintracht Frankfurt
Real Madrid 3–1 Barcelona
Barcelona 1–3 Real Madrid

Final

18 May 1960, GLASGOW, 135 000
REAL MADRID (3) 7,
EINTRACHT FRANKFURT (1) 3
Real Madrid: Dominguez; Marquitos,
Pachin; Vidal, Santamaria, Zarraga;
Canario, Del Sol, Di Stefano, Puskas,
Gento.
Eintracht: Loy; Lutz, Hoefer;
Wellbaecher, Eigenbrodt, Stinka;
Kress, Lindner, Stein, Pfaff, Meier.
Scorers: Di Stefano (3), Puskas (4) for
Real; Kress, Stein (2) for Eintracht.

1960–61

Preliminary Round

Frederikstad 4–3 Ajax
Ajax 0–0 Frederikstad
Limerick 0–6 Young Boys Berne
Young Boys Berne 4–2 Limerick
Kamraterna 1–3 IFK Malmö
IFK Malmö 2–1 Kamraterna
Reims 6–1 Jeunesse Esch
Jeunesse Esch 0–5 Reims
Rapid Vienna 4–0 Besiktas
Besiktas 1–0 Rapid Vienna
Juventus 2–0 CDNA Sofia
CDNA Sofia 4–1 Juventus
Aarhus 3–0 Legia Warsaw
Legia Warsaw 1–0 Aarhus
Red Star Belgrade 1–2 Ujpest Dozsa
Ujpest Dozsa 3–0 Red Star Belgrade
Barcelona 2–0 Lierse SK
Lierse SK 0–3 Barcelona
Hearts 1–2 Benfica
Benfica 3–0 Hearts
CCA Bucharest 0–3 Spartak Kralove
CCA Bucharest withdrew
Walkover: *Wismut Karl-Marx-Stadt (v
Glenavon)*
Byes: *Real Madrid, Panathinaikos,
Hamburg, Burnley*

First Round

Aarhus 3–0 Frederikstad
Frederikstad 0–1 Aarhus
IFK Malmö 1–0 CDNA Sofia
CDNA Sofia 1–1 IFK Malmö
Young Boys Berne 0–5 Hamburg
Hamburg 3–3 Young Boys Berne
Spartak Kralove 1–0 Panathinaikos
Panathinaikos 0–0 Spartak Kralove
Benfica 6–2 Ujpest Dozsa
Ujpest Dozsa 2–1 Benfica
Real Madrid 2–2 Barcelona
Barcelona 2–1 Real Madrid
Rapid Vienna 3–1 Wismut Karl-Marx
Stadt
Wismut Karl-Marx-Stadt 2–0 Rapid
Vienna
Rapid Vienna 1–0 Wismut Karl-Marx-
Stadt

Burnley 2–0 Reims
Reims 3–2 Burnley

Quarter-finals

Burnley 3–1 Hamburg
Hamburg 4–1 Burnley
Barcelona 4–0 Spartak Kralove
Spartak Kralove 1–1 Barcelona
Benfica 3–1 Aarhus
Aarhus 2–4 Benfica
Rapid Vienna 2–0 IFK Malmö
IFK Malmö 0–2 Rapid Vienna

Semi-finals

Barcelona 1–0 Hamburg
Hamburg 2–1 Barcelona
Barcelona 1–0 Hamburg
Benfica 3–0 Rapid Vienna
Rapid Vienna 1–1 Benfica

Final

31 May 1961, BERNE, 28 000
BENFICA (2) 3, BARCELONA (1) 2
Benfica: Costa Pereira; Joao, Angelo;
Neto, Germano, Cruz; Augusto,
Santana, Aguas, Coluna, Cavem.
Barcelona: Ramallets; Foncho, Gracia;
Verges, Garay, Gensana; Kubala,
Kocsis, Evaristo, Suarez, Czibor.
Scorers: Aguas, Ramallets (own goal),
Coluna for Benfica; Kocsis, Czibor for
Barcelona.

1961–62

Preliminary Round

Nuremberg 5–0 Drumcondra
Drumcondra 1–4 Nuremberg
Vorwaerts Berlin 3–0 Linfield
*(Linfield gave Vorwaerts a walkover in the
second leg when the East Germans were
refused visas)*
Spora Luxembourg 0–6 Odense BK
Odense BK 9–2 Spora Luxembourg
Monaco 2–3 Rangers
Rangers 3–2 Monaco
Vasas 0–2 Real Madrid
Real Madrid 3–1 Vasas
CDNA Sofia 4–4 Dukla Prague
Dukla Prague 2–1 CDNA Sofia
Standard Liège 2–1 Frederikstad
Frederikstad 0–2 Standard Liège
IFK Gothenburg 0–3 Feyenoord
Feyenoord 8–2 IFK Gothenburg
Servette Geneva 5–0 Valetta
Valetta 1–2 Servette Geneva
Gornik Zabrze 4–2 Tottenham Hotspur
Tottenham Hotspur 8–1 Gornik Zabrze
Sporting Lisbon 1–1 Partizan Belgrade
Partizan Belgrade 2–0 Sporting Lisbon
Panathinaikos 1–1 Juventus
Juventus 2–1 Panathinaikos
CCA Bucharest 0–0 FK Austria
FK Austria 2–0 CCA Bucharest
Byes: *Benfica, Valkeakosken, Fenerbahce.*

First Round

Odense BK 0–3 Real Madrid
Real Madrid 9–0 Odense BK
Fenerbahce 1–2 Nuremberg
Nuremberg 1–0 Fenerbahce
Standard Liège 5–1 Valkeakosken
Valkeakosken 0–2 Standard Liège
FK Austria 1–1 Benfica
Benfica 5–1 FK Austria
Servette Geneva 4–3 Dukla Prague
Dukla Prague 2–0 Servette Geneva
Feyenoord 1–3 Tottenham Hotspur
Tottenham Hotspur 1–1 Feyenoord
Partizan Belgrade 1–2 Juventus
Juventus 5–0 Partizan Belgrade
Vorwaerts Berlin 1–2 Rangers
Rangers 4–1 Vorwaerts Berlin

Quarter-finals

Nuremberg 3–1 Benfica
Benfica 6–0 Nuremberg
Standard Liège 4–1 Rangers
Rangers 2–0 Standard Liège
Dukla Prague 1–0 Tottenham Hotspur
Tottenham Hotspur 4–1 Dukla Prague
Juventus 0–1 Real Madrid
Real Madrid 0–1 Juventus
Real Madrid 3–1 Juventus

Semi-finals

Benfica 3–1 Tottenham Hotspur
Tottenham Hotspur 2–1 Benfica
Real Madrid 4–0 Standard Liège
Standard Liège 0–2 Real Madrid

Final

2 May 1962, AMSTERDAM, 65 000
BENFICA (2) 5, REAL MADRID (3) 3
Benfica: Costa Pereira; Joao, Angelo;
Cavem, Germano, Cruz; Augusto,
Eusebio, Aguas, Coluna, Simoes.
Real: Araquistain; Casado, Miera; Felo,
Santamaria, Pachin; Tejada, Del Sol,
Di Stefano, Puskas, Gento.
Scorers: Puskas (3) for Real; Aguas,
Cavem, Coluna, Eusebio (2) for
Benfica.

1962–63

Preliminary Round

Linfield 1–2 Esbjerg
Esbjerg 0–0 Linfield
Real Madrid 3–3 Anderlecht
Anderlecht 1–0 Real Madrid
Floriana 1–4 Ipswich Town
Ipswich Town 10–0 Floriana
Dundee 8–1 Cologne
Cologne 4–0 Dundee
Shelbourne 0–2 Sporting Lisbon
Sporting Lisbon 5–1 Shelbourne
Vorwaerts Berlin 0–3 Dukla Prague
Dukla Prague 1–0 Vorwaerts Berlin
Norrköping 9–2 Partizan Tirana
Partizan Tirana 1–1 Norrköping

Dinamo Bucharest 1–1 Galatasaray
Galatasaray 3–0 Dinamo Bucharest
Servette Geneva 1–3 Feyenoord
Feyenoord 1–3 Servette Geneva
Servette Geneva 1–3 Feyenoord
Polonia Bytom 2–1 Panathinaikos
Panathinaikos 1–4 Polonia Bytom
Frederikstad 1–4 Vasas
Vasas 7–0 Frederikstad
FK Austria 5–3 Kamraterna Helsinki
Kamraterna Helsinki 0–2 FK Austria
CDNA Sofia 2–1 Partizan Belgrade
Partizan Belgrade 1–4 CDNA Sofia
Milan 8–0 US Luxembourg
US Luxembourg 0–6 Milan
Byes: *Benfica, Reims*

First Round
FK Austria 3–2 Reims
Reims 5–0 FK Austria
Sporting Lisbon 1–0 Dundee
Dundee 4–1 Sporting Lisbon
Norrköping 1–1 Benfica
Benfica 5–1 Norrköping
Galatasaray 4–1 Polonia Bytom
Polonia Bytom 1–0 Galatasaray
Esbjerg 0–0 Dukla Prague
Dukla Prague 5–0 Esbjerg
Feyenoord 1–1 Vasas
Vasas 2–2 Feyenoord
CDNA Sofia 2–2 Anderlecht
Anderlecht 2–0 CDNA Sofia
Milan 3–0 Ipswich Town
Ipswich Town 2–1 Milan

Quarter-finals
Anderlecht 1–4 Dundee
Dundee 2–1 Anderlecht
Galatasaray 1–3 Milan
Milan 5–0 Galatasaray
Benfica 2–1 Dukla Prague
Dukla Prague 0–0 Benfica
Reims 0–1 Feyenoord
Feyenoord 1–1 Reims

Semi-finals
Milan 5–1 Dundee
Dundee 1–0 Milan
Benfica 3–1 Feyenoord
Feyenoord 0–0 Benfica

Final
22 May 1963, WEMBLEY, 45 000
MILAN (0) 2, BENFICA (1) 1
Milan: Ghezzi; David, Trebbi; Benitez,
    Maldini, Trapattoni; Pivatelli, Sani,
    Altafini, Rivera, Mora.
Benfica: Costa Pereira; Cavem, Cruz;
    Humberto, Raul, Coluna; Augusto,
    Santana, Torres, Eusebio, Simoes.
Scorers: Eusebio for Benfica; Altafini (2)
    for Milan.

1963–64

Preliminary Round
Galatasaray 4–0 Ferencvaros
Ferencvaros 2–0 Galatasaray
Partizan Belgrade 3–0 Anorthosis
Anorthosis 1–3 Partizan Belgrade
Dundalk 0–3 FC Zürich
FC Zürich 1–2 Dundalk
Lyn Oslo 2–4 Borussia Dortmund
Borussia Dortmund 3–1 Lyn Oslo
Dukla Prague 6–0 Valetta
Valetta 0–2 Dukla Prague
Everton 0–0 Internazionale
Internazionale 1–0 Everton
Gornik Zabrze 1–0 FK Austria
FK Austria 1–0 Gornik Zabrze
Gornik Zabrze 2–1 FK Austria
Monaco 7–2 AEK Athens
AEK Athens 1–1 Monaco
Dinamo Bucharest 2–0 Motor Jena
Motor Jena 0–1 Dinamo Bucharest
Valkeakosken 4–1 Jeunesse Esch
Jeunesse Esch 4–0 Valkeakosken
Standard Liège 1–0 Norrköping
Norrköping 2–0 Standard Liège
Partizan Tirana 1–0 Spartak Plovdiv
Spartak Plovidv 3–1 Partizan Tirana
PSV Eindhoven 7–1 Esbjerg
Esbjerg 3–4 PSV Eindhoven
Distillery 3–3 Benfica
Benfica 5–0 Distillery
Rangers 0–1 Real Madrid
Real Madrid 6–0 Rangers
Bye: *Milan*

First Round
Benfica 2–1 Borussia Dortmund
Borussia Dortmund 5–0 Benfica
Internazionale 1–0 Monaco
Monaco 0–3 Internazionale
Norrköping 1–1 Milan
Milan 5–2 Norrköping
FC Zürich 3–0 Galatasaray
Galatasaray 2–0 FC Zürich
Gornik Zabrze 2–0 Dukla Prague
Dukla Prague 4–1 Gornik Zabrze
Jeunesse Esch 2–1 Partizan Belgrade
Partizan Belgrade 6–2 Jeunesse Esch
Spartak Plovdiv 0–1 PSV Eindhoven
PSV Eindhoven 0–0 Spartak Plovdiv
Dinamo Bucharest 1–3 Real Madrid
Real Madrid 5–3 Dinamo Bucharest

Quarter-finals
Real Madrid 4–1 Milan
Milan 2–0 Real Madrid
Partizan Belgrade 0–3 Internazionale
Internazionale 2–1 Partizan Belgrade
PSV Eindhoven 1–0 FC Zürich
FC Zürich 3–1 PSV Eindhoven
Dukla Prague 0–4 Borussia Dortmund
Borussia Dortmund 1–3 Dukla Prague

Semi-finals
Borussia Dortmund 2–2 Internazionale
Internazionale 2–0 Borussia Dortmund
FC Zürich 1–2 Real Madrid
Real Madrid 6–0 FC Zürich

Final
27 May 1964, VIENNA, 74 000
INTER (1) 3, REAL MADRID (0) 1
Inter: Sarti; Burgnich, Facchetti; Tagnin,
    Guarneri, Picchi; Jair, Mazzola,
    Milani, Suarez, Corso.
Real: Vicente; Isidro, Pachin; Muller,
    Santamaria, Zoco; Amancio, Felo, Di
    Stefano, Puskas, Gento.
Scorers: Mazzola (2), Milani for Inter;
    Felo for Real.

1964–65

Preliminary Round
Anderlecht 1–0 Bologna
Bologna 2–1 Anderlecht
Anderlecht 0–0 Bologna (*in Barcelona*)
(*Anderlecht won on toss of a coin*)
Rangers 3–1 Red Star Belgrade
Red Star Belgrade 4–2 Rangers
Rangers 3–1 Red Star (*at Highbury*)
Chemie Leipzig 0–2 Vasas Gyor
Vasas Gyor 4–2 Chemie Leipzig
Dukla Prague 4–1 Gornik Zabrze
Gornik Zabrze 3–0 Dukla Prague
Gornik Zabrze 0–0 Dukla Prague (*in
    Duisburg, Dukla won on toss of a coin*)
Reipas Lahti 2–1 Lyn Oslo
Lyn Oslo 3–0 Reipas Lahti
Partizan Tirana 0–0 Cologne
Cologne 2–0 Partizan Tirana
Saint Etienne 2–2 Chaux de Fonds
Chaux de Fonds 2–1 Saint Etienne
Glentoran 2–2 Panathinaikos
Panathinaikos 3–2 Glentoran
Odense BK 2–5 Real Madrid
Real Madrid 4–0 Odense BK
Aris Bonnevoie 1–5 Benfica
Benfica 5–1 Aris Bonnevoie
DWS Amsterdam 3–0 Fenerbahce
Fenerbahce 0–1 DWS Amsterdam
Rapid Vienna 3–0 Shamrock Rovers
Shamrock Rovers 0–2 Rapid Vienna
Lokomotiv Sofia 8–3 Malmö FF
Malmö FF 2–0 Lokomotiv Sofia
Reykjavik 0–5 Liverpool
Liverpool 6–1 Reykjavik
Dinamo Bucharest 5–0 Sliema
    Wanderers
Sliema Wanderers 0–2 Dinamo
    Bucharest
Bye: *Internazionale*

First Round
Panathinaikos 1–1 Cologne
Cologne 2–1 Panathinaikos
Internazionale 6–0 Dinamo Bucharest

Dinamo Bucharest 0–1 Internazionale
Vasas Gyor 5–3 Lokomotiv Sofia
Lokomotiv Sofia 4–3 Vasas Gyor
Rangers 1–0 Rapid Vienna
Rapid Vienna 0–2 Rangers
Real Madrid 4–0 Dukla Prague
Dukla Prague 2–2 Real Madrid
Liverpool 3–0 Anderlecht
Anderlecht 0–1 Liverpool
DWS Amsterdam 5–0 Lyn Oslo
Lyn Oslo 1–3 DWS Amsterdam
Chaux de Fonds 1–1 Benfica
Benfica 5–0 Chaux de Fonds

Quarter-finals
Cologne 0–0 Liverpool
Liverpool 0–0 Cologne
Liverpool 2–2 Cologne (*in Rotterdam*)
(*Liverpool won toss*)
Internazionale 3–1 Rangers
Rangers 1–0 Internazionale
Benfica 3–1 Real Madrid
Real Madrid 2–1 Benfica
DWS Amsterdam 1–1 Vasas Gyor
Vasas Gyor 1–0 DWS Amsterdam

Semi-finals
Vasas Gyor 0–1 Benfica
Benfica 4–0 Vasas Gyor
Liverpool 3–1 Internazionale
Internazionale 3–0 Liverpool

Final
27 May 1965, MILAN, 80 000
INTER (1) 1, BENFICA (0) 0
Inter: Sarti; Burgnich, Facchetti; Bedin,
  Guarneri, Picchi; Jair, Mazzola, Peiro,
  Suarez, Corso.
Benfica: Costa Pereira; Cavem, Cruz;
  Neto, Germano, Raul; Augusto,
  Eusebio, Torres, Coluna, Simoes.
Scorer: Jair.

1965–66

Preliminary Round
Lyn Oslo 5–3 Derry City
Derry City 5–1 Lyn Oslo
Feyenoord 2–1 Real Madrid
Real Madrid 5–0 Feyenoord
Keflavik 1–4 Ferencvaros
Ferencvaros 9–1 Keflavik
Fenerbahce 0–0 Anderlecht
Anderlecht 5–1 Fenerbahce
Nendori Tirana 0–0 Kilmarnock
Kilmarnock 1–0 Nendori Tirana
Djurgarden 2–1 Levski
Levski 6–0 Djurgarden
Drumcondra 1–0 Vorwaerts Berlin
Vorwaerts Berlin 2–0 Drumcondra
Linz 1–3 Gornik Zabrze
Gornik Zabrze 2–1 Linz
Partizan Belgrade 2–0 Nantes
Nantes 2–2 Partizan Belgrade
HJK Helsinki 2–3 Manchester United

Manchester United 6–0 HJK Helsinki
Lausanne 0–0 Sparta Prague
Sparta Prague 4–0 Lausanne
Dudelange 0–2 Benfica
Benfica 10–0 Dudelange
Panathinaikos 4–1 Sliema
Sliema 1–0 Panathinaikos
Apoel Nicosia 0–5 Werder Bremen (*in
  Hamburg*)
Werder Bremen 5–0 Apoel Nicosia
Dinamo Bucharest 4–0 Odense BK
Odense BK 2–3 Dinamo Bucharest
Bye: *Internazionale*

First Round
Partizan Belgrade 3–0 Werder Bremen
Werder Bremen 1–0 Partizan Belgrade
Levski 2–2 Benfica
Benfica 3–2 Levski
Ferencvaros 0–0 Panathinaikos
Panathinaikos 1–3 Ferencvaros
Kilmarnock 2–2 Real Madrid
Real Madrid 5–1 Kilmarnock
Vorwaerts Berlin 0–2 Manchester United
Manchester United 3–1 Vorwaerts Berlin
Sparta Prague 3–0 Gornik Zabrze
Gornik Zabrze 1–2 Sparta Prague
Dinamo Bucharest 2–1 Internazionale
Internazionale 2–0 Dinamo Bucharest
Anderlecht 9–0 Derry City
(*No return match*)

Second Round
Manchester United 3–2 Benfica
Benfica 1–5 Manchester United
Anderlecht 1–0 Real Madrid
Real Madrid 4–2 Anderlecht
Sparta Prague 4–1 Partizan Belgrade
Partizan Belgrade 5–0 Sparta Prague
Internazionale 4–0 Ferencvaros
Ferencvaros 1–1 Internazionale

Semi-finals
Partizan Belgrade 2–0 Manchester United
Manchester United 1–0 Partizan Belgrade
Real Madrid 1–0 Internazionale
Internazionale 1–1 Real Madrid

Final
11 May 1966, BRUSSELS, 55 000
REAL MADRID (0) 2, PARTIZAN
  BELGRADE (0) 1
Real: Araquistain; Pachin, Sanchis; Pirri,
  De Felipe, Zoco; Serena, Amancio,
  Grosso, Velasquez, Gento.
Partizan: Soskic; Jusufi, Milhailovic;
  Becejac, Rasovic, Vasovic; Bakic,
  Kovacevic, Hasanagic, Galic, Primajer.
Scorers: Amancio and Serena for Real;
  Vasovic for Partizan.

1966–67

Preliminary Round
Sliema Wanderers 1–2 CSKA Sofia

CSKA Sofia 4–0 Sliema Wanderers
Waterford 1–6 Vorwaerts Berlin
Vorwaerts Berlin 6–0 Waterford

First Round
Reykjavik 2–3 Nantes
Nantes 5–2 Reykjavik
Aris Bonnevoie 3–3 Linfield
Linfield 6–1 Aris Bonnevoie
Admira 0–1 Vojvodina
Vojvodina 0–0 Admira
Anderlecht 10–1 Valkeakovski
Valkeakovski 0–2 Anderlecht (*in Brussels*)
1860 Munich 8–0 Omonia Nicosia
Omonia Nicosia 1–2 1860 Munich (*in
  Munich*)
Liverpool 2–0 Petrolul Ploesti
Petrolul Ploesti 3–1 Liverpool
Liverpool 2–0 Petrolul Ploesti (*in Brussels*)
Celtic 2–0 FC Zürich
FC Zürich 0–3 Celtic
Malmö 0–2 Atlético Madrid
Atlético Madrid 3–1 Malmö
Esbjerg 0–2 Dukla Prague
Dukla Prague 4–0 Esbjerg
Ajax 2–0 Besiktas
Besiktas 1–2 Ajax
Vasas 5–0 Sporting Lisbon
Sporting Lisbon 0–2 Vasas
CSKA Sofia 3–1 Olimpiakos
Olimpiakos 1–0 CSKA Sofia
Gornik Zabrze 2–1 Vorwaerts Berlin
Vorwaerts Berlin 2–1 Gornik Zabrze
Gornik Zabrze 3–1 Vorwaerts Berlin (*in
  Budapest*)
Internazionale 1–0 Torpedo Moscow
Torpedo Moscow 0–0 Internazionale
Walkover: *Valerengen (v Nendori Tirana)*
Bye: *Real Madrid.*

Second Round
Valerengen 1–4 Linfield
Linfield 1–1 Valerengen
Internazionale 2–1 Vasas
Vasas 0–2 Internazionale
Dukla Prague 4–1 Anderlecht
Anderlecht 1–2 Dukla Prague
1860 Munich 1–0 Real Madrid
Real Madrid 3–1 1860 Munich
CSKA Sofia 4–0 Gornik Zabrze
Gornik Zabrze 3–0 CSKA Sofia
Vojvodina 3–1 Atlético Madrid
Atlético Madrid 2–0 Vojvodina
Atlético Madrid 2–3 Vojvodina
Nantes 1–3 Celtic
Celtic 3–1 Nantes
Ajax 5–1 Liverpool
Liverpool 2–2 Ajax

Quarter-finals
Internazionale 1–0 Real Madrid
Real Madrid 0–2 Internazionale
Linfield 2–2 CSKA Sofia
CSKA Sofia 1–0 Linfield

Ajax 1–1 Dukla Prague
Dukla Prague 2–1 Ajax
Vojvodina 1–0 Celtic
Celtic 2–0 Vojvodina

Semi-finals
Celtic 3–1 Dukla Prague
Dukla Prague 0–0 Celtic
Internazionale 1–1 CSKA Sofia
CSKA Sofia 1–1 Internazionale
Internazionale 1–0 CSKA Sofia (in
   Bologna)

Final
25 May 1967, LISBON, 56 000
CELTIC (0) 2, INTERNAZIONALE (1) 1
Celtic: Simpson; Craig, Gemmell;
   Murdoch, McNeill, Clark; Johnstone,
   Wallace, Chalmers, Auld, Lennox.
Inter: Sarti; Burgnich, Facchetti; Bedin,
   Guarneri, Picchi; Bicicli, Mazzola,
   Cappellini, Corso, Domenghini.
Scorers: Mazzola (pen) for Inter;
   Gemmell, Chalmers for Celtic.

1967–68

(First European Cup to be seeded.)

First Round
Glentoran 1–1 Benfica
Benfica 0–0 Glentoran
Besiktas 0–1 Rapid Vienna
Rapid Vienna 3–0 Besiktas
Celtic 1–2 Dynamo Kiev
Dynamo Kiev 1–1 Celtic
Olympiakos 0–0 Juventus
Juventus 2–0 Olympiakos
Dundalk 0–1 Vasas
Vasas 8–1 Dundalk
Manchester United 4–0 Hibernians
   Valletta
Hibernians Valletta 0–0 Manchester
   United
Saint Etienne 2–0 Kuopio
Kuopio 3–0 Saint Etienne
Karl-Marx-Stadt 1–3 Anderlecht
Anderlecht 2–1 Karl-Marx-Stadt
Basle 1–2 Hvidovre
Hvidovre 3–3 Basle
Skeid Oslo 0–1 Sparta Prague
Sparta Prague 1–1 Skeid Oslo
Olympiakos Nicosia 2–2 Sarajevo
Sarajevo 3–1 Olympiakos Nicosia
Ajax 1–1 Real Madrid
Real Madrid 2–1 Ajax
Valur Reykjavik 1–1 Jeunesse Esch
Jeunesse Esch 3–3 Valur Reykjavik
Gornik Zabrze 3–0 Djurgarden
Djurgarden 0–0 Gornik Zabrze
Plovdiv 2–0 Rapid Bucharest
Rapid Bucharest 3–0 Plovdiv
Walkover: *Eintracht Brunswick (v Dinamo
   Tirana)*

Second Round
Sarajevo 0–0 Manchester United
Manchester United 2–1 Sarajevo
Hvidovre 2–2 Real Madrid
Real Madrid 4–1 Hvidovre
Rapid Vienna 1–0 Eintracht Brunswick
Eintracht Brunswick 2–0 Rapid Vienna
Benfica 2–0 Saint Etienne
Saint Etienne 1–0 Benfica
Vasas 6–0 Valur Reykjavik
Valur Reykjavik 1–5 Vasas
Dynamo Kiev 1–2 Gornik Zabrze
Gornik Zabrze 1–1 Dynamo Kiev
Juventus 1–0 Rapid Bucharest
Rapid Bucharest 0–0 Juventus
Sparta Prague 3–2 Anderlecht
Anderlecht 2–3 Sparta Prague

Quarter-finals
Eintracht Brunswick 3–2 Juventus
Juventus 1–0 Eintracht Brunswick
Eintracht Brunswick 0–1 Juventus
Manchester United 2–0 Gornik Zabrze
Gornik Zabrze 1–0 Manchester United
Real Madrid 3–0 Sparta Prague
Sparta Prague 2–1 Real Madrid
Vasas 0–0 Benfica
Benfica 3–0 Vasas

Semi-finals
Manchester United 1–0 Real Madrid
Real Madrid 3–3 Manchester United
Benfica 2–0 Juventus
Juventus 0–1 Benfica

Final
29 May 1968, WEMBLEY, 100 000
MANCHESTER UNITED (0) 4,
   BENFICA (0) 1 (after extra time, 1–1 at
   90 mins)
Manchester United: Stepney; Brennan,
   Dunne; Crerand, Foulkes, Stiles; Best,
   Kidd, Charlton, Sadler, Aston.
Benfica: Henrique; Adolfo, Humberto,
   Jacinto, Cruz; Graça, Coluna; Augusto,
   Eusebio, Torres, Simoes.
Scorers: Charlton (2), Best, Kidd for
   Manchester United; Graça for Benfica.

1968–69

Preliminary Round
Saint Etienne 2–0 Celtic
Celtic 4–0 Saint Etienne
Waterford 1–3 Manchester United
Manchester United 7–1 Waterford
Manchester City 0–0 Fenerbahce
Fenerbahce 2–1 Manchester City
Anderlecht 3–0 Glentoran
Glentoran 2–2 Anderlecht
AEK Athens 3–0 Jeunesse Esch
Jeunesse Esch 3–2 AEK Athens
Nuremberg 1–1 Ajax
Ajax 4–0 Nuremberg
Malmö 2–1 Milan

Milan 4–1 Malmö
Steaua Bucharest 3–1 Spartak Trnava
Spartak Trnava 4–0 Steaua Bucharest
FC Zürich 1–3 AB Copenhagen
AB Copenhagen 1–2 FC Zürich
Rosenborg 1–3 Rapid Vienna
Rapid Vienna 3–3 Rosenborg
Floriana 1–1 Reipas Lahti
Reipas Lahti 2–0 Floriana
Real Madrid 6–0 Limassol
Limassol 0–6 Real Madrid (in Madrid)
Valur Reykjavik 0–0 Benfica
Benfica 8–0 Valur Reykjavik
Walkover: *Red Star (v Carl Zeiss Jena)*

Second Round
Manchester United 3–0 Anderlecht
Anderlecht 3–1 Manchester United
Celtic 5–1 Red Star Belgrade
Red Star Belgrade 1–1 Celtic
Rapid Vienna 1–0 Real Madrid
Real Madrid 2–1 Rapid Vienna
Reipas Lahti 1–9 Spartak Trnava
Spartak Trnava 7–1 Reipas Lahti
AEK Athens 0–0 AB Copenhagen
AB Copenhagen 0–2 AEK Athens
Ajax 2–0 Fenerbahce
Fenerbahce 0–2 Ajax
Byes: *Benfica, Milan*

Quarter-finals
Manchester United 3–0 Rapid Vienna
Rapid Vienna 0–0 Manchester United
Ajax 1–3 Benfica
Benfica 1–3 Ajax
Ajax 3–0 Benfica
Milan 0–0 Celtic
Celtic 0–1 Milan
Spartak Trnava 2–1 AEK Athens
AEK Athens 1–1 Spartak Trnava

Semi-finals
Milan 2–0 Manchester United
Manchester United 1–0 Milan
Ajax 3–0 Spartak Trnava
Spartak Trnava 2–0 Ajax

Final
28 May 1969, MADRID, 50 000
MILAN (2) 4, AJAX (0) 1
Milan: Cudicini; Anquilletti, Schnellinger,
   Maldera, Rosato, Trapattoni, Hamrin,
   Lodetti, Sormani, Rivera, Prati.
Ajax: Bals; Suurbier (Nunina), Vasovic,
   Van Duivenbode, Hulshoff, Pronk,
   Groot, Swart, Cruyff, Danielsson,
   Keizer.
Scorers: Prati (3), Sormani for Milan;
   Vasovic (penalty) for Ajax.

1969–70

Preliminary Round
Turku Palloseura 0–1 KB Copenhagen
KB Copenhagen 3–0 Turku Palloseura

First Round

Milan 5-0 Avenir Beggen
Avenir Beggen 0-3 Milan
Leeds United 10-0 Lyn Oslo
Lyn Oslo 0-6 Leeds United
Red Star Belgrade 8-0 Linfield
Linfield 2-4 Red Star Belgrade
Basle 0-0 Celtic
Celtic 2-0 Basle
Hibernians Valletta 2-2 Spartak Trnava
Spartak Trnava 4-0 Hibernians Valletta
Galatasaray 2-0 Waterford
Waterford 2-3 Galatasaray
CSKA Sofia 2-1 Ferencvaros
Ferencvaros 4-1 CSKA Sofia
UT Arad 1-2 Legia Warsaw
Legia Warsaw 8-0 UT Arad
Vorwaerts Berlin 2-0 Panathinaikos
Panathinaikos 1-1 Vorwaerts Berlin
Bayern Munich 2-0 Saint Etienne
Saint Etienne 3-0 Bayern Munich
Standard Liège 3-0 Nendori Tirana
Nendori Tirana 1-1 Standard Liège
Feyenoord 12-0 Reykjavik
Reykjavik 0-4 Feyenoord
FK Austria 1-2 Dynamo Kiev
Dynamo Kiev 3-1 FK Austria
Fiorentina 1-0 Oster Vaxjo
Oster Vaxjo 1-2 Fiorentina
Benfica 2-0 KB Copenhagen
KB Copenhagen 2-3 Benfica
Real Madrid 8-0 Olympiakos Nicosia
Olympiakos Nicosia 1-6 Real Madrid

Second Round

Leeds United 3-0 Ferencvaros
Ferencvaros 0-3 Leeds United
Celtic 3-0 Benfica
Benfica 3-0 Celtic
(*Celtic won on toss of a coin*)
Dynamo Kiev 1-2 Fiorentina
Fiorentina 0-0 Dynamo Kiev
Milan 1-0 Feyenoord
Feyenoord 2-0 Milan
Spartak Trnava 1-0 Galatasaray
Galatasaray 1-0 Spartak Trnava
(*Galatasaray won on toss of a coin*)
Legia Warsaw 2-1 Saint Etienne
Saint Etienne 0-0 Legia Warsaw
Vorwaerts Berlin 2-1 Red Star Belgrade
Red Star Belgrade 3-2 Vorwaerts Berlin
Standard Liège 1-0 Real Madrid
Real Madrid 2-3 Standard Liège

Quarter-finals

Standard Liège 0-1 Leeds United
Leeds United 1-0 Standard Liège
Celtic 3-0 Fiorentina
Fiorentina 1-0 Celtic
Galatasaray 1-1 Legia Warsaw
Legia Warsaw 2-0 Galatasaray
Vorwaerts Berlin 1-0 Feyenoord
Feyenoord 2-0 Vorwaerts Berlin

Semi-finals

Leeds United 0-1 Celtic
Celtic 2-1 Leeds United
Legia Warsaw 0-0 Feyenoord
Feyenoord 2-0 Legia Warsaw

Final

6 May 1970, MILAN, 50 000
FEYENOORD (1) 2, CELTIC (1) 1 (after extra time, 1-1 at 90 mins)
Feyenoord: Pieters Graafland; Romeyn (Haak), Israel, Laseroms, Jansen, Van Duivenbode; Hasil, Van Hanegem; Wery, Kindvall, Moulijn.
Celtic: Williams; Hay, Gemmell; Murdoch, McNeill, Brogan; Johnstone, Wallace, Hughes, Auld (Connelly), Lennox.
Scorers: Gemmell for Celtic; Israel, Kindvall for Feyenoord.

1970–71

Preliminary Round

Levski Spartak 3-1 FK Austria
FK Austria 3-0 Levski Spartak

First Round

Everton 6-2 Keflavik
Keflavik 0-3 Everton
Celtic 9-0 Kokkola
Kokkola 0-5 Celtic
Glentoran 1-3 Waterford
Waterford 1-0 Glentoran
Cagliari 3-0 Saint Etienne
Saint Etienne 1-0 Cagliari
Slovan Bratislava 2-1 BK Copenhagen
BK Copenhagen 2-2 Slovan Bratislava
Nendori Tirana 2-2 Ajax
Ajax 2-0 Nendori Tirana
IFK Gothenburg 0-4 Legia Warsaw
Legia Warsaw 2-1 IFK Gothenburg
Ujpest Dozsa 2-0 Red Star Belgrade
Red Star Belgrade 4-0 Ujpest Dozsa
Rosenborg 0-2 Standard Liège
Standard Liège 5-0 Rosenborg
Borussia Mönchenbladbach 6-0 EP Larnax (*in Augsburg*)
Borussia Mönchengladbach 10-0 EP Larnax
Spartak Moscow 3-2 Basle
Basle 2-1 Spartak Moscow
Feyenoord 1-1 UT Arad
UT Arad 0-0 Feyenoord
Atlético Madrid 2-0 FK Austria
FK Austria 1-2 Atlético Madrid
Jeunesse Esch 1-2 Panathinaikos
Panathinaikos 5-0 Jeunesse Esch
Fenerbahce 0-4 Carl Zeiss Jena
Carl Zeiss Jena 1-0 Fenerbahce
Sporting Lisbon 5-0 Floriana
Floriana 0-4 Sporting Lisbon

Second Round

Borussia Mönchengladbach 1-1 Everton

Everton 1-1 Borussia Mönchengladbach
(*Everton qualified on new penalty-kicks rule*)
Waterford 0-7 Celtic
Celtic 3-2 Waterford
Red Star Belgrade 3-0 UT Arad
UT Arad 1-3 Red Star Belgrade
Carl Zeiss Jena 2-1 Sporting Lisbon
Sporting Lisbon 1-2 Carl Zeiss Jena
Panathinaikos 3-0 Slovan Bratislava
Slovan Bratislava 2-1 Panathinaikos
Standard Liège 1-0 Legia Warsaw
Legia Warsaw 2-0 Standard Liège
Cagliari 2-1 Atlético Madrid
Atlético Madrid 3-0 Cagliari
Ajax 3-0 Basle
Basle 1-2 Ajax

Quarter-finals

Everton 1-1 Panathinaikos
Panathinaikos 0-0 Everton
Ajax 3-0 Celtic
Celtic 1-0 Ajax
Atlético Madrid 1-0 Legia Warsaw
Legia Warsaw 2-1 Atlético Madrid
Carl Zeiss Jena 3-2 Red Star Belgrade
Red Star Belgrade 4-0 Carl Zeiss Jena

Semi-finals

Red Star Belgrade 4-1 Panathinaikos
Panathinaikos 3-0 Red Star Belgrade
Atletico Madrid 1-0 Ajax
Ajax 3-0 Atlético Madrid

Final

2 June 1971, WEMBLEY, 90 000
AJAX (1) 2, PANATHINAIKOS (0) 0
Ajax: Stuy; Neeskens, Vasovic, Hulshoff, Suurbier; Rijnders (Blankenburg), Muhren; Swart (Haan), Cruyff, Van Dijk, Keizer.
Panathinaikos: Oeconomopoulos; Tomaras, Vlahos, Eleftherakis, Kamaras, Sourpis, Grammos, Filakouris, Antoniadis, Domazos, Kapsis.
Scorers: Van Dijk, Haan.

1971–72

Preliminary Round

Valencia 3-1 US Luxembourg
US Luxembourg 0-1 Valencia

First Round

Olympique Marseille 2-1 Gornik Zabrze
Gornik Zabrze 1-1 Olympique Marseille
Galatasaray 1-1 CSKA Moscow
CSKA Moscow 3-0 Galatasaray
Akranes 0-4 Sliema Wanderers
Sliema Wanderers 0-0 Akranes
Ujpest Dozsa 4-0 Malmö
Malmö 1-0 Ujpest Dozsa
CSKA Sofia 3-0 Partizan Tirana
Partizan Tirana 0-1 CSKA Sofia
Stromsgodset 1-3 Arsenal

Arsenal 4–0 Stromsgodset
BK 1903 Copenhagen 2–1 Celtic
Celtic 3–0 BK 1903 Copenhagen
Standard Liège 2–0 Linfield
Linfield 2–3 Standard Liège
Valencia 0–0 Hajduk Split
Hajduk Split 1–1 Valencia
Internazionale 4–1 AEK Athens
AEK Athens 3–2 Internazionale
Reipas Lahti 1–1 Grasshoppers
Grasshoppers 8–0 Reipas Lahti
Ajax 2–0 Dynamo Dresden
Dynamo Dresden 0–0 Ajax
Wacker Innsbruck 0–4 Benfica
Benfica 3–1 Wacker Innsbruck
Feyenoord 8–0 Olympiakos Nicosia
Olympiakos Nicosia 0–9 Feyenoord (in Rotterdam)
Dinamo Bucharest 0–0 Spartak Trnava
Spartak Trnava 2–2 Dinamo Bucharest
Cork Hibernians 0–5 Borussia Mönchengladbach
Borussia Mönchengladbach 2–1 Cork Hibernians

Second Round
Grasshoppers 0–2 Arsenal
Arsenal 3–0 Grasshoppers
Celtic 5–0 Sliema Wanderers
Sliema Wanderers 1–2 Celtic
Inter 4–2 Borussia Mönchengladbach
Borussia Mönchengladbach 0–0 Inter
Dinamo Bucharest 0–3 Feyenoord
Feyenoord 2–0 Dinamo Bucharest
Valencia 0–1 Ujpest Dozsa
Ujpest Dozsa 2–1 Valencia
CSKA Moscow 1–0 Standard Liège
Standard Liège 2–0 CSKA Moscow
Olympique Marseille 1–2 Ajax
Ajax 4–1 Olympique Marseille
Benfica 2–1 CSKA Sofia
CSKA Sofia 0–0 Benfica

Quarter-finals
Ajax 2–1 Arsenal
Arsenal 0–1 Ajax
Ujpest Dozsa 1–2 Celtic
Celtic 1–1 Ujpest Dozsa
Internazionale 1–0 Standard Liège
Standard Liège 2–1 Internazionale
Feyenoord 1–0 Benfica
Benfica 5–1 Feyenoord

Semi-finals
Internazionale 0–0 Celtic
Celtic 0–0 Internazionale
(Inter won on penalties 5–4)
Ajax 1–0 Benfica
Benfica 0–0 Ajax

Final
31 May 1972, ROTTERDAM, 67 000
AJAX (0) 2, INTERNAZIONALE (0) 0
Ajax: Stuy; Suurbier, Hulshoff, Blankenburg, Krol; Haan, Neeskens,

G. Muhren; Swart, Cruyff, Keizer.
Inter: Bordon; Bellugi, Burgnich, Giubertoni (Bertini), Facchetti; Oriali, Mazzola, Bedin, Jair (Pellizzaro), Boninsegna, Frustalupi.
Scorer: Cruyff (2).

1972–73
First Round
Derby County 2–0 Zeljeznicar
Zeljeznicar 1–2 Derby County
Celtic 2–1 Rosenborg
Rosenborg 1–3 Celtic
Real Madrid 3–0 Keflavik
Keflavik 0–1 Real Madrid
Anderlecht 4–2 Vejle
Vejle 0–3 Anderlecht
Ujpest Dozsa 2–0 Basle
Basle 2–3 Ujpest Dozsa
Galatasaray 1–1 Bayern Munich
Bayern Munich 6–0 Galatasaray
Olympique Marseille 1–0 Juventus
Juventus 3–0 Olympique Marseille
Malmö 1–0 Benfica
Benfica 4–1 Malmö
TS Innsbruck 0–1 Dynamo Kiev
Dynamo Kiev 2–0 TS Innsbruck
CSKA Sofia 2–1 Panathinaikos
Panathinaikos 0–2 CSKA Sofia
Sliema Wanderers 0–5 Gornik Zabrze
Gornik Zabrze 5–0 Sliema Wanderers
Magdeburg 6–0 Turun Palloseura
Turun Palloseura 1–3 Magdeburg
Aris Bonnevoie 0–2 Arges Pitesti
Arges Pitesti 4–0 Aris Bonnevoie
Waterford 2–1 Omonia Nicosia
Omonia Nicosia 2–0 Waterford
Byes: *Ajax, Spartak Trnava*

Second Round
Derby County 3–0 Benfica
Benfica 0–0 Derby County
Omonia Nicosia 0–9 Bayern Munich
Bayern Munich 4–0 Omonia Nicosia
Celtic 2–1 Ujpest Dozsa
Ujpest Dozsa 3–0 Celtic
Dynamo Kiev 2–0 Gornik Zabrze
Gornik Zabrze 2–1 Dynamo Kiev
Juventus 1–0 Magdeburg
Magdeburg 0–1 Juventus
Arges Pitesti 2–1 Real Madrid
Real Madrid 3–1 Arges Pitesti
CSKA Sofia 1–3 Ajax
Ajax 3–0 CSKA Sofia
Spartak Trnava 1–0 Anderlecht
Anderlecht 0–1 Spartak Trnava

Quarter-finals
Spartak Trnava 1–0 Derby County
Derby County 2–0 Spartak Trnava
Dynamo Kiev 0–0 Real Madrid
Real Madrid 3–0 Dynamo Kiev
Ajax 4–0 Bayern Munich

Bayern Munich 2–1 Ajax
Juventus 0–0 Ujpest Dozsa
Ujpest Dozsa 2–2 Juventus

Semi-finals
Juventus 3–1 Derby County
Derby County 0–0 Juventus
Ajax 2–1 Real Madrid
Real Madrid 0–1 Ajax

Final
30 May 1973, BELGRADE, 93 500
AJAX (1) 1, JUVENTUS (0) 0
Ajax: Stuy; Suurbier, Hulshoff, Blankenburg, Krol; Neeskens, Haan, G. Muhren; Rep, Cruyff, Keizer.
Juventus: Zoff; Longobucco, Marchetti, Furino, Morini, Salvadore, Causio (Cuccureddu), Altafini, Anastasi, Capello, Bettega (Haller).
Scorer: Rep.

1973–74
First Round
Jeunesse Esch 1–1 Liverpool
Liverpool 2–0 Jeunesse Esch
TPS Turku 1–6 Celtic
Celtic 3–0 TPS Turku
Crusaders 0–1 Dinamo Bucharest
Dinamo Bucharest 11–0 Crusaders
Benfica 1–0 Olympiakos
Olympiakos 0–1 Benfica
Waterford 2–3 Ujpest Dozsa
Ujpest Dozsa 3–0 Waterford
Dynamo Dresden 2–0 Juventus
Juventus 3–2 Dynamo Dresden
Vejle 2–2 Nantes
Nantes 0–1 Vejle
Bayern Munich 3–1 Atvidaberg
Atvidaberg 3–1 Bayern Munich
(Bayern won on penalties)
Zaria 2–0 Apoel Nicosia
Apoel Nicosia 0–1 Zaria
Red Star Belgrade 2–1 Stal Mielec
Stal Mielec 0–1 Red Star Belgrade
FC Bruges 8–0 Floriana
Floriana 0–2 FC Bruges
Atlético Madrid 0–0 Galatasaray
Galatasaray 1–1 Atlético Madrid
Viking Stavanger 1–2 Spartak Trnava
Spartak Trnava 1–0 Viking Stavanger
Fram Reykjavik 0–5 Basle
Basle 6–2 Fram Reykjavik
CSKA Sofia 3–0 Wacker Innsbruck
Wacker Innsbruck 0–1 CSKA Sofia
Bye: *Ajax*

Second Round
Red Star Belgrade 2–1 Liverpool
Liverpool 1–2 Red Star Belgrade
Celtic 0–0 Vejle
Vejle 0–1 Celtic
Benfica 1–1 Ujpest Dozsa

Ujpest Dozsa 2-0 Benfica
Bayern Munich 4-3 Dynamo Dresden
Dynamo Dresden 3-3 Bayern Munich
Ajax 1-0 CSKA Sofia
CSKA Sofia 2-0 Ajax
Dinamo Bucharest 0-2 Atlético Madrid
Atlético Madrid 2-2 Dinamo Bucharest
Spartak Trnava 0-0 Zaria
Zaria 0-1 Spartak Trnava
Bruges 2-1 Basle
Basle 6-4 Bruges

Quarter-finals
Basle 3-2 Celtic
Celtic 4-2 Basle
Bayern Munich 4-1 CSKA Sofia
CSKA Sofia 2-1 Bayern Munich
Red Star Belgrade 0-2 Atlético Madrid
Atlético Madrid 0-0 Red Star Belgrade
Spartak Trnava 1-1 Ujpest Dozsa
Ujpest Dozsa 1-1 Spartak Trnava
(*Ujpest won on penalties*)

Semi-finals
Celtic 0-0 Atlético Madrid
Atlético Madrid 2-0 Celtic
Ujpest Dozsa 1-1 Bayern Munich
Bayern Munich 3-0 Ujpest Dozsa

Final
15 May 1974, BRUSSELS, 65 000
BAYERN MUNICH (0) 1, ATLÉTICO
 MADRID (0) 1 (after extra time, 0-0 at
 90 mins)
Bayern: Maier; Hansen, Breitner,
 Schwarzenbeck, Beckenbauer, Roth,
 Torstensson (Durnberger), Zobel,
 Müller, Hoeness, Kappelmann.
Atlético: Reina; Melo, Capon, Adelardo,
 Heredia, Eusebio, Ufarte (Becerra),
 Luis, Garate, Irureta, Salcedo (Alberto).
Scorers: Luis for Atlético; Schwarzenbeck
 for Bayern.

Replay
17 May 1974, BRUSSELS, 23 000
BAYERN MUNICH (1) 4, ATLÉTICO
 MADRID (0) 0
Bayern: Maier; Hansen, Breitner,
 Schwarzenbeck, Beckenbauer, Roth,
 Torstensson, Zobel, Müller, Hoeness,
 Kappelmann.
Atlético: Reina; Melo, Capon, Adelardo
 (Benegas), Heredia, Eusebio, Salcedo,
 Luis, Garate, Alberto (Ufarte), Becerra.
Scorers: Hoeness (2), Müller (2).

1974–75
First Round
Leeds United 4-1 FC Zürich
FC Zürich 2-1 Leeds United
Celtic 1-1 Olympiakos
Olympiakos 2-0 Celtic
Universitatea Craiova 2-1 Atvidaberg

Atvidaberg 3-1 Universitatea Craiova
Valletta 1-0 HJK Helsinki
HJK Helsinki 4-1 Valletta
Levski Spartak 0-3 Ujpest Dozsa
Ujpest Dozsa 4-1 Levski Spartak
Jeunesse Esch 2-3 Fenerbahce
Fenerbahce 2-0 Jeunesse Esch
Viking Stavanger 0-2 Ararat Erevan
Ararat Erevan 4-2 Viking Stavanger
Hvidovre 0-0 Ruch Chorzow
Ruch Chorzow 2-1 Hvidovre
Slovan Bratislava 4-2 Anderlecht
Anderlecht 3-1 Slovan Bratislava
Feyenoord 7-0 Coleraine
Coleraine 1-4 Feyenoord
Saint Etienne 2-0 Sporting Lisbon
Sporting Lisbon 1-1 Saint Etienne
Voest Linz 0-0 Barcelona
Barcelona 5-0 Voest Linz
Hajduk Split 7-1 Keflavik
Keflavik 0-2 Hajduk Split

Second Round
Ujpest Dozsa 1-2 Leeds United
Leeds United 3-0 Ujpest Dozsa
Bayern Munich 3-2 Magdeburg
Magdeburg 1-2 Bayern Munich
Hajduk Split 4-1 Saint Etienne
Saint Etienne 5-1 Hajduk Split
Feyenoord 0-0 Barcelona
Barcelona 3-0 Feyenoord
Cork Celtic 1-2 Ararat Erevan
Ararat Erevan 5-0 Cork Celtic
Ruch Chorzow 2-1 Fenerbahce
Fenerbahce 0-2 Ruch Chorzow
HJK Helsinki 0-3 Atvidaberg
Atvidaberg 1-0 HJK Helsinki
Anderlecht 5-1 Olympiakos
Olympiakos 3-0 Anderlecht

Quarter-finals
Bayern Munich 2-0 Ararat Erevan
Ararat Erevan 1-0 Bayern Munich
Leeds United 3-0 Anderlecht
Anderlecht 0-1 Leeds United
Ruch Chorzow 3-2 Saint Etienne
Saint Etienne 2-0 Ruch Chorzow
Barcelona 2-0 Atvidaberg
Atvidaberg 0-3 Barcelona

Semi-finals
Saint Etienne 0-0 Bayern Munich
Bayern Munich 2-0 Saint Etienne
Leeds United 2-1 Barcelona
Barcelona 1-1 Leeds United

Final
28 May 1975, PARIS, 50 000
BAYERN MUNICH (0) 2, LEEDS
 UNITED (0) 0
Bayern: Maier; Durnberger, Andersson
 (Weiss), Schwarzenbeck, Beckenbauer,
 Roth, Torstensson, Zobel, Hoeness
 (Wunder), Muller, Kappelmann.
Leeds: Stewart; Reaney, F. Gray, Bremner,

Madeley, Hunter, Lorimer, Clarke,
 Jordan, Giles, Yorath (E. Gray).
Scorers: Roth, Muller.

1975–76
First Round
Slovan Bratislava 1-0 Derby County
Derby County 3-0 Slovan Bratislava
Glasgow Rangers 4-1 Bohemians
Bohemians 1-1 Glasgow Rangers
Linfield 1-2 PSV Eindhoven
PSV Eindhoven 8-0 Linfield
Ujpest Dozsa 4-0 FC Zürich
FC Zürich 5-1 Ujpest Dozsa
Real Madrid 4-1 Dinamo Bucharest
Dinamo Bucharest 1-0 Real Madrid
KB Copenhagen 0-2 Saint Etienne
Saint Etienne 3-1 KB Copenhagen
Olympiakos 2-2 Dynamo Kiev
Dynamo Kiev 1-0 Olympiakos
Ruch Chorzow 5-0 Kuopion Palloseura
Kuopion Palloseura 2-2 Ruch Chorzow
Benfica 7-0 Fenerbahce
Fenerbahce 1-0 Benfica
Jeunesse Esch 0-5 Bayern Munich
Bayern Munich 3-1 Jeunesse Esch
RWD Molenbeek 3-2 Viking Stavanger
Viking Stavanger 0-1 RWD Molenbeek
Borussia Mönchengladbach 1-1
 Innsbruck
Innsbruck 1-6 Borussia
 Mönchengladbach
CSKA Sofia 2-1 Juventus
Juventus 2-0 CSKA Sofia
Floriana 0-5 Hajduk Split
Hajduk Split 3-0 Floriana
Malmö 2-1 Magdeburg
Magdeburg 2-1 Malmö
(*Malmö won on penalties*)
Omonia Nicosia 2-1 Akranes
Akranes 4-0 Omonia Nicosia

Second Round
Derby County 4-1 Real Madrid
Real Madrid 5-1 Derby County
Saint Etienne 2-0 Glasgow Rangers
Glasgow Rangers 1-2 Saint Etienne
Borussia Mönchengladbach 2-0 Juventus
Juventus 2-2 Borussia Mönchengladbach
Dynamo Kiev 3-0 Akranes
Akranes 0-2 Dynamo Kiev
Ruch Chorzow 1-3 PSV Eindhoven
PSV Eindhoven 4-0 Ruch Chorzow
Benfica 5-2 Ujpest Dozsa
Ujpest Dozsa 3-1 Benfica
Hajduk Split 4-0 RWD Molenbeek
RWD Molenbeek 2-3 Hajduk Split
Malmö 1-0 Bayern Munich
Bayern Munich 2-0 Malmö

Quarter-finals
Benfica 0-0 Bayern Munich
Bayern Munich 5-1 Benfica

Dynamo Kiev 2–0 Saint Etienne
Saint Etienne 3–0 Dynamo Kiev
Hajduk 2–0 PSV Eindhoven
PSV Eindhoven 3–0 Hajduk
Borussia Mönchengladbach 2–2 Real
  Madrid
Real Madrid 1–1 Borussia
  Mönchengladbach

Semi-finals
Saint Etienne 1–0 PSV Eindhoven
PSV Eindhoven 0–0 Saint Etienne
Real Madrid 1–1 Bayern Munich
Bayern Munich 2–0 Real Madrid

Final
12 May 1976, GLASGOW, 54 864
BAYERN MUNICH (0) 1, SAINT
  ETIENNE (0) 0
Bayern: Maier; Beckenbauer; Hansen,
  Horsmann, Schwarzenbeck, Roth,
  Kappelmann, Durnberger, Muller,
  U. Hoeness, Rummenigge.
Saint Etienne: Curkovic; Janvion,
  Repellini, Piazza, Lopez, Bathenay,
  Santini, Larqué, P. Revelli, H. Revelli,
  Sarramagna (Rocheteau).
Scorer: Roth.

1976–77

First Round
Liverpool 2–0 Crusaders
Crusaders 0–5 Liverpool
Glasgow Rangers 1–1 FC Zürich
FC Zürich 1–0 Glasgow Rangers
Akranes 1–3 Trabzonspor
Trabzonspor 3–2 Akranes
Austria Vienna 1–0 Borussia
  Mönchengladbach
Borussia Mönchengladbach 3–0 Austria
  Vienna
FC Bruges 2–1 Steaua Bucharest
Steaua Bucharest 1–1 FC Bruges
CSKA Sofia 0–0 Saint Etienne
Saint Etienne 1–0 CSKA Sofia
Dynamo Dresden 2–0 Benfica
Benfica 0–0 Dynamo Dresden
Dundalk 1–1 PSV Eindhoven
PSV Eindhoven 6–0 Dundalk
Ferencvaros 5–1 Jeunesse Esch
Jeunesse Esch 2–6 Ferencvaros
Dynamo Kiev 3–0 Partizan Belgrade
Partizan Belgrade 0–2 Dynamo Kiev
Omonia Nicosia 0–2 PAOK Salonika
PAOK Salonika 1–1 Omonia Nicosia
Stal Mielec 1–2 Real Madrid
Real Madrid 1–0 Stal Mielec
Viking Stavanger 2–1 Banik Ostrava
Banik Ostrava 2–0 Viking Stavanger
Torino 2–1 Malmö
Malmö 1–1 Torino
Koge BK 0–5 Bayern Munich

Bayern Munich 2–1 Koge BK
Sliema Wanderers 2–1 Turun Palloseura
Turun Palloseura 1–0 Sliema Wanderers

Second Round
Trabzonspor 1–0 Liverpool
Liverpool 3–0 Trabzonspor
Dynamo Kiev 4–0 PAOK Salonika
PAOK Salonika 0–2 Dynamo Kiev
Ferencvaros 1–0 Dynamo Dresden
Dynamo Dresden 4–0 Ferencvaros
Real Madrid 0–0 FC Bruges
FC Bruges 2–0 Real Madrid
Saint Etienne 1–0 PSV Eindhoven
PSV Eindhoven 0–0 Saint Etienne
Torino 1–2 Borussia Mönchengladbach
Borussia Mönchengladbach 0–0 Torino
FC Zürich 2–0 Turun Palloseura
Turun Palloseura 0–1 FC Zürich
Banik Ostrava 2–1 Bayern Munich
Bayern Munich 5–0 Banik Ostrava

Quarter-finals
Saint Etienne 1–0 Liverpool
Liverpool 3–1 Saint Etienne
Bayern Munich 1–0 Dynamo Kiev
Dynamo Kiev 2–0 Bayern Munich
Borussia Mönchengladbach 2–2 FC
  Bruges
FC Bruges 0–1 Borussia
  Mönchengladbach
FC Zürich 2–1 Dynamo Dresden
Dynamo Dresden 3–2 FC Zürich

Semi-finals
FC Zürich 1–3 Liverpool
Liverpool 3–0 FC Zürich
Dynamo Kiev 1–0 Borussia
  Mönchengladbach
Borussia Mönchengladbach 2–0 Dynamo
  Kiev

Final
25 May 1977, ROME, 57 000
LIVERPOOL (1) 3, BORUSSIA
  MÖNCHENGLADBACH (0) 1
Liverpool: Clemence; Neal, T. Smith,
  Hughes, J. Jones; Case, McDermott,
  R. Kennedy, Callaghan; Keegan,
  Heighway.
Borussia: Kneib; Vogts, Klinkhammer,
  Wittkamp, Bonhof, Wohlers (Hannes),
  Simonsen, Wimmer (Kulik), Stielike,
  Schafer, Heynckes.
Scorers: McDermott, Smith, Neal (pen)
  for Liverpool; Simonsen for Borussia.

1977–78

First Round
Celtic 5–0 Jeunesse Esch
Jeunesse Esch 1–6 Celtic
Valur 1–0 Glentoran
Glentoran 2–0 Valur
Red Star Belgrade 3–0 Sligo Rovers

Sligo Rovers 0–3 Red Star Belgrade
Lillestrom 2–0 Ajax
Ajax 4–0 Lillestrom
Basle 1–3 Innsbruck
Innsbruck 0–1 Basle
Vasas 0–3 Borussia Mönchengladbach
Borussia Mönchengladbach 1–1 Vasas
Omonia Nicosia 0–3 Juventus
Juventus 2–0 Omonia Nicosia
Trabzonspor 1–0 BK Copenhagen
BK Copenhagen 2–0 Trabzonspor
Kuopion Palloseura 0–4 FC Bruges
FC Bruges 5–2 Kuopion Palloseura
Levski Spartak 3–0 Slask Wroclaw
Slask Wroclaw 2–2 Levski Spartak
Floriana 1–1 Panathinaikos
Panathinaikos 4–0 Floriana
Dukla Prague 1–1 Nantes
Nantes 0–0 Dukla Prague
Dynamo Dresden 2–0 Halmstad
Halmstad 2–1 Dynamo Dresden
Benfica 0–0 Torpedo Moscow
Torpedo Moscow 0–0 Benfica
(*Benfica won on penalties*)
Dinamo Bucharest 2–1 Atlético Madrid
Atlético Madrid 2–0 Dinamo Bucharest

Second Round
Liverpool 5–1 Dynamo Dresden
Dynamo Dresden 2–1 Liverpool
Celtic 2–1 Innsbruck
Innsbruck 3–0 Celtic
Glentoran 0–1 Juventus
Juventus 5–0 Glentoran
Levski Spartak 1–2 Ajax
Ajax 2–1 Levski Spartak
Red Star 0–3 Borussia Mönchengladbach
Borussia Mönchengladbach 5–1 Red Star
FC Bruges 2–0 Panathinaikos
Panathinaikos 1–0 FC Bruges
Benfica 1–0 BK Copenhagen
BK Copenhagen 0–1 Benfica
Nantes 1–1 Atlético Madrid
Atlético Madrid 2–1 Nantes

Quarter-finals
Benfica 1–2 Liverpool
Liverpool 4–1 Benfica
Innsbruck 3–1 Borussia
  Mönchengladbach
Borussia Mönchengladbach 2–0
  Innsbruck
Ajax 1–1 Juventus
Juventus 1–1 Ajax
(*Juventus won on penalties*)
FC Bruges 2–0 Atlético Madrid
Atlético Madrid 3–2 FC Bruges

Semi-finals
Borussia Mönchengladbach 2–1
  Liverpool
Liverpool 3–0 Borussia
  Mönchengladbach
Juventus 1–0 FC Bruges
FC Bruges 2–0 Juventus

Final

10 May 1978, WEMBLEY, 92 000
LIVERPOOL (0) 1, FC BRUGES (0) 0
Liverpool: Clemence; Neal, Hughes,
    Thompson, R. Kennedy, Hansen,
    Dalglish, Case (Heighway),
    McDermott, Souness, Fairclough.
Bruges: Jensen; Bastijns, Maes (Volder),
    Krieger, Leekens, Cools, De Cubber,
    Vandereycken, Simoen, Ku (Sanders),
    Sorensen.
Scorer: Dalglish.

1978–79

Preliminary Round
Monaco 3–0 Steaua Bucharest
Steaua Bucharest 2–0 Monaco

First Round
Nottingham Forest 2–0 Liverpool
Liverpool 0–0 Nottingham Forest
Juventus 1–0 Rangers
Rangers 2–0 Juventus
Linfield 0–0 Lillestrom
Lillestrom 1–0 Linfield
Real Madrid 5–0 Progres Niedercorn
Progres Niedercorn 0–7 Real Madrid
AEK Athens 6–1 Porto
Porto 1–1 AEK Athens
Fenerbahce 2–1 PSV Eindhoven
PSV Eindhoven 6–1 Fenerbahce
Vllaznia 2–0 Austria Vienna
Austria Vienna 4–1 Vllaznia
Malmö 0–0 Monaco
Monaco 0–1 Malmö
Cologne 4–1 Akranes
Akranes 1–1 Cologne
Zbrojovka Brno 2–2 Ujpest Dozsa
Ujpest Dozsa 0–2 Zbrojovka Brno
Partizan Belgrade 2–0 Dynamo Dresden
Dynamo Dresden 2–0 Partizan Belgrade
(*Dynamo Dresden won on penalties*)
Grasshoppers 8–0 Valletta
Valletta 3–5 Grasshoppers
FC Bruges 2–1 Wisla Krakow
Wisla Krakow 3–1 FC Bruges
Odense 2–2 Lokomotiv Sofia
Lokomotiv Sofia 2–1 Odense
Valkeakosken 0–1 Dynamo Kiev
Dynamo Kiev 3–1 Valkeakosken
Omonia Nicosia 2–1 Bohemians
Bohemians 1–0 Omonia Nicosia

Second Round
AEK Athens 1–2 Nottingham Forest
Nottingham Forest 5–1 AEK Athens
Rangers 0–0 PSV Eindhoven
PSV Eindhoven 2–3 Rangers
Real Madrid 3–1 Grasshoppers
Grasshoppers 2–0 Real Madrid
Dynamo Kiev 0–0 Malmö
Malmö 2–0 Dynamo Kiev
Lokomotiv Sofia 0–1 Cologne

Cologne 4–0 Lokomotiv Sofia
Bohemians 0–0 Dynamo Dresden
Dynamo Dresden 6–0 Bohemians
Austria Vienna 4–0 Lillestrom
Lillestrom 0–0 Austria Vienna
Zbrojovka Brno 2–2 Wisla Krakow
Wisla Krakow 1–1 Zbrojovka Brno

Quarter-finals
Nottingham Forest 4–1 Grasshoppers
Grasshoppers 1–1 Nottingham Forest
Cologne 1–0 Glasgow Rangers
Glasgow Rangers 1–1 Cologne
Wisla Krakow 2–1 Malmö
Malmö 4–1 Wisla Krakow
Austria Vienna 3–1 Dynamo Dresden
Dynamo Dresden 1–0 Austria Vienna

Semi-finals
Nottingham Forest 3–3 Cologne
Cologne 0–1 Nottingham Forest
Austria Vienna 0–0 Malmö
Malmö 1–0 Austria Vienna

Final
30 May 1979, MUNICH, 57 500
NOTTINGHAM FOREST (1) 1,
    MALMÖ (0) 0
Forest: Shilton; Anderson, Clark,
    McGovern, Lloyd, Burns, Francis,
    Bowyer, Birtles, Woodcock, Robertson.
Malmö: Moller; R. Andersson, Jonsson,
    M. Andersson, Erlandsson, Tapper
    (Malmberg), Ljungberg, Prytz,
    Kindvall, Hansson (T. Andersson),
    Cervin.
Scorer: Francis.

1979–80

Preliminary Round
Dundalk 1–1 Linfield
Linfield 0–2 Dundalk (*in Haarlem*)

First Round
Liverpool 2–1 Dynamo Tbilisi
Dynamo Tbilisi 3–0 Liverpool
Nottingham Forest 2–0 Oster Vaxjo
Oster Vaxjo 1–1 Nottingham Forest
Partizan Tirana 1–0 Celtic
Celtic 4–1 Partizan Tirana
Dundalk 2–0 Hibernians Malta
Hibernians Malta 1–0 Dundalk
Levski Spartak 0–1 Real Madrid
Real Madrid 2–0 Levski Spartak
Arges Pitesti 3–0 AEK Athens
AEK Athens 2–1 Arges Pitesti
Start Kristiansand 1–2 Strasbourg
Strasbourg 4–0 Start Kristiansand
Dynamo Berlin 4–1 Ruch Chorzow
Ruch Chorzow 0–0 Dynamo Berlin
Ujpest Dozsa 3–2 Dukla Prague
Dukla Prague 2–0 Ujpest Dozsa
Red Boys Differdange 2–1 Omonia
    Nicosia

Omonia Nicosia 6–1 Red Boys
    Differdange
HJK Helsinki 1–8 Ajax
Ajax 8–1 HJK Helsinki
Valur Reykjavik 0–3 Hamburg
Hamburg 2–1 Valur Reykjavik
Hajduk Split 1–0 Trabzonspor
Trabzonspor 0–1 Hajduk Split
Vejle 3–2 Austria Vienna
Austria Vienna 1–1 Vejle
Porto 0–0 Milan
Milan 0–1 Porto
Servette Geneva 3–1 Beveren
Beveren 1–1 Servette Geneva

Second Round
Nottingham Forest 2–0 Arges Pitesti
Arges Pitesti 1–2 Nottingham Forest
Celtic 3–2 Dundalk
Dundalk 0–0 Celtic
Dynamo Berlin 2–1 Servette Geneva
Servette Geneva 2–2 Dynamo Berlin
Dukla Prague 1–0 Strasbourg
Strasbourg 2–0 Dukla Prague
Hamburg 3–1 Dynamo Tbilisi
Dynamo Tbilisi 2–3 Hamburg
Hajduk Split 3–0 Vejle
Vejle 2–1 Hajduk Split
Ajax 10–0 Omonia Nicosia
Omonia Nicosia 4–0 Ajax
Porto 2–1 Real Madrid
Real Madrid 1–0 Porto

Quarter-finals
Nottingham Forest 0–1 Dynamo Berlin
Dynamo Berlin 1–3 Nottingham Forest
Celtic 2–0 Real Madrid
Real Madrid 3–0 Celtic
Hamburg 1–0 Hajduk Split
Hajduk Split 3–2 Hamburg
Strasbourg 0–0 Ajax
Ajax 4–0 Strasbourg

Semi-finals
Nottingham Forest 2–0 Ajax
Ajax 1–0 Nottingham Forest
Real Madrid 2–0 Hamburg
Hamburg 5–1 Real Madrid

Final
28 May 1980, MADRID, 50 000
NOTTINGHAM FOREST (1) 1,
    HAMBURG (0) 0
Forest: Shilton; Anderson, F. Gray
    (Gunn), McGovern, Lloyd, Burns,
    O'Neill, Bowyer, Birtles, Mills
    (O'Hare), Robertson.
Hamburg: Kargus; Kaltz, Nogly, Jakobs,
    Buljan, Hieronymus (Hrubesch),
    Memering, Magath, Reimann,
    Milewski, Keegan.
Scorer: Robertson.

1980–81

Preliminary Round
Honved 8–0 Valletta
Valletta 0–3 Honved

First Round
Linfield 0–1 Nantes
Nantes 2–0 Linfield
Aberdeen 1–0 Austria Vienna
Austria Vienna 0–0 Aberdeen
FC Bruges 0–1 Basle
Basle 4–1 FC Bruges
CSKA Sofia 1–0 Nottingham Forest
Nottingham Forest 0–1 CSKA Sofia
Dynamo Berlin 3–0 Apoel Nicosia
Apoel Nicosia 2–1 Dynamo Berlin
Dynamo Tirana 0–2 Ajax
Ajax 1–0 Dynamo Tirana
Internazionale 2–0 Universitatea Craiova
Universitatea Craiova 1–1 Internazionale
Jeunesse Esch 0–5 Moscow Spartak
Moscow Spartak 4–0 Jeunesse Esch
Limerick 1–2 Real Madrid
Real Madrid 5–1 Limerick
Olympiakos 2–4 Bayern Munich
Bayern Munich 3–0 Olympiakos
OPS Oulu 1–1 Liverpool
Liverpool 10–1 OPS Oulu
Sporting Lisbon 0–2 Honved
Honved 1–0 Sporting Lisbon
Trabzonspor 2–1 Szombierki Bytom
Szombierki Bytom 3–0 Trabzonspor
Viking Stavanger 2–3 Red Star Belgrade
Red Star Belgrade 4–1 Viking Stavanger
IBV 1–1 Banik Ostrava
Banik Ostrava 1–0 IBV
Halmstad 0–0 Esbjerg
Esbjerg 3–2 Halmstad

Second Round
Nantes 1–2 Internazionale
Internazionale 1–1 Nantes
Real Madrid 1–0 Honved
Honved 0–2 Real Madrid
Bayern Munich 5–1 Ajax
Ajax 2–1 Bayern Munich
Aberdeen 0–1 Liverpool
Liverpool 4–0 Aberdeen
CSKA Sofia 4–0 Szombierki Bytom
Szombierki Bytom 0–1 CSKA Sofia
Banik Ostrava 0–0 Dynamo Berlin
Dynamo Berlin 1–1 Banik Ostrava
Moscow Spartak 3–0 Esbjerg
Esbjerg 2–0 Moscow Spartak
Basle 1–0 Red Star Belgrade
Red Star Belgrade 2–0 Basle

Quarter-finals
Liverpool 5–1 CSKA Sofia
CSKA Sofia 0–1 Liverpool
Bayern Munich 2–0 Banik Ostrava
Banik Ostrava 2–4 Bayern Munich
Moscow Spartak 0–0 Real Madrid
Real Madrid 2–0 Moscow Spartak

Internazionale 1–1 Red Star Belgrade
Red Star Belgrade 0–1 Internazionale

Semi-finals
Liverpool 0–0 Bayern Munich
Bayern Munich 1–1 Liverpool
Real Madrid 2–0 Internazionale
Internazionale 1–0 Real Madrid

Final
27 May 1981, PARIS, 48 360
LIVERPOOL (0) 1, REAL MADRID (0) 0
Liverpool: Clemence; Neal, A. Kennedy,
   Thompson, R. Kennedy, Hansen,
   Dalglish (Case), Lee, Johnson,
   McDermott, Souness.
Real: Rodriguez; Garcia Cortes,
   Camacho, Stielike, Sabido (Pineda),
   Del Bosque, Juanito, De Los Santos,
   Santillana, Navajas, Cunningham.
Scorer: Alan Kennedy.

1981–82

Preliminary Round
Saint Etienne 1–1 Dynamo Berlin
Dynamo Berlin 2–0 Saint Etienne

First Round
Widzew Lodz 1–4 Anderlecht
Anderlecht 2–1 Widzew Lodz
Dynamo Berlin 2–0 FC Zürich
FC Zürich 3–1 Dynamo Berlin
Aston Villa 5–0 Valur Reykjavik
Valur Reykjavik 0–2 Aston Villa
OPS Oulu 0–1 Liverpool
Liverpool 7–0 OPS Oulu
Oster Vaxjo 0–1 Bayern Munich
Bayern Munich 5–0 Oster Vaxjo
Ferencvaros 3–2 Banik Ostrava
Banik Ostrava 3–0 Ferencvaros
Austria Vienna 3–1 Partizani
Partizani 1–0 Austria Vienna
Hibernians Malta 1–2 Red Star Belgrade
Red Star Belgrade 8–1 Hibernians Malta
Celtic 1–0 Juventus
Juventus 2–0 Celtic
Benfica 3–0 Omonia Nicosia
Omonia Nicosia 0–1 Benfica
Niedercorn 1–1 Glentoran
Glentoran 4–0 Niedercorn
Dynamo Kiev 1–0 Trabzonspor
Trabzonspor 1–1 Dynamo Kiev
Start Kristiansand 1–3 AZ 67 Alkmaar
AZ 67 Alkmaar 1–0 Start Kristiansand
KB Copenhagen 1–1 Athlone Town
Athlone Town 2–2 KB Copenhagen
CSKA Sofia 1–0 Real Sociedad
Real Sociedad 0–0 CSKA Sofia
Universitatea Craiova 3–0 Olympiakos
Olympiakos 2–0 Universitatea Craiova

Second Round
Banik Ostrava 3–1 Red Star Belgrade
Red Star Belgrade 3–0 Banik Ostrava

Anderlecht 3–1 Juventus
Juventus 1–1 Anderlecht
AZ 67 Alkmaar 2–2 Liverpool
Liverpool 3–2 AZ 67 Alkmaar
CSKA Sofia 2–0 Glentoran
Glentoran 2–1 CSKA Sofia
KB Copenhagen 1–0 Universitatea
   Craiova
Universitatea Craiova 4–1 KB
   Copenhagen
Benfica 0–0 Bayern Munich
Bayern Munich 4–1 Benfica
Austria Vienna 0–1 Dynamo Kiev
Dynamo Kiev 1–1 Austria Vienna
Dynamo Berlin 1–2 Aston Villa
Aston Villa 0–1 Dynamo Berlin

Quarter-finals
Dynamo Kiev 0–0 Aston Villa
Aston Villa 2–0 Dynamo Kiev
Anderlecht 2–1 Red Star Belgrade
Red Star Belgrade 1–2 Anderlecht
Liverpool 1–0 CSKA Sofia
CSKA Sofia 2–0 Liverpool
Universitatea Craiova 0–2 Bayern
   Munich
Bayern Munich 1–1 Universitatea
   Craiova

Semi-finals
CSKA Sofia 4–3 Bayern Munich
Bayern Munich 4–0 CSKA Sofia
Aston Villa 1–0 Anderlecht
Anderlecht 0–0 Aston Villa

Final
26 May 1982, ROTTERDAM, 46 000
ASTON VILLA (0) 1, BAYERN
   MUNICH (0) 0
Villa: Rimmer (Spink); Swain, Williams,
   Evans, McNaught, Mortimer, Bremner,
   Cowans, Morley; Shaw, Withe.
Bayern: Muller; Dremmler, Horsmann,
   Weiner, Augenthaler, Kraus
   (Niedermayer), Durnberger, Breitner,
   D. Hoeness, Mathy (Guttler),
   Rummenigge.

1982–83

Preliminary Round
Dinamo Bucharest 3–1 Valerengen
Valerengen 2–1 Dinamo Bucharest

First Round
Dundalk 1–4 Liverpool
Liverpool 1–0 Dundalk
Aston Villa 3–1 Besiktas
Besiktas 0–0 Aston Villa
Avenir Beggen 0–5 Rapid Vienna
Rapid Vienna 8–0 Avenir Beggen
Celtic 2–2 Ajax
Ajax 1–2 Celtic
Dinamo Bucharest 2–0 Dukla Prague
Dukla Prague 2–1 Dinamo Bucharest

Dynamo Zagreb 1-0 Sporting Lisbon
Sporting Lisbon 3-0 Dynamo Zagreb
Grasshoppers 0-1 Dynamo Kiev
Dynamo Kiev 3-0 Grasshoppers
Hibernians Malta 1-4 Widzew Lodz
Widzew Lodz 3-1 Hibernians Malta
Hvidovre 1-4 Juventus
Juventus 3-3 Hvidovre
Monaco 0-0 CSKA Sofia
CSKA Sofia 2-0 Monaco
Nendori Tirana 1-0 Linfield
Linfield 2-1 Nendori Tirana
Vikingur 0-1 Real Sociedad
Real Sociedad 3-2 Vikingur
Omonia Nicosia 2-0 HJK Helsinki
HJK Helsinki 3-0 Omonia Nicosia
Standard Liège 5-0 Raba Gyor
Raba Gyor 3-0 Standard Liège
Dynamo Berlin 1-1 Hamburg
Hamburg 2-0 Dynamo Berlin
Olympiakos 2-0 Oster Vaxjo
Oster Vaxjo 1-0 Olympiakos

Second Round
Dinamo Bucharest 0-2 Aston Villa
Aston Villa 4-2 Dinamo Bucharest
HJK Helsinki 1-0 Liverpool
Liverpool 5-0 HJK Helsinki
CSKA Sofia 2-2 Sporting Lisbon
Sporting Lisbon 0-0 CSKA Sofia
Hamburg 1-0 Olympiakos
Olympiakos 0-4 Hamburg
Rapid Vienna 2-1 Widzew Lodz
Widzew Lodz 5-3 Rapid Vienna
Real Sociedad 2-0 Celtic
Celtic 2-1 Real Sociedad
Standard Liège 1-1 Juventus
Juventus 2-0 Standard Liège
Walkover: *Dynamo Kiev (v Nendori Tirana)*

Quarter-finals
Aston Villa 1-2 Juventus
Juventus 3-1 Aston Villa
Widzew Lodz 2-0 Liverpool
Liverpool 3-2 Widzew Lodz
Sporting Lisbon 1-0 Real Sociedad
Real Sociedad 2-0 Sporting Lisbon
Dynamo Kiev 0-3 Hamburg
Hamburg 1-2 Dynamo Kiev

Semi-finals
Juventus 2-0 Widzew Lodz
Widzew Lodz 2-2 Juventus
Real Sociedad 1-1 Hamburg
Hamburg 2-1 Real Sociedad

Final
25 May 1983, ATHENS, 75 000
HAMBURG (1) 1, JUVENTUS (0) 0
Hamburg: Stein; Kaltz, Wehmeyer,
  Jakobs, Hieronymus, Rolff, Milewski,
  Groh, Magath, Hrubesch, Bastrup (Van
  Heesen).
Juventus: Zoff; Gentile, Bonini, Brio,
  Scirea; Bettega, Tardelli, Rossi

(Marocchino), Platini, Boniek.
Scorer: Magath.

1983–84
First Round
Ajax 0-0 Olympiakos
Olympiakos 2-0 Ajax
Athlone 2-3 Standard Liège
Standard Liège 8-2 Athlone
Dynamo Berlin 4-1 Jeunesse Esch
Jeunesse Esch 0-2 Dynamo Berlin
Dynamo Minsk 1-0 Grasshoppers
Grasshoppers 2-2 Dynamo Minsk
CSKA Sofia 3-0 Omonia Nicosia
Omonia Nicosia 4-1 CSKA Sofia
Fenerbahce 0-1 Bohemians Prague
Bohemians Prague 4-0 Fenerbahce
Hamrun Spartans 0-3 Dundee United
Dundee United 3-0 Hamrun Spartans
Kuusysi Lahti 0-1 Dinamo Bucharest
Dinamo Bucharest 3-0 Kuusysi Lahti
Lech Poznan 2-0 Athletic Bilbao
Athletic Bilbao 4-0 Lech Poznan
Odense BK 0-1 Liverpool
Liverpool 5-0 Odense BK
Partizan Belgrade 5-1 Viking Stavanger
Viking Stavanger 0-0 Partizan Belgrade
Raba Gyor 2-1 Vikingur
Vikingur 0-2 Raba Gyor
Rapid Vienna 3-0 Nantes
Nantes 3-1 Rapid Vienna
Roma 3-0 IFK Gothenburg
IFK Gothenburg 2-1 Roma

Second Round
Bohemians Prague 2-1 Rapid Vienna
Rapid Vienna 1-0 Bohemians Prague
CSKA Sofia 0-1 Roma
Roma 1-0 CSKA Sofia
Dinamo Bucharest 3-0 Hamburg
Hamburg 3-2 Dinamo Bucharest
Liverpool 0-0 Athletic Bilbao
Athletic Bilbao 0-1 Liverpool
Olympiakos 1-0 Benfica
Benfica 3-0 Olympiakos
Raba Gyor 3-6 Dynamo Minsk
Dynamo Minsk 3-1 Raba Gyor
Standard Liège 0-0 Dundee United
Dundee United 4-0 Standard Liège
Roma 3-0 Dynamo Berlin
Dynamo Berlin 2-1 Roma

Quarter-finals
Dynamo Minsk 1-1 Dinamo Bucharest
Dinamo Bucharest 1-0 Dynamo Minsk
Liverpool 1-0 Benfica
Benfica 1-4 Liverpool
Rapid Vienna 2-1 Dundee United
Dundee United 1-0 Rapid Vienna
Roma 3-0 Dynamo Berlin
Dynamo Berlin 2-1 Roma

Semi-finals
Dundee United 2-0 Roma
Roma 3-0 Dundee United

Liverpool 1-0 Dinamo Bucharest
Dinamo Bucharest 1-2 Liverpool

Final
30 May 1984, ROME, 69 693
ROMA (1) 1, LIVERPOOL (1) 1 (after
  extra time, 1-1 at 90 mins)
Liverpool won 4-2 on penalties.
Roma: Tancredi; Nappi, Bonetti, Righetti,
  Nela, Di Bartolomei, Falcao, Cerezo
  (Strukeli), Conti, Pruzzo (Chierico),
  Graziani.
Liverpool: Grobbelaar; Neal, A. Kennedy,
  Lawrenson, Hansen, Whelan, Dalglish
  (Robinson), Souness, Lee, Johnston
  (Nicol), Rush.
Scorers: Neal for Liverpool; Pruzzo for
  Roma.

1984–85
First Round
Aberdeen 2-1 Dynamo Berlin
Dynamo Berlin 2-1 Aberdeen
(*Dynamo won on penalties*)
IA Akranes 2-2 Beveren
Beveren 5-0 IA Akranes
Avenir Beggen 0-8 IFK Gothenburg
IFK Gothenburg 9-0 Avenir Beggen
Bordeaux 3-2 Athletic Bilbao
Athletic Bilbao 0-0 Bordeaux
Dinamo Bucharest 4-1 Omonia Nicosia
Omonia Nicosia 2-1 Dinamo Bucharest
FK Austria 4-0 Valletta
Valletta 0-4 FK Austria
Feyenoord 0-0 Panathinaikos
Panathinaikos 2-1 Feyenoord
Grasshoppers 3-1 Honved
Honved 2-1 Grasshoppers
Ilves 0-4 Juventus
Juventus 2-1 Ilves
Levski Spartak 1-1 Vfb Stuttgart
Vfb Stuttgart 2-2 Levski Spartak
Linfield 0-0 Shamrock Rovers
Shamrock Rovers 1-1 Linfield
Labinoti 0-3 Lyngby
Lyngby 3-0 Labinoti
Lech Poznan 0-1 Liverpool
Liverpool 4-0 Lech Poznan
Red Star Belgrade 3-2 Benfica
Benfica 2-0 Red Star Belgrade
Trabzonspor 1-0 Dnepr
Dnepr 3-0 Trabzonspor
Valerengen 3-3 Sparta Prague
Sparta Prague 2-0 Valerengen

Second Round
Bordeaux 1-0 Dinamo Bucharest
Dinamo Bucharest 1-1 Bordeaux
Dynamo Berlin 3-3 FK Austria
FK Austria 2-1 Dynamo Berlin
IFK Gothenburg 1-0 Beveren
Beveren 2-1 IFK Gothenburg

Juventus 2–0 Grasshoppers
Grasshoppers 2–4 Juventus
Levski Spartak 3–1 Dnepr
Dnepr 2–0 Levski Spartak
Liverpool 3–1 Benfica
Benfica 1–0 Liverpool
Panathinaikos 2–1 Linfield
Linfield 3–3 Panathinaikos
Sparta Prague 0–0 Lyngby
Lyngby 1–2 Sparta Prague

Quarter-finals
Bordeaux 1–1 Dnepr
Dnepr 1–1 Bordeaux
(*Bordeaux won on penalties*)
FK Austria 1–1 Liverpool
Liverpool 4–1 FK Austria
IFK Gothenburg 0–1 Panathinaikos
Panathinaikos 2–2 IFK Gothenburg
Juventus 3–0 Sparta Prague
Sparta Prague 1–0 Juventus

Semi-finals
Juventus 3–0 Bordeaux
Bordeaux 2–0 Juventus
Liverpool 4–0 Panathinaikos
Panathinaikos 0–1 Liverpool

Final
29 May 1985, BRUSSELS, 58 000
JUVENTUS (0) 1, LIVERPOOL (0) 0
Juventus: Tacconi; Scirea; Favero, Bonini, Brio, Briaschi (Prandelli), Tardelli, Rossi (Vignola), Platini, Boniek.
Liverpool: Grobbelaar; Neal, Lawrenson (Gillespie), Hansen, Beglin, Wark, Dalglish, Whelan, Nicol, Rush, Walsh.
Scorer: Platini (pen).

1985–86

First Round
Akranes 1–3 Aberdeen
Aberdeen 4–1 Akranes
Bordeaux 2–3 Fenerbahce
Fenerbahce 0–0 Bordeaux
Dynamo Berlin 0–2 FK Austria
FK Austria 2–1 Dynamo Berlin
Gornik Zabrze 1–2 Bayern Munich
Bayern Munich 4–1 Gornik Zabrze
Honved 2–0 Shamrock Rovers
Shamrock Rovers 1–3 Honved
IFK Gothenburg 3–2 Trakia Plovdiv
Trakia Plovdiv 1–2 IFK Gothenburg
Jeunesse Esch 0–5 Juventus
Juventus 4–1 Jeunesse Esch
Kuusysi Lahti 2–1 Sarajevo
Sarajevo 1–2 Kuusysi Lahti
Linfield 2–2 Servette Geneva
Servette Geneva 2–1 Linfield
Porto 2–0 Ajax
Ajax 0–0 Porto
Rabat Ajax 0–5 Omonia Nicosia
Omonia Nicosia 5–0 Rabat Ajax

Sparta Prague 2–1 Barcelona
Barcelona 1–0 Sparta Prague
Vejle 1–1 Steaua Bucharest
Steaua Bucharest 4–1 Vejle
Verona 3–1 PAOK Salonika
PAOK Salonika 1–2 Verona
Zenit Leningrad 2–0 Valerengen
Valerengen 0–2 Zenit Leningrad

Second Round
Anderlecht 1–0 Omonia Nicosia
Omonia Nicosia 1–3 Anderlecht
Barcelona 2–0 Porto
Porto 3–1 Barcelona
Bayern Munich 4–2 FK Austria
FK Austria 3–3 Bayern Munich
IFK Gothenburg 4–2 Fenerbahce
Fenerbahce 2–1 IFK Gothenburg
Servette Geneva 0–0 Aberdeen
Aberdeen 1–0 Servette Geneva
Honved 1–0 Steaua Bucharest
Steaua Bucharest 4–1 Honved
Verona 0–0 Juventus
Juventus 2–0 Verona
Zenit Leningrad 2–1 Kuusysi Lahti
Kuusysi Lahti 3–1 Zenit Leningrad

Quarter-finals
Aberdeen 2–2 IFK Gothenburg
IFK Gothenburg 0–0 Aberdeen
Barcelona 1–0 Juventus
Juventus 1–1 Barcelona
Bayern Munich 2–1 Anderlecht
Anderlecht 2–0 Bayern Munich
Steaua Bucharest 0–0 Kuusysi Lahti
Kuusysi Lahti 0–1 Steaua Bucharest

Semi-finals
Anderlecht 1–0 Steaua Bucharest
Steaua Bucharest 3–0 Anderlecht
IFK Gothenburg 3–0 Barcelona
Barcelona 3–0 IFK Gothenburg
(*Barcelona won on penalties*)

Final
7 May 1986, SEVILLE, 70 000
STEAUA BUCHAREST (0) 0, BARCELONA (0) 0 (after extra time)
Steaua won 2–0 on penalties.
Steaua: Ducadam; Iovan, Belodedici, Bumbescu, Barbulescu, Balan (Ionescu), Balint, Boloni, Majearu, Lacatus, Piturca (Radu).
Barcelona: Urruticoechea; Gerardo, Migueli, Alexanco, Julio Alberto, Victor, Schuster (Moratalla), Marcos, Pedraza, Archibald (Pichi Alonso), Carrasco.

1986–87

First Round
Anderlecht 2–0 Gornik Zabrze
Gornik Zabrze 1–1 Anderlecht
Apoel Nicosia 1–0 HJK Helsinki

HJK Helsinki 3–2 Apoel Nicosia
Avenir Beggen 0–3 FK Austria
FK Austria 3–0 Avenir Beggen
Beroe Stara Zagora 1–1 Dynamo Kiev
Dynamo Kiev 2–0 Beroe Stara Zagora
Besiktas 2–0 Dynamo Tirana
Dynamo Tirana 0–1 Besiktas
Brondby 4–1 Honved
Honved 2–2 Brondby
Juventus 7–0 Valur
Valur 0–4 Juventus
Orgryte 2–3 Dynamo Berlin
Dynamo Berlin 4–1 Orgryte
Paris Saint Germain 2–2 Vitkovice
Vitkovice 1–0 Paris Saint Germain
Porto 9–0 Rabat Ajax
Rabat Ajax 0–1 Porto
PSV Eindhoven 0–2 Bayern Munich
Bayern Munich 0–0 PSV Eindhoven
Red Star Belgrade 3–0 Panathinaikos
Panathinaikos 2–1 Red Star Belgrade
Rosenborg 1–0 Linfield
Linfield 1–1 Rosenborg
Shamrock Rovers 0–1 Celtic
Celtic 2–0 Shamrock Rovers
Young Boys Berne 1–0 Real Madrid
Real Madrid 5–0 Young Boys Berne

Second Round
Anderlecht 3–0 Steaua Bucharest
Steaua Bucharest 1–0 Anderlecht
Bayern Munich 2–0 FK Austria
FK Austria 1–1 Bayern Munich
Brondby 2–1 Dynamo Berlin
Dynamo Berlin 1–1 Brondby
Celtic 1–1 Dynamo Kiev
Dynamo Kiev 3–1 Celtic
Real Madrid 1–0 Juventus
Juventus 1–0 Real Madrid
(*Real Madrid won on penalties*)
Rosenborg 0–3 Red Star Belgrade
Red Star Belgrade 4–1 Rosenborg
Vitkovice 1–0 Porto
Porto 3–0 Vitkovice
Walkover: *Besiktas (v Apoel Nicosia)*

Quarter-finals
Bayern Munich 5–0 Anderlecht
Anderlecht 2–2 Bayern Munich
Besiktas 1–5 Dynamo Kiev
Dynamo Kiev 2–0 Besiktas
Porto 1–0 Brondby
Brondby 1–1 Porto
Red Star Belgrade 4–2 Real Madrid
Real Madrid 2–0 Red Star Belgrade

Semi-finals
Bayern Munich 4–1 Real Madrid
Real Madrid 1–0 Bayern Munich
Porto 2–1 Dynamo Kiev
Dynamo Kiev 1–2 Porto

Final
27 May 1987, VIENNA, 59 000
PORTO (0) 2, BAYERN MUNICH (1) 1

Porto: Mlynarczyk; Joao Pinto, Edoardo Luis, Celso, Inacio (Frasco), Quim (Juary), Magalhaes, Sousa, Andre, Futre, Madjer.
Bayern: Pfaff; Winkelhofer, Nachtweih, Eder, Pfugler, Flick (Lunde), Brehme, Hoeness, Matthaus, Kogl, Rummenigge.
Scorers: Madjer, Juary for Porto; Kogl for Bayern Munich.

1987–88

First Round
Aarhus 4–1 Jeunesse Esch
Jeunesse Esch 1–0 Aarhus
Bayern Munich 4–0 CSKA Sofia
CSKA Sofia 0–1 Bayern Munich
Benfica 4–0 Partizan Tirana
(*Partizan expelled by UEFA. Benfica walked over*)
Bordeaux 2–0 Dynamo Berlin
Dynamo Berlin 0–2 Bordeaux
Fram Reykjavik 0–2 Sparta Prague
Sparta Prague 8–0 Fram Reykjavik
Dynamo Kiev 1–0 Rangers
Rangers 2–0 Dynamo Kiev
Lillestrom 1–1 Linfield
Linfield 2–4 Lillestrom
Malmö 0–1 Anderlecht
Anderlecht 1–1 Malmö
Neuchatel 5–0 Kuusysi Lahti
Kuusysi Lahti 2–1 Neuchatel
Olympiakos 1–1 Gornik Zabrze
Gornik Zabrze 2–1 Olympiakos
Porto 3–0 Vardar Skopje
Vardar Skopje 0–3 Porto
PSV Eindhoven 3–0 Galatasaray
Galatasaray 2–0 PSV Eindhoven
Rapid Vienna 6–0 Hamrun Spartans
Hamrun Spartans 0–1 Rapid Vienna
Real Madrid 2–0 Napoli
Napoli 1–1 Real Madrid
Shamrock Rovers 0–1 Omonia Nicosia
Omonia Nicosia 0–0 Shamrock Rovers
Steaua Bucharest 4–0 MTK Budapest
MTK Budapest 2–0 Steaua Bucharest

Second Round
Aarhus 0–0 Benfica
Benfica 1–0 Aarhus
Lillestrom 0–0 Bordeaux
Bordeaux 1–0 Lillestrom
Rangers 3–1 Gornik Zabrze
Gornik Zabrze 1–1 Rangers
Rapid Vienna 1–1 PSV Eindhoven
PSV Eindhoven 2–0 Rapid Vienna
Real Madrid 2–1 Porto (*in Valencia*)
Porto 1–2 Real Madrid
Sparta Prague 1–2 Anderlecht
Anderlecht 1–0 Sparta Prague
Steaua Bucharest 3–1 Omonia Nicosia
Omonia Nicosia 0–2 Steaua Bucharest
Neuchatel 2–1 Bayern Munich

Bayern Munich 2–0 Neuchatel

Quarter-finals
Bayern Munich 3–2 Real Madrid
Real Madrid 2–0 Bayern Munich
Benfica 2–0 Anderlecht
Anderlecht 1–0 Benfica
Bordeaux 1–1 PSV Eindhoven
PSV Eindhoven 0–0 Bordeaux
Steaua Bucharest 2–0 Rangers
Rangers 2–1 Steaua Bucharest

Semi-finals
Real Madrid 1–1 PSV Eindhoven
PSV Eindhoven 0–0 Real Madrid
Steaua Bucharest 0–0 Benfica
Benfica 2–0 Steaua Bucharest

Final
25 May 1988, STUTTGART, 70 000
PSV EINDHOVEN (0) 0, BENFICA (0) 0
PSV won 6–5 on penalties.
PSV: Van Breukelen; Gerets, Van Aerle, R. Koeman, Nielsen, Vanenburg, Linskens, Lerby, Heintze, Kieft, Gilhaus (Jansen).
Benfica: Silvino; Veloso, Dito, Mozer, Alvaro, Elzo, Sheu, Chiquinho, Aguas (Vando), Pacheco, Magnusson (Haiiri).

1988–89

First Round
FC Bruges 1–0 Brondby
Brondby 2–1 FC Bruges
Dundalk 0–5 Red Star Belgrade
Red Star Belgrade 3–0 Dundalk
Dynamo Berlin 3–0 Werder Bremen
Werder Bremen 5–0 Dynamo Berlin
Gornik Zabrze 3–0 Jeunesse Esch
Jeunesse Esch 1–4 Gornik Zabrze
Hamrun Spartans 2–1 Nentori Tirana
Nentori Tirana 2–0 Hamrun Spartans
Honved 1–0 Celtic
Celtic 4–0 Honved
Larissa 2–1 Neuchatel
(*Neuchatel won on penalties*)
Neuchatel 2–1 Larissa
Moscow Spartak 2–0 Glentoran
Glentoran 1–1 Moscow Spartak
Pezoporikos 1–2 IFK Gothenburg
IFK Gothenburg 5–1 Pezoporikos
Porto 3–0 HJK Helsinki
HJK Helsinki 2–0 Porto
Rapid Vienna 2–1 Galatasaray
Galatasaray 2–0 Rapid Vienna
Real Madrid 3–0 Moss
Moss 0–1 Real Madrid
Sparta Prague 1–5 Steaua Bucharest
Steaua Bucharest 2–2 Sparta Prague
Valur 1–0 Monaco
Monaco 2–0 Valur
Vitosha 0–2 Milan
Milan 5–1 Vitosha

Second Round
FC Bruges 1–0 Monaco
Monaco 6–1 FC Bruges
Celtic 0–1 Werder Bremen
Werder Bremen 0–0 Celtic
Gornik Zabrze 0–0 Real Madrid
Real Madrid 3–2 Gornik Zabrze
Milan 1–1 Red Star Belgrade
Red Star Belgrade 1–1 Milan
(*Milan won on penalties*)
Nentori 0–3 IFK Gothenburg
IFK Gothenburg 1–0 Nentori
Neuchatel 3–0 Galatasaray
Galatasaray 5–0 Neuchatel
PSV Eindhoven 5–0 Porto
Porto 2–0 PSV Eindhoven
Steaua Bucharest 3–0 Moscow Spartak
Moscow Spartak 1–2 Steaua Bucharest

Quarter-finals
IFK Gothenburg 2–0 Steaua Bucharest
Steaua Bucharest 5–0 IFK Gothenburg
Werder Bremen 0–0 Milan
Milan 1–0 Werder Bremen
PSV Eindhoven 1–1 Real Madrid
Real Madrid 2–1 PSV Eindhoven
Monaco 0–1 Galatasaray
Galatasaray 1–0 Monaco (*in Cologne*)

Semi-finals
Real Madrid 1–1 Milan
Milan 5–0 Real Madrid
Steaua Bucharest 4–0 Galatasaray
Galatasaray 1–1 Steaua Bucharest

Final
24 May 1989, BARCELONA, 97 000
MILAN (3) 4, STEAUA (0) 0
Milan: Galli; Tassotti, Costacurta (F. Galli), F. Baresi, Maldini, Rijkaard, Colombo, Ancelotti, Gullit (Virdis), Donadoni, Van Basten.
Steaua: Lung; Petrescu, Iovan, Bumbescu, Ungureanu, Stoica, Minea, Hagi, Rotariu (Balaci), Lacatus, Piturca.
Scorers: Gullit (2), Van Basten (2).

1989–90

First Round
Rangers 1–3 Bayern Munich
Bayern Munich 0–0 Rangers
Marseille 3–0 Brondby
Brondby 1–1 Marseille
Milan 4–0 HJK Helsinki
HJK Helsinki 0–1 Milan
Spora Luxembourg 0–3 Real Madrid
Real Madrid 6–0 Spora Luxembourg
Derry City 1–2 Benfica
Benfica 4–0 Derry City
Steaua Bucharest 4–0 Fram Reykjavik
Fram Reykjavik 0–1 Steaua Bucharest
Rosenborg 0–0 Mechelen
Mechelen 5–0 Rosenborg

PSV Eindhoven 3-0 Lucerne
Lucerne 0-2 PSV Eindhoven
Sparta Prague 3-1 Fenerbahce
Fenerbahce 2-1 Sparta Prague
Dynamo Dresden 1-0 AEK Athens
AEK Athens 5-3 Dynamo Dresden
Malmö 1-0 Internazionale
Internazionale 1-1 Malmö
Tirol 6-0 Omonia Nicosia
Omonia Nicosia 2-3 Tirol
Ruch Chorzow 1-1 Sredets Sofia
Sredets Sofia 5-1 Ruch Chorzow
Honved 1-0 Vojvodina
Vojvodina 2-1 Honved
Sliema Wanderers 1-0 Nentori Tirana
Nentori Tirana 5-0 Sliema Wanderers
Linfield 1-2 Dnepr
Dnepr 1-0 Linfield

Second Round
Bayern Munich 3-1 Nentori Tirana
Nentori Tirana 0-3 Bayern Munich
Dnepr 2-0 Tirol
Tirol 2-2 Dnepr
Honved 0-2 Benfica
Benfica 7-0 Honved
Malmö 0-0 Mechelen
Mechelen 4-1 Malmö
Marseille 2-0 AEK Athens
AEK Athens 1-1 Marseille
Milan 2-0 Real Madrid
Real Madrid 1-0 Milan
Sparta Prague 2-2 Sredets Sofia
Sredets Sofia 3-0 Sparta Prague
Steaua Bucharest 1-0 PSV Eindhoven
PSV Eindhoven 5-1 Steaua Bucharest

Quarter-finals
Bayern Munich 2-1 PSV Eindhoven
PSV Eindhoven 0-1 Bayern Munich
Benfica 1-0 Dnepr
Dnepr 0-3 Benfica
Mechelen 0-0 Milan
Milan 2-0 Mechelen
Sredets Sofia 0-1 Marseille
Marseille 3-1 Sredets Sofia

Semi-finals
Marseille 2-1 Benfica
Benfica 1-0 Marseille
Milan 1-0 Bayern Munich
Bayern Munich 2-1 Milan

Final
23 May 1990, VIENNA, 57 500
MILAN (0) 1, BENFICA (0) 0
Milan: G. Galli; F. Baresi, Tassotti,
    Costacurta, Maldini, Colombo
    (F. Galli), Rijkaard, Ancelotti
    (Massaro), Evani, Gullit, Van Basten.
Benfica: Silvino; Jose Carlos, Aldair,
    Ricardo, Samuel; Vitor Paneira (Vata
    Garcia), Valdo, Thern, Pacheco (Cesar
    Brito), Hernani, Magnusson.
Scorer: Rijkaard.

1990–91
First Round
Apoel Nicosia 2-3 Bayern Munich
Bayern Munich 4-0 Apoel Nicosia
Red Star Belgrade 1-1 Grasshoppers
Grasshoppers 1-4 Red Star Belgrade
Marseille 5-1 Dynamo Tirana
Dynamo Tirana 0-0 Marseille
Sparta Prague 0-2 Moscow Spartak
Moscow Spartak 2-0 Sparta Prague
Porto 5-0 Portadown
Portadown 1-8 Porto
Valletta 0-4 Rangers
Rangers 6-0 Valletta
Tirol 5-1 Kuusysi Lahti
Kuusysi Lahti 1-2 Tirol
Lillestrom 1-1 FC Bruges
FC Bruges 2-0 Lillestrom
Napoli 3-0 Ujpest Dozsa
Ujpest Dozsa 0-2 Napoli
Lech Poznan 3-0 Panathinaikos
Panathinaikos 1-2 Lech Poznan
Akureyri 1-0 Sredets Sofia
Sredets Sofia 3-0 Akureyri
Odense BK 1-4 Real Madrid
Real Madrid 6-0 Odense BK
Dinamo Bucharest 4-0 St Patrick's
    Athletic
St Patrick's Athletic 1-1 Dinamo
    Bucharest
Malmö 3-2 Besiktas
Besiktas 2-2 Malmö
US Luxembourg 1-3 Dynamo Dresden
Dynamo Dresden 3-0 US Luxembourg
Bye: *Milan*

Second Round
Dynamo Dresden 1-1 Malmö
Malmö 1-1 Dynamo Dresden
(*Dynamo Dresden won on penalties*)
Red Star Belgrade 3-0 Rangers
Rangers 1-1 Red Star Belgrade
Dinamo Bucharest 0-0 Porto
Porto 4-0 Dinamo Bucharest
Real Madrid 9-1 Tirol
Tirol 2-2 Real Madrid
Bayern Munich 4-0 Sredets Sofia
Sredets Sofia 0-3 Bayern Munich
Lech Poznan 3-2 Marseille
Marseille 6-1 Lech Poznan
Napoli 0-0 Moscow Spartak
Moscow Spartak 0-0 Napoli
(*Moscow Spartak won on penalties*)
Milan 0-0 FC Bruges
FC Bruges 0-1 Milan

Quarter-finals
Red Star Belgrade 3-0 Dynamo Dresden
Dynamo Dresden 1-2 Red Star Belgrade
(*Abandoned due to crowd trouble, 82 mins;
    match awarded to Red Star*)
Bayern Munich 1-1 Porto
Porto 0-2 Bayern Munich

Moscow Spartak 0-0 Real Madrid
Real Madrid 1-3 Moscow Spartak
Milan 1-1 Marseille
Marseille 1-0 Milan

Semi-finals
Bayern Munich 1-2 Red Star Belgrade
Red Star Belgrade 2-2 Bayern Munich
Moscow Spartak 1-3 Marseille
Marseille 2-1 Moscow Spartak

Final
29 May 1991, BARI, 58 000
RED STAR BELGRADE (0) 0,
    MARSEILLE (0) 0 (after extra time)
Red Star won 5-3 on penalties.
Red Star: Stojanovic; Jugovic, Marovic,
    Sabanadzovic, Belodedic, Najdoski,
    Prosinecki, Mihajlovic, Pancev,
    Savicevic (Stosic), Binic.
Marseille: Olmeta; Amoros, Di Meco
    (Stojkovic), Boli, Mozer, Germain,
    Casoni, Waddle, Papin, Pelé, Fournier
    (Vercruysse).

INDEX